GENDERING MODERN
JEWISH THOUGHT

NEW JEWISH PHILOSOPHY AND THOUGHT
Zachary J. Braiterman

GENDERING MODERN JEWISH THOUGHT

—∿—

ANDREA DARA COOPER

INDIANA UNIVERSITY PRESS

This book is a publication of

Indiana University Press
Office of Scholarly Publishing
Herman B Wells Library 350
1320 East 10th Street
Bloomington, Indiana 47405 USA

iupress.org

Manufactured in the United States of America

Cataloging information is available from the Library of Congress.

ISBN 978-0-253-05758-7 (hardback)
ISBN 978-0-253-05757-0 (paperback)
ISBN 978-0-253-05756-3 (ebook)

First printing 2021

CONTENTS

ACKNOWLEDGMENTS

I AM GRATEFUL TO MY teachers, colleagues, friends, and family for their help and encouragement. This project originated at New York University, where I benefited from the intellectually enriching environment in the Skirball Department of Hebrew and Judaic Studies. I am deeply indebted to the teaching and guidance of my doctoral advisor, Elliot Wolfson. In graduate seminars and directed readings, he challenged me to refine my analysis and to broaden my intellectual horizons. I am grateful for his mentorship, insight, and wisdom. I would also like to thank the other members of my dissertation committee—Yael Feldman, Avital Ronell, David Engel, and Stefanos Geroulanos—and the NYU faculty in the Department of Hebrew and Judaic Studies, the Department of German, and the Program in Poetics and Theory. Faculty at the University of King's College set me on my academic path with a grounding in philosophy, literature, and theory, and I would like to thank Dorota Glowacka for encouraging my academic pursuits in the humanities.

I am thankful to have lived and written this book on the ancestral lands of many Indigenous peoples, including the Lenape, the Huron-Wendat, the Seneca, the Mississaugas of the Credit River, the Eno, the Catwawba, and the Shakori nations.

I thank my colleagues who have made the Department of Religious Studies at the University of North Carolina at Chapel Hill a wonderful place to work. I am grateful to department chairs Barbara Ambros and Randall Styers; my colleagues Yaakov Ariel, Brandon Bayne, Jessica Boon, Bart Ehrman, Carl Ernst, Juliane Hammer, Harshita Kamath, Joseph Lam, David Lambert, Lauren Leve, Jodi Magness, Evyatar Marienberg, Hugo Méndez, Todd Ochoa,

Zlatko Plese, Brendan Thornton, Waleed Ziad; and department administrators Tracey Cave, Myra Quick, Amy Miskow, and Hope Toscher. I extend my thanks to colleagues in UNC's Carolina Center for Jewish Studies. Thank you to program director Ruth von Bernuth and to colleagues Karen Auerbach, Gabrielle Berlinger, Flora Cassen, Danielle Christmas, Marcie Cohen Ferris, Maria DeGuzman, Michael Figueroa, Jeanne Fischer, Jonathan Hess, Rosa Perelmuter, Michele Rivkin-Fish, Yaron Shemer, Hanna Sprintzik, Martin Sueldo, and communications director Karen Gajewski. Through the North Carolina Jewish Studies Seminar and Consortium I have met a wide network of fellow scholars. Members of the Duke/UNC Theory reading group have been invaluable conversation partners. Many thanks to the participants of the Paula E. Hyman Mentoring Program for Jewish Women's and Gender Studies, and to Vanessa Ochs for her mentorship.

I gratefully acknowledge support for my research from the Memorial Foundation for Jewish Culture, the NYU-Cambridge Mainzer Visiting Fellowship at the University of Cambridge Centre for Gender Studies, the Tikvah Center for Law and Jewish Civilization's Scholar-in-Residence program, the Posen Foundation, and the MacCracken doctoral fellowship. The Department of Religious Studies and the Carolina Center for Jewish Studies at UNC have been supportive of my research. My thanks go to the Leonard and Tobee Kaplan Distinguished Professorship in Modern Jewish Religious Thought, the William D. McLester Fund for Faculty Excellence in Religious Studies, the Sarah Graham Kenan Arts and Sciences Endowment Fund, the Jay Gould Endowment Fund for Jewish Studies, and the Jerry and Huddy Cohen Faculty Excellence Fund in Jewish Studies. The UNC College of Arts & Sciences and the Carolina Center for Jewish Studies provided much appreciated travel funds for research conferences. I extend my gratitude to the Association for Jewish Studies First Book Subvention Prize and to the Association for Jewish Studies Women's Caucus Cashmere Subvention Award in Jewish Gender, Sexuality, and Women's Studies for supporting the book's publication.

I owe thanks to the members of the Modern Judaism Electronic Workshop for their helpful feedback and collegiality: Yonatan Brafman, Samuel Brody, Rachel Gordan, Sarah Imhoff, Alexander Kaye, Jessica Marglin, Paul Nahme, and Elias Sacks. Thank you to Mara Benjamin for her encouragement and feedback in conversations about this project. My thanks to Ellen Pollak for her insightful comments. I have benefited enormously from the careful eye and suggestions of Catherine Osborne, who encouraged my voice to emerge more clearly. Zachary Braiterman has been a strong supporter of this project, and I thank him for his encouragement, advice, and invaluable suggestions as I revised the manuscript. I am very grateful to Dee Mortensen for leading this book through the publication process and for her guidance and insight, to Ashante Thomas for all her help throughout, and to Darja Malcolm-Clarke and Stephen Williams at Indiana University Press and Jennifer Crane at Amnet. Thank you to Brian Flanagan for his work on the index. I also thank the anonymous reviewers for their careful and thoughtful feedback on the manuscript.

An earlier version of chapter 1 appeared as Andrea Dara Cooper, "From Sister-Wife to Brother-Neighbor: Rosenzweig Reads the Song of Songs," *Journal of Jewish Thought and Philosophy* 28, no. 2 (2020): 228–258. I am thankful for the editor's and anonymous reviewers' insights and for permission to incorporate the article here.

Thank you to friends, colleagues, and family who have offered help and assurance along the way, including Magalí Armillas Tiseyra, Sarah Bloesch, Jeremy Brown, Miles Cooper Mendel, Ezra Cooper Mendel, Ella Cooper, Yali Dekel, Guadalupe González Diéguez, Rosane Gertner, David Gertner, Leo Gertner, Lynn Kaye, Ayelet Kuper, Michelle Landy-Shavim, Michael Mendel, Rachel Paneth-Pollak, Vera Paneth-Gertner, Katherine Turk, Emily Robins Sharpe, and Erin Shnier. I will always be grateful to my Zaidy Max Zeller, z"l, for his generosity and for teaching me about survival and strength. Thank you to my sister Jess Riva Cooper for her companionship and inspiring creativity and for creating the artwork for the cover of this book. My deepest thanks to my parents, Esther Zeller Cooper and Morris Cooper, for their continual love, enthusiasm, and support and for instilling in me the values of education, imagination, and curiosity. Finally, I am so grateful to my human-canine family, Alex Gertner, Nemo, Gemma, and Ada. Thank you for making this possible.

GENDERING MODERN
JEWISH THOUGHT

INTRODUCTION

Gendered Genealogies

What better notion to conjure with than "fraternity," and what better
conjuring trick than to insist that "fraternity" is universal and nothing more
than a metaphor for community.

—CAROLE PATEMAN, *THE SEXUAL CONTRACT*[1]

The fratriarchy may *include* cousins and sisters but, as we will see, including
may also come to mean neutralizing. Including may dictate forgetting, for
example, with "the best of all intentions," that the sister will never provide a
docile example for the concept of fraternity.

—JACQUES DERRIDA, *THE POLITICS OF FRIENDSHIP*[2]

IN *THE POLITICS OF FRIENDSHIP*, Jacques Derrida examines the brotherly
nature of friendship and political community, arguing that any social organization based on fraternity is exclusionary. If communities are structured through
"the economic, genealogical, ethnocentric, androcentric features of fraternity,"
then how can we begin to think beyond the fraternal?[3] Derrida's critical formulation of "a *familial, fraternalist* and thus *androcentric* configuration"[4] could be
well applied to the field of modern Jewish thought and its historical construction. Twentieth-century thinkers such as Franz Rosenzweig, Martin Buber, and
Emmanuel Levinas focus on human intersubjectivity and its theological and
ethical possibilities. They have much to contribute to current conversations on
relational ethics, embodiment, otherness, and affective modes of engagement.
At the same time, a twenty-first century reader cannot help but become aware
of the limitations to this canon when read with attention to gender.

1

Many areas within both Jewish studies and religious studies have been productively challenged and illuminated by using gender as an analytical category, and there have been important and groundbreaking contributions to the fields of gender and Jewish philosophy.[5] Yet the all-male fraternity of modern Jewish thinkers has remained largely immune to critiques informed by gender and feminist analysis.[6] In reassessing what she calls (with intentional capitalization) "The Great Men of Modern Jewish Thought," Mara Benjamin convincingly identifies "the limits of the all-male canon of modern Jewish thinkers, thinkers as often beatified as analyzed in scholarship on Jewish philosophy and religious thought."[7] I contend that we can deeply value these thinkers' significant contributions while also interrogating and making explicit the structures that drive their philosophical approaches. In these works, kinship functions on the level of both form and content: as a network of male thinkers who operate in relation to one another and as a trope that shapes their methodologies. This coincidence is not accidental. How do these themes shore up ethical approaches that privilege the masculine? This is both a hermeneutical and an ethical limitation. What would the accepted canon of modern Jewish thought look like beyond, in Derrida's words, "the homo-fraternal and phallogocentric schema" of the fratriarchy?[8] What approaches and interpretations are overlooked?[9] Questions of identity and agency can reanimate the field by uncovering power relations already at work in canonical texts, pointing toward an inclusive reimagining of canons that often reflect exclusive social norms.[10]

This book aims to bring current readers into conversation with the twentieth-century Jewish philosophical canon[11] through a critical gender analysis of key works in the field. I examine the German Jewish tradition through the work of Franz Rosenzweig and the French Jewish tradition through Emmanuel Levinas, investigating the genealogies of familial tropes in their theological and ethical frameworks. As Elliot R. Wolfson observes, Rosenzweig is "one of the more lionized thinkers of the twentieth century."[12] Likewise, Robert Erlewine identifies a trend of celebrating Rosenzweig's thought: "Franz Rosenzweig has been embraced by Jewish Studies scholars like no other figure in modern Jewish thought," as has his work *The Star of Redemption*.[13] The laudatory reception of Rosenzweig's work in recent years may be a result of readers conflating him with Levinas.[14] Rosenzweig's voice is granted prominent authority in the academy, and his thought "continues to attract more attention and followers than that of any other modern thinker" in modern Jewish philosophy, "perhaps with the exception of Emmanuel Levinas."[15]

I do not seek to explain away these thinkers' markedly paternalistic approaches to certain themes, nor do I suggest dismissing their writing on these issues. Rather, I approach them by considering their influences and evolutions and thinking through some of the more troubling aspects of their work. Using interdisciplinary methods from feminist and gender studies, literary and psychoanalytic theories, and religious and cultural studies, I offer here a new reading of major works, highlighting both their problems and possibilities. I show how a feminist reading of Jewish philosophical texts reveals them to be shaped by traditionally Jewish patriarchal approaches to kinship that have been invested in biblical and rabbinic models of normativity. Structured around the relational models of erotic love, paternity, and brotherhood, among others, an intrinsically gendered kinship becomes a root metaphor for ethical and communal relationships.[16]

When kinship goes to work as a metaphor, it can proliferate at many levels. Referring to twentieth-century Jewish philosophers' uncritical use of the term *the feminine*, Leora Batnizky writes, "these thinkers relegate women to the roles of mother and keeper of the home. Rosenzweig's and Levinas's traditionalism is particularly apt in this regard."[17] Organizing metaphors like these tend to reproduce themselves if we do not pay explicit attention to them, and they can have real effects on real people. If female bodies become metaphorical vessels for the reproduction of men, then women and non-normative individuals come to be elided from organizing language, and their interests are ignored in the intersubjective, communal, and scholarly spheres. This patriarchal logic is further implicated in the propagation of these ideas. The philosophical texts I treat in this book both encode and construct models of relationship that have ongoing normative status in the world. Responsibly and critically reading our foundational texts, I argue, can lead to a more inclusive field of study, in which nonmale voices are not reflexively elided and in which male intellectual dissemination and female biological reproduction are not the overarching goals.

READING FOR GENDER

Franz Rosenzweig, one of the two foundational figures I investigate, was born in Germany in 1887 and died in 1929. Developing an early interest in political philosophy, he studied with Hermann Cohen and drew on his concept of correlation but later came to offer a critique of his teacher's neo-Kantianism.[18] In his major work, *The Star of Redemption*, written in 1918–19 and published in 1921, Rosenzweig related the elements of God, world, and man to the theological notions of creation, revelation, and redemption. He viewed the *Star* as a philosophical system but also referred to it as a "great world poem."[19] It was first composed on postcards sent home during the end of his military service in World War I.[20] My other key figure, Emmanuel Levinas, was born in 1906 in Lithuania, became a French citizen in the 1930s, and died in 1995. Within French thought and twentieth-century continental philosophy more broadly, he is known for his philosophical approach toward an ethics of otherness (or alterity, as he formulates it) and for a radical reshaping of subjectivity, especially in his later work. Levinas's first magnum opus, *Totality and Infinity: An Essay on Exteriority*, published in 1961, is well known through its analysis of the "face-to-face" relation with the other. His second main work, *Otherwise Than Being or Beyond Essence*, was published in 1974. Levinas acknowledged Rosenzweig as a formative influence, although Levinas's thinking diverges from Rosenzweig's in important ways.[21] Levinas continued on Rosenzweig's path but subsumed the theological under the ethical.[22] His concept of alterity with a transcendent other reflects Rosenzweig's articulation of the human-divine dialogical encounter. Notably, for Levinas, responsibility for the other does not originate in the revelation of divine love. Rather, the other calls the self into responsibility prior to choice, like the involuntary action of breathing.

Levinas's gendered concepts in particular have come in for quite a bit of scholarly examination. In *The Second Sex* (1949), Simone de Beauvoir criticized his perpetuation of the philosophical trend to relegate the feminine to secondary status against the normative masculine. In a footnote, Beauvoir writes, "it is striking that [Levinas] deliberately takes a man's view, disregarding the reciprocity of subject and object. When he writes that woman is mystery, he implies that she is mystery for man. Thus his description, which is intended to be objective, is in fact an assertion of masculine privilege."[23] This assessment of Levinas's work *Time and the Other* has been called into question by later readers who point out that Beauvoir did not appreciate the privileged position of the other in Levinas's project.[24]

While Beauvoir's critique may not reflect Levinas's radical elevating of the other over the subject, she nevertheless points out a central problem in his thought. Luce Irigaray also criticizes Levinas's relegation of the feminine to the object-like status of "beloved woman" while the man is provided with the active term "lover." Irigaray asks why the relation that leads toward the future in *Totality and Infinity* must be of the father and son and not the daughter.[25] In his account, Irigaray argues, the erotic encounter with the feminine is useful only insofar as it produces a (masculine) child.[26] For both Irigaray and Jacques Derrida, the horizon of sexual difference sharply limits Levinas's ethics, not least because Levinas views sexual difference as secondary to the primary category of ethics. Not incidentally, Levinas makes this move by signifying sexuality as feminine and the site of the ethical as masculine.[27] In a multivocal essay that I will engage in the second and third chapters, Derrida reveals that Levinas's work is housed atop a cellar in which the daughter is encrypted and excluded from the relation of paternity-filiality.[28]

Rosenzweig has received less criticism, but these responses to Levinas's work can also be applied to his approach. For both thinkers, the subordination of the sexual to the fraternal-filial correlates to the subordination of the feminine by the masculine, the female beloved by the male lover, the mother by the father, and the daughter by the son. Rosenzweig and Levinas both locate the possibility of the future in the son and designate the feminine as the subject's "beloved." In Levinas's account, fathers achieve transcendence while passing on "the possibility for further transcendence to sons and brothers," an exclusionary transmission that, as Sarah Allen points out, "passes in silence over the feminine."[29] For Rosenzweig, love moves beyond itself in marriage, binding a couple together in blood and propagating the community's future. He details how the past is tied to the present and the future through a genealogy of males, reaching back to the grandfather in the transmission of a distinctly masculine familial line.[30]

But it is women's bodies that allow for this masculine dissemination of bloodlines. Zachary Braiterman criticizes Rosenzweig's omission of women from this celebration of propagation and thus from the central drama of revelation.[31] Rosenzweig's version of intersubjectivity gives way to a *Männerbund*, a homosocial community: "This community of men has been made possible by the exclusion of women, who are taken for granted, their presence effaced. In a gendered body of work, from which actual women are explicitly excluded, 'man' is more than a generic brand of human community."[32] For both Rosenzweig and Levinas, erotic love must eventually be overcome by the universality of brotherhood in the social realm. In light of all this, it is tempting to agree with Stella Sandford, who finds aspects of Levinas's thought to be "gratingly patriarchal"; after reading his description of the feminine in *Totality and Infinity*, she finds that "the feminist case for Levinas does not look good."[33]

A gender-conscious reading of what Levinas terms "the feminine" can offer a focused examination on a specific, foundational current within his thought by taking into account the Jewish elements pervading his broader work. As Claire Elise Katz shows in *Levinas, Judaism, and the Feminine: The Silent Footsteps of Rebecca*, the traditional Jewish themes shaping Levinas's thought on the feminine can offer a more nuanced reading of his work. Katz reads his thought within a Judaic framework, analyzing his philosophical and religious texts side by side, despite Levinas's attempts to demarcate them.[34] Katz explains that in turning away from Heideggerian ontology and the quest for representational knowledge to an ethics of responsibility, Levinas inverts the ontological focus on the masculine to an ethical reflection on the feminine. Levinas's evocation of the maternal bond in his later work, then, demonstrates a shift from the classical philosophical focus on death to an emphasis on life.

Katz's work on the place of the feminine and Judaism in Levinas's thought has been instructive to me, and my reading has been informed by her insight on the contributions and interruptions that Jewish philosophers offer Western philosophy. Levinas's relational models can serve as a challenge to traditional Western approaches, which are often centered on atomistic individuals: "Today, Jewish philosophy is positioned outside the boundary of modern Western philosophy, which has been dominated by thinkers of Protestant background. This position allows Jewish thought to expose the myth of philosophy's neutrality and objectivity."[35] Levinas's method allows him to critique his philosophical lineage: "If Jewish philosophy is the critic of Western Protestant philosophy, then Levinas is the critic of the critics. Writing as a phenomenologist after the Shoah, he witnessed the spectacular failure of the Enlightenment.... Is secular society really secular? Is it really secular for Jews? Similar to how Mendelssohn called out the unfairness of the quotas imposed on Jewish citizenship, Levinas is able to see that what appears as secular to Christian society is not secular to those who sit at its margins."[36] This insight leads me to comment in this book on what I call (perhaps anachronistically) Levinas's positionality. That is, his philosophical voice is informed by the specifics that make up his own unique position—his life as a male, Jewish, heterosexual, non-native French speaker who worked in religious education for much of his life and lost close family members during the Shoah, among other formative experiences.[37] By insisting on the stubborn location and embodiedness of thought, he presents a refreshing contrast with many other thinkers.

Indeed, Derrida points out that Levinas's thought is explicitly sexed as male. Levinas's phenomenology of eros, a controversial section but nevertheless one that "occupies such an important place in the book's economy," is representative of this position: "let us note in passing that *Totality and Infinity* pushes the respect for dissymmetry so far that it seems to us impossible, essentially impossible, that it could have been written by a woman. Its philosophical subject is man."[38] The author's masculine signature is apparent in his work: "His signature thus assumes the sexual mark, a remarkable phenomenon in the history of philosophical writing, if the latter has always been interested in occupying that position without re-marking upon it or assuming it on, without signing its mark."[39] Derrida is right to criticize Levinas for relying on patriarchal logic while also acknowledging that Levinas inscribes his own work with an explicitly masculine viewpoint. By intentionally marking his thought as male and Jewish, Levinas forces readers to confront the usually invisible assumptions underlying Western thought. He invites us to reflect on the contingency and specificity of *all* philosophical work, to pay attention to language, and to read closely.

My own reading of these thinkers turns on an investigation of how their positionality drove their persistent and underexamined organizing metaphors of kinship: erotic love, marriage, brotherhood, paternity, and maternity. These metaphors provide the framework of the book. Levinas's *Totality and Infinity*, for example, concludes with the paternal-son relation, and its correlative end in social fraternity, as the essential link to the future. Rosenzweig, as I will explore at length, emphasizes homogenous brotherhood in reading the Song of Songs, effacing the text's celebration of differentiated lovers. A particular issue I address in this book is Rosenzweig's highlighting of the importance of fraternity as a formative relationship and Levinas's echo of this emphasis: "The other is from the first the brother to all the other men."[40] For both, any relation of solidarity among nonbiological brothers is thinkable only within the model of fraternity. They are not alone in this move. Even Beauvoir's *The Second Sex* maintains that freedom is modeled on a masculine bond. While the introduction to her book appeals for women to become at last full members of the "human race,"[41] Beauvoir concludes with a hope that men and women will unite in *"fraternité."*[42]

But while brotherhood may appear to be an admirable ethical aim, it comes at a high price. Feminist political theorists Carole Pateman and Juliet Flower MacCannell have shown that fraternity is inherently limiting. In *The Sexual Contract*, Pateman makes the case for giving fraternity its rightful place alongside the revolutionary values of liberty and equality, which have been the subject of much further analysis and theorization.[43] She argues that the alliance of the three elements predates the 1789 proclamation of *"liberté, égalité, fraternité"*[44] and that patriarchy has always depended on fraternity. "A very nice conjuring trick has been performed so that one kinship term, fraternity, is held to be merely a metaphor for the universal bonds of humankind, for community, solidarity or fellowship."[45] Proponents of fraternity claim it has replaced patriarchy, the ancient and long past rule of fathers. "The modern civil order can then be presented as universal ('fraternal') not patriarchal. Almost no one—except some feminists—is willing to admit that fraternity means what it says: the brotherhood of *men*."[46]

In Pateman's view, the language of fraternity has allowed social contract theorists to mask its essential patriarchal structure.[47] Fraternity has always been an exclusive and exclusionary masculine bond. This is apparent in Freud's *Civilization and Its Discontents*, in which women's attachments are particularized and limited to the family while men are free to develop an affective fraternal community outside the domestic sphere.[48] The separation of women helped to stabilize the political system. Fraternity's adherents have an interest in retaining the terms of this sexual contract and in claiming that fraternity is only a metaphor for community, when in reality it is more like a fraternal patriarchy. The fraternal model, as a function of patriarchy, is linked to the subjection of women.

Building on Pateman's work, Juliet Flower MacCannell uses a psychoanalytic approach to argue that the regime of the brother has replaced patriarchy. The Enlightenment advanced the egalitarian norm of common humanity, and modern society was constructed with an "alibi of fraternal love."[49] In the "universal" brotherhood of man, sisterhood is suppressed along with sexual difference, an exclusion that is integral to the economy of the modern society. The law of the brother warps the world "into a fiction of fraternity, the dream of a universal, which becomes the nightmare lie of the family of man."[50] Because the "family of man" sequesters the sister, it erroneously claims to be a civilization founded on justice, equality, and freedom. "Women are coded men, and lesser men at that . . . and the real other, the sister, is absorbed into a general brotherhood."[51] Brotherhood is a founding structure of modernity, and it continues to reproduce itself. More recently, scholars have argued that fraternity has not replaced patriarchy but rather reinscribed it. When fraternity is installed as the controlling political structure, the vertical relations of patriarchy "are sustained by the lateral relations of fraternity."[52] Fraternity, as Stephani Engelstein writes in her study of modernity's siblinghood discourses, "cannot serve as a symbol of inclusive politics when it blatantly excludes half the population."[53]

The model of brotherhood pervades the move from the dyadic relationship to the communal sphere that we find in much of twentieth-century Jewish dialogical philosophy and ethical monotheism.[54] In advancing from the familial to the social level, society is construed as a relationship of brothers in which every self is commanded to ethical relations with others because of this shared kinship. The discourse of brotherhood is a regulative theological and philosophical ideal for modern Jewish thought, predicated on the concept that all are children of the one God, and therefore brothers to one another, sharing a common nature and purpose. As Marc Shell has observed, there are implications to a religiously inflected call for universal brotherhood: "The motto 'All men are brothers' has had political significance for national unity and religious universalism. But however profound its cultural origin or ineradicable its linguistic presence, it is often prematurely dismissed as merely metaphorical, as if simply to say that 'brother' does not mean 'brother.'"[55] The use of kinship terminology is hardly neutral. The distinction between figural and literal kinship should be challenged because the ideal of universal siblinghood is mobilized to shape and restrict homogenized group membership. The monotheistic ideal of universal brotherhood is based on exclusion. This schema implicitly values the erasure of difference. It requires dissolving the particularities of identity, and it raises critical questions about the status of those who, by definition, are not capable of performing "brotherhood."

I uncover the meaning of the fraternal metaphor for Rosenzweig in my first chapter, showing that it is central to his evocative reading of the Song of Songs in *The Star of Redemption*. One compelling feature of Rosenzweig's interpretation of the Song of Songs is that, while the Song is usually understood to focus on a heteroerotic relationship between lovers, Rosenzweig concentrates on the lovers' wish to be united in societal fraternity. His idiosyncratic interpretation is marked by fraternal tropes and the subsequent effacement of gender. The erotic sphere of revelation is surpassed by neighborly "brotherliness" in communal redemption. Ultimately, Rosenzweig transposes the erotic energy in the Song from a celebration of difference to a longing for sameness—a move that has exegetical, normative, and philosophical implications. Informed by critical feminist and intersectional analysis, I argue that his notion of blood community supports a patriarchal genealogy that relies on the regulation of Jewish women's bodies to produce Jewish children in the service of continuity.

In the second chapter, I examine the role of erotic love in Levinas's earlier work. I read Levinas alongside Plato, who strongly influenced his phenomenology of eros, and I examine how Plato views the feminine and the body to understand how Levinas draws on and diverges from these frameworks. I consider the consequences to Levinas's insistence that erotic love lies outside the ethical realm. Levinas ultimately goes even further than Plato in his dismissal of erotic love, and I question the priority he gives to the future of fecundity—to procreation. I offer a critique of Levinas's gender economy by highlighting the sublated space of the feminine and the absent presence of the reproductive female body.

The third chapter brings Derrida and Hannah Arendt into conversation to pry open the unifying concept of brotherhood. This concept simultaneously eclipses and usurps the feminine on the one hand and becomes the basis for politics on the other. Levinas's phenomenology of eros reflects Rosenzweig's emphasis on the erotic relationship being surpassed in marriage, entering the community, and becoming eternal through male offspring. The possibility of moving from ethics to politics is predicated on the fraternal. Levinas comes to emphasize a neighborly love purified of carnal eros, and embodied maternity becomes the ethical relationship par excellence. But, as I argue, the maternal emphasis is pervaded by the filial-fraternal model. I read Derrida's politics of friendship alongside Arendt's critique of brotherhood and its classical exclusion of Jewish politics, which she draws from the leitmotif of friendship in Gotthold Ephraim Lessing's play *Nathan the Wise*. For Arendt, "brotherhood" exists only in dark times between persecuted peoples, and as such it cannot be political. It is friendship, rather, that should be the basis of the political realm. Arendt also draws our attention to the unmarked post-Christian nature of so much contemporary philosophical discourse on the "brotherhood of man."

Chapter 4 examines the scandal of the biographical trace, the regulations of kinship and bloodlines, and the struggle between erotic love and family obligations. I unpack the eroticism of the sister-brother relation in Rosenzweig's life, letters, and work. His exegesis of the Song of Songs in the *Star* especially calls for this kind of comparative reading because it was written via letters to Margrit Rosenstock-Huessy, whom he called his "sister-bride"—a term lifted from the Song. Cultural critics of the period immediately preceding Rosenzweig's composition of the *Star* have observed that in a number of spheres, the brother-sister relationship was a cultural touchstone. To help me examine the meaning and symbolism of this sibling relationship, I turn to Sophocles's *Antigone*, which Hegel famously celebrated. We can better understand Rosenzweig's idealization of the brother-sister relationship in both his philosophical work and his life if we look back to the reception history of *Antigone*, which became the urtext of the brother-sister relationship following Hegel. I argue that Rosenzweig's text and its production history mutually illuminate each other when it comes to the troubling gender dynamics that subsume the sister-wife in both philosophy and life. In doing so, I consider what is at stake when we read for biography in philosophical work. There is good reason to avoid reducing the philosophical text to the philosopher's life, but there are risks to this approach. If we stay safely removed from the biographical sphere, then we reify the patriarchal structures that too often allow the work of philosophy to be done.

In chapter 5, the Hebrew Bible, Greek tragedy, and popular culture inform my understanding of Levinas's ethics of maternity, substitution, and sacrifice. Although there are helpful elements to Levinas's idea of embodied maternity, there are also drawbacks to his approach. He slips between pregnant bodies and figural ethical gestation, much as he tended to slip in his earlier work between actual women and the symbolic feminine. He plainly states that the body is not merely a metaphor in his work, and I take this assertion seriously. If it is not merely figural, then we must be especially cautious when an ethical relationship of embodied maternity is characterized as self-sacrificial. While the Levinasian model of maternal self-sacrifice does not take us far enough, it can point to new possibilities for imagining gender, kinship, and embodied responsibility. I track alternative modes of familial sacrifice, showing how interventions in twenty-first century popular narrative and culture both recapitulate and subvert traditional models of Greek and biblical paternal sacrifice. Contemporary sacrificial echoes point to the persistence of these models, but they also indicate a way beyond the limitations of patriarchal approaches to kinship. The figure of sorority can interrupt "this history of brothers that has been told to us for thousands of years."[56] The sisterly relationship offers a challenge to the fraternalist and fratriarchal framework.

In the epilogue, I argue that to explore the capacious possibilities that emerge from modern Jewish thought, we need to expose the narrative models that persist beneath our explicit acknowledgment. To engage with these thinkers in dialogue, and to see how they provide valuable models for intersubjective ethics, reciprocity, embodiment, and positionality, we must first do the work of critical reading. We have to come to terms with gender terminology expressed in normatively limiting and damaging ways. In her foundational essay "A Matter of Discipline: Reading for Gender in Jewish Philosophy," Susan Shapiro lays out the scope and stakes of this reading practice:

> To read for gender is to read for constructions and performances of gender with an interest in the intellectual, religious, and cultural labor these tropes enact in these texts. It is to read, as well, with an interest in the social, political, and cultural consequences of these figures and tropes, both within these texts and for women and men in the past as well as for readers today. That is, the work performed by these gendered tropes, I argue, is philosophical, requiring a re-thinking of what we understand (Jewish) philosophical texts to be and, therefore, how they can best be read.[57]

For example, when a writer refers to one category (say, philosophy) as the "handmaiden" to another (such as theology), this is not a neutral statement.[58] Whenever I come across this fairly common phrase, I flinch. This trope supports sexual, political, and classist (not to mention biblical) hierarchization. Other commonly used tropes reify ableist, racist, and speciesist attitudes.

I could go on. The point is, these metaphors matter because they have material consequences; they regulate bodies and organize communities.

We must pay attention to gender without reflexively aligning "gender" with "women." Masculinity often goes unmarked, and men are framed as the normative default. As Sarah Imhoff argues, "By not studying men and not paying attention to how their gender roles and ideals are constructed, we can leave ourselves with the impression that masculinity is transhistorical and essential."[59] Investigating masculinity is central to the study of gender and Judaism, since masculinity has often been invisible, and "Jewish men are (and have been) the normative Jews."[60] Rather than reflexively assigning the Great (Male) Thinkers a normative neutrality, we can begin by emphasizing their positionality. In doing so, we will reveal and disrupt relations of power in these texts. It is my contention that to avoid reproducing the exclusionary logic within foundational works that make uncritical use of gendered terms, critical reading practices are vital. Investigating the gendered metaphors of kinship that organize these texts, as I do in this book, can open space for different conversations and point toward a more inclusive field.

NOTES

1. Carol Pateman, *The Sexual Contract* (Cambridge, UK: Polity, 1988), 114.

2. Jacques Derrida, *Politics of Friendship*, trans. George Collins (London: Verso, 2005), viii.

3. Derrida, *Politics of Friendship*, viii.

4. Derrida, viii.

5. For foundational texts in gender and Jewish history, see Marion A. Kaplan, *The Making of the Jewish Middle Class: Women, Family, and Identity in Imperial Germany* (Oxford: Oxford University Press, 1991); Paula E. Hyman, *Gender and Assimilation in Modern Jewish History* (Seattle: University of Washington Press, 1995); Miriam Peskowitz, "Engendering Jewish Religious History," *Shofar: An Interdisciplinary Journal of Jewish Studies* 14, no. 1 (fall 1995): 8–34; Laura Levitt, *Jews and Feminism: The Ambivalent Search for Home* (New York: Routledge, 1997); and Riv-Ellen Prell, *Fighting to Become Americans: Jews, Gender, and the Anxiety of Assimilation* (Boston: Beacon, 1999). For representative examples in gender and Jewish philosophy, see Heidi Ravven, "Creating a Jewish Feminist Philosophy," *Anima* 12, no. 2 (1986): 99–112; Hava Tirosh-Rothschild, "Dare to Know: Feminism and the Discipline of Jewish Philosophy," in *Feminist Perspectives on Jewish Studies*, ed. Lynn Davidman and Shelly Tenenbaum (New Haven, CT: Yale University Press, 1996); Susan E. Shapiro, "A Matter of Discipline: Reading for Gender in Jewish Philosophy," in *Judaism Since Gender*, ed. Miriam Peskowitz

and Laura Levitt (New York: Routledge, 1997); Claire Elise Katz, *Levinas, Judaism, and the Feminine: The Silent Footsteps of Rebecca* (Bloomington: Indiana University Press, 2003); Leora Batnizky, "Dependency and Vulnerability: Jewish and Feminist Existentialist Constructions of the Human," in *Women and Gender in Jewish Philosophy* (Bloomington: Indiana University Press, 2004); Elliot R. Wolfson, *Language, Eros, Being: Kabbalistic Hermeneutics and Poetic Imagination* (New York: Fordham University Press, 2005); Michael Oppenheim, "Feminist Jewish Philosophy: A Response," *Nashim: A Journal of Jewish Women's Studies & Gender Issues* 14 (fall 2007): 209–32; Tamar Rudavsky, "Feminism and Modern Jewish Philosophy," in *The Cambridge Companion to Modern Jewish Philosophy*, ed. Michael Morgan and Peter Gordon (Cambridge, UK: Cambridge University Press, 2007), 324–47; Hava Tirosh-Samuelson, Feminism and Gender," in *The Cambridge History of Jewish Philosophy, Volume 2: The Modern Era*, ed. Martin Kavka, Zachary Braiterman, and David Novak, 154–89 (Cambridge: Cambridge University Press, 2012); and Mara Benjamin, *The Obligated Self: Maternal Subjectivity and Jewish Thought* (Bloomington: Indiana University Press, 2018). See also Andrea Dara Cooper, "Gender and Modern Jewish Thought," in *Oxford Bibliographies in Jewish Studies*, ed. Naomi Seidman (New York: Oxford University Press, 2021), for a detailed overview of developments and interventions in critical gender analysis in relation to modern Jewish thought.

6. See Susan Shapiro: "The instruction to ignore images, figures and tropes of gender difference and hierarchy as well as of sexuality in Jewish philosophical texts has been a hermeneutic practice of long standing. In the past twenty years or so, however, there has been some feminist engagement with Jewish philosophy. Despite this feminist intervention, there has been an ongoing reluctance, or even resistance, to reading for gender and sexuality in Jewish philosophy" ("Gender and Jewish Philosophy: Introduction," *Bamidbar* 4, no. 2 [2019]: 7). See also Hava Tirosh-Samuelson: "In the late 1980s and early 1990s, only a few (male) scholars of Jewish philosophy took note of feminism and acknowledged its potential relevance to Jewish philosophy, but despite these lone sympathetic voices, the field as a whole has remained oblivious to the vast literature of feminist philosophy or to the philosophical debates among feminists" ("Feminism and Gender," 157).

7. Mara Benjamin, "Agency as Quest and Question: Feminism, Religious Studies, and Modern Jewish Thought," *Jewish Social Studies* vol. 24, no. 2 (Winter 2019): 11–12. Benjamin identifies the "intractably androcentric nature" of this subfield (10).

8. Derrida, *Politics of Friendship*, 306.

9. Ken Koltun-Fromm illustrates the divide between what counts as "Jewish thought" and "Jewish philosophy": "The rubric 'Jewish thought' already expands upon the more limited category of 'Jewish philosophy' to include texts usually

on the outside of an accepted canon. There is certainly a turf war here, in which some protect a rubric and canon to safeguard against noisy insurgents. But there is also a serious concern about method and access: how do we best articulate the boundaries between thought and culture, and the methods by and through which we access those domains?" (*Imagining Jewish Authenticity: Vision and Text in American Jewish Thought* [Bloomington: Indiana University Press, 2015], 10). On this topic, see also Claire E. Katz, "Philosophy, the Academy, and the Future of Jewish Learning," in *Jewish Philosophy for the Twenty-First Century: Personal Reflections,* ed. Hava Tirosh-Samuelson and Aaron W. Hughes (Leiden: Brill, 2014), 155, and Zachary Braiterman, "After Germany: An American Jewish Philosophical Manifesto," in *Jewish Philosophy for the Twenty-First Century,* 42–60.

10.   Nancy Tuana explains the importance of analyzing how philosophical canons are shaped by power relations: "Along with the process of uncovering women's philosophical history, we must also begin to analyze the impact of gender ideologies upon the process of canonization. . . . Paying attention to the workings of gender within the texts of philosophy will make visible the complexities of the inscription of gender ideologies" ("Preface," in *Feminist Interpretations of Emmanuel Levinas,* ed. Tina Chanter [University Park: Pennsylvania State University Press, 2001], xv).

11.   A canonical text in Jewish philosophy, according to Robert Erlewine, is "a work that has set the terms according to which scholarly discussion and debate have proceeded and continue to proceed" (*Judaism and the West: From Hermann Cohen to Joseph Soloveitchik* [Bloomington: Indiana University Press, 2016], 165n1). A thinker is canonical if their works "have significantly shaped the landscape of the field. . . . The term 'canonical' can be used in the sense that one can reasonably expect to find either the author or one of his or her texts represented on most syllabi devoted to modern Jewish philosophy or modern Judaism" (165n1). In this regard, Levinas is tied to the canon of modern German Jewish philosophy beginning with Hermann Cohen and continuing through Rosenzweig and Martin Buber. In contrast to seeing Levinas as situated firmly in the canon, Katz maintains that "Levinas's thinking, influenced by Husserl, Heidegger, and the postmodern tradition, is viewed as highly speculative and not as rigorous as 'real' philosophical thought requires. . . . His work is often excluded from the traditional canon in modern Jewish philosophy. The major figures in this canon include Moses Mendelssohn, Hermann Cohen, Martin Buber, and Franz Rosenzweig" ("Philosophy, the Academy, and the Future of Jewish Learning," 155–6). On Levinas's role in the canon of Jewish philosophy, see Martin Kavka, "Screening the Canon: Levinas and Medieval Jewish Philosophy," in *New Directions in Jewish Philosophy,* ed. Elliot R. Wolfson and Aaron W. Hughes (Bloomington: Indiana University Press, 2010), 17–51.

12. Elliot R. Wolfson, *Giving beyond the Gift: Apophasis and Overcoming Theomania* (New York: Fordham University Press, 2014), 42.

13. Erlewine, *Judaism and the West*, 52–3.

14. Peter Eli Gordon has pointed out this link: "Perhaps the most powerful catalyst to the recent resurgence of interest in Rosenzweig's philosophy is his connection with the widely discussed French-Jewish philosopher Emmanuel Levinas" ("Rosenzweig Redux: The Reception of German-Jewish Thought," *Jewish Social Studies* 8, no. 1 [fall 2001], 30.)

15. Erlewine, *Judaism and the West*, 53. Referring to Rosenzweig's undeniable Orientalism in the *Star*, Erlewine writes convincingly that "the tendency to dismiss his remarks about non-Western religions as a mere prejudice of bygone times and antiquated ways of thinking is untenable" (53). I take seriously Erlewine's point that "Rosenzweig's vision must be recognized for what it is. Indeed, it is imperative that we take stock of his actual position before we rush to reconstruct it in ways that are more palatable to our contemporary sensibilities" (53).

16. Carol Delaney explains the biblical origins of theories of kinship, which lent them divine authority: "kinship theory developed in the nineteenth century in cultures heavily influenced by the Bible in which notions of kinship and family appear simultaneously natural and divinely ordained" ("Cutting the Ties That Bind: The Sacrifice of Abraham and Patriarchal Kinship," in *Relative Values: Reconfiguring Kinship Studies*, ed. Sarah Franklin and Susan McKinnon [Durham, NC: Duke University Press, 2001], 445). From a sociological standpoint, Leonore Davidoff observes that in any society, "the basic framework of family and kin depends on prescribed gender categories, that is on current conceptions of what constitutes the feminine and masculine and the practices of people within these categories" (*Thicker Than Water: Siblings and Their Relations, 1780–1920* [Oxford: Oxford University Press, 2012], 5). On the role of kinship in anthropology, see Janet Carsten, *After Kinship* (Cambridge, UK: Cambridge University Press, 2003), and Adam Kuper, *The Reinvention of Primitive Society: Transformations of a Myth* (London: Routledge, 2005).

17. Batnizky, "Dependency and Vulnerability," 146–7. Batnitzky here notes, "It is not a coincidence that these two philosophers (and Rosenzweig more particularly) are considered more theologically 'Jewish' than some of their more rationalist predecessors." See also Tamar Rudavsky: "as Batnitzky and others have argued, Levinas's very use of the 'feminine' was itself influenced by Rosenzweig's *Star of Redemption*, in which 'the feminine' was utilized as an important theoretical category but was devoid of feminist concerns. Levinas has confined women to the private domain and to the hearth, adding legitimacy to such halakhic claims that because women are 'private' individuals, they cannot count in a 'public' prayer quorum. The implications of this exclusion

become all the more palpable when we turn to the area of Jewish liturgy and ritual" ("Feminism and Modern Jewish Philosophy," 337); and see Hava Tirosh-Samuelson: "Jewish philosophy remained almost exclusively dominated by men until the second half of the twentieth century, and modern Jewish philosophers—Franz Rosenzweig and Emmanuel Levinas—made the category of 'the feminine' central to their philosophical projects. These two philosophers were either closely associated with Martin Buber or deeply influenced by Buber, respectively. And all three took for granted the bourgeois model of female domesticity that dominated Europe in the late nineteenth and early twentieth centuries and the importance of women to the cultural ideal of *Bildung* and the bourgeois religiosity advanced by the proponents of Jewish enlightened reformers. Given the cult of domesticity, it is not surprising that Jewish philosophers use the category of 'the feminine' in their analysis of Judaism and in their reflections on the human condition. . . . The ubiquity of 'the feminine' as a trope to explore otherness does not entail that these Jewish philosophers were feminist; in fact, they all perpetuated traditional gender stereotyping of women as passive and receptive and did not promote the women's drive toward political equality" ("Feminism and Gender," 160).

18. For a discussion of Cohen's influence on Rosenzweig's theological approach, see Randi Rashkover, *Revelation and Theopolitics: Barth, Rosenzweig, and the Politics of Praise* (New York: T&T Clark International, 2005), 9–53.

19. Franz Rosenzweig, "The New Thinking," in *Philosophical and Theological Writings*, trans. and ed. Paul W. Franks and Michael L. Morgan (Indianapolis, IN: Hackett Publishing Company, 2000), 125.

20. For more on the background of Rosenzweig's life and thought, see Mara Benjamin, *Rosenzweig's Bible: Reinventing Scripture for Jewish Modernity* (Cambridge, UK: Cambridge University Press, 2009), 5–20.

21. In the preface to *Totality and Infinity*, Levinas writes, "We were impressed by the opposition to the idea of totality in Franz Rosenzweig's *Stern der Erlösung* [Star of Redemption], a work too often present in this book to be cited" (*Totality and Infinity: An Essay on Exteriority*, trans. Alphonso Lingis [Pittsburgh, PA: Duquesne University Press, 1995], 28). Leaving aside the question of citation (or lack thereof), it is clear that Rosenzweig had a strong influence on Levinas's thinking. Levinas wrote the following essays on Rosenzweig: "'Between Two Worlds' (The Way of Franz Rosenzweig)," in *Difficult Freedom: Essays on Judaism*, trans. Seán Hand (Baltimore, MD: Johns Hopkins University Press, 1997), first delivered as a paper to the second Colloquium of French-Speaking Jewish Intellectuals in 1959; "Franz Rosenzweig: A Modern Jewish Thinker," in *Outside the Subject*, trans. Michael B. Smith (Stanford, CA: Stanford University Press, 1994), first published in 1965 in *Revue de Théologie et de Philosophie*; and the foreword to Stéphane Mosès, *System and Revelation: The Philosophy of Franz*

Rosenzweig, trans. Catherine Tihanyi (Detroit, MI: Wayne State University Press, 1992 [1982]).

Many scholars have commented on Levinas's indebtedness to Rosenzweig's thought. Robert Gibbs refers to correlations between the two, emphasizing Levinas's adaptation and translation of Rosenzweig's German thought into the language of French phenomenology (*Correlations in Rosenzweig and Levinas* [Princeton, NJ: Princeton University Press, 1992], 32). Richard A. Cohen compares the thought of the two in a shared emphasis on ethical obligation and justice, arguing that they share a "central inspiration" in the intersubjective relation of non-indifference, opposing totality in transcendence (*Elevations: The Height of the Good in Rosenzweig and Levinas* [Chicago: University of Chicago Press, 1994], 162). Cohen notes that Levinas first read Rosenzweig's *Star* in 1935 (237). Leora Batnizky suggests that in the post-Holocaust era, Levinas translates many of Rosenzweig's explicitly theological notions into an interpersonal ethic. "Levinas represents the ethical obligation to the other as the eternal mark of humanity while Rosenzweig describes the Jewish people as themselves living this timeless ethic for the sake of others ("Dependency and Vulnerability," 139). Martin Kavka makes the case for both Levinas's similarity to and his critique of Rosenzweig. Referring to Levinas's famous remark on Rosenzweig's influence, Kavka writes, "Scholars can use this single sentence—which is truly as enigmatic as the most difficult of sentences in Levinas—to forge links between the two authors that remain unspoken on the surface of their published work . . . . The Levinas-Rosenzweig relationship is extremely complex, but there is more than enough room to articulate how the Levinasian adaptation of Rosenzweig includes a moment of critique" (*Jewish Messianism and the History of Philosophy* [Cambridge, UK: Cambridge University Press, 2004], 130–2). Claudia Welz suggests viewing the relation between the two in terms of crossroads, observing similarities but also points of divergence between their approaches (*Love's Transcendence and the Problem of Theodicy* [Tübingen: Mohr Siebeck, 2008], 285).

22. Samuel Moyn argues that Levinas's famous declaration of allegiance to Rosenzweig's thought in *Totality and Infinity* requires parsing. Despite Levinas's tribute, a straightforward continuity between the two cannot be taken for granted; rather, Levinas "radicalized, secularized, and moralized" Rosenzweig's thought (*Origins of the Other: Emmanuel Levinas between Revelation and Ethics* [Ithaca, NY: Cornell University Press, 2005], 117). Benjamin discusses Levinas's acknowledged debt to Rosenzweig alongside these differences: "for Levinas, contact with the other remains 'terrestrial,' that is, devoid of a 'vertical' (theological) component. This formulation secularizes Rosenzweig's theological model, but obligation nonetheless remains central" (*The Obligated Self*, 12).

23. Simone de Beauvoir, *The Second Sex,* trans. and ed. H. M. Parshley (New York: Vintage Books, 1989), xxii n3. For an analysis of Beauvoir's philosophy,

see Nancy Bauer, *Simone de Beauvoir, Philosophy, and Feminism* (New York: Columbia University Press, 2001).

24. See, for example, Richard A. Cohen, who maintains that although this issue is indeed important, it is "certainly not as simple as de Beauvoir, in this instance, makes it out to be, because for Levinas the other has a priority over the subject" (Emmanuel Levinas, *Time and the Other*, trans. Richard A. Cohen [Pittsburgh, PA: Duquesne University Press, 1987], 85n69.) Katz notes that "Beauvoir does not see the positive implications of alterity, and Cohen does not allow that de Beauvoir's intuition may have some merit" (*Levinas, Judaism, and the Feminine*, 36). Stella Sandford is sympathetic to Beauvoir's interpretation. She refers to her "first shocked reading of the passages on the feminine in Levinas's *Totality and Infinity* which appeared to me—as parts of Levinas's work had appeared to Simone de Beauvoir, I later learned—almost parodically exemplary of the crass, unthinking sexism so familiar in this history" (*The Metaphysics of Love: Gender and Transcendence in Levinas* [London: Continuum International Publishing Group, 2000], 2). On this topic, see also Hava Tirosh-Samuelson, who points out that Rosenzweig, Buber, and Levinas "employed the category of the 'the feminine' as a Jewish critique of Western philosophy, which is both Christian and masculine. The 'feminine' represents the Other that cannot be universalized, remaining distinctly particular in its otherness. Most importantly, whereas non-Jewish philosophers such as Jean Paul Sartre understood the category of Other negatively, signifying alienation, marginalization, and hostility, these three Jewish philosophers made the Other into the source of source of care, love, and above all, responsibility" ("Feminism and Gender," 160). Despite this shift, Tirosh-Samuelson notes that these thinkers nevertheless perpetuated the traditional gender stereotyping of women.

25. Luce Irigaray, *An Ethics of Sexual Difference*, trans. Carolyn Burke and Gillian C. Gill (Ithaca, NY: Cornell University Press, 1993), 197.

26. The secondary status of the feminine is also noted in Sarah Allen's analysis of transcendence: "the role of the feminine in fecundity remains a supporting role, subordinate to the transcendent movement of what can only be described as a masculine subject" (*The Philosophical Sense of Transcendence: Levinas and Plato on Loving beyond Being* [Pittsburgh, PA: Duquesne University Press, 2009], 234).

27. In the second chapter, I discuss sexual difference in Levinas's ethics in more detail in conversation with his Talmudic reading "And God Created Woman" in *Nine Talmudic Readings*, trans. Annette Aronowicz (Bloomington: Indiana University Press, 1994).

28. Derrida, "At This Very Moment in This Work Here I Am," in *Re-Reading Levinas*, trans. Ruben Berezdivin, ed. Robert Bernasconi and Simon Critchley (Bloomington: Indiana University Press, 1991), 47. See Simon Critchley, "'Bois'—Derrida's Final Word on Levinas," in *Re-Reading Levinas*, 186.

29. Allen, *The Philosophical Sense of Transcendence*, 240.

30. "The begetting of the future is a direct bearing witness to the past. The son is begotten so that he might bear witness to the past father of his begetter. The grandson renews the grandfather's name. The patriarchs call the last offspring by his name, which is also theirs. Above the darkness of the future there burns the starry heaven of the promise: so shall be your seed" (Franz Rosenzweig, *The Star of Redemption*, trans. Barbara E. Galli [Madison: University of Wisconsin Press, 2005], 317).

31. Zachary Braiterman, *The Shape of Revelation: Aesthetics and Modern Jewish Thought* (Redwood City, CA: Stanford University Press, 2007), 226–7.

32. Braiterman, *The Shape of Revelation*, 235.

33. Stella Sandford, "Levinas, Feminism and the Feminine," in *The Cambridge Companion to Levinas*, ed. Simon Critchley and Robert Bernasconi (Cambridge, UK: Cambridge University Press, 2006), 147. Alternatively, Craig R. Vasey suggests Levinas can be read as employing a feminist approach, but only unintentionally. He suggests that "the misogyny of Levinas's text . . . undermines or counters itself by containing a feminist vision or argument, albeit in ignorance" ("Faceless Women and Serious Others: Levinas, Misogyny, and Feminism," in *Ethics and Danger: Essays on Heidegger and Continental Thought*, ed. Arleen B. Dallery and Charles E. Scott [Albany: State University of New York Press, 1992], 317).

34. As Katz observes, "Levinas's intention to keep these writings separate does not preclude his Judaism from influencing his approach to philosophy" (Claire Elise Katz, "Reinhabiting the House of Ruth: Exceeding the Limits of the Feminine in Levinas," in *Feminist Interpretations of Emmanuel Levinas*, 164n6). The methodological question of whether to read Levinas's thought within a Judaic framework is more broadly raised by Elliot R. Wolfson and Aaron W. Hughes: "Can there be a Jewish philosophy? Surely, we would not want to say that every Jew who is a philosopher is necessarily a Jewish philosopher in the sense that he or she articulates a Jewish philosophy—Spinoza or Derrida, in contrast to Maimonides or Levinas—any more than we want to say a Jew who is a mathematician professes a Jewish mathematics, that a Jew who is a physicist does Jewish physics, or that Jew who writes poetry necessarily produces Jewish poetry" ("Introduction: Charting an Alternative Course for the Study of Jewish Philosophy," in *New Directions in Jewish Philosophy*, 2). Wolfson and Hughes put forward "a taxonomy that shifts the emphasis from seeing philosophy itself as a derivative to a native dimension of the Jewish religious sensibility" (2). Lila Corwin Berman addresses this methodological question when reading for Jewishness in Jewish history: "How does Jewishness help us explain a subject of interrogation? . . . Our goal is not to refine and sharpen Jewishness, in the hopes of one day knowing what it is. Rather, the goal is to blur it, such that, in motion,

its shape loses the solidity of a foundation and, instead, gains the flexibility of a
process that moves through bodies, ideas, objects, and spaces" ("Jewish History
Beyond the Jewish People," *AJS Review* 42:2 [November 2018], 290).

35. Katz, "Philosophy, the Academy, and the Future of Jewish Learning," 157.

36. Katz, 157. Relatedly, see Janet Jakobsen and Ann Pellegrini, *Love the Sin:
Sexual Regulations and the Limits of Religious Tolerance* (Boston: Beacon, 2004),
114; the authors refer to "stealth Protestantism" as the upholding of specifically
Christian values in the name of the "secular."

37. The epigraph to Levinas's *Otherwise Than Being or Beyond Essence*
illustrates his linguistic specificity in remembering loved ones who perished in
the Shoah. In French, Levinas dedicates this work to "those who were closest
among the six million assassinated by the National Socialists" and the "millions
of all confessions and all nations" who are victims "of the same hatred of the
other man, the same anti-Semitism" (Levinas, *Otherwise Than Being or Beyond
Essence*, trans. Alphonso Lingis [Dordrecht: Kluwer Academic Publishers, 1991],
v). The Hebrew following this dedication lists by name those in the author's
immediate family who perished in mass executions in Lithuania. See Salomon
Malka, *Emmanuel Levinas: His Life and Legacy*, trans. Michael Kigel and Sonja
M. Embree (Pittsburgh, PA: Duquesne University Press, 2006), 81. On Levinas's
choice of language in the epigraph and the relation to translation in Shoah
testimony, see Dorota Glowacka, "The Trace of the Untranslatable: Emmanuel
Levinas and the Ethics of Translation," *PhaenEx* 7, no. 1 (Spring/Summer 2012),
10; and Dorota Glowacka, *Disappearing Traces: Holocaust Testimonials, Ethics,
and Aesthetics* (Seattle: University of Washington Press, 2012).

38. Jacques Derrida, "Violence and Metaphysics: An Essay on the Thought
of Emmanuel Levinas," in *Writing and Difference*, trans. Alan Bass (Chicago:
University of Chicago Press, 1978), 320–1n92.

39. Derrida, "At This Very Moment," 40. Katz echoes this observation in
reading Irigaray's response to Levinas's work: "Levinas was criticized for taking
the position of the male, yet what other position could he take?" (*An Introduction
to Modern Jewish Philosophy* [London: I.B. Tauris, 2014], 132).

40. Levinas, *Otherwise Than Being or Beyond Essence*, 158; in the original,
"Autrui est d'emblée le frère de tous les autres hommes" (*Autrement qu'être, ou,
Au-delà de l'essence* [La Haye: Nijhoff, 1974], 246).

41. Beauvoir, *The Second Sex*, xxxv.

42. "To gain the supreme victory, it is necessary, for one thing, that by and
through their natural differentiation men and women unequivocally affirm
their brotherhood" (Beauvoir, *The Second Sex*, 732); in the original, "Pour
remporter cette suprême victoire, il est entre autres nécessaire que par-delà
leurs différenciations naturelles hommes et femmes affirment sans équivoque
leur fraternité" (Beauvoir, *Le Deuxième Sexe, tome II: L'Expérience Vécue* [Paris:
Gallimard, 1949], 577).

43. Wilson Carey McWilliams articulates fraternity's lasting influence, although he valorizes it: "Of all the terms of kinship, none has had so enduring an appeal and so firm a place in political symbolism as fraternity" (*The Idea of Fraternity in America* [Berkeley: University of California Press, 1973], 1).

44. Mona Ozouf unpacks the supposedly "banal" French republican motto: "Fraternity is clearly of another order ... of community rather than individuality. It is more carnal than intellectual, more religious than juridical, more spontaneous than contemplative" ("Liberty, Equality, Fraternity," in *Realms of Memory: The Construction of the French Past*, vol. 3, trans. Arthur Goldhammer [New York: Columbia University Press, 1998], 86). See also Leah Hunt-Hendrix, "The Ethics of Solidarity: Republican, Marxist, and Anarchist Interpretations" (PhD diss., Princeton University, 2014), 39: "In the revolutionary cry for '*liberté, égalité, fraternité*,' the third term would indicate a commitment to one another in the search for a new world that was more just and equitable. *Fraternité*, a term with familial connotations, signified an affective attachment that could ground the project for a new national identity."

45. Pateman, *The Sexual Contract*, 78.

46. Pateman, 78.

47. See Kimberly Hutchings: "Pateman's argument is that the story of the social contract in classical social contract theory (Hobbes, Locke, Rousseau) is the story of the overthrow of *paternal* and the institution of *fraternal* political right. ... Pateman claims that the stories told in classical social contract theory capture ongoing truths about the nature of the modern liberal state, in which the sovereign individuality of men is linked to the denial of that status to women" (*Hegel and Feminist Philosophy* [Cambridge, UK: Polity, 2003], 136–7).

48. Pateman, *The Sexual Contract*, 99.

49. Juliet Flower MacCannell, *The Regime of the Brother: After the Patriarchy* (London: Routledge, 1991), 5.

50. MacCannell, *The Regime of the Brother*, 16–17.

51. MacCannell, 26–7.

52. Mary C. Rawlinson, "Beyond Antigone: Ismene, Gender, and the Right to Life," in *The Returns of Antigone: Interdisciplinary Essays*, ed. Tina Chanter and Sean D. Kirkland (Albany: State University of New York Press, 2014), 118n14.

53. Stefani Engelstein, *Sibling Action: The Genealogical Structure of Modernity* (New York: Columbia University Press, 2017), 62. As Katja Garloff observes, "the political ideal of fraternity, which is based on the idea of brotherly love, enacts a whole new set of exclusions, notably of women. ... The concept of fraternity points to a problem at the core of liberalism—namely, how to reconcile the citizen's identification with the state with more particularistic attachments of love and kinship. Eighteenth century political philosophers responded to this problem by identifying women with purely personal feelings and excluding them from the sphere of politics" (*Mixed Feelings: Tropes of Love in German Jewish Culture* [Ithaca, NY: Cornell University Press, 2016], 28n8).

54. See Levinas, *Totality and Infinity*, 214, in which Levinas refers to a monotheistic fraternal society held together by a common divine father:

> The very status of the human implies fraternity and the idea of the human race. . . . Human fraternity has then two aspects: it involves individualities whose logical status is not reducible to the status of ultimate differences in a genus, for their singularity consists in each referring to itself. (An individual having a common genus with another individual would not be removed enough from it.) On the other hand, it involves the commonness of a father, as though the commonness of race would not bring together enough. Society must be a fraternal community to be commensurate with the straightforwardness, the primary proximity, in which the face presents itself to my welcome. Monotheism signifies this human kinship, this idea of a human race that refers back to the approach of the Other in the face, in a dimension of height, in responsibility for oneself and for the Other.

Tamar Rudavsky notes that "Levinas has appropriated the patriarchalism of monotheism, and once again 'the feminine' has been removed from canonical philosophical discourse" ("Feminism and Modern Jewish Philosophy," 337).

55. Marc Shell, *Children of the Earth: Literature, Politics, and Nationhood* [Oxford: Oxford University Press, 1993], vii. In discussing the creed of 1789, McWilliams observes that "fraternity is intelligible only in relation to the idea of a Creator, a Divine 'father' who established fraternity among men" (*The Idea of Fraternity in America*, 4). Marc Shell points out that the very goal of universal fraternity thus "undoes itself because fraternity implies a common (in Christian terms, divine) father" (*The End of Kinship: 'Measure for Measure,' Incest, and the Ideal of Universal Siblinghood* [Redwood City, CA: Stanford University Press, 1988], 189). The supposed equality of fraternity is already called into question by the hierarchical relationship to the presumed father: "the group of human beings that becomes an egalitarian brotherhood merely by assuming a common Father is only replacing an earthly hierarchy, that of the sons against the father, with a heavenly hierarchy, that of the sons against the Father" (Shell, *Children of the Earth*, 186).

In the *Star*, Rosenzweig similarly refers to the bond of brotherliness in Christianity, expressed in the act of brotherly love: "In all the given relationships that quietly continue to exist, brotherliness joins men independently of these relationships as equals, as brothers, 'in the Lord.' The mutual faith in the mutual way is the content on which they turn from men into brothers. In this fraternal covenant of Christianity Christ is both beginning and end of the way, and consequently content and goal, founder and Lord of the covenant, as well center of the way and hence everywhere present where two are together in his name" (365). See also Garloff, *Mixed Feelings*, 28–9: "The ideas of brotherhood and brotherly love hark back to the early Christians, who—similarly to the Jews of their time—conceived of their coreligionists as 'brothers' with whom they shared an affective bond. Since the Middle Ages, and especially during the eighteenth century, the term 'brotherly love' had become intermittently secularized and politicized, notably among the Freemasons (who called each other *Bruder* and promised to love each other in a brotherly way) and in the egalitarian ideal of the French Revolution, *fraternité*." Garloff discusses how in the eighteenth century, Moses Mendelssohn reclaimed the idea of brotherly love, which at the time had mostly Christian connotations, as a core value of Judaism: "Translating a religious into a political concept, Mendelssohn appeals to the brotherly love of his Christian readers to solicit support for Jewish emancipation" (24). For Mendelssohn, brotherly love became a way to create bonds between Jews and Christians. Mendelssohn "transfers the idea of an affective bond between coreligionists to a modern, secular, broadly inclusive state" (29). Garloff finds Mendelssohn's conception of brotherly love subversive because "he traces the Judaic origins of this idea and deplores its absence in contemporary Christianity" (31).

56. Derrida, *Politics of Friendship*, ix.

57. Shapiro, "A Matter of Discipline," 158–9.

58. In his essay "The New Thinking," Rosenzweig pairs this with another gendered and classist trope: "Theology may not debase philosophy to play the part of the *handmaid*, yet just as degrading is the role of *charwoman* which, in modern and in most recent times, philosophy has become accustomed to give theology" (Rosenzweig, "The New Thinking," 129, emphasis mine); in the original, "Nicht zur Hausmagd darf Theologie Philosophie erniedern, aber genau so entwürdigend ist die Rolle der Monatsfrau, welche die Philosophie in neuerer und neuester Zeit der Theologie zuzumuten sich gewöhnt hatte" (Rosenzweig, "*Das Neue Denken*," in *Der Morgen* 1, no. 4 [October 1925], 441).

59. Sarah Imhoff, "Women and Gender, Past and Present: A Jewish Studies Story," *Jewish Social Studies* 24, no. 2 (winter 2019): 81. See also Miriam Peskowitz: "'Gender' is often used as a synonym for 'women.' In this formulation, masculinity is retained as the assumption of universality and femininity continues to function as a mark of difference" ("Engendering Jewish Religious History," 29).

60. Sarah Imhoff, *Masculinity and the Making of American Judaism* (Bloomington: Indiana University Press, 2017), 20. See also Judith Plaskow: "If women are not part of the congregation . . . this is because men—and not women with them—define Jewish humanity" (*The Coming of Lilith: Essays on Feminism, Judaism, and Sexual Ethics, 1972–2003*, ed. Judith Plaskow and Donna Berman [Boston: Beacon Press, 2005], 57); and see Kerry Wallach: "For many, 'the Jew' is almost always gendered male" (*Passing Illusions: Jewish Visibility in Weimar Germany* [Ann Arbor: University of Michigan Press, 2017], 7).

ONE

LOVERS AND BROTHERS

AT THE HEART OF FRANZ Rosenzweig's major work, *The Star of Redemption* (1921), lies an evocative reading of the Song of Songs, situating the themes of revelation and love at the foreground of his philosophical and theological project. The Song of Songs is one of the shortest books in the Hebrew Bible.[1] It has no explicit religious content and includes many overtly sensual verses. For this reason, it has traditionally been interpreted as an allegorical representation of the relationship between God and God's people, or God and the human soul. In many interpretations, the female voice in the Song of Songs is elided, and the Song is read instead as a dialogue between the femininized male soul and the masculine divine. Rosenzweig's reading, for all its innovation, reflects this hermeneutic tradition by ultimately effacing gender difference. His interpretation is marked by fraternal tropes and the subsequent effacement of the feminine. He transposes the erotic energy in the Song from a celebration of difference to a longing for sameness, in service of a unifying fraternal community.

This chapter begins by underlining the hierarchical ordering of gender in Rosenzweig's reading of the lover-beloved relationship. While within the text of the Song of Songs itself the lover can be both male and female, Rosenzweig generally attributes the masculine pronoun to the lover and the feminine pronoun to the beloved, in accordance with the preexisting exegetical framework within which he read the Song. Rosenzweig's conventional binary of the passively receiving female as beloved and the actively bestowing male as lover means that for him, the female lover has no ability to act without becoming masculine.[2] The themes foregrounded in Rosenzweig's project have key gendered dimensions that resonate within the Jewish mystical tradition but raise central ethical issues.

One compelling feature of Rosenzweig's interpretation of the Song of Songs is that, while the Song is usually understood to focus on a heteroerotic relationship between lovers, Rosenzweig concentrates on the lovers' wish to become like siblings. In this chapter, I uncover the meaning of the sibling metaphor for Rosenzweig. The motif of the sister-bride that he draws from the Song is psychoanalytically rich, and he does not avoid its suggestive incestuous dimensions. Ultimately, in his reading, the heteroerotic sibling-spouses become neighborly blood brothers. In moving from revelation to communal redemption, the erotic sphere is surpassed by neighborly "brotherliness." Rosenzweig espouses marriage as stronger than mere erotic love, "more than love," and the Song's lovers yearn to be united in societal fraternity.[3] This move has normative and exclusionary implications, eliding women from a public communal role as anything other than the bearers of children.

By pursuing a robust critical gender analysis, I take into account not just a key section of the Star but its overall philosophical, theological, and political implications. This offers a more complete understanding of the whole work—not only of the section on revelation. Because previous analyses of gender in that section have read it more or less in isolation from the latter part of the Star, the issue of moving from difference to sameness has been obscured. My analysis demonstrates that Rosenzweig's notion of blood community supports a patriarchal genealogy.

ALLEGORICAL LOVE

The Star's central section on revelation begins by quoting the Song of Songs: "Love is as strong as death."[4] Why is this passage so important to this section and to the entire book? Rosenzweig writes that this is the only passage in the entire Song in which an objective statement interrupts the otherwise pervasive first-person voice. These are the only words that cannot be spoken about love but are spoken by love. Revelation is the expression of God's love for humanity, and it takes place in lived experience as a victory over death. It is crucial that love is temporally set in the present, not in an idealized time outside of time. This revelatory love is experienced as a violent awakening that surrenders completely to the immediate moment.

Rosenzweig describes this love as "entirely 'deus fortior me'—to use the words of the great love who upheld his love and whom his love upheld through hell, world and heaven ... ecce deus fortior me 'qui veniens dominabitur mihi.'"[5] In one of many paratextual references in this dense chapter, Rosenzweig illustrates the "intrinsic necessity" of love with a reference to Dante Alighieri's

Vita Nuova.[6] To understand why this reference speaks to Rosenzweig, it will be helpful to revisit how *Vita Nuova* begins, with Dante's recollection of the life-altering moment in which he first saw a young Beatrice:

> To my eyes first appeared the glorious lady of my mind, who was called Beatrice.... At that moment I say truly that the spirit of life, which dwells in the most secret chamber of the heart, began to tremble so strongly that it appeared terrifying in its smallest veins; and trembling it said these words: "Ecce deus fortior me, qui veniens dominabitur mihi" [Behold a god more powerful than I, who comes to rule over me].... I say that from that time forward, Love ruled over my soul, which was so early espoused to him, and he began to assume over me such assurance and such mastery, through the power that my imagination gave him, that I was obliged to do all his bidding fully.[7]

For Rosenzweig, Dante's proclamation becomes a "philosophical Archimedean point."[8] He reflects on this experience in his "*Urzelle*" to the *Star*, written in 1917 as a letter to his cousin Rudolph Ehrenberg: "I knew nothing further than the mark of the 'reluctant,' of the '*Ecce deus fortior me qui veniens dominabitur mihi*'.... The assumption, then, [is] that man of his own accord follows only 'his impulses' and that the voice of God calls him always in a directly opposed direction."[9] Rosenzweig feels that he had been inadequately considering revelation as a concept, which "brought me insights that were only into the history of philosophy and were never purely conceptual."[10] Revelation, he now realizes, involves the possibility for the human encounter with the divine, and it is not reducible to reason. It lies outside history while breaking into the historical realm.

When Rosenzweig began to write the chapter on revelation in the *Star* in 1918, he revisited Dante, whose words attribute to love the divine power to overmaster the lover, a power that always occurs in the immediate instant. Importantly, Dante's lasting love for Beatrice is inaugurated with this pronunciation in his youth. For Rosenzweig, Dante depicts a love that is "always young, always first."[11] This love "breaks into the revealed world" in the "immediately and presently experienced moment of life."[12] Although both Dante and Beatrice were married to others, and she suffered an early death, Beatrice was his great love, his muse and spiritual guide, and to him she symbolized the overwhelming divine love of the beatific vision.

Invoking Dante's figure of Beatrice, who was both woman and allegorical symbol, likely emphasizes Rosenzweig's recognition of the Song's convergence of the literal and the figurative. Modern readers, according to Rosenzweig, have lost this sense of the Song, diluting its power by reading it through only one of its allegorical registers. Rosenzweig insists that the Song of Songs must be recovered from the "purely human" status it has acquired in the modern period, as readers have mistakenly made the Song a testament to mere human love. Although the Song features the interactions of two lovers, Rosenzweig stresses that it does not portray only a human connection—an insight already intrinsic to premodern interpretations.[13]

To elucidate his approach to the Song of Songs, Rosenzweig first examines where its interpretation historically went wrong. The Song always was meant to attest to the relationship between the terrestrial and spiritual realms. In the nineteenth century, however, this view became distorted; the Song was read as a purely human love song, excluding the relationship of love between God and the individual soul.[14] In attributing the Song to mere worldly love, these interpreters were stating that "God—does not love."[15] The modern interpretation made a critical mistake, trying to shift "the I and You of the poem, into an obvious He and She."[16] For Rosenzweig, the love depicted in the Song must be recast as the revelatory experience between the individual and the divine. The Song's very "worldliness" attests to it being an "authentic 'spiritual' love song of God's love for man. Man loves because, and as, God loves."[17] God's love for the human soul is the model by which humans love one another.

For Rosenzweig, then, the Song of Songs does not depict only human love, nor is it a pure allegory of divine love; rather, it explores *both* human-human *and* divine-human love. Any interpretation of the Song that does not account for this twofold dimension fails to recognize that all love between humans attests to the love that God has for the human individual: "it is not possible for love to be 'purely human' . . . when love speaks, it is already changed into something superhuman; for the sensuous character of the word is full to the brim with its divine supra-sensuous meaning."[18] The human loves as God loves.

The Song of Songs has raised significant theological debate due to its frankly erotic imagery. Both Jewish and Christian theologians tend to distinguish human eros from divine love.[19] Rosenzweig responds differently. He finds that the Song's sensuality allows it to paradigmatically evoke the meaning of revelation in the divine-human encounter: "Like all human love, this is only a simile."[20] Scholars have commented on the centrality of allegory for Rosenzweig's reading.[21] According to Stéphane Mosès, "[Rosenzweig's] analysis is based on a description of human love, and the term 'love' as applied to God is obviously metaphorical. As in the Song of Songs, human love is here the paradigm that serves as a model for the description of a relation whose departure point is not accessible to experience."[22] Samuel Moyn disagrees with Mosès's reading, arguing that divine love serves as the paradigm for the love relation between humans: "humanity's love for one another is derivative of God's love for humanity. If anything, then, human love is metaphorical of divine love. . . . If there is an original or a model, it is divine love for humanity and not the love of individual humans for each other."[23] Moyn's explanation is convincing. For Rosenzweig, any reading of the Song as merely a worldly love poem fails to recognize that insofar as the Song is worldly, it is spiritual. The Song does not depict *either* divine-human love *or* human love (the mistake of the contemporary "atheistic" readings criticized by Rosenzweig) but both. In this sense, the Song is also more than merely allegory: in relating to God, the individual is already relating to the other person and vice versa.

Rosenzweig's notion of speech-thinking (*sprachdenken*) helps illustrate why this double register is so important. In dialogical speech-thinking, there is an inseparable connection between human-divine and human-human speech. Speaking to another person testifies to divine-human speech because the revelatory encounter with God shapes human conversation.[24] In speech-thinking, the speaker's boring, predictable monologue is spontaneously interrupted. This spontaneity is vital for real dialogue. In speaking to another person, one is also speaking with God *at the same moment*. Mere analogy is traversed, for human discourse *is* the dialogue between God and the individual.[25] Similarly, loving another stems from being attuned to God's speech in one's heart. Revelation in the present is experienced as speech, which offers a unique convergence of divinity and humanity. The distinctions between human and divine love, and between imagination and reality, collapse. Love is both sensible and supra-sensible, transient and enduring.

When Rosenzweig describes the Song of Songs as an "allegory of love," he is drawing on its traditional rabbinic interpretation as a heteroerotic representation of God's love for the people of Israel.[26] The Song had become sanctioned within the Jewish and Christian canons because its frank eroticism was transferred to the relationship between God and the religious community.[27] In the mystical exegesis of the Song, the heterosexual language of the biblical narrative becomes a kind of spiritualized homoeroticism.[28] In Christian mysticism, the male mystic takes on the voice of the female beloved and Jesus that of the male lover, and in the Jewish mystical tradition, the male kabbalist shares a homoerotic bond with the divine presence.[29] The mystics who appropriated this discourse of sensual love sought to convey the passionate nature of religious experience.

The echoes of mystical sensibilities in Rosenzweig's *Star* illustrate some important convergences in the representation of gender. For kabbalists, in

contrast to many Christians following Paul's early advocacy for eschatological celibacy, marriage was not viewed as yielding to the weakness of the flesh
but as symbolically realizing the union of the masculine and feminine divine
potencies.[30] But they nevertheless shared with their Christian counterparts an
uneasy relation to the physical body, which they correlated with the feminine.
This can be seen in the kabbalists' symbolic interpretation of the Song, which
"underscores the extent to which [they] sought to augment, and in some measure displace, carnal sexuality with spiritual eroticism."[31] In rabbinic culture,
too, the body was hardly unproblematic, "nor was asceticism unknown," as
Daniel Boyarin has shown.[32] In both rabbinic Midrash and kabbalistic exegesis of the Song, Yudit Kornberg Greenberg observes, "the physical body of the
lovers and their sexual desire are displaced. In rabbinic Midrash, sexual desire
is transformed" as sensual desire is replaced with the textual desire to reveal
multiple layers of meaning.[33] Stephen Moore has convincingly demonstrated
that the interpretive history of the Song is a "consummately queer body of allegorical commentary."[34] This allegorical exposition strains to overcome "the
sexual, the sensual, the fleshly, the female. By annexing a mystified femininity
to his own male body . . . the allegorical expositor renders the literal female body
redundant. The woman of the Song—and, by extension, woman in general—is
symbolically annihilated in the very gesture through which she is idealized."[35]
This overcoming of femininity is echoed in Rosenzweig's reading. In the *Star*,
Rosenzweig claims to reject asceticism and mysticism.[36] But mystical sensibilities are nevertheless reflected in his thought.[37]

Significantly, the masculine role kabbalistic literature assigns to motherhood resonates with a rare maternal reference Rosenzweig makes in the *Star*.
While he mainly uses the example of male and female lovers, at one point he
offers an alternate metaphor for the soul's state of contentment: "The soul is
tranquil in God's love, like a child in the arms of its mother, and now it can go
to the farthest sea and to the gates of the grave—it always stays near Him."[38] It
is possible that God-the-Mother here is meant to be passively inflected toward
the soul, which would then take on the counter role of the active masculine
child. But it is more likely that it is another illustration of the active divine lover.
Casting motherhood as actively masculine is another way Rosenzweig reflects
a kabbalistic approach where "the female assumes the role of the engendering
male" by giving birth.[39] As Elliot R. Wolfson explains, although pregnancy
and childbirth are traditionally thought of as biologically unique to the female
sex, "in kabbalistic literature they are valorized as positive, masculine traits.
The biological woman assumes the male gender through these bodily functions."[40] Rosenzweig later invokes the masculine maternal metaphor in the *Star*

to illustrate God as lover and active creator. God becomes the masculine lover who has created the beloved soul and has "given birth in pain" to the feminine beloved.[41] In this way, Rosenzweig appropriates maternity as a distinctly masculine and virile activity.

LOVER AND BELOVED

In Rosenzweig's reading of the lover-beloved relationship, gender is organized hierarchically. The feminized beloved submits to the dominating, masculine lover. To understand why Rosenzweig felt compelled to refocus on the Song's sibling language—as I will explore in the sections below—it is first critical to understand how his gendered reading of the heteroerotic relationship at the Song's center, shaped within the Jewish exegetical tradition, backed him into a corner. This reading, by mapping divine-human love onto human-human love, mandates hierarchical relationships between the sexes and forced him into another set of relational metaphors in order to consider dyadic equality.

When Rosenzweig speaks about the lover and beloved, he is referring metaphorically to the figures of God and the beloved soul. The male lover is God, and the female beloved is the soul, which may be embodied by either a man or a woman.[42] But since divine-human love and human-human love are not separable, what applies to one applies to the other. In the relation between God as lover and the soul as beloved, a hierarchy is notably preserved: "The love of the beloved sits peacefully at the feet of the love of the lover."[43] The soul (the beloved) receives God's love in allowing herself to be loved. The soul here is troped as female: "She does not respond to the lover's love with any recognition in herself. . . . The beloved has no other resource than to let herself be loved by the lover."[44] God demands submission on the part of the beloved soul. The beloved's faith yields entirely to the lover, "bound to the moment, and reinforces it so far as to make it a lasting love."[45] The lover commands, "Love me."[46] Of the beloved's grateful response, Rosenzweig writes, "Only the confession ravishes the soul in the blissfulness of feeling loved."[47] The beloved feels "seized" in love[48] and becomes serene while the lover, "by sheer fighting . . . uproots his love from the stem of his Self."[49] As we can see, Rosenzweig describes this relationship in unequivocally aggressive terms, through the language of domination and acquiescence.

The nature of divine love is illustrated in the metaphorical relation of the lover and beloved: as the lover loves, "This, too, is the way God loves."[50] But while the relationship between lover and beloved is fixed in the love between the soul and God, it is interchangeable between man and woman:

Between the man and the woman, the taller the flowers are that the stem of
love makes grow between them, the more love resembles a palm tree rising
up in the sky and distancing itself from its subterranean roots, and the more
the roles of the one giving love and the one receiving love go back and forth,
although the roots of their sexuality always re-establish the unambiguous
relationship of nature. But between God and the soul, the relationship
remains always the same. God does not stop loving, and the soul never stops
being loved.[51]

In Rosenzweig's analogy, the taller the plant of love grows, the further its flowers grow above the subterranean roots of sexuality. Although men and women
are bound by their sexual roles, their gender roles are not set; they can attempt
to transcend these roles in love. But a relationship of love between a man and a
woman must inevitably be reduced to the rigid roots of biology. By characterizing sexuality as the "subterranean roots" of love, Rosenzweig suggests that
gender can transcend sex but will always be drawn back to it in love. Rosenzweig's remark may also suggest that a love less bound up in sex would allow the
lover/beloved dyad access to greater gender interchangeability.

Rosenzweig does allow for role flexibility in the Song, in which the "beloved" is not always represented as female. Indeed, the woman's voice in the
Song of Songs characterizes the man as her beloved. Scholarship has struggled
with the thorny question of what Rosenzweig is doing on the subject of gender
and what readers are meant to take away from it.[52] Mara Benjamin, for example,
comments on Rosenzweig's normative framework: "The gendering of God as
male and the soul as female is essential to the heterosexual erotic encounter that
Rosenzweig employs to describe revelation. To the degree that scholarship has
focused at all on this point, feminist scholars disagree on the significance of
Rosenzweig's assignation of gender to God and soul and its heteronormative
implications."[53] Rosenzweig himself complicates the question by both reading the divine and human erotic dramas through each other and insisting on a
distinction between them.[54]

Although in the Song itself the lover can be both male and female, Rosenzweig generally attributes the masculine pronoun to the lover and the feminine
pronoun to the beloved. This is in accordance with the long-standing Jewish
exegetical framework for the Song. It can be argued that Rosenzweig's identification of the female with passivity and references to God as masculine may simply
be a result of the grammatical terms of biblical Hebrew, in which God is gendered
masculine and the soul feminine.[55] But while a grammatical locus for gender
terminology offers an explanation for its origin, it does not dissolve its harmful
application. Although he allows for flexibility as men and women in turn take on

the roles of lover and beloved, he ultimately accedes to a typical and rather tired binary: a passively receiving female as beloved and an actively bestowing male as lover. As Benjamin observes, "Rosenzweig's brief qualification notwithstanding, the rigidly imagined gender roles propel the logic of this section."[56] Benjamin's point here is instructive. Rosenzweig's schema has rigid heteronormative implications that should be questioned. The woman can be lover in the relationship of love, but she will inescapably be drawn back to her sexuality and to her passivity as beloved. The female can become lover only under the bearing of the masculine and can remain feminine only in the status of beloved. The female sex has no access to activity without becoming gendered masculine.

Rosenzweig's comments on the "subterranean roots" of love can be read in light of his earlier references to women. As Leora Batnitzky observes, Rosenzweig begins the section on revelation "with an argument not only about an abstract feminine element but also with an argument about real women."[57] Rosenzweig writes that "nature has given only the woman, and not the man, the capacity to die of love. What has been said of the twofold encounter of the man with his Self applies strictly and universally only to the masculine."[58] The "woman" lacks this encounter with her Self, and as such, "her life is simpler than that of the man."[59] The woman's experience in love is unique. Unlike the man, the woman's heart is already "firm in the tremors of love; it no longer needs the tremors of death."[60] In love, "a young woman can reach her maturity for eternity" while a man can reach this maturity only at death: "Once touched by love, a woman is what a man will only be at the centenary age of Faust: ready for the final encounter as strong as death."[61] Batnitzky rightfully calls this passage "very strange" and "deeply perplexing."[62]

What should readers make of this passage, in which Rosenzweig refers to a literal woman, especially in light of his later comments on metaphorical femininity and masculinity? For Batnitzky, Rosenzweig's construction of Judaism in the next part of the Star suggests an answer: "For Rosenzweig, while all people are capable of participating in a dialogical relation, and while 'masculine' and 'feminine' can apply to both men and women, the Jewish people, like real women, have a special, ontological share in revelation. The argument about real women that he makes in Part Two of the Star is intimately connected to the argument that Rosenzweig makes in Part Three, about the reality of the Jewish people. Real women, who are not reducible to a metaphorical 'feminine,' function for Rosenzweig in this text as a foil for real Jews."[63] Rosenzweig writes of Judaism, "The community of the same blood alone feels even today the guarantee of its eternity running warmly through its veins."[64] According to Batnitzky, the key to understanding Rosenzweig's references to the "feminine" is in his argument against Christian supersessionism. "What does it mean for a woman to be ready for eternity in a way that a man is not? And how might this readiness for eternity relate to being 'strong as death'? For Rosenzweig, a woman is a priori ready for eternity just as the Jewish people are a priori eternal."[65] This is an insightful reading, and it helps to make sense of these passages on Rosenzweig's own terms.

Batnitzky acknowledges that Rosenzweig relies on troubling ideas about the "true nature" of the Jewish people and their propagation, but she suggests we should read his references to "natural" femininity in light of his conviction that the blood running through Jewish veins gives the Jewish people access to eternity. Rosenzweig's obsession with blood could also be a subversive reversal of a long-standing Christian fixation on consanguinity.[66] But while he may have set out to strategically feminize Judaism to challenge a hegemonic Christianity, Rosenzweig runs the risk of reifying stereotypical characterizations of Jews as feminized and innately natural/corporeal/animalistic in comparison with more "spiritual" Christians.[67] In attempting to challenge Christian polemics against Judaism through references to "femininity" and "women," Rosenzweig creates another set of problems with normative implications. Furthermore, this approach is not consistent with how Rosenzweig portrays Judaism throughout the Star. He does not figure the Jewish people as feminine. Instead, he portrays the Jewish community as a distinctly homosocial group that effaces women, which I will discuss further in the last section of this chapter.

In the text of the Song of Songs, the genders are interchangeable in the relation of love, as attested to by the female, who calls the male her "beloved." So why does Rosenzweig characterize the divine lover only as masculine and the human beloved as feminine? This likely speaks more to the reader's interpretation than to the text itself. Michael Fishbane suggests it is possible to read the rabbinic interpretation of the erotic poem according to Gadamer's horizon of understanding: the rabbinic sages perceived a religious dialogue in the Song because they were predisposed to do so. In the rabbinic exegesis of the Song, the reader can find "hermeneutical transformations that reflect the religious view and mentality of the interpreters, and aspects of their historical sense."[68] According to Fishbane, "the figures of the Song provide the literary types, so to speak, for the ever-changing challenges of the Jewish religious mentality—and provide a linguistic source for its evolving spiritual imagination and eros."[69] The Song has been a mirror in which interpreters (usually men) have historically seen their religious views and ideologies reflected back to them.

In this sense, Rosenzweig's other comments on the status of women are instructive. Rosenzweig elsewhere describes women in paternalistic, traditional

Jewish terms. In "The Builders: Concerning the Law," addressed to Martin Buber, Rosenzweig refers to "the legal exclusion of the woman from the religious congregation" and her "ruling rank in the home, given to her by age-old custom, and acknowledged by the husband on Friday evening in the biblical song of the Woman of Valour."[70] Rosenzweig translates the Song's erotic flexibility to a rigid hierarchy of sexes aligning with a traditional Jewish framework. In his view, this gender hierarchy ultimately maintains and controls erotic relationships. For a relationship of equality, which he wants to achieve in the next section of the *Star*, the erotic register must be reconfigured. Sexual difference will then become the casualty of this move.

SISTER-WIVES

The Song of Songs is bursting with evocative imagery, leaving interpreters and exegetes spoiled by choice. A philosophical/theological reading, such as Rosenzweig undertakes, could focus on the metaphors of fruitfulness and fecundity, relating these to both the terrestrial and supernal spheres; take up the rich animal and vegetative imagery;[71] or make much of the suggestive erotic language in the lovers' words, applying this to the soul's yearning for the divine.

The selection Rosenzweig chooses to make central to his reading instead is compelling, strange, and instructive. The Song of Songs, as discussed in the last section, is usually understood to focus on a heteroerotic relationship between lovers, and this aspect of Rosenzweig's thought has been well explored by scholarship. But the most critical element of Rosenzweig's analysis, which I investigate here, highlights his view that the lovers' deepest wish is to become like siblings. He underlines the moments when the lovers refer to each other as both sibling and spouse: "With an infinite tenderness, and the calling of her name constantly repeated in a whisper: 'My sister, my betrothed,' the lover evokes the foundation of their love. . . . To him, the beloved was once 'in past times my sister, my wife.'"[72] For Rosenzweig, I argue, the sibling motif became a way of writing himself out of the hierarchical relational models just explored. And yet he will then move beyond the sphere of erotic siblinghood toward a "neighborliness" that defines women away.

The Song of Songs, as Rosenzweig noted, indeed contains many references to the beloved as sibling:[73]

> Thou hast ravished my heart, my sister, my bride. . . . How fair is thy love, my sister, my bride! . . . A garden enclosed is my sister, my bride; a spring shut up, a fountain sealed. . . . I am come into my garden, my sister, my bride. . . . Hark, my beloved is knocking, saying, Open to me, my sister, my love, my dove, my

undefiled. . . . O that thou were as my brother, that sucked the breasts of my mother! When I should find thee outside, I would kiss thee; and none would scorn me. I would lead thee and bring thee into the house of my mother who brought me up.[74]

In Rosenzweig's reading of the Song, the beloved enjoys a special status as both betrothed and sister. In calling out to her, the lover can lift her out of the fleeting moment: "With names of endearment, the beloved man has clearly intimated his love to her by evoking the secret substitution-foundation of a fraternal feeling."[75]

Calling her by these endearments, however, is ultimately insufficient:

And from the blissfully overflowing heart of the beloved, a sob rises and starts to spell out the words—words which upset things and allude to an incompleteness that cannot be fulfilled in the immediate revelation of the love: "Oh, if only you were a brother to me!" It is not enough that, in the half-light of the allusion, he calls the betrothed by the name of sister; the name would have to be truth, heard in the bright light of the streets, not whispered into the beloved ear, in the twilight of caresses in the solitude of the twosome; it would have to be fully true in the eyes of the multitude.[76]

The lovers long to proclaim their intimate love to the public.[77] The sibling-lovers' relationship cannot be fulfilled in the revealed love of the immediate present: "The sob of the beloved sobs toward a beyond of love, toward a future of its present revelation; it sighs toward an eternal love."[78] This love seeks to be externalized, no longer shared by the lovers, but yearning to be "in view of the entire earth. . . . Marriage is not love. Marriage is infinitely more than love; marriage is the fulfillment on the outside, in it love comes out from its blissful inner completeness and stretches out its hand, in a helpless and unquenchable longing—Oh, would that you were my brother."[79] The love seeks to become external. Crucially, it reaches outward and toward eternity through union in marriage. Eternity can be reached only when the pair's solitary relation becomes public, and as such it lies beyond the capacity of love.

If we are to adhere to Rosenzweig's earlier assertion that the human loves as God loves, and divine-human love is the model for human-human love, then presumably Rosenzweig is referring not primarily to interhuman marriage when he describes the beloved yearning for brotherly connection but to human marriage with the divine.[80] The interpretation of marriage as strictly between God and the soul would neatly resolve any incestuous human sibling-lover implications. And yet, as Rosenzweig has made clear, what holds true for divine-human love necessarily applies to human-human love: "Man loves because, and as, God loves."[81] If interhuman love is based on divine-human love, then the extension from love to marriage holds true for the interhuman relation as well. In that case, Rosenzweig's statement about marriage stands for both marriage with the divine and interhuman marriage, and the incestuous desire is maintained at the level of both the human and the divine. It is also possible that, as with his discussion of neighborliness in the next section of the *Star*, marriage is meant here as an expression of divine love between humans. The redemptive function of marriage that Rosenzweig refers to is consonant with his later characterization in the *Star* of interhuman marriage as bringing the people into eternity.[82]

By highlighting this aspect of the Song, Rosenzweig's account makes sexually differentiated siblinghood a place of potential erotic desire. In emphasizing this erotic dimension, Rosenzweig's interpretation is both innovative and subversive. But while this relationship is central, it is not the end. Incestuous sibling desire is the mechanism but not the telos of the relationship. The model of male-female marriage/siblinghood is ultimately divested of this erotic energy as the neighborly plane approaches. Rosenzweig's discussion of revelation in love ends with a call to move beyond heteroerotic love, toward redemption: "The soul aspires to this realm of the brotherliness, beyond the love between I and You, where the dark portents of the impersonal communal life that the natural community of the same blood intimates had been marvelously fulfilled."[83] In revelation, the individual has responded to God's call but is closed off from the world. The lover-beloved revelatory relation must become that of brothers, and then of neighbors, in order for revelation to pass over into redemption.[84] As such, the next part of the *Star*, "Redemption, or the Eternal Future of the Kingdom," begins with the words "love your neighbor."[85] Only the soul that is loved by God is able to receive the commandment of neighborly love. Rosenzweig's analysis of the Song describes "the moment and the path of the soul's awakening by God and her approach in love to her neighbours in the world."[86] The love for God that begins in an erotic dyad between the human soul and the divine must end in externalization and generalization, in love for the neighbor, which is the fulfillment of God's love in the world.

The Song of Songs is not the only time the sister-wife motif resounds in the Hebrew Bible.[87] In Genesis, three narratives appear in which wives are substituted for sisters. In two accounts featuring Abraham and Sarah and one involving their son Isaac and his wife, Rebecca, the following narrative repeats itself: the couple travels to a foreign land, and the husband entreats his wife to pretend she is his sister to protect him from being killed for her beauty; when found out by the king, he explains why he had lie to save his life. In Genesis 20,

Abraham tells the duped King Abimelech, who might have otherwise taken Sarah for a wife, that in his falsehood he was in fact telling the truth—she is both his sister *and* his wife: "she is indeed my sister, the daughter of my father, but not the daughter of my mother; and so she became my wife."[88] Later, in Genesis 24, Isaac and Rebecca go into the land of King Abimelech and pose as brother and sister, echoing the similar actions of his parents. These instances in Genesis of blurring relationships between sibling and spouse suggest a repetition-compulsion and expose the potentially erotic dimension of this relationship in the layers of truth that are slowly revealed.

Rosenzweig made a note of the potential for a psychoanalytic reading of Abraham and Sarah as sibling-spouses in a 1922 journal entry. The Midrash *Bereishit Rabbah*'s backstory to Abraham's childhood and the suggestive incestuous account with Sarah would make, in his view, for magnificent Freudian material.[89] Rosenzweig had previously reflected on the motif of incest in a letter to Eugen Rosenstock-Huessy in January 1920.[90] In the letter, Rosenzweig suggests that brother-sister romantic relationships really do happen in the best of families—this can be seen in the Nordic legend of siblings Siegmund and Sieglinde; in the Greek saga of the Titan Kronos with his sister Rhea; and in ancient Egypt, in which it was customary among the pharaohs for siblings to marry one another in order to preserve their dynasty. The letter is written in a playful manner, suggesting that since brother-sister romance takes place in royal and archetypal figures, it is legitimated by society. But he notes that mother and son relationships are Oedipal and, he therefore implies, deemed incestuous. At the very least, he differentiates biologically incestuous relationships based on the variable power differentials between participants. By referring to the Oedipal relation as the downfall, Rosenzweig evokes the narrative structure of the tragedy; that kind of incest leads to familial, state, and narrative destruction, whereas brother and sister love shores up empires. That Freud focused on the Oedipal relationship so much may have been precisely due to this tragic narrative structure. He was concerned with identifying which behaviors are societally permissible and survivable, and which lead to psychic and mortal ruin.

Feminist theorists have shown that Rosenzweig was probably, if unwittingly, right: the way a culture defines incest—by definition impermissible—has less to do with the closeness of biological relations and more to do with maintaining patriarchal power structures and delimiting accepted sexual practices. The idea of incest and its prohibition, as with many other taboos around sexuality, implies the assumption of men's ownership of women's bodies.[91] As Ellen Pollak puts it, "The very idea of incest depends on the institution of prohibition,"[92] precisely because "'before the prohibition, it is not incest.'"[93] The law contains both the explicit prohibition of incestuous heterosexuality and the implicit prohibition of nonnormative sexuality.[94] Incest and its prohibition are mutually sustaining categories, and the suppression of nonnormative sexuality "is therefore a product of the same system whose rules and relations oppress women."[95] The prohibition of incest regulates "not so much incest itself as the multiplicity of forms that, in the absence of that prohibition, it might be possible for sexuality to take."[96]

Wilda Gafney's womanist reading of the Sarah-Abraham sibling-spouse incident further exposes the dynamics of power at work in these narratives. After detailing how incestuous, intrafamily unions run in their family,[97] Gafney makes explicit how Abraham manufactured the deception and sold Sarah into sexual slavery for his own benefit: "Abram did not object to Sarai's seizure. He relinquished her to the pharaoh and accepted a rich settlement for his loss. Her brother-husband sold her to a man he knew would use her for sex."[98] Gafney identifies Sarah as a survivor of both sexual violence and domestic abuse whose partner is complicit in that abuse and monetarily profits from it, receiving payment in the form of herd animals in exchange for her body.

Critical feminist and womanist analyses, then, expose the assumptions underpinning psychoanalytic representations of incest and its prohibition.[99] This trope is deployed to maintain an entire system of social, sexual, and power relations. Textual representations of incest contribute to the production and consolidation of power structures in class, gender, and kinship organization. The incest trope is the hallmark of the androcentric, heteronormative system of kinship that Rosenzweig takes as the organizing structure of his religious vision of redemption. As I will show in the next section, Rosenzweig's homosocial fraternity presupposes women's constitution as enabling objects of exchange rather than as active agents or subjects within the Jewish community.

SHARED BLOOD AND THE EFFACEMENT OF WOMEN

For Rosenzweig, the call to the loved one as "brother" signifies transcending the relation of lovers. Ironically, it is the relation of marriage that allows for this transition from the transient love of lovers to, in his view, the deeper love of siblings. As Rosenzweig understands it, the lover in the Song of Songs longs to call her beloved "brother," for their bond would be that much closer if shared in blood. It is not merely that she yearns to be seen in public with him, to be able to kiss him in the streets without reproach, to be permitted to share a house with him;[100] in Rosenzweig's interpretation, she longs for a relationship with him that would be open to the world, that would exceed the present moment and exist forever.

The bond represents her desire to be tied by blood to him, and therefore to the entire community, in an eternal bond realized through marriage, which later on in the *Star* is portrayed as a human relationship:

> So all human relationships, absolutely all, blood relationship, brotherhood, nation, marriage . . . all are rooted in the blood community, which among them is that which is closest in Creation; and invested with soul in Redemption, they all tend to look alike according to the great analogy of marriage which among them is that which is closest in the order of Redemption: mystery of the soul that has become existing figure completely in view of all eyes, structured life completely filled with soul. It is for that reason that at the pinnacle of love the soul aspired to rejoin the created blood community; it is only in the destined, or rather God-given union of the soul and the community, in marriage, that it finds its Redemption.[101]

As previously discussed, Rosenzweig begins his reading of the Song by invoking its key line: "Love is as strong as death."[102] This dimension is emphasized once again here; in marriage, death is overcome in an assertion of continued life. This is symbolized in Judaism by the custom of the bridegroom wearing a burial garment under the wedding canopy. This garbing of the bridegroom in the attire of the dead while entering into the eternal life of the Jewish people announces that matrimony is as strong as death, for "it is marriage first of all that makes him a full-standing member of the people."[103] The shared blood of the community "gives to hope for the future a guarantee in the present."[104] Rosenzweig places great emphasis on the uniqueness of the community of blood. Only a people bonded by blood can be eternal:

> There is only one community in which such a relationship of eternal life reaches from the grandfather to the grandson, only one that cannot express the "We" of its unity without hearing as well within its core "are eternal" as its complement. It must be a community of the same blood, for only the blood gives to hope for the future a guarantee in the present. Every other one, every community can be propagated differently than by blood if it wants to establish its We for eternity, and it can do so only by safeguarding a place for itself in the future; all bloodless eternity is founded on the will and on hope. The community of the same blood alone feels even today the guarantee of its eternity running warmly through its veins.[105]

Only "the community of the same blood" need not worry about passing from the present to the future: "in the natural propagation of the body it has the guarantee of its eternity."[106] For Rosenzweig, love moves beyond itself in marriage, tying the past and present to the future, binding the couple together in blood, and propagating the community's future.[107]

If "blood" becomes the essence of Judaism for Rosenzweig, it is critically important, especially in the historical context of the nineteenth and early twentieth centuries, to ask what he means by this.[108] Most scholars agree that this blood community is not meant to be interpreted along racial lines but rather as "an essence devoid of specific racial content . . . blood detached from soil."[109] The "purity" of Jewish blood depends on the avoidance of territorial nationalism.[110] The motif of the blood community is meant to explicitly contrast with the idea of Judaism as a community oriented by land.[111] Rosenzweig writes in the *Star*, "being a people means still something other than remaining in a land—for the eternal people the homeland never becomes its own in that sense . . . the people is a people only through the people."[112] Rosenzweig's blood community can be interpreted as a philosophical idea, not to be taken literally.[113] Many scholars thus agree that Rosenzweig's concept of blood community should not be interpreted solely along the lines of race or ethnicity. But just because Rosenzweig's blood community may not be intentionally racially inflected, that does not let it off the ethical hook. As Gil Anidjar observes, "Rosenzweig does not have to be construed as a racist, if only because blood, as a figure for the community, precedes and exceeds 'race thinking'—and it is not less troubling for that. Beginning with the equation of blood and procreation . . . it may in fact be more pervasive."[114]

I suggest that we read Rosenzweig on blood through the lens of gender, a "more pervasive" category, especially since this is precisely how he frames it. First and foremost, he affirms the classical halakhic rule that defines a Jew as someone born to a Jewish mother, making this law into a "substantive characterization of Judaism on a biological basis."[115] In an analysis of blood and procreation as motifs in the *Star*, Haggai Dagan observes, "This continuity, rooted in blood, is first and foremost the responsibility of the woman, who gives birth, who gives life."[116] For Rosenzweig, the existence of the Jewish people relies "only upon blood ties and natural procreation."[117] In my view, this goes much further. The central uniqueness of Judaism in the *Star* depends on Jewish continuity, defined as the production of Jewish children by Jewish women.[118] Because Judaism is traditionally matrilineal and mothers' wombs are the carriers of both children and their religious identity, the model of Jewish continuity is predicated on the proposition "that women were meant to be vessels for the Jewish future, and that women's wombs mattered more than women's autonomy."[119] As Lila Corwin Berman, Kate Rosenblatt, and Ronit Y. Stahl demonstrate, the pro-endogamy continuity paradigm, which gained traction in the twentieth century, "is a political stance predicated upon women's bodies as communal property."[120]

There are alarming implications to a system of blood community that relies on the regulation of Jewish women's bodies. Marla Brettschneider's observations on the links between patriarchy, heterosexism, and race are relevant here. In *Jewish Feminism and Intersectionality*, Brettschneider writes, "Significant parts of Jewish discourse operate through obsessions with stock components of patriarchy, such as bloodlines and birthrights, and not just sex but also heterosexual sex or various forms of Jewish heterosexual panic. These are always also race issues."[121] Critical intersectionality helps us see that the idea of blood continuity is intricately connected to the control of women's bodies in a heteroregulative system. Patricia Hill Collins and Sirma Bilge demonstrate that "power relations are to be analyzed both via their intersections, for example, of racism and sexism, as well as across domains of power, namely, structural, disciplinary, cultural, and interpersonal."[122] In the "race/reproduction bind," as Alys Eve Weinbaum formulates it, race and sex are inextricable in the organizing framework of genealogy. In prevailing accounts of group affiliation and social organization, human reproduction is a "biological, sexual, and racialized process" that orchestrates inclusion in political societies.[123] In this constellation, blood becomes equated with bloodline and questions of race are implicated in questions of sex and gender.[124] The anxious maintenance of lineage is a patriarchal, restrictive, and damaging paradigm.

Laura Levitt's critical analysis of heterocompulsory marriage is instructive in this case. Levitt shows that theological and ethical approaches in which "heterosexual procreative marriage is the critical metaphor" are by definition exclusionary and limiting.[125] The covenantal metaphor then becomes a prescription to create the Jewish biological future. In such cases, the heterosexual family is assumed to be the procreative family; nonheterosexual families are omitted, as are, presumably, heterosexual nonprocreative families. Levitt thus makes clear "the material implications, the limitations, and the dangers posed by this kind of theologizing of the sexual contract as a vision of Jewish community and home."[126] In Jewish theologies for which heterosexual procreative marriage remains the ideal, nonnormative sexual identities are necessarily excluded.

Rosenzweig's blood community reinscribes a traditionally Jewish patriarchal genealogy. Biale puts it this way: "since procreation is the essence of Judaism, it follows that it is women who are the primary propagators of Jewish life. Men may be knowledgeable in Torah, but since Torah is not the essence, women, who are excluded from study, actually occupy center stage: they are rooted in nature, by which Rosenzweig means that their essential task is procreation. Judaism is, almost by definition, female."[127] I am inclined to a far less generous reading than Biale gives here. Biale does not read Rosenzweig uncritically; he continues, "To be sure, a full gender analysis of the *Star* would reveal a much more ambiguous role for women, especially in Rosenzweig's passages on the dynamics of love."[128] I agree, but I maintain that a "full gender analysis of the *Star*" enables us to see not only how women's roles are accorded but how Rosenzweig's entire system is structured. In the *Star*, women as agents and actors do not occupy center stage; rather, their bodies—specifically their wombs—are central. In this schema, Judaism is by definition female only in the pragmatics of procreation, not in any meaningful essence. Women only matter as *mater*, maternal material.

Critical feminist and intersectional analysis allow us to see how Rosenzweig's notion of blood community supports a patriarchal and potentially racial genealogy. In the *Star*, we read, "For [the Jewish community] alone, that which is future is nothing foreign, but something that is its own, something that it carries in its womb, and it can give birth to it every day."[129] As Zachary Braiterman aptly puts it, while women's bodies are essential, "actual women are explicitly excluded. . . . The woman determines the Jewish character of blood; her blood and womb carry the man's seed. But for Rosenzweig she does so invisibly and utterly passively—the standard excuse used to justify the exclusion of women from the all-important active center of Jewish religious life, the study of Torah and its commandments."[130] The "natural propagation of the body" so central to Rosenzweig's logic is achieved, significantly, through the woman's body.[131]

In Rosenzweig's genealogy, blood is the sticky stuff that adheres grandfathers to grandsons in the Jewish community by passing through the bodies of Jewish women. In this way, sperm becomes reconfigured as blood, "the fleshly flowing on of the one blood which testifies to the ancestor in the begotten grandson."[132] He emphasizes the biological transmission of the distinctly masculine familial line. This is achieved in a relation of filiation from the son reaching back to the grandfather: "The begetting of the future is a direct bearing witness to the past. The son is begotten so that he might bear witness to the past father of his begetter. The grandson renews the grandfather's name. The patriarchs call the last offspring by his name, which is also theirs. Above the darkness of the future there burns the starry heaven of the promise: so shall be your seed."[133] The blood in the *Star* refers, in Braiterman's view, "not to race and soil, but to sex and propagation. Only the blood community is eternal, Jewish birth and being, the bond between grandfather and grandson."[134] Sexual reproduction creates a community "out of its own viscous substance combining seed and blood."[135] The real telos of maternal blood is to further male blood.

Rosenzweig's idea of the eternal Jewish blood community contains echoes of Martin Buber's early work. In *Drei Reden über das Judentum* (*Three Speeches on Judaism*), delivered between 1909 and 1911 and published in 1920, Buber emphasizes the future of the Jewish people in terms of blood continuity.[136] Buber describes a hypothetical child who imagines his Jewish genealogy: "He perceives then what commingling of individuals, what confluence of blood, has produced him, what round of begettings and births has called him forth."[137] Unlike Rosenzweig, Buber gives credit to the maternal line, referring to a "succession of generations" made up of a "line of fathers and of mothers."[138] Likewise, the community's shared blood is "implanted within us by the chain of fathers and mothers."[139] And yet, immediately following that statement, he writes mothers out of the deeper story by describing a uniquely paternal legacy.[140]

Like Rosenzweig, Buber ties blood to sperm as a community-binding substance: "What does it mean for us to want perpetuity, not merely as human beings—human spirit and human seed—but, in defiance of both Time and this particular time, as Jews?"[141] In Buber's genealogical narrative, the (male) child envisions his hematological antecedents, which allows him to recognize "that the deepest layers of our being are determined by blood; that our innermost thinking and our will are colored by it."[142] Unlike his shallower worldly relationships, the Jewish child feels a deep connection to the "community of those whose substance he shares."[143] For this community, blood is "the deepest, most potent stratum of our being."[144] The Jewish individual can envision "all the future promise of his blood."[145] Ultimately, to live as a Jew is to choose this eternal sanguine substance over the ephemeral environment.

Although Rosenzweig insists on the desire of the Song's lovers to share "blood" ties, the binding fluid they long to share in the Song of Songs is not in fact blood but milk—nourishment from a shared mother's breast. The call of longing uttered in the Song refers to a siblinghood inaugurated not through a common bloodline but in the act of sharing breast milk: "O that thou were as my brother, that sucked the breasts of my mother!"[146] By emphasizing the wish for the lovers to become siblings related by blood, Rosenzweig superimposes a masculine interest in bloodlines over the Song's reference to shared mother's milk. This likely speaks to the gendered elements of these disparate bodily fluids: milk is inherently maternal and generative, proceeding from birth. But in the genealogical and biological line, as Rosenzweig presents it, fathers pass on their blood, while only mothers can pass on their milk. His focus on shared blood, rather than milk, tacitly privileges the paternal over the maternal, as the "mother's house" referred to in the Song becomes entirely lost.[147]

In the *Star*'s definition of Jewish community, Rosenzweig depicts a celebration of filial propagation, from grandfather to grandson and beyond. Rosenzweig's eroticism, with its focus on male issue, is "active, severe, and violent."[148] His attraction to Dante's characterization of overpowering love becomes even more apparent in this context. In Dante's proclamation that became so central to Rosenzweig, love is a dominating ruler and master that requires complete subservience.[149] This section of the *Star* is based on a trope of asymmetric eros tied up with domination.[150] Benjamin offers the counterexample of maternal love and practice to the form of dyadic, erotic intersubjectivity found in the *Star*. In interrogating Rosenzweig through this counter-relation of parent and child, she reveals the *Star*'s "crucial limitations and problems" and challenges the "overly sanguine readings" of its section on revelation.[151] Raising the point that Rosenzweig might have focused on mother's milk rather than blood further emphasizes the text's relatively narrow definition of Jewish community.

Communal relationships are of the utmost importance to Rosenzweig because the erotic relationship is inherently closed, not open.[152] To reach redemption, the lover and beloved must become neighbors. In the Song of Songs, the lovers seek to become sister and brother, but Rosenzweig's reading effaces this difference. Rosenzweig's ideal society does not allow for variation or diversity.[153] That all are united in the realm of "brotherliness" implies that all must first become homogenous and masculinized.

Although Rosenzweig does not advocate an ascetic lifestyle, his elucidation of the lover-beloved erotic relationship transcended in redemption reflects a mystical dimension in his thought. Wolfson explains that the ascetic dimension in kabbalistic literature is emphasized "by the symbolic association of *Binah*, which is the world-to-come, and Yom Kippur, a day in which physical pleasures are prohibited . . . the kabbalist who is bound to God experiences the life of the world-to-come, which is a plane of existence beyond physical eros and the concomitant gender bifurcation."[154] Rosenzweig writes in the *Star* that on the Day of Atonement, Yom Kippur, the soul moves from temporal life to eternity.[155] The realm of "brotherliness" achieved in redemption suggests that, as the lover-beloved erotic plane is left behind, all are equal as brothers.

My reading of Rosenzweig is influenced by Wolfson's explanation of a fundamental motif in kabbalistic literature in which the feminine becomes masculine in a reconstituted male androgyne: "in the ideal state, gender differentiation is neutralized and the female is absorbed back into the male."[156] A similar transmutation takes place in Rosenzweig's reading of the Song, as all are united in brotherliness and attain equality under the bearing of the masculine. Here, my argument diverges from Katja Garloff's reading of erotic love and neighbor-love

in the *Star*. In her view, Rosenzweig depicts erotic love "as a force that prolifer-
ates differences rather than creates a union, and, in so doing, offer[s] new models for living together in an inescapably pluralist world."[157] Neighbor-love is the
foundation of human communities and makes redemption possible. Revelatory
love becomes Rosenzweig's model for social relations, as "love reorients the self
toward the other without collapsing the difference between the two."[158] Garloff
reads Rosenzweig's vision of love as preserving difference: "The romantic attraction between individuals gives rise to social structures—from the lovers'
dyad to larger communities—that respect and in fact encourage the expression
of difference."[159] While I agree with Garloff that Rosenzweig may hope to bring
people together across religious, national, and cultural boundaries, as I see it,
his vision of revelatory love gives way in redemptive love to homogeneity, not
to a respect for difference.

While mystical ideas are most apparent in the third part of the *Star*, they
are also evident throughout the work. In the *Star*, the monologue of Creation
becomes a dialogue in Revelation, leading to a chorus of communal voices in
Redemption and an ultimate silencing of speech, which gives way to vision. In
redemption, seeing the divine face trumps hearing the divine word; word and
language are overcome.[160] The move beyond the dialogical reflects the mystical, in which all distinctions are absorbed into the light of God.[161] Here, it is
notable that as language is overcome in redemption, the erotic plane, and with
it the very existence of women, is also left behind.

In Rosenzweig's reading, the lovers in the Song of Songs long to expand their
love by expressing it in the public realm. In the *Star*'s movement from revelation to redemption, he insists that the erotic relationship must be similarly
externalized and transcended in marriage, branching out toward eternity in
propagation of the male seed. Erotic love can become redemptive only through
procreative marriage represented by an expression of fraternity from the Song.
Clearly, this scheme works only out of tightly conceived gender assumptions.
For Rosenzweig, the anthropocentric and the theocentric are never entirely
separable, and the language of brotherhood is not exclusive to one sphere or
another.

If we attend to a close reading of the Song of Songs itself, however, we notice
that there are indeed points of inequality among the lovers, which is significant
to a reading focused on the relation of difference. The male figure in the Song
utters, "my sister, my bride" (אחתי כלה, *achoti kalla*) without difficulty, over and
over again, as his call is echoed throughout the poem. The female never actually
refers to him as the equivalent—brother-groom—or, for that matter, as brother
at all. She only *longs* to call him brother. Yael Feldman points out that the "sister

bride" of the Song "once, and once only (8:1), wishes for her lover to be her
brother ('*ah*) rather than her beloved (*dod*) so that she could publicly kiss him
without censure."[162] He is not limited from this most intimate of utterances,
and yet she is. What is she asking for in this call, so central to Rosenzweig's
reading? What is her demand, or desire, in this moment of longing? The action
of merging suggested by her wish for the private to become public, and for her
lover to become brother, would dissolve all societal and familial differences
between the two.

Rosenzweig is attentive to the Hebrew text of the Song of Songs. His reading
is nevertheless filtered through many linguistic and conceptual layers: to name
two of significance, the German rendering of the biblical text and the traces
of rabbinic exegesis. His is not a straightforward reading. He makes numerous
maneuvers and impositions, and mapping these disjunctions serves to highlight his own greater interpretive and philosophical aims. I see these points of
dislocation as largely marked by the sign of gender difference and its attendant
displacement or effacement of female sexuality and maternity.

In her classic work of biblical criticism, *God and the Rhetoric of Sexuality*,
Phyllis Trible calls Rosenzweig out for twisting the Song's egalitarianism into a
stereotypical representation of womanhood: "Contra, e.g., Franz Rosenzweig,
The Star of Redemption," in the Song of Songs itself, "there is no male domi-
nance, no female subordination, and no stereotyping of either sex. . . . Never
is this woman called a wife, nor is she required to bear children. In fact, to the
issues of marriage and procreation the Song does not speak."[163] While in the
Song, the beloved is specifically seeking to share mother's milk with her lover,
Rosenzweig emphasizes the longing for shared bloodlines between the lovers.
The maternal gesture inherent in the Song is transposed into an emblem of
virility, propagation of the generative male seed. Rosenzweig inverts Judaism's
traditional law of matriarchal lineage by making it about a continuation of the
male blood flowing in children's veins. Judaism is construed as a homosocial
consanguinity.

Rosenzweig's reading reflects the hermeneutic tradition of the Song by ultimately eliminating gender difference. The lovers' differences are smoothed
away in their move to the communal sphere so they are united as brothers—not
brother and sister—in the *Reich der Brüderlichkeit*. As the lover-beloved erotic
plane is left behind, all become equal as brothers. While this may suggest a
neutrality of gender, it masks a unifying, compulsory masculinity. The female
lover becomes absorbed as the sister-bride is sublimated into a male sibling. The
feminine is the engine for this telic finality, left aside and sacrificed to fraternity.

NOTES

1. According to scholarly consensus, the Song of Songs is a collection of lyrics composed over many centuries, "beginning (perhaps) in the mid-tenth century BCE and continuing to the fifth or fourth centuries BCE, when the Song achieved something like its present form" (Michael Fishbane, "Introduction to the Commentary: Song of Songs," in *Song of Songs: The Traditional Hebrew Text with the New JPS Translation* [Philadelphia: The Jewish Publication Society, 2015], xxi).

2. After making a similar observation on Rosenzweig's traditional gender dichotomy, David Biale notes, "A feminist reading of the *Star*," such as I provide here, "is an important desideratum" (*Blood and Belief: The Circulation of a Symbol between Jews and Christians* [Berkeley, CA: University of California Press, 2007], 257n151).

3. Rosenzweig, *Star*, 219.

4. Rosenzweig, 169.

5. Rosenzweig, 173.

6. Rosenzweig, 173.

7. Dante Alighieri, *Vita Nuova*, trans. Dino S. Cervigni and Edward Vasta (Notre Dame, IN: University of Notre Dame Press, 1995), 47–9.

8. Franz Rosenzweig, "'*Urzelle*' to the *Star of Redemption*," 48.

9. Rosenzweig, 48–9.

10. Rosenzweig, 49.

11. Rosenzweig, *Star*, 173.

12. Rosenzweig, 173.

13. Samuel Moyn, "Divine and Human Love: Franz Rosenzweig's History of the Song of Songs," *Jewish Studies Quarterly* 12 (2005): 198. As Rosenzweig sees it, the secularization of the Song's interpretations obscured a philosophical truth: "before modern times, intersubjectivity between humans necessarily presupposed the 'intersubjectivity' between God and his children; the latter served as the template for the former.... Rosenzweig took the Song to illustrate a brute theological fact about the divine origins of human love and the everlasting dependence of human love on this origin" (Moyn, 198–9).

14. Alternatively, Ilana Pardes maintains that this shift has been over-emphasized in scholarship on the Song's exegetical history. Pardes challenges the tendency to regard the transition from the allegorical to the literal as clear-cut, instead considering how "these two interpretive lines are inextricably intertwined in a whole array of episodes in the text's biography" (*The Song of Songs: A Biography* [Princeton, NJ: Princeton University Press, 2019], 17).

15. Rosenzweig, *Star*, 214.

16. Rosenzweig, 215.

17. Rosenzweig, 214.

18. Rosenzweig, 216.

19. Paul Mendes-Flohr explains that this distinction "is captured by Augustine's transformative translation of the Greek *eros* by *agape*, or by the Latin *caritas*" ("Between Sensual and Heavenly Love: Franz Rosenzweig's Reading of the Song of Songs," in *Scriptural Exegesis: The Shapes of Culture and the Religious Imagination: Essays in Honour of Michael Fishbane*, ed. Deborah A. Green and Laura S. Lieber [Oxford: Oxford University Press, 2009], 310, referring to Jean-Luc Marion, *The Erotic Phenomenon*, trans. Stephen E. Lewis [Chicago: University of Chicago Press, 2005], 220–1).

20. Rosenzweig, *Star*, 169; in the original, "Das ist, wie alle irdische Liebe, nur ein Gleichnis" (Franz Rosenzweig, *Der Stern der Erlösung* [Heidelberg: L. Schneider, 1954], 88).

21. Mendes-Flohr views this simile, or analogy (Gleichnis), as "also a homology. Human *eros* and divine *eros* coincide" ("Between Sensual and Heavenly Love," 313). Mara Benjamin observes that Rosenzweig "treats the allegorical interpretive history of the Song of Songs as contained within the text's 'plain sense.' Indeed, only by claiming the presence of this double register within the Song itself can he claim that this text constitutes a unique instance of signifier and signified in one" (*Rosenzweig's Bible*, 59). Yudit Kornberg Greenberg clarifies that for Rosenzweig, eros is "more than an analogy; it is an instantiation of divine embodiment . . . divine love conveyed through the language and the experience of physical love" (*Better than Wine: Love, Poetry, and Prayer in the Thought of Franz Rosenzweig* [Atlanta, GA: Scholars Press, 1996], 96).

22. Stéphane Mosès, *System and Revelation: The Philosophy of Franz Rosenzweig*, trans. Catherine Tihanyi (Detroit, MI: Wayne State University Press, 1992), 102.

23. Moyn, *Origins of the Other*, 150–1.

24. Rosenzweig writes that while thinking is timeless and conducted in solitude, "speaking is time-bound, time-nourished. . . . it does not know in advance where it will arrive; it lets its cues be given by others. It lives in general from the life of the other" ("The New Thinking," 125–6). Unlike the monologue, dialogue is spontaneous, and it is impossible to anticipate what the other person will say: "In actual conversation, something happens; I do not know in advance what the other will say to me because I myself do not even know what I am going to say" (126).

25. Barbara Galli observes that for speech-thinking, "human-divine conversation is the root of human-human speech, and is that which nourishes and authenticates all speech" (*Franz Rosenzweig and Jehuda Halevi: Translating, Translations, and Translators* [Montreal: McGill-Queen's University Press,

1995], 345); Rosenzweig "preferred to speak *to* rather than *about* God, and in conversation with human beings, to permit God as a third speaker. Thus, Rosenzweig's reading of the Song of Songs as 'more than simile'.... It is from Rosenzweig's analysis of the Song of Songs that we learn he maintains that God is a partner in authentic inter-human speech" (346). As Elliot R. Wolfson explains, "It is not simply speaking about God that matters here, but the encountering of the divine through the speech of revelation" ("Facing the Effaced: Mystical Eschatology and the Idealistic Orientation in the Thought of Franz Rosenzweig," *Zeitschrift für Neure Theologiegeschichte* 4 [1997]: 77). On speech-thinking in the context of Rosenzweig's relationship with Eugen Rosenstock-Huessy, see Wayne Cristaudo, "The Basis of the New Speech Thinking," in *Religion, Redemption, and Revolution: The New Speech Thinking of Franz Rosenzweig and Eugen Rosenstock-Huessy* (Toronto: University of Toronto Press, 2012), 57–81.

26. Rosenzweig, *Star*, 213. Wolfson explains how, for Rosenzweig, the Song is the "'core book of Revelation'" because its literal meaning is figurative (Elliot R. Wolfson, *Giving Beyond the Gift*, 65); "The distinction between dream and reality, what appears and what is, collapses when the divine word is thought to allude to the relationship of God and human in the erotically charged images of male lover and female beloved" (Wolfson, "Light Does Not Talk but Shines: Apophasis and Vision in Rosenzweig's Theopoetic Temporality," in *New Directions in Jewish Philosophy*, ed. Elliot R. Wolfson and Aaron W. Hughes [Bloomington: Indiana University Press, 2010], 103–4). The Song holds a special stature as the most hallowed of books because its metaphorical nature "reveals something basic concerning the very possibility of speaking about divine revelation" (Wolfson, "Suffering Eros and Textual Incarnation: A Kristevan Reading of Kabbalistic Poetics," in *Toward a Theology of Eros: Transfiguring Passion at the Limits of Discipline*, ed. Virginia Burrus and Catherine Keller [New York: Fordham University Press, 2006], 346). Rosenzweig thus identifies both the "essentially metaphorical nature of eros" and the "essentially erotic nature of metaphor" (Wolfson, *Language, Eros, Being*, 336). As Paul Mendes-Flohr writes, for Rosenzweig, "it is precisely the sensual, emphatically human eros of this love song that renders it such a powerful religious document, for it recognizes that erotic and religious passion are ultimately homologous" (review of *The Kiss of God: Spiritual and Mystical Death in Judaism*, by Michael Fishbane, *History of Religions* 37, no. 2 [1997]: 174).

27. See Benjamin, *Rosenzweig's Bible*, 59. Greenberg notes that in contemporary gender analysis of the Song, "the binary of human and divine love that results from traditional interpretations has been questioned. Scholars have underscored the amplification of the woman's voice that is stifled in the vast majority of biblical texts" ("Erotic Representations of the Divine," in *Oxford*

Research Encyclopedia of Religion 22 [December 2016]: 5–6, https://doi.org/10
.1093/acrefore/9780199340378.013.120). As Phyllis Trible effectively puts it, "in
the Song, male power vanishes" (*God and the Rhetoric of Sexuality* [Philadelphia:
Fortress Press, 1978], 160).

28. See Elliot R. Wolfson, "Asceticism and Eroticism in Medieval Jewish
Philosophical and Mystical Exegesis of the Song of Songs," in *With Reverence for
the Word: Medieval Scriptural Exegesis in Judaism, Christianity, and Islam*, ed. Jane
Dammen McAuliffe, Barry D. Walfish, and Joseph W. Goering (Oxford: Oxford
University Press, 2003), 97.

29. Wolfson, "Asceticism and Eroticism," 97.

30. David Biale explains that the kabbalists had a "powerful ambivalence
about sexuality and a desire to reconcile the attraction of celibacy with marital
obligations by subsuming the physical act of sex into a mystical theology"
(*Eros and the Jews: From Biblical Israel to Contemporary America* [New York:
BasicBooks, 1992], 111).

31. Wolfson, "Asceticism and Eroticism," 105. The contemplative regimen
of the kabbalists "linked to an erotic passion that demanded the abrogation
of physical desire" (105). Reflecting the medieval philosophical approach,
Maimonides appropriated the erotic symbolism of the Song of Songs to portray
the ideal of intellectual love of the divine, asserting in his *Mishneh Torah* that the
Song is a parable for the soul's love for God (94). Along similar registers, in his
Guide of the Perplexed, Maimonides suggests that when an individual is alone, at
times that do not involve conversing "with your wife and your small children," he
should take care "during these precious times" not to think "on anything other
than that intellectual worship consisting in nearness of God and being in His
presence" (*The Guide of the Perplexed*, trans. Shlomo Pines [Chicago: University
of Chicago Press, 1963], III: 51, 623).

32. Daniel Boyarin, *Carnal Israel: Reading Sex in Talmudic Culture* (Berkeley:
University of California Press, 1995), 34. See also Steven D. Fraade, "Ascetical
Aspects of Ancient Judaism," in *Jewish Spirituality: From the Bible through the
Middle Ages*, ed. Arthur Green (New York: Crossroad, 1986).

33. Greenberg, "Erotic Representations of the Divine," 6.

34. Stephen D. Moore, "The Song of Songs in the History of Sexuality," *Church
History* 69, no. 2 (June 2000): 339.

35. Moore, "The Song of Songs," 339. In Moore's view, the allegorical history
of the Song is intrinsically queer because it depends on the male reader's ability
to internalize the central feminine voice of the Song and to throw himself
"into the role of a vivacious young woman in love" (349). Braiterman echoes
this genderqueer dimension in arguing that the figure of the beloved from the
Song of Songs in the section on revelation, the Shulamite, is not Rosenzweig's
lover Gritli but rather "Rosenzweig himself, a female avatar of his own eros, his

passion for male authority, passive receptivity, his own desire to be a woman with the force of her own character" (*The Shape of Revelation*, 230–1). See also Braiterman, "Revelation Camp: Gender, Franz Rosenzweig, and the Con-fusion of Concepts," *Bamidbar* 4, no. 2 (2019): 54: "One would have thought one knew that the project of Jewish philosophy is both masculinist and heteronormative. And yet, one discovers that in Rosenzweig's text this masculinity relates primarily back to the figure of a woman, that her desire represents the author's own desire for a homosocial community of men."

36. "Man defined only as an object of divine love is cut off from the whole world and closed in himself. For any normal sensibility, there is in any mysticism something disquietingly and even objectively dangerous. His soul is open to God, but because it is open only to God, it is invisible for the rest of the world and cut off from it" (Rosenzweig, *Star*, 223). Wolfson discusses this explicit rejection: "Rosenzweig decried the implicit immorality that derives from the mystic's ascetic renunciation and the ensuing retreat into the silence of seclusion, an immorality that is to be distinguished from the amorality implied by his own notion of the meta-ethical nature of redeeming human love" (*Venturing Beyond: Law and Morality in Kabbalistic Mysticism* [Oxford: Oxford University Press, 2006], 11). Benjamin Pollock addresses the treatment of mysticism and world denial in the *Star*: "The mystic's celebration of the intimacy of his relation to God, Rosenzweig suggests here, comes at the expense of the world" (*Franz Rosenzweig's Conversions: World Denial and World Redemption* [Bloomington: Indiana University Press, 2014], 171).

37. Rosenzweig's emphasis on the visual in the last part of the *Star* betrays an affinity to kabbalah, reflecting a mystically oriented conception that leads to a reappropriation of the idealism he had initially renounced (see Wolfson, "Facing the Effaced," 39–81). Rivka Horwitz examines Rosenzweig's apophaticism as a turn toward these mystical strains. Horwitz argues that although he had minimal knowledge of kabbalah, his "construction of the dialectic within each element in God, man, and the world" is indebted to this way of thinking and plays an important role in all three parts of *The Star* ("From Hegelianism to a Revolutionary Understanding of Judaism: Franz Rosenzweig's Attitude toward Kabbala and Myth," *Modern Judaism* 2, no. 1 [2006]: 39–40); see also Wolfson, "Light Does Not Talk but Shines," 93. For Rosenzweig, redemption redeems not just humanity and the world but God as well—an idea that resonates with a central kabbalistic theme (Wolfson, "Facing the Effaced," 69). Rosenzweig reflects the kabbalistic principle that God becomes who God is "through the actions of human beings. . . . just as the lover who sacrifices himself in love is recreated anew by the trust of the beloved, so God's existence is dependent on the affirmation of the soul" (77). Indeed, the important place given to mysticism in Rosenzweig's thought can be seen in his *Urzelle* to the *Star*, in which he notes

the "exceptional position of mysticism *between* actual theology and actual philosophy" (Rosenzweig, "*Urzelle* to the *Star of Redemption*," 71).

38. Rosenzweig, *Star*, 185; in the original, "Die Seele ist in Gottes Liebe stille wie ein Kind in den Armen der Mutter, und nun kann sie über das äußerste Meer und an die Pforten des Grabes—und ist doch immer bei Ihm" (*Stern*, 107–8).

39. Elliot R. Wolfson, *Circle in the Square: Studies in the Use of Gender in Kabbalistic Symbolism* (Albany: State University of New York Press, 1995), 98.

40. Wolfson, *Circle in the Square*, 98.

41. Rosenzweig, *Star*, 197. Rosenzweig also turns to a maternal register in discussing mythical messengers of fate, and he elucidates maternity from the masculine perspective: "it is not by accident that they are mostly women; for the maternal is always that which is there already, the paternal is only an addition; for man, the woman is always mother" (172). Earlier in the *Star*, the world is compared to nature/motherhood in its feminine aspect and to spirit/ paternity in its masculinity: "[The world's] womb is insatiable in conceiving, it is inexhaustible in giving birth. Or better—for both masculine and feminine are in it—it is, as 'nature,' as much the mother who endlessly gives birth to its figures as it is the indefatigable procreative force of the 'spirit' that is at home in it" (53).

42. As Wolfson explains, "the exegetical context of the Song of Songs necessitates the metaphorical application of the feminine persona to the soul and that of the masculine to the divine. The female beloved who encounters the male lover is none other than the self (which may be embodied in either a man or a woman) who visually confronts the face of God" ("Facing the Effaced," 44).

43. Rosenzweig, *Star*, 182.

44. Rosenzweig, 183.

45. Rosenzweig, 185.

46. Rosenzweig, 190. On the place of this command in Rosenzweig's religious anthropology, see Michael Fishbane, *The Garments of Torah: Essays in Biblical Hermeneutics* (Bloomington: Indiana University Press, 1989), 102.

47. Rosenzweig, *Star*, 193; in the original, "Erst das Bekenntnis reißt die Seele hinein in die Seligkeit des Geliebtseins" (*Stern*, 117).

48. Rosenzweig, *Star*, 169; in the original, "Die Geliebte wird ergriffen" (*Stern*, 174). Zachary Braiterman comments on the explicit gendering of the lovers in this passage, referring to the "violent form of Rosenzweig's literary expression": "'The beloved is seized, *her* love is already a response to being seized'. . . . The switch in gender is deliberate. God's 'untrammeled passion' bursts forth. . . . The eros of revelation is violent" (*The Shape of Revelation*, 227–8).

49. Rosenzweig, *Star*, 175; in the original, "er entringt seine Liebe dem Stamm seines Selbst" (*Stern*, 181).

50. Rosenzweig, *Star*, 176.

51. Rosenzweig, *Star*, 183. In illustrating the transcending of gender boundaries with the image of a palm tree, Rosenzweig may be referring to the rabbinic idea of the palm tree's androgyny, according to which this tree was thought to comprise both male and female characteristics (b. Pesaḥ. 56a, cited in Wolfson, *Language, Eros, Being*, 151).

52. For Claire Katz, Rosenzweig's depiction of love "identifies the role of the lover as giver and the Beloved as the receiver, regardless of the sex (or gender) of who is in that position. . . . The logic here is less a logic of 'genders' than it is a logic of 'positions'" ("For Love Is as Strong as Death: Taking Another Look at Levinas on Love," *Philosophy Today* 45 [2001]: 126). Samuel Moyn makes a similar argument: "though in several forgivably sexist passages he noted that . . . the male is figured as naturally active and the female passive, Rosenzweig suggests that the asymmetry in the dyad is not ultimately gendered, since 'between man and woman the roles of giver and receiver of love pass back and forth'" (*Origins of the Other*, 148). Paul Mendes-Flohr advises taking into account the autobiographical context of this section of the *Star*, directed toward Rosenzweig's lover Margrit Rosenstock: "Rosenzweig's oft-criticized sexist language is at least partially explained when one realizes that he wrote these words for his lover, Gritli, as he affectionately called her. Further, he would undoubtedly concede, the roles of lover and beloved—of Eros and Anteros—can alternate" ("Between Sensual and Heavenly Love," 312–3).

53. Benjamin, *Rosenzweig's Bible*, 35n21.

54. See Benjamin, *Rosenzweig's Bible*, 35n21: "Rosenzweig states, 'It is only to the soul and the love of God that all this [God as (active, male) lover, soul as (passive, female) beloved] applies in the strict sense.'"

55. See Norbert Samuelson's comment: "once the human (male or female) becomes open to an external voice, he/she becomes a soul (feminine)" (*A User's Guide to Franz Rosenzweig's Star of Redemption* [Richmond, VA: Curzon, 1999], 153). For Rosenzweig, "what is active is male, whether they be men or women, and what is passive is female, again, whether they be men or women. . . . It is not how I would prefer the active/passive distinction to be made, but without a doubt that is how Rosenzweig makes it and thinks it" (177–8n7).

56. Benjamin, *Rosenzweig's Bible*, 35n21.

57. Batnitzky, "Dependency and Vulnerability," 138.

58. Rosenzweig, *Star*, 169. Gesine Palmer writes aptly of this passage, "To the modern reader this claim will prove contentious, no matter how hard-boiled she may be. It was a bit too much for me when I first read it, even though I was already well-trained in silently passing over all those disturbing gender biases that philosophers of earlier generations took for granted" ("'Dying for Love'— Making Sense of an [Unwitting?] Inversion in Franz Rosenzweig's Star of Redemption," *Bamidbar* 4, no. 2 (2019): 30).

59. Rosenzweig, *Star*, 169.

60. Rosenzweig, 169.

61. Rosenzweig, 169.

62. Batnitzky, "Dependency and Vulnerability," 139.

63. Batnitzky, 139–40.

64. Rosenzweig, *Star*, 317.

65. Batnitzky, "Dependency and Vulnerability," 140. Braiterman shows how Rosenzweig's idea of the eternal Jewish "blood community" is already present in Buber's work:

> It was Buber who first embraced the fact that, in exile, the Jew's land, language, and mores do not belong to the community of his blood, that the 'confluence of blood' directs one's vision beyond the span of the individual's life toward something greater and far more enduring. Of one mind, both thinkers ascribed the eternity of Israel and the abiding fact of its physical endurance to blood; and both sought to 'plant' eternity back into time. The difference between the two was Zionism. Buber sought to set the people in the space of its land, whereas Rosenzweig sought to plant that blood in the temporal rhythm of a ritual calendar. (*The Shape of Revelation*, 154)

Buber emphasizes the future of the Jewish people in terms of blood continuity in *Drei Reden über das Judentum* (Frankfurt am Main: Rütten and Loening, 1920); translated in *On Judaism*, ed. Nahum N. Glatzer, trans. Eva Jospe (New York: Schocken Books, 1967).

66. See Gil Anidjar, *Blood: A Critique of Christianity* (New York: Columbia University Press, 2014), 32: "At the center of the community of blood, there is a political hematology as well as a hematocentric embryology, a conception of kinship based on consanguinity." Anidjar explores this obsession with blood and its often murderous results.

67. See Katz's comment: "Jewish men were historically viewed as feminized. And this view was not positive. The historical context in which we find this characterization reveals the loaded nature of the term. The Jews were characterized as feminine by those—for example, the Nazis—who viewed themselves as virile. . . . And they were characterized in a historical context in which it was not only negative to be feminine if one was a man, it was also negative to be feminine if one was a woman. Thus, it is not clear if the problem is the feminization of men as much as it is the historical attitude toward women and all the stereotypical attributes ascribed to them" (*Levinas, Judaism, and the Feminine*, 150–51). On this topic, see also Howard Eilberg-Schwartz, "Introduction: People of the Body," in *People of the Body: Jews and Judaism from an Embodied Perspective*, ed. Howard Eilberg-Schwartz (Albany: State University of New York Press, 1992), 1–15; Daniel Boyarin, *Unheroic Conduct: The*

Rise of Heterosexuality and the Invention of the Jewish Man (Berkeley: University of California Press), 1997; and Daniel Boyarin, Daniel Itzkovitz, and Ann Pellegrini, "Strange Bedfellows: An Introduction," in *Queer Theory and the Jewish Question*, ed. Daniel Boyarin, Daniel Itzkovitz, and Ann Pellegrini (New York: Columbia University Press, 2003), 1–18.

68. Michael Fishbane, "The Song of Songs and Ancient Jewish Religiosity: Between Eros and History," in *Von Enoch bis Kafka: Festschrift für Karl E. Grözinger zum 60. Geburtstag* (Wiesbaden: Harrassowitz, 2002), 74.

69. Fishbane, "The Song of Songs," 78.

70. Franz Rosenzweig, "The Builders: Concerning the Law," in *On Jewish Learning*, ed. N. N. Glatzer (Madison: University of Wisconsin Press, 1955), 84–5. This language reflects Levinas's similar ascription of the feminine/woman to the site of domesticity; see the section "Habitation and the Feminine" in Levinas, *Totality and Infinity*: "the other whose presence is discreetly an absence, with which is accomplished the primary hospitable welcome which describes the field of intimacy, is the Woman [la Femme]. The woman [La femme] is the condition for recollection, the interiority of the Home, and inhabitation" (155; *Totalité et infini*, 166).

71. For an analysis of the Song of Songs that takes into account ecology and geography, see Elaine T. James, *Landscapes of the Song of Songs: Poetry and Place* (Oxford: Oxford University Press, 2017); for a reading of animality, see Eric Daryl Meyer, "Gregory of Nyssa and Jacques Derrida on the Human-Animal Distinction in the Song of Songs," in *The Bible and Posthumanism*, ed. Jennifer L. Koosed (Atlanta, GA: Society of Biblical Literature, 2014), 199–223.

72. Rosenzweig, *Star*, 218.

73. Fishbane maintains that the Song of Songs should be viewed against the backdrop of Egyptian and Mesopotamian love lyrics. In the secular love poems of ancient Egypt, "there are dialogues of celebration and longing between two youths, often portrayed with the epithets of brother and sister," among other parallels with the Song of Songs ("Introduction to the Commentary: Song of Songs," in *Song of Songs: The Traditional Hebrew Text with the New JPS Translation*, xxxii). Fishbane offers comparisons to highlight similar conventions in love discourse. "Notable among these external features are the use of fraternal rubrics to depict the female (she is called a 'sister' in both cultures)" (xxxii).

74. Song of Songs 4:9–12; 5:1–2; 8:1–2. Joan B. Burton focuses on parallels in gender themes between the Song and Hellenistic poetry, addressing scholarly speculation that the Song was written in a Hellenized atmosphere in third-century BCE: "In the context of Ptolemaic Egypt, the Song's repeated amatory references to the beloved female as sister would not seem out of place. . . Egypt had a tradition of erotic addresses to siblings and the usage need not be related to sibling marriage; yet Egypt also had a long pharaonic tradition of brother-sister

marriage as well as a strong mythic tradition of reciprocal love between Isis and Osiris, full brother and sister. The Greeks too had a mythic tradition of marriage between full brother and sister (Zeus and Hera). In the early-third-century BCE, the marriage of Ptolemy II to his full sister Arsinoe II brought this tradition (with its parallels in pharaonic practice and mythology) into the Greek political landscape as well" ("Themes of Female Desire and Self-Assertion in the Song of Songs and Hellenistic Poetry," in *Perspectives on the Song of Songs*, ed. Anselm C. Hagedorn [Berlin: Walter de Gruyter, 2005], 192).

75. Rosenzweig, *Star*, 218.

76. Rosenzweig, 218–9.

77. As Galli explains, "in the immediate revelation of love . . . the love between the two lacks something and is not fulfilled. 'Would that you were my brother,' the beloved sobs. Calling by name is not enough. It demands reality" (*Franz Rosenzweig and Jehuda Halevi*, 357).

78. Rosenzweig, *Star*, 219.

79. Rosenzweig, 219.

80. Rosenzweig, 219.

81. Rosenzweig, 214.

82. See Rosenzweig, *Star*, 259.

83. Rosenzweig, *Star*, 219. Fishbane notes that Rosenzweig's term *Reich der Brüderlichkeit* is "a prophetic allusion to the kingdom of heaven" (*The Garments of Torah*, 104). Pollock discusses this "kingdom of brotherliness" in the context of the self's longing to have the relationship with the divine "grounded in and recognized in the context of the world" (*Franz Rosenzweig's Conversions*, 165). See also Samuelson's comment: "The move towards the eternal from the momentary is a move beyond love. Beyond love, the soul longs for brotherliness" (*A User's Guide*, 177).

84. The Song is liturgically correlated to redemption, as it is read on Passover, not on Shavuot, the holiday that explicitly celebrates revelation. In this sense, Rosenzweig's reading of the Song as articulating a move from revelation to redemption reflects its liturgical location. On the recitation of the Song on Passover, see Fishbane, "Introduction to the Commentary," xlviii–xlix.

85. Rosenzweig, *Star*, 221. Benjamin explains how Rosenzweig turns to specific biblical texts to link the theological moments of creation, revelation, and redemption to one another. Rosenzweig understands the passage in Song 8:1 "as describing the soul's thirst for the presence of God in the world. But the soul's longing must remain unrealized. . . . Precisely this frustration leads the soul to turn toward the neighbor—a turn that, for Rosenzweig, signifies the onset of redemption. He signifies this turn with the citation, once again, of a biblical text as the opening words of the next volume—Part II, volume III begins: 'Love thy neighbor.' Here the erotic 'love' of Song of Songs becomes the neighborly love of Leviticus 19:18" (Benjamin, *Rosenzweig's Bible*, 42).

86. Galli, *Franz Rosenzweig and Jehuda Halevi*, 435.

87. See E. A. Speiser, "The Wife-Sister Motif in the Patriarchal Narratives," in *Biblical and Other Studies*, ed. Alexander Altmann (Cambridge, MA: Harvard University Press, 1963), for a comparison of the motif to the contemporaneous Hurrian legal concept of wife-sister: "The demonstrated prestige status of the wife-sister in Hurrian society, which was normative for the Patriarchs in many ways, provides a self-evident reason for the importance of the theme to early Biblical tradition" (28).

88. Genesis 20:12.

89. "Die Akeda würde nach Freud herrlich zu interpretieren sein. Man müsste noch die Kindheit Abrahams aus dem Midrasch hinzunehmen. Der Inzest wäre mit Sara gegeben" (Rosenzweig, *Briefe und Tagebücher*, ed. Rachel Rosenzweig and Edith Rosenzweig-Scheinmann [The Hague: Springer, 1979], 770). Braiterman observes of this note, "Unapologetic, Rosenzweig never denied that psychoanalysis lends itself to the interpretation of Scripture and midrash (Abraham, Terah, Isaac, and the conflict between fathers and sons; Abraham and Sarah in Egypt and the problem of incest)" (*The Shape of Revelation*, 228). For a discussion of psychoanalytic implications in Rosenzweig's thought, see Eric L. Santner, *On the Psychotheology of Everyday Life: Reflections on Freud and Rosenzweig* (Chicago: University of Chicago Press, 2001). Santner notes, "Psychoanalysis differs from other approaches to human being by attending to the constitutive 'toomuchness' that characterizes the psyche; the human mind is, we might say, defined by the fact that it includes more reality than it can contain, is the bearer of an excess, a too much of pressure that is not merely physiological" (8).

90. "Bruder und Schwester—das kommt wirklich in den 'besten Familien' vor (bei den Wälsungen, den Kroniden und Pharaonen), aber Mutter und Sohn, das ist der Untergang, Ödipus" (Franz Rosenzweig, *Die 'Gritli'-Briefe: Briefe an Margrit Rosenstock-Huessy*, ed. Inken Ruhle and Reinhold Mayer [Tübingen: Bilam, 2002], 516). I thank Paul Nahme for pointing out this reference to me, and I thank Juliane Hammer for her insightful reflections on how gender, sexuality, and power are implicated in this statement.

91. Davidoff, *Thicker Than Water*, 199.

92. Ellen Pollak, *Incest and the English Novel, 1684–1814* (Baltimore, MD: Johns Hopkins University Press, 2003), 203n12.

93. Ibid., 9. Judith Butler has shown that the law prohibiting incest "is the selfsame law that invites it, and it is no longer possible to isolate the repressive from the productive function of the juridical incest taboo" (*Gender Trouble: Feminism and the Subversion of Identity* [New York: Routledge, 1999], 97).

94. As Gayle Rubin has made clear, a prohibition "against *some* heterosexual unions assumes a taboo against *non*-heterosexual unions" ("The Traffic in

Women: Notes on the 'Political Economy' of Sex," in *Toward an Anthropology of Women*, ed. Rayna R. Reiter [New York: Monthly Review, 1975], 180).

95. Rubin, "The Traffic in Women," 180.

96. Pollak, *Incest and the English Novel*, 10.

97. "Sarah and Abraham are sister and brother, and they are married. . . . Iscah and Milcah are Abram's nieces, the daughters of his brother Haran. Milcah is also Abram's sister-in-law. Milcah is Abram's niece and sister-in-law because she married her uncle Nahor, Abram's brother. Abram, Nahor, and Haran are brothers, the sons of Terah (and grandsons of another Nahor.) Milcah and Iscah are also Lot's sisters. The normative or at least regular practice of incestuous marriage in Lot's family may have some bearing on his subsequent conduct with his daughters. It is not clear whether the women in these relationships had any say in the matter. Neither is it clear whether the practice represented local culture or was characteristic of this family. The Torah will eventually proscribe such unions" (Wilda C. Gafney, *Womanist Midrash: A Reintroduction to the Women of the Torah and the Throne* [Louisville, KY: Westminster John Knox Press, 2017], 30).

98. Gafney, *Womanist Midrash*, 32–33.

99. Pollak, 17.

100. Song of Songs, 8:1–2: "When I should find thee outside, I would kiss thee; and none would scorn me. I would lead thee, and bring thee into the house of my mother who brought me up." Julia Kristeva discusses this wish for connection: "she wishes indeed to introduce him 'into my mother's house' (8:2); she would have preferred him to be brother, familial, and thus loved without constraint" ("A Holy Madness: She and He," in *Tales of Love*, trans. Leon S. Roudiez [New York: Columbia University Press, 1987], 96).

101. Rosenzweig, *Star*, 258–9.

102. Rosenzweig, 169.

103. Rosenzweig, 345.

104. Rosenzweig, 317.

105. Rosenzweig, 317.

106. Rosenzweig, 318. Katz explains, "Love as that which goes beyond the moment is the eternal victory over death, and one way this victory is achieved is through fecundity" ("For Love Is as Strong as Death," 127).

107. See Biale's view that in the *Star*, "Marriage is not only a union between two people but is also the act that establishes community" (*Blood and Belief*, 201–2).

108. See Aaron W. Hughes: "His reification of *the* Jewish people . . . potentially risks nourishing a proto-racist and atavistic nationalism. . . . An early twentieth-century philosophical system that is founded in racial and religious superiority, and that seeks rejuvenation based on an acknowledgement of shared ancestry,

culture, and blood should immediately alert us to its implicit and explicit fascism" (*Rethinking Jewish Philosophy: Beyond Particularism and Universalism* [Oxford: Oxford University Press, 2014], 87).

109. Biale, *Blood and Belief*, 200. An alternative view, in which blood community can be read as ethnicity, is found in Mosès, *System and Revelation*, 176–8. For Dana Hollander, Mosès's formulation of Rosenzweig's blood community as ethnic community "resorts to a sociological idiom that is in my view not compatible with Rosenzweig's mode of argumentation" (*Exemplarity and Chosenness: Rosenzweig and Derrida on the Nation of Philosophy* [Redwood City, CA: Stanford University Press, 2008], 237n32). Hollander discusses Derrida's critique of Mosès's reading: "Derrida speculates whether Mosès may have been motivated by the wish to shield Rosenzweig's talk of blood and generation from any suspicion of geneticism or racism" (*Exemplarity and Chosenness*, 140; referring to Derrida, *Monolingualism of the Other: or, The Prosthesis of Origin*, trans. Patrick Mensah [Redwood City, CA: Stanford University Press, 1998], 79n9). As Hollander maintains, "we should be cautious about reading Rosenzweig's talk of blood and Volk in an organicist way" (*Exemplarity and Chosenness*, 121). Readers should be careful not to take Rosenzweig's reference to blood "to be simply organicist or racist, even if we cannot deny that it has such connotations" (139).

110. See Biale, *Blood and Belief*, 203. Wolfson explains Rosenzweig's view of Judaism's diasporic nature: "In contrast to other nations, the sense of peoplehood for the Jews is based on the ancestral blood community (*Blutsgemeninschaft*), which is construed neither as the ethnic attachment to land secured by territorial occupation, as Zionism advocates, nor the racial purity decreed by the Nazis, but rather as the ontological-temporal self-sufficiency that preserves Jewish identity through participation in liturgy, ritual, and textual study" (*The Duplicity of Philosophy's Shadow: Heidegger, Nazism, and the Jewish Other* [New York: Columbia University Press, 2018], 71). See also Haggai Dagan: "the motif of blood, in addition to being a negation of the centrality of the spirit (and, as such, a negation of the entire tradition of Western thought), also becomes a negation of the national ethos in its usual territorial form, and especially of the Zionist ethos, which wished to actively restore the connection between the people and its land. The people, Rosenzweig claimed, was not founded on its soil, and its land is more a locus of longing than a place to live" ("The Motif of Blood and Procreation in Franz Rosenzweig," *AJS Review* 26, no. 2 [2002]: 246–7.) For Peter Eli Gordon, the blood community refers to "a form of nomadic group-identification, a 'self-rootedness' that evokes the self-enclosed and circulatory structure of the Jewish liturgical calendar itself" ("Rosenzweig and the Philosophy of Jewish Existence," in *The Cambridge Companion to Modern Jewish Philosophy*, 136).

111. Judith Butler discusses both Rosenzweig's and Buber's opposition in the 1910s and 1920s to the idea of a state for the Jewish people, wary of the negative effect on Judaism of "the establishment of a state with legal coercion and sovereignty as its basis" (*Parting Ways: Jewishness and the Critique of Zionism* [New York: Columbia University Press, 2012], 75).

112. Rosenzweig, *Star*, 319. Exile is central to this conception of the eternal people. As Batnitzky notes, "Rooted not in land but in blood, the Jewish people exist in a state of embodied disembodiment. The natural propagation of the Jewish body guarantees it eternity, but the Jewish people remain physically dispersed in exile" (Batnitzky, "Dependency and Vulnerability," 141). Wolfson discusses Rosenzweig's appeal to the unique role of exile in the Jewish tradition: "The Jew belongs to this home, we might say, by not belonging" (Wolfson, *The Duplicity of Philosophy's Shadow*, 73).

113. See Leora Batnitzky, *Idolatry and Representation: The Philosophy of Franz Rosenzweig Reconsidered* (Princeton, NJ: Princeton University Press, 2000), 75: "Just as Rosenzweig argues that the notion of the blood community has symbolically maintained the integrity of Judaism against coercive proselytism, so too the notion of the blood community symbolically maintains the integrity of Judaism in the wake of modern philosophy. . . . The Jewish community in general, and the blood community in particular, are not regulative ideals but instead mark the limit of philosophy itself."

114. Anidjar, *Blood*, 312n9.

115. Dagan, "The Motif of Blood," 243.

116. Dagan, 244.

117. Dagan, 244.

118. The twentieth-century context of the continuity crisis is discussed further in the epilogue. For more on the history of the Jewish continuity narrative and its implications in contemporary contexts, see Lila Corwin Berman, Kate Rosenblatt, and Ronit Y. Stahl, "Continuity Crisis: The History and Sexual Politics of an American Jewish Communal Project," *American Jewish History* 104, no. 2/3 (April/July 2020): 167–94.

119. Berman, Rosenblatt, and Stahl, "Continuity Crisis," 194.

120. Berman, Rosenblatt, and Stahl, 192.

121. Marla Brettschneider, *Jewish Feminism and Intersectionality* (Albany: State University of New York Press, 2016), 143. Robert Gibbs calls Rosenzweig's evocation of a blood community "philosophically troubling (a potentially catastrophic racism lurks here)" (*Correlations in Rosenzweig and Levinas*, 137). The Jewish people "roots itself in its body, in its generations" in Rosenzweig's "potentially racist idea of blood" (*Correlations in Rosenzweig and Levinas*, 137–8).

122. Patricia Hill Collins and Sirma Bilge, *Intersectionality* (Cambridge, UK: Polity, 2016), 200.

123. Alys Eve Weinbaum, *Wayward Reproductions: Genealogies of Race and Nation in Transatlantic Modern Thought* (Durham, NC: Duke University Press, 2004), 2–5.

124. Engelstein, *Sibling Action*, 9.

125. Levitt, *Jews and Feminism*, 87.

126. Levitt, 89. In her reading of Eugene Borowitz's liberal theology and ethics, Levitt points out the consequences of defending monogamous, procreative heterosexual marriage over and against feminism and nonheterosexual relationships. Borowitz "claims that his objections to queer families is about protecting the biological future of the Jewish people" (88). But Levitt points out the trouble with identifying a narrative of continuity along biological lines, especially in reference to Jews' minority status: "This appeal to biology or race is especially striking, because Borowitz uses the Holocaust as a justification. This is for many a counterintuitive move since it was precisely arguments that pinned Jewish identity to notions of biology and race that were used to justify genocide" (194n33).

127. Biale, *Blood and Belief*, 200–1.

128. Biale, 201. Biale also notes that "Rosenzweig anticipates Chajim Bloch in replicating the well-known nineteenth-century homily that it was Jewish women who preserved Judaism through the family."

129. Rosenzweig, *Star*, 318.

130. Braiterman, *The Shape of Revelation*, 235.

131. Rosenzweig, *Star*, 318.

132. Rosenzweig, 362. It is through the alliance of grandson and grandfather that the Jewish people "becomes the eternal people; for when grandson and grandfather behold one another, they behold in each other at the same moment the last grandson and the first grandfather. So the grandson and the grandfather, both of them, and both together are for the one who stands between them the true embodiment of the eternal people" (367).

133. Rosenzweig, 317. This passage is preceded by an image of the people of Israel, from which fire in the core of the star continually burns. Braiterman helpfully observes of this passage, "Sexual reproduction thus shifts revelation from the astral plane back down to earth and eros. Eternity is the bearing of children across the span of generations. . . . Male issue transforms into and out of starlike substance" (*The Shape of Revelation*, 226).

134. Braiterman, *The Shape of Revelation*, 153.

135. Braiterman, 236.

136. Martin Buber, *Drei Reden über das Judentum* (Frankfurt am Main.: Rütten and Loening, 1920).

137. Martin Buber, "Judaism and the Jews," in Martin Buber, *On Judaism*, trans. Eva Jospe, ed. Nahum N. Glatzer (New York: Schocken Books, 1967), 15.

138. Buber, "Judaism and the Jews," 15.

139. Buber, 17.

140. "We Jews need to know that our being and our character have been formed not solely by the nature of our fathers but also by their fate, and by their pain, their misery and their humiliation" (Buber, "Judaism and the Jews," 17).

141. Buber, "Judaism and the Jews," 11–12; in the original, "Was bedeutet das, dass wir dauern wollen, nicht bloß als Menschen, Menschengeist und Menschensame, sondern, den Zeiten und der Zeit selber zum Trotz, als Juden?" (Buber, *Drei Reden über das Judentum*, 12).

142. Buber, 15.

143. Buber, 15.

144. Buber, 17.

145. Buber, 19.

146. Song of Songs 8:1.

147. In an exploration of leitmotifs within the Song of Songs, Phyllis Trible observes that in the Song "the births of the lovers are linked to their mothers, though the fathers are never mentioned" (*God and the Rhetoric of Sexuality*, 157–8). Similarly, Simon Critchley observes, "The figure absent from the Song of Songs is the father. . . . The household is not paternally but maternally regulated" (*The Problem with Levinas* [Oxford: Oxford University Press, 2015], 92).

148. Braiterman, *The Shape of Revelation*, 227.

149. "Love ruled over my soul, which was so early espoused to him, and he began to assume over me such assurance and such mastery, through the power that my imagination gave him, that I was obliged to do all his bidding fully" (Alighieri, *Vita Nuova*, 47–9).

150. Laura Levitt points out the issues with this vision of asymmetric love, calling for "rethinking the human-divine relationship in nonhierarchical terms, challenging the abusiveness of the metaphor of the lover and the beloved in Rosenzweig's text" (*Jews and Feminism*, 191n13). Levitt observes that such theological approaches have disturbing implications: "the asymmetries within the sexual contract pose dangers for Jewish women precisely because they are uttered in the name of love" (*Jews and Feminism*, 82). As Mara Benjamin asks, "what is excluded or suppressed when we equate this particular conception of eros with love? What do we obscure when we fail to recognize the gap between them? And what would the *Star* need to account for love and revelation imagined in more capacious and complex terms than those found within this text's pristine, severe structure? ("Love in the *Star*? A Feminist Challenge," *Bamidbar* 4, no. 2 [2019]: 11–12).

151. Benjamin, "Love in the *Star*?," 13.

152. In revelation the individual "has heard God's call and has been ravished in his love," but he is closed off "from access to the world" (Rosenzweig, *Star*, 228).

153. As Benjamin explains, "the community as Rosenzweig envisions it hardly allowed for difference or tension among the members; the *Männerbund* he envisioned, with its almost military-style actions performed in unison, evoke a stylized homogeneity rather than offering room for multiplicity and dyadic connection among the members" (*The Obligated Self*, 123).

154. Wolfson, "Asceticism and Eroticism," 106.

155. Rosenzweig, *Star*, 346–7.

156. Wolfson, *Circle in the Square*, 80.

157. Garloff, *Mixed Feelings*, 147.

158. Garloff, 154.

159. Garloff, 171.

160. See Wolfson, *Giving Beyond the Gift*, 82–3: "The disclosure of the face of God that will shine in the eschaton is itself a form of concealment, the manifestation becoming hidden and the speech leading to silence. To be granted a vision of the face inscribed within the contours of the star is to behold the inexpressible truth. . . . his own sense of affirmation as the negation of negation, which is reflected in his characterization of the end as a silence that no longer needs words, is itself a form of apophasis that embraces the mystical."

161. The end of the *Star* betrays an affinity to a more mystically oriented conception "that, in some measure, led to a reappropriation of the very idealism that he set out to repudiate" (Wolfson, *Giving Beyond the Gift*, 36); "Rosenzweig's indebtedness to kabbalah, or at the very least the affinity of his thinking to the Jewish esoteric tradition, can be seen in his embrace of an apophatic discourse at the end of the voyage, and this in spite of his explicit rejection of negative theology at the beginning" (52). Despite Rosenzweig's effort to use theological language, "that very language implicates him finally in what he called atheistic theology, that is, configuring God in human terms in such a way that the reality of the divine, which he presumes cannot be reduced to the human or to the world, and to which he does refer as the 'wholly other,' is inevitably compromised. This is what leads back at the end of the journey to the apophasis laid aside at the beginning" (52). See also Wolfson, "Light Does Not Talk but Shines," 93.

162. Yael Feldman, *No Room of Their Own: Gender and Nation in Israeli Women's Fiction* (New York: Columbia University Press, 1999), 80.

163. Trible, *God and the Rhetoric of Sexuality*, 165n22; 161–2.

TWO

EROS, BODIES, AND BEYOND

"*RETROUVER LE PLATONISME.*"[1] THIS IS how Levinas articulates the philo-sophical project of *Totality and Infinity* (1961) and the task of contemporary philosophy more broadly. Stella Sandford interprets this to mean "to redis-cover, recover or re-encounter Platonism, to find or meet it again, but also to find oneself back in the place of Platonism, to recuperate it."[2] In particular, Levinas's phenomenology of eros is strongly influenced by Plato's *Symposium*.[3] Both Plato and Levinas view erotic love as a disruptive force that conflicts with ethical responsibility, and each finds a way out of the problems of erotic love in the possibility of procreation.[4] Levinas ultimately goes even further than Plato in his dismissal of erotic love, and I will question the priority he gives to the future of fecundity—to procreation. In this chapter, the specific materials I put in conversation with one another contribute to my critique of Levinas's gender economy by highlighting the sublated space of the feminine and the absent presence of the reproductive female body.

I will begin by examining the role of erotic love in Levinas's earlier work. Here, eros is the original form of alterity, or otherness. Eros is characterized by the feminine, which calls the subject's self-containment into question. In this way, Levinas gives the feminine a positive inflection, because it interrupts the virile sphere of totality.[5] But while it is certainly philosophically refreshing that Levinas valorizes the feminine, it is radically insufficient. Although the language Levinas uses for eros is feminine, the language that his ethics is aim-ing toward, in both infinity (father/son) and the communal sphere (brothers), is masculine. He moves from masculine, virile totality to filial, fatherly, and fraternal infinity.[6] This gendered language has real-world consequences, and it demands critical attention.

Exploring how Plato views the feminine and the body helps us understand how Levinas draws on these frameworks and diverges from them. For Plato, love of the intangible good is privileged over love of the physically beautiful, but loving beautiful bodies can have a purpose, because they can lead toward metaphysical beauty. The *Symposium* prefers intellectual fecundity to human procreation, and as we saw in the previous chapter, the slippage between metaphor and reality has consequences for the roles of real women. For Levinas, erotic love is evocative and important but closed off, so the couple needs to bridge the erotic to the ethical. This is where the child comes in. Human fecundity is the link to the future, and this also has consequences for women.

In the course of this analysis, I address Levinas's treatment of the "feminine" in his earlier philosophical work and of "femininity" in his Talmudic work, and the implications of the latter for the former. I consider the consequences of Levinas's insistence that erotic love lies outside the ethical realm. Then, I analyze the entrenched place of physicality in Plato's account of eros and the role of Diotima, the mouthpiece at the center of his narrative. Diotima ultimately promotes intellectual (male) fecundity over physical (female) reproduction. But as Carol Pateman points out, a central patriarchal argument has historically been the refusal to acknowledge women's creative power: "Men appropriate to themselves women's natural creativity, their capacity physically to give birth—but they also do more than that. Men's generative power extends into another realm; they transmute what they have appropriated into another form of generation, the ability to create new political life, or to give birth to political right."[7] I argue here that Levinas, like Rosenzweig, ultimately succumbs to this logic, eliding women, along with the erotic, from generativity in favor of an entirely masculinized fecundity.

EROS AND THE FEMININE IN LEVINAS

In *Time and the Other*, first presented as a series of lectures in 1946–47 at the *Collège Philosophique*, Levinas seeks to subvert the commonly held view of erotic love as a mutual synthesis, instead illustrating erotic love as a tension maintained between opposites. As he sees it, the erotic relationship has an exceptional status because it does not involve power or knowledge. It has a unique communicative framework. It is "a relationship with alterity, with mystery—that is to say, with the future."[8] But within the erotic relation, the subject is never sufficiently brought out of subjectivity by the other person, instead retaining a sense of egoism: "the *I* survives in it."[9]

Here the unique nature of the erotic relationship coincides with the exceptional role of the feminine, itself characterized by mystery and otherness, slipping away from the realm of light. As Levinas formulates it, the feminine is unknowable, and its hiddenness is the very source of its privileged position. In flying from the light, it eludes easy interpretation. The feminine's alterity and mystery constitute its power.[10] Feminist interpreters, most notably Luce Irigaray, have frequently criticized this ascription of the feminine to darkness. Irigaray asks why the feminine cannot be brought out into the light with the masculine subject: "he will have taken from the beloved woman this visibility that she offers him, which strengthens him, and will have sent her back to darkness."[11] Irigaray offers a necessary corrective. Levinas seems to be just another in a long line of thinkers, from Plato onward, associating virility with the light of knowledge.

But Irigaray does not acknowledge Levinas's critique of both ocularcentrism and the metaphysics of presence from Plato to Husserl, and his ascription of the feminine to darkness and mystery is located within that critique.[12] In this sense the feminine is not necessarily subjugated by retreating from representation but rather—at least in theory—elevated beyond the masculine subject who remains within the sphere of comprehension and mastery. Within Levinas's phenomenology of eros, the feminine puts into question the self-contained totality of subjectivity in favor of a relation with an unknowable, unrepresentable other. The feminine interrupts the virile sphere of ontology.

In *Totality and Infinity*, Levinas builds on his earlier investigation of the feminine to further explore the erotic relationship. His chapter on the phenomenology of eros is prefaced with a section on "The Ambiguity of Love."[13] This ambiguity echoes Diotima's emphasis on the intermediary character of eros in Plato's *Symposium*. Levinas clarifies Plato's conception of eros as a child of need,[14] and he explains that he will provide an enhanced role to the feminine in the erotic relationship, which he sees as absent from Plato's account.

In the next section, "Phenomenology of Eros," Levinas writes that the erotic relationship is "the very contrary of the social relation."[15] In a particularly lyrical passage, Levinas describes why erotic love for the other is ultimately self-reflective: "If to love is to love the love the Beloved bears me, to love is also to love oneself in love, and thus to return to oneself."[16] For Levinas, the erotic relation excludes itself from the ethical because the lovers are enclosed within a self-contained unity without any reference to the external world.[17] The feminine is the heart of this sequestered mini-society, both at one with society and inherently apart from it: "The feminine is the other refractory to society, member of a dual society, an intimate society, a society without language."[18]

To understand why Levinas excludes the erotic relationship from ethics, we have to keep in mind what ethics and eros mean for Levinas. Erotic relationships involve the desire for reciprocity, whereas ethical relationships cannot be based on reciprocity, for that would involve reducing the other to the Same. For Levinas, the self becomes constituted and elected in responsibility within an ethical horizon. The transcendent, wholly other is infinitely distant, beyond representational knowledge structures. If we follow Levinas's understanding of eros and ethics, Claire Katz explains, "it is not clear that this bridge from ethics to eros can be completed."[19] The truly intersubjective relationship cannot be symmetrical or expect reciprocation.[20]

When we understand why, for Levinas, erotic love must be excluded from asymmetrical intersubjectivity, we have a better sense of why eros must be excluded from ethics. Within this insular relation, the love for the other is ultimately self-reflective. Ethics requires the subject to be interrupted by the other, and this does not happen in erotic love. The only way the erotic relationship can take part in ethics, then, is through fecundity, in the form of the child: "the encounter with the Other as feminine is required in order that the future of the child come to pass from beyond the possible."[21] The relationship to the child brings the lover outside of the self toward an external being, allowing the possibility for an ethical relation to come out of the erotic encounter. The emphasis is on the future, the anticipation of *"what is not yet."*[22]

In theory, both lovers might be equally bound into the relationship and equally in need of transcendence into the ethical. But Levinas, like Rosenzweig, suggests a hierarchy within the erotic, describing the feminine as frail, vulnerable, and characterized by a "weight of non-signifyingness."[23] Levinas's phenomenological depiction of the feminine as passive beloved (*l'aimée*) to the active male lover (*l'aimé*) echoes the ascriptions of gender roles in Rosenzweig's reading of the Song of Songs.[24] Levinas goes on to rhetorically compare the feminine beloved to a modest virgin, a young animal, and a shy plaything: "The beloved, at once graspable but intact in her nudity, beyond object and face and thus beyond the existent, abides in virginity. . . . The beloved is opposed to me . . . as an irresponsible animality which does not speak true words. The beloved, returned to the stage of infancy without responsibility—this coquettish head, this youth, this pure life 'a bit silly'—has quit her status as a person. . . . The relations with the Other are enacted in play; one plays with the Other as with a young animal."[25] The beloved is animalized and lacks coherent human language, responsibility, and seriousness. The beloved is played with and at play.[26]

Levinas's comparison of the beloved with the animal at play helps explain why he excludes eros from ethics. Elsewhere, he asserts that humans have a unique ethical relationship with one another that cannot be found with an animal other; relationships with animals are derivative only of the primary relationships we have with humans. Considering the importance of the "face" to Levinas's ethics, it is significant that he believes our relationship to the face of a dog is secondary and analogous: "It is via the face that one understands, for example, a dog. Yet the priority here is not found in the animal, but in the human face."[27] A human face can challenge and surprise—unlike, he claims, the face of an animal.[28]

In excluding the nonhuman animal other, Levinas diverges from Martin Buber's model of dialogical encounter in *I and Thou*. Buber demarcates I-It relationships, characterized by utility and instrumentality, from I-Thou relationships, based on openness and mutuality. For Buber, we can experience I-Thou relationships in our relation to nature, which includes trees and animals; in our relation to other humans; and in our relation to the divine. About the first relation, Buber famously writes, "An animal's eyes have the power to speak a great language. . . . This condition of the mystery is known only by the animal, it alone can disclose it to us."[29] Buber says he has experienced this encounter with an animal's gaze many times: "Sometimes I look into a cat's eyes. . . . The beginning of this cat's glance, lighting up under the touch of my glance, indisputably questioned me: 'Is it possible that you think of me?'"[30] Derrida self-consciously echoes Buber when he invokes the irreducible singularity of his feline inspiration.[31] According to Derrida, the denial of the animal gaze is foundational to the Western philosophical tradition, from Descartes on (excluding Buber and a few other notable exceptions).[32] But Levinas does not think nonhuman beings can provide ethical encounters. This is one of the reasons that, in his view, Buber's I-Thou model is lacking. In this regard I agree with Peter Atterton, who writes, "Levinas's criticism seriously underestimates a major strength of Buber's philosophy, which is precisely to have included the possibility of extending ethical consideration to other animals in their own right. . . . His objection to Buber's philosophy is specious—and speciesist."[33]

When he compares the beloved to an animal, Levinas means that everyone, man or woman, becomes silly and playful in erotic love, like a happy, fun-loving puppy.[34] Nonetheless, his alignment of femininity, animality, and eros draws on the longstanding philosophical association of femininity with animal nature, set apart from civilized, rational masculinity. Notably, Levinas both draws on this association and challenges it by disrupting the privileging of virile rationality in the Western tradition. But although he elevates femininity above masculine rationality, which is a corrective to previous approaches, he still sets up the animalized feminine against masculine reason, and he is not alone in this move. Discourses of gender and the human-animal boundary intersect routinely in the history of philosophy. As Sherryl Vint observes, "there are many parallels between the ways in which women have been constructed, controlled, spoken for and objectified by patriarchal culture, and similar constraints placed on animals by Western culture more generally."[35] Kecia Ali shows how in religious thinking, in particular, "dense webs of signification" have long connected women and animals, which, "often discursively connected, play vital roles in the symbolic language of religious identity."[36] While Levinas does at least invert this equation, the troubling binary remains.

This is only part of the problem. Why must the beloved be feminized, regardless of the sexual or gendered identities of the lovers? This erotic structure is (unsurprisingly) heteronormative, and its conclusion is the production of a child. It is no wonder that many readers of Levinas have taken issue with his descriptions of the feminine. Sandford points out that the "frank and unself-conscious account of the nature and the place of the feminine in *Totality and Infinity* is gratingly patriarchal."[37] By arriving at fecundity through the phenomenology of eros, Levinas subordinates eros to fecundity and love to procreation.

This brings us to the next section, "Fecundity," which follows his phenomenology of eros.[38] Here, Levinas specifies that the relation to the child is exemplified in the father-son relationship.[39] This relationship is unique because it involves both identification and foreignness: "My child is a stranger (Isaiah 49), but a stranger who is not only mine, for he *is* me. He is me a stranger to myself."[40] Soon after, Levinas slips from the gender-neutral "child" (*l'enfant*) to the far more particularized "son" (*le fils*): "I do not have my child; I am my child. Paternity is a relation with a stranger who while being Other *is* me . . . the son is not me; and yet I *am* my son."[41] Sarah Allen raises an important point here: it is curious and telling that for Levinas, "the primary source of intersubjectivity in erotic love is not the relation between man and woman, or between man, woman, and child, but between father and son."[42] Does the ethical transcendence of *Totality and Infinity* exclude women? The feminine and maternal may be the conditions of possibility for transcendence in paternal fecundity, but it is the "overtly masculine fathers and sons" who are the central figures.[43] Similarly, Irigaray argues that Levinas reinscribes a hegemony of paternal-filial relations that ignores and displaces a genealogy of mothers and daughters. The feminine enables the masculine subject to gain access to the transcendent other while not participating in this relation, and the feminine's only access to transcendence is through the possibility of a son.[44]

Levinas further elucidates his conception of femininity within biblical and Talmudic frameworks.[45] In his essay "Judaism and the Feminine," Levinas discusses empirical women, not merely the category of the "feminine," despite the essay's title. Here, Levinas positions woman as the place of the home and gentleness, much as he does in his philosophical work in which the feminine is the site of ethical habitation. Indeed, the slippage between woman and the abstract trope of the feminine also occurs throughout *Totality and Infinity*.[46] Levinas explains that the women of the Hebrew scriptures "all play an active role in the attainment of the biblical purpose and are placed at the very pivot of Sacred History."[47] The participation of women allows biblical events to occur. The biblical Jewish woman has a "secret presence, on the edge of invisibility," and is characterized by interiority.[48] She is the site of the home, keeping peace and ensuring the safety of the interior in order for the exterior path of history to take place. In her gentleness and untainted goodness, the woman is the alternative to the masculine "geometry of infinite and cold space" and to the virile "anonymous circuit of the economy."[49] Woman restores equilibrium to society, overcoming the alienation caused by the "universal and all-conquering *logos*" of the masculine sphere.[50] Woman reflects God's presence in the world: "'man without woman diminishes the image of God in the world.'"[51] She is the original manifestation of gentleness itself, without which ethics would not be possible.

It is true that Levinas is here providing a refreshing and necessary critique of the virile and cold economy of masculine logos. But this critique need not require the ascription of biblical women to restrictive and reductive stereotypes in an essay that is, moreover, self-consciously about Judaism. This has consequences for the representation and potential exclusion of Jewish women from communal spheres and their relegation to sites of domesticity. My response is similar to my reading of Levinas on animality. Although he sets femininity above virility, in doing so, he also reifies the masculine/feminine binary. Putting the feminine on a pedestal may be preferable to subjugation, but it is radically insufficient, and it comes with especially concerning implications.

In this essay, Levinas goes on to compare the Talmudic interpretation of human creation in Genesis with a similar narrative from Plato's *Symposium*:

> The discussion between the schools of Rav and Shmuel on the creation of Eve can be viewed from this perspective. Did she come from Adam's rib? Was this rib not a *side* of Adam, created as a single being with two faces that God separated while Adam, still androgynous, was sleeping? This theme perhaps evolved from Plato's *Symposium*. . . . The two faces of the primitive Adam from the beginning look towards the side to which they will always remain turned. They are faces from the very outset, whereas Plato's god turns them round after separation. Their new existence, separated existence, will not come to punish the daring of too perfect a nature, as in Plato. For the Jews, separated existence will be worth more than the initial union.[52]

Levinas contrasts his exegesis of the creation story with the Aristophanic account in which two beings are cleaved by divine agents, forever after searching for their other half.[53] Rather than the self and other fusing in erotic love, the other maintains distance, which is precisely what fuels the erotic relationship: "In voluptuosity the other is me and separated from me."[54] For Levinas, Aristophanes's etiology of love is incorrect because the infinite, insatiable longing of eros should not be nostalgic. Instead of reaching back to recover a lost origin point, it is directed toward an unknown future.[55]

In Levinas's view, "'flesh of my flesh and bone of my bone' therefore means an identity of nature between woman and man . . . and also a subordination of sexual life to the personal relation which is equality in itself."[56] As he sees it, from the rabbinic standpoint erotic love is tied to its futural possibilities. Romantic love is not the end of the conjugal union; sex, tied to marriage, involves multiplying the image of God and fulfilling the people of Israel's future. He clarifies, "Not that conjugal love has no importance in itself, or that it is reduced to the rank of a means of procreation, or that it merely *prefigures* its fulfillments, as in a certain theology. On the contrary, the ultimate end of the family is the actual *meaning* and the joy of this present."[57] Inherent in the very act of erotic love is the participation of the present (eros) in the future (fecundity). "The meaning of love does not, then, stop with the moment of voluptuousness, nor with the person loved."[58]

Levinas also interprets the creation narrative in "And God Created Woman," his Talmudic reading of Tractate *Berakhot* 61a. He writes that the feminine must become clear "against the background of a human essence, the *Isha* from the *Ish*," the woman from the man.[59] Levinas argues that traditional biblical commentators interpret the dual nature of the human to mean that woman is derived from man. But he takes an approach that will inform how he views the feminine within his ethics: "The feminine does not derive from the masculine; rather, the division into feminine and masculine—the dichotomy—derives from what is human."[60] Woman is not derived from the masculine, nor is she half of a male whole; rather, the human is posited prior to any division of sex, and thus both man and woman are derived from the human. In fundamental interhuman relations, the masculine and feminine are contemporaries while their sexual aspects are secondary: "The sexual is only an accessory of the human."[61] Irigaray would argue that sexuality is never secondary to humanity but rather inherent to it. For Levinas, though, sexual difference is "subordinated in the interhuman relation."[62]

In this Talmudic reading, Levinas explains the Gemara's ordering of dangers: it is preferable for a man to walk behind a lion than to walk behind a woman (presumably because he may be distracted by the woman's body). The Gemara prefers the danger of a wild animal to the danger of intimacy or the distracting thoughts resulting from the potential of intimacy. Levinas explains that this reasoning "stems perhaps from masculine psychology. It assumes that a woman bears the erotic within herself as a matter of course."[63] He suggests that a woman can rise above her inherent eroticism and thus become elevated—she can become, essentially, like a man. But if it is the man who is so attracted to the woman that he should prefer the possibility of a violent death, why is it the woman who has to overcome sexuality? She seems to be innocent of these charges—all she has done is taken a stroll.

Levinas attempts to offer an explanation for the issues of hierarchy and the inequality of the sexes: "Real humanity does not allow for an abstract equality, without some subordination of terms. What family scenes there would have been between the members of that first perfectly equal couple! Subordination was needed, and a wound was needed; suffering was and is needed to unite equals and unequals."[64] In this Talmudic reading, Susan Shapiro finds "both the promise and the problems of Levinas's attempts to think sexual difference otherwise."[65] Shapiro rightfully questions Levinas's choice of this text as a forum for raising issues on sexual difference, for its description of woman as accessory to man, constructed out of his tail, "is one of the most misogynistic rabbinic readings of the creation stories."[66] Levinas explains away the subordination of woman to man as necessary, rationalizing the injustice of the hierarchy of the sexes as originary and natural.[67]

THE ENCRYPTED DAUGHTER

Both Irigaray and Derrida maintain that we must pay attention to the horizon of sexual difference in Levinas's work. While Irigaray takes issue with Levinas's subordination of the sexual to the ethical relation, Derrida worries that sexual difference "may actually define, and so limit, Levinas's ethics."[68] In his essay "*Geschlecht*: Sexual Difference, Ontological Difference," Derrida discusses how Heidegger and Levinas figure the feminine as the degraded secondary function and then efface the question of sexual difference, even as it actually allows their systems of thought to function.[69] Derrida asks why Heidegger has been silent on this question, specifically in *Being and Time*, in which the term for sex or gender rarely comes up.[70] Although *Dasein* (the human who uniquely asks the question of existence) is meant to be free of sexual difference, this issue in fact pervades Heidegger's thought. In Heidegger, *Dasein* is pure being, prior to any sense of difference, in a primary relation with only itself and not any other. But since *Dasein* is the concrete foundation to the human, it will also be the source for modes of difference, primarily sexual difference. It is in *Dasein*'s dispersion from its pure self into the world that it engages in relations with others and enters into relations of difference.

Similarly, Derrida points out that in the case of Levinas, "the classical interpretation gives a masculine sexual marking to what is presented either as a neutral originariness, or, at least, as prior and superior to all sexual markings."[71] Levinas does not erase sexual difference—rather, he maintains it: "the human in general remains a sexual being. But he can only do so, it would seem, by placing (differentiated) sexuality beneath humanity which sustains itself at the level of the Spirit."[72] Derrida argues that for Levinas, the masculine is constructed as the normative human while the feminine is other. He points out that Levinas seeks to view sexual difference as secondary to the primary category of the human, the ethical relation prior to sexual difference. Reading Levinas's explicitly Jewish texts allows Derrida to see Levinas making this move; in "And God Created Woman," Levinas exegetically reads the creation of woman from man's rib/side as indicating that the feminine, standing in for the sexual relation, is secondary to the human, which in turn represents the primary ethical relation.

The human in Levinas, then, is precisely that which is male, from which the female is derived. For this reason, Derrida questions Levinas's aim to articulate a relation to the other prior to sexual differentiation. The other "who is *not yet marked* is *already* found to be marked by masculinity."[73] The human other in Levinasian ethics is primarily the masculine, despite attempts to locate an ethical relation prior to sexual difference. And while Levinas devalues femininity by casting it as derivative, he simultaneously devalues sexual difference by signifying sexuality as feminine and the human (the site of the ethical) as masculine. In this Talmudic reading, then, we can see both the foundational nature of sexual difference to Levinas's thought and the process by which it (and, by extension, the feminine with which it is associated) is encrypted as the unacknowledged void beneath his work.

In his essay "At This Very Moment in This Work Here I Am," Derrida presents two moments of reading: one in which the male reader demonstrates what is successful in Levinas's thought and another in which the female reader reveals what is lacking. Levinas's filiated ethics surmounts a void, a space both there and not there, a cellar in which the apparently absent daughter is encrypted. The essay ends with two voices, male and female, speaking over and within each other, gazing into the symbolic grave of the daughter, who is excluded from the relation of paternity-filiality:[74] "BUT IN THE BOTTOMLESS CRYPT THE

INDECIPHERABLE STILL GIVES READING FOR A LAPSE ABOVE
HER BODY WHICH SLOWLY DECOMPOSES IN ANALYSIS. . . . SHE
DOESN'T SPEAK THE UNNAMEABLE YET YOU HEAR HER BETTER
THAN ME AHEAD OF ME AT THIS VERY MOMENT WHERE NONE-
THELESS ON THE OTHER SIDE OF THE MONUMENTAL WORK I
WEAVE MY VOICE SO AS TO BE EFFACED THIS TAKE IT HERE I AM
EAT ≈ GET NEARER ≈ IN ORDER TO GIVE HIM/HER ≈ DRINK."[75] In
the essay's conclusion, the daughter is the crypt, "both in the sense of the secret
and the tomb," above which Levinas's work is built.[76]

Derrida's image of the encrypted daughter is an especially vivid way of raising a question Irigaray asks directly: why must the relation that leads toward
futurity in *Totality and Infinity* be that of the father with the son, and not with
the daughter? Why does Levinas slip, without marking the difference, between
the terms "child" (*l'enfant*) and "son" (*le fils*)?[77] The woman is "pregnant with a
son, perhaps (but why a son and not a daughter, her other self?)"[78] After all, the
daughter is not the only invisible foundation of the house; her mother is as well.

In a later interview, "Love and Filiation," Levinas attempts to clarify his
writings on the feminine. After describing the feminine as the origin of alterity, he says, "All these allusions to the ontological differences between the
masculine and the feminine would appear less archaic if, instead of dividing
humanity into two species (or into two genders), they would signify that the
participating in the masculine and in the feminine were the attribute of every
human being. Could this be the meaning of the enigmatic verse of *Genesis* 1.27:
'male and female created He them'?"[79] For Levinas, the masculine-feminine
duality represents the original interhuman self-and-other relation described
in the biblical creation narrative. He seems to say that the masculine-feminine
relationship is the only configuration possible and that in each encounter, the
self, whether male or female, encounters an absolute otherness in their partner,
signified by "the feminine." But, as Tanja Staehler points out, "several open
questions remain, regarding the nature of masculinity but also regarding the
relationship between femininity and womanhood . . . the qualification given
in this interview does not really resolve the objections raised by feminist critics."[80] His response, then, does not entirely respond to the issue.

BODY AND VOICE IN PLATO

Levinas's philosophy of erotic love shares important sensibilities with Diotima's speech in Plato's *Symposium*. Levinas's approach operates according to the same sublimation of sensuality to fecundity that we find in Plato's

spiritual procreation.[81] Sarah Allen agrees that the two approaches share similarities; they both emphasize affectivity—sensibility, emotion, inspiration, and
embodiment—as a path toward transcendence and a divine good. But while
eros is indeed put through a purification process in both Plato and Levinas,
physicality operates differently in each thinker.[82] I am inclined to agree with
Allen, and I will investigate the roles of fecundity and femininity in the *Symposium* with this nuanced distinction in mind. We can get a better sense of how
erotic love and fecundity work in Levinas, and the implications for gender and
embodiment, by examining these linked concepts in Plato.

Plato's *Symposium* begins with multiple framing devices. Each speaker's
voice is channeled through another, until they are finally reported by Apol-
lodorus to an unnamed friend. The authoritative voice embedded at the center
is Diotima of Mantinea, who offers the central opinion on love. Her voice is
doubly enframed within the voices of others. Her speech (if it is indeed hers,
and not merely a device of Socrates) is filtered through the voice of Socrates,
then through the circuits of Aristodemus and Appolodorus shared by the other
male speakers, and finally through the author, Plato. Her status as potential
philosophical muse calls into question the role of the feminine voice in Plato's
text and similarly disrupts the ability to impose a network of easy categorizations upon the work. The text oscillates between the transcendent and the material, the mind and the body, and its classical philosophical correlatives, masculine and feminine. The *Symposium* moves between these two poles, reflecting
an overall textual ambivalence demonstrated most in the figure of Socrates,
who drinks but does not get drunk and chases beautiful bodies without ever
entirely indulging his sexual appetites.

Before the serious philosophical discussion in the *Symposium* can begin, the
female musician must be sent out.[83] Musicality, and presumably frivolity, is
here inextricably linked to the body of the female and to the feminine sphere.[84]
It is not unusual, then, that the only female at the *Symposium* is present only in
her absence; she is not invited to eat or drink with the men.[85] The forum cannot
tolerate female bodies. Yet it not only makes room for the female voice on the
experience of love but goes so far as to elevate it, even as it is funneled through
the voices of multiple male speakers. It is not clear if Diotima and Socrates
actually had this conversation or if he is merely invoking her as a dialectical in-
strument, but either way it is curious and notable that a female voice is brought
into the philosophical conversation in any capacity.

Diotima suggests that the desire for the good and beautiful must be transcended beyond the bodily aspect of the beloved toward the incorporeal nature
of beauty and goodness. Beauty itself, she maintains, ultimately is the "goal

of all Loving."[86] Love, which is initially expressed as the desire to sexually possess the body of another person, turns out to ultimately be a desire for the metaphysical. Unlike fleshly love, which involves contingency, mutability, and (most importantly) mortality, the form of Love "always *is* and neither comes to be nor passes away, neither waxes nor wanes."[87] Beauty itself is free from contamination, "absolute, pure, unmixed, not polluted by human flesh or colors or any other great nonsense of mortality."[88]

While Socrates assumes that love desires beauty, Diotima corrects him by arguing that what love truly wants is "reproduction and birth in beauty," a bridge to immortality and timelessness.[89] While some are "pregnant in body," others are "pregnant in soul."[90] If an individual who is pregnant in soul comes into contact with another who also gives birth in beauty, then such people "have much more to share than do the parents of human children, and have a firmer bond of friendship, because the children in whom they have a share are more beautiful and more immortal. Everyone would rather have such children"—progeny of creative, artistic, and intellectual means—because these offspring "provide their parents with immortal glory and remembrance," unlike mere "human ones."[91]

Plato here appropriates and subverts the metaphor of reproduction on two levels. Men can participate in this activity by being pregnant in mind but also in body. Men who are pregnant in body "turn more to women and pursue love in that way, providing themselves through childbirth with immortality and remembrance and happiness, as they think, for all time to come."[92] Reproduction in body necessarily involves women in the procreative act. Importantly, even though it is the reproduction of ideas and not children under discussion, it is still according to the biological metaphor of pregnancy.

In her reading of the *Symposium*, Irigaray elucidates the nature of love as an in between term. Diotima takes on the role of mediator in the dialogue, offering a philosophy of intermediaries. Diotima's interlocutor, Socrates, a stand-in for the other men present, "is incapable of grasping the existence or the in-stance of that which stands *between*, that which makes possible the passage between ignorance and knowledge."[93] Socrates immediately sets up oppositions in his attempt to acquire knowledge of love; if Eros is not beautiful and good, he reasons, then it must be ugly and bad. Diotima refutes these assumptions, pointing out that even genealogically, Eros resides in the equivocation between wisdom and nonwisdom, poverty and wealth, as exemplified by the contrasting traits of Eros's parents.

During their discussion about Eros, Diotima laughs.[94] For Irigaray, Diotima's laughter is dismantling. It interrupts the logical flow of argumentation

with an unquantifiable burst of exultation, putting into question the interlocutor's claims:

> And, in response to Socrates' protestation that love is a great God, that
> *everyone says so or thinks so*, she *laughs*. Her retort is not at all angry, the
> effect of hesitating between contradictory positions; it is laughter based
> on other grounds. While laughing, then, she asks Socrates what he means
> by *everyone*. Just as she ceaselessly dismantles the assurance or *closure* of
> opposing terms, she undoes all *sets* of units reduced to sameness in order
> to constitute a whole. . . . Thus she ceaselessly examines Socrates on his
> positions but without positing authoritative, already constituted truths.
> Instead, she teaches the renunciation of already established truths. And
> each time Socrates thinks he can take something as certain, she undoes his
> certainty. . . . All entities, substantives, adverbs, sentences are patiently, and
> joyously, called into question.[95]

Diotima does not refute Socrates dialectically but with irrefutable laughter.
Diotima's laughter does not conform to the solidified norms of ordered cognitive processes. It bursts out and refuses to be contained.

Diotima concludes that love seeks reproduction and birth in beauty. In love,
one can become immortal through corporeal fecundity or, better yet, through
fecundity of the soul—wisdom.[96] Diotima uses the metaphor of pregnancy to
refer to love in general, ultimately concluding that to be pregnant in body is
of less value than to be pregnant in soul—to create a work of art and to gain
immortality by passing on wisdom. Even if the reproduction is intellectual
or creative and not biological, Plato nevertheless employs the terminology
of pregnancy and birth.[97] The avenue of specifically male reproduction—in
beauty, rather than in body—is privileged above the more limited biological
method.[98] It is deeply ironic that it should be a woman teaching Socrates and
this group of men that specifically male philosophical conception and engendering are superior to the corporeal reproduction marked as female.[99]

Irigaray accounts for Diotima's adoption of the Platonic approach she had
previously managed to subvert by reminding us that "*she is not there. Socrates
relates her words. Perhaps he distorts them unwittingly or unknowingly.*"[100]
Diotima surrenders the intermediary status of eros, arguing that love between
two people leads only to the higher love of knowledge and discourse.[101] Diotima's discourse is split between the preservation of the intermediary and the
resolution of the dialectic by treating love as a means: "She doubled its intermediary function and subjected it to a *telos*."[102] Plato uses Diotima as a female
mouthpiece to articulate a desexualized eros. But the invocation of the female

voice complicates these matters through the text's elevation of the female as the philosophical voice par excellence, even if that voice is embedded within a masculine framework. Does the love of the body play only a cursory role in the love of the ultimate form of beauty, the Good? The question of the place of the feminine in this text is inextricably linked to the issue of materiality—the "*mater*-ial,"[103] and the maternal.

In casting out the female bodies, the *Symposium* doubly casts out the material from the immaterial, the idle flute playing from the more contemplative mode of conversation. But the approach to the material is not a straightforward assignment of the body to the woman and the intellect to the man; while the bodies of women are sent away, the bodies of the men are central to the action.[104] The lofty conversation undertaken in the *Symposium* from which the flute girl must be "dispensed" notably takes place in a setting of bodily indulgence, involving eating, reclining, and (initially moderate) drinking.[105]

Indeed, Plato's text operates on ambivalent lines in its relation to both the material and the feminine, and, unlike with Levinas, it becomes difficult to argue that either is consistently left behind as both are at various points summoned and cast out.[106] Diotima's voice may be filtered through that of Socrates, but her voice nevertheless stands as the central word on the object of discussion. The entire structure of the *Symposium* is pervaded by both an approach toward and a retreat from the body, mirrored in the person of Socrates himself. This becomes most evident in Alcibiades's contribution at the end of the text. Alcibiades is an inebriated latecomer to the affair who is enjoined to roast Socrates. He describes Socrates as standing up to hunger better than anyone else in the troops at the invasion of Potidaea—"And yet he was the one man who could really enjoy a feast; and though he didn't much want to drink, when he had to, he could drink the best of us under the table."[107] This doubling (he stands up best to hunger and yet enjoys food better than any other) is further qualified: "Still, and most amazingly, no one ever saw him drunk (as we'll straightaway put to the test)."[108] This is only one in a number of references throughout the dialogue to Socrates as the only one who never becomes inebriated while drinking.

Alcibiades's entire speech of praise and reproach is marked by oppositions: lascivious/celibate, ascetic/indulgent. This apparently stems from the speaker's own ambivalence toward the subject. Alcibiades adores Socrates, who remains frustratingly immune to his advances.[109] Socrates' rejection of Alcibiades's seduction attempts reflects a continual oscillation toward and away from the beautiful male body, along with an enthusiasm for food and drink but with none of their accompanying consequences. His is the only body that can resist the effects of hunger and cold as well as inebriation and exhaustion. The text ends with Socrates proceeding from an all-nighter fresh and ready to face the day while every other member of the group has succumbed to sleep.[110] Socrates alone rises above drunkenness and sexuality, and yet he always manages to find a way to sit next to the most beautiful body.[111] The entire dialogue ends in a jubilant party atmosphere.[112] In the oscillation between the temptations of the material and the contemplations of the immaterial, neither is finally privileged. This is reflected in the setting of the *Symposium*, a decidedly nonascetic meal that embraces the material while hosting the intellectual work of philosophizing.

Reflecting this double movement, we see that in the *Symposium* the female body is cast out, only to be brought back through a disembodied voice into the heart of the dialogue. The central word on love comes from the mouth of a woman who is not present. In this sense she is an unfeminine female, according to classical typologies aligning the female with the physical. Diotima's incorporeal female voice may be the clearest manifestation of the text's unwillingness to tether philosophy to one or the other—to the metaphysical or the material realm.

LAUGHTER AND THE FEMALE BODY

Irigaray reads Diotima's laughter as interrupting the male philosophical system; the laugh cannot be contained or dialectically refuted. It tears a hole in the ordered texture of the argument.[113] The Hebrew Bible has its own exemplary case of misinterpreted female laughter.[114] Irigaray's themes of maternity, sexuality, and laughter as disruptions of masculine discourses converge in the biblical account of Isaac's conception, where laughter precedes the birth of Sarah's son-to-be. Abraham responds to the news that Sarah will bear a son by falling on his face, and he laughs at the thought that the elderly couple can yet be fertile.[115] After this conversation, Abraham generously offers hospitality to three male visitors. Sarah does not eat with them. Like the female flute players in the *Symposium*, and even Diotima herself, Sarah is not invited to partake in food and drink.

One of the visitors reiterates God's announcement about the happy couple. This allows Sarah, listening from the tent door, to learn that she will bear a son, and she responds by laughing: "Sarah laughed within herself, saying, After I am grown old shall I have pleasure, my lord being old also?"[116] The entire discussion of Sarah's procreation is conducted by masculine figures. She learns she will issue a line of kings through male mediation. This time, the laughter is misunderstood. There are marked differences between Abraham's and Sarah's laughter, and God's response to each differs significantly as well. Abraham is told the news firsthand from God, and he laughs out loud in response.[117] Sarah, who may not be meant to know the information, "laughs within herself";[118] perhaps she is concerned that someone will overhear. Sarah's laughter has to be suppressed within the body and within the tent in which she prepares the food eaten outside, of which she does not partake.[119]

While Abraham laughs at the miraculous notion of fertility, Sarah also laughs at the anticipation of pleasure.[120] In Katz's view, Sarah thus displays a *jouissance* central to maternity.[121] In the interpretation of Sarah's outburst (or, in this case, inburst), laughter runs interference lines between the male and female figures. The masculine agents in the story, God included, are perplexed by her laughter—they are not in on the joke. For them, perhaps, sexuality is not distinguished from procreation. Notably, God does not ask her, "Why did you laugh?" Instead, God is paranoid, as if fearing to be made into an object of ridicule. God essentially asks Abraham, "Is she laughing at me?" Subsequently, God becomes angry, especially in light of Sarah's silence—but she is too embarrassed to relay the truth.[122] Sarah's laugh puts God, the visitors, and Abraham all out of joint. While in Plato, the laughing figure of Diotima can represent an ultimately desexualized view of eros, Sarah's laughter embodies sexual pleasure, threatening the alignment of femininity with maternity and reclaiming her displaced desire.[123]

The male figures surrounding the question of Sarah's pregnancy are collectively taken aback by her responding to the possibilities of both sexuality and maternity. Rachel Adler points out that instead of being merely awed by this gift of returned fertility, Sarah reacts less than demurely by immediately daydreaming about the act by which the child will be produced, laughing "at the prospect of again having *ednah* . . . not simply pleasure, but physical pleasure, erotic pleasure."[124] Sarah's laughter, like Diotima's, is threatening. Like Diotima's emphasis on eros as in between, Sarah's laughter functions as an intermediary between maternity and sexuality, thwarting the desire of interpreters to define her by one or the other.

In other biblical passages, laughter is also associated with sexuality. Laughter comes back to Sarah later on with graver consequences. After Isaac is weaned, Sarah sees Ishmael, the son of her husband and Hagar, and he is *mitzaḥek*—laughing, playing, or, in some translations, "making sport."[125] After seeing this, Sarah cruelly kicks Ishmael and his mother out. Later, after Isaac loses his mother, replacing her with his wife, Rebecca—he "takes comfort for [the loss of] his mother"[126] by taking his new wife into Sarah's former tent—laughter becomes a euphemism for sexual play. Isaac and Rebecca go into the land of King Abimelech and pose as brother and sister, echoing the similar actions of his parents. They are caught when the king spots them through the window. Isaac lives up to the laughter in his name because he is seen *mitzahek*, or "playing," with his wife.[127] They are acting out the very same term for "play" or "making sport" for which Sarah banished Ishmael. Their actions cause the king to glean that they are not brother and sister, as they had claimed, and Isaac is found out. Although the confusion gets resolved, the plot is temporarily unhinged by this unreadable act.

Laughter reverberates through Genesis and is marked by ambiguity. When it is done with proper deference, you can get away with it, like Abraham. But when coupled with its linguistic implications of sexual play, it becomes suspect, and then maybe even deviant—something that should not be heard nor seen. Brought under question, it causes breakdowns in communication lines. Laughter causes people to get into trouble, as they get called out for doing something wrong, unnamable, and indefinable. In these linked accounts, Sarah's indecipherable laughter echoes down the family line.

These instances of female laughter from the Greek and biblical traditions both raise the specter of eroticism. In the *Symposium*, the female speaker's voice is referred through a male agent, affirming love as highest when it is of a nonsexual nature, but nevertheless positioned in a dialogue firmly rooted in the physical. In Genesis, we are privy to Sarah's voice firsthand, and to her inner laughter that must be hidden—an illicit, erotically charged laugh. If female laughter (per Irigaray) is an intermediary, disrupting the dialectical synthesis of masculine discourse, then the laughter of both Diotima and Sarah interrupts the male feast and its accompanying discussion, suggesting why Plato and Levinas alike are so eager to find a way to transcend the erotic and progress into a less unsettling realm.

The move from the phenomenological feminine to empirical women that we see in Levinas is echoed by the move from the disembodied Diotima to the more actualized Sarah, whose innermost thoughts we appear to have access to without the filter of multiple voices. The figure of Sarah can disrupt the economy of fertility-as-femininity, as Sarah keeps fecundity in the erotic sphere. Her son Isaac's name is marked by laughter of his mother and of his father, but along different registers. After all, how can we be sure Isaac is named after Sarah's laugh, and not Abraham's exclamation at the wonder at fertility?[128] After Abraham laughs, God tells him that his son shall be called Isaac.[129] Sarah laughs only after her unborn son has already been named for laughter, without her knowledge. It is more likely that Abraham's laughter is perpetuated in the name of the son, rather than the more ambiguous, incredulous laughter of Sarah. The figure of Sarah allows us to glimpse a way out of the patriarchal framework of both Plato and Levinas, but she may not take us far enough.

Both Plato and Levinas emphasize a purification of eros through fecundity. In Sandford's reading, the same trajectory in which the feminine is transcended by the masculine in Plato's *Symposium* can be found in Levinas's philosophy, "a subordination of the phenomenology of eros to the metaphysics of love."[130] For Plato, reproduction leading to immortality may begin in human form, but ultimately the highest kind of fecundity comes about through intellectual procreation and the generation of ideas rather than children. Nevertheless, the body is never entirely left behind, and it preserves a necessary role. In his *Symposium*, Plato presents a Socrates who never really transcends the corporeal but always manages to remain in between the physical and spiritual realms. The physicality retained in Plato's *Symposium* is ambivalent in its relation to sexual love. The push and pull away from and toward erotic love is retained throughout.

In Plato, we find an ambivalence between the physical/erotic and the metaphysical. In Levinas the emphasis on the body remains, but it ends up being a post-erotic body. Levinas's attribution of fecundity to eternality resembles Plato's striving for immortality through procreative efforts, although in Levinas these are limited to physical, not intellectual, procreation. Fecundity in Levinas amounts to the transcendence of erotic love, "a love entirely purified of eros."[131] In Plato, erotic love can be viewed as ambivalent, as humans transcend physicality but never leave it behind. In Levinas, sexual eros leads toward the telos of fecundity.[132]

In Plato, although men can give birth in humanity (through female partners), the primarily male mode of giving birth to the abstraction of ideas is clearly elevated beyond the primarily female mode of giving birth to human life. From this we can see that Levinas provides a valuable and important corrective to Plato in the move beyond eros, since Levinas is not valorizing an explicitly male mode of disembodied propagation above an explicitly female mode of reproduction. But the way that reproduction is rigidly gendered and hierarchized in Plato also allows us to see that Levinas adheres to certain gender norms with real consequences. In the place of Platonic masculine intellectual procreation, arrived at through a disembodied female intermediary, we have in Levinas masculine physical fecundity, arrived at through the corporeal mediation of the female body. It is certainly an improvement, as far as valorizing femininity is concerned, but it still omits the feminine/female from the relation with the future. Sandford writes that in both Plato and Levinas, ultimately "maternity must give way to paternity, that is, to the law of the father.... In the end, as in the beginning, the feminine is made to give way to the masculine."[133] Both Plato and Levinas valorize a type of masculine procreative possibility, as female-marked gestation is appropriated by the male mind in Plato, and the feminine functions to bring about the son who will link the father to the future in Levinas.

Significantly, in Plato, only the *male* body gains entrance and remains at the end. The kind of fecundity that women have access to is clearly devalued. In Levinas, the feminine/female gains entrance and is vital to the future by enabling procreation and, with it, the filial relation between father and son. In different ways, then, Plato and Levinas both devalue the woman's role; in Plato the female voice is present only in her absence, and in Levinas both the feminine and the female body are a bridge to father-son eternity. Any philosophical system or ethical framework that privileges reproduction as the end to the couple's amorousness is exclusionary, limiting, and potentially damaging to nonreproductive individuals. In *Totality and Infinity*, the eternal time inaugurated through bodily fecundity is brought about by a distinctly paternal generativity of fathers and sons, ultimately leading to a fraternal community far removed from femininity. The implications of this universal fraternity will be the focus of the next chapter.

NOTES

1. Emmanuel Levinas, "Résumé de 'Totalité et infini,'" *Annales de l'université de Paris (Sorbonne, Paris V)* 31 (1961): 386n3, cited in Sandford, *The Metaphysics of Love*, 7.

2. Sandford, *The Metaphysics of Love*, 7.

3. In her interpretation of Levinas's *Totality and Infinity*, Tina Chanter argues, "Levinas's account of eros and desire draws so heavily upon Plato's *Symposium* that it almost reads as an extended footnote to that dialogue" ("Feminism and the Other," in *The Provocation of Levinas: Rethinking the Other*, ed. Robert Bernasconi and David Wood, trans. Andre Benjamin and Tamra Wright, [London: Routledge, 1988], 49). Sandford similarly observes, "Levinas's phenomenology of eros and fecundity is heavily indebted to Plato" ("Masculine Mothers? Maternity in Levinas and Plato," in *Feminist Interpretations of Emmanuel Levinas*, 192). Levinas makes clear his Platonic reference point on eros in an earlier work, *Existence and Existents*: "the plane of *eros* allows us to see that the other par excellence is the feminine, through which a world behind the scenes prolongs the world. In Plato, Love, a child of need, retains the features of destitution. Its negativity is the simple 'less' of need, and not the very moment unto alterity. Eros, when separated from the Platonic interpretation which

completely fails to recognize the role of the feminine, can be the theme of a philosophy which, detached from the solitude of light, and consequently from phenomenology properly speaking, will concern us elsewhere" (*Existence and Existents*, trans. Alphonso Lingis [The Hague: Martinus Nijhoff, 1978], 85).

4. See Tanja Staehler's observation: "Levinas and Plato identify similar features of love which concern its inexplicable and apparently 'irrational' character, its ambiguous position between physical attraction and desire from soul to soul, and regarding the way in which Eros can never ultimately be fulfilled or sated" (*Plato and Levinas: The Ambiguous Out-Side of Ethics* [New York: Routledge, 2010], 79–80). Staehler points out that Levinas refers to Plato many times within his corpus, and it can be argued that his references to Plato outnumber those to any other philosopher, including Heidegger and Husserl (16).

5. In *Totality and Infinity*, the relation to the infinite other ruptures the self's totality. This reflects a similar emphasis in Rosenzweig's *Star* on questioning the Idealist "All" (the sphere of Hegelian totality), in which spirit sets off on a journey to the foreign only to be returned to itself.

6. Here I am referring to Levinas's earlier work, and in chapters 3 and 5 I will discuss Levinas's later adoption of embodied maternity as the ethical relation *par excellence*. However, I see a continued valorization of the fraternal sphere throughout his oeuvre, as the maternal emphasis comes to be pervaded by the fraternal model in *Otherwise Than Being*.

7. Pateman, *The Sexual Contract*, 88.

8. Levinas, *Time and the Other*, 88.

9. Levinas, 89.

10. "The feminine in existence is an event different from that of spatial transcendence or of expression that go toward the light. It is a flight before light" (Levinas, *Time and the Other*, 86).

11. Irigaray, "The Fecundity of the Caress," 210.

12. Edith Wyschogrod explains that for Levinas, philosophy must attempt a "high-wire act" by demonstrating how the other constitutes the ethical response of the self "without rendering the other as a phenomenon, as the sum of her or his properties as apprehended by perceptual or cognitive consciousness. To apprehend the other cognitively or affectively is to traduce the radical character of alterity, the insurmountable difference between self and other" (*Crossover Queries: Dwelling with Negatives, Embodying Philosophy's Others* [New York: Fordham University Press, 2006], 30). As Wolfson explains, "Levinas opts to reform phenomenology by utilizing language that is replete with aniconic resonances and critical of the ocularcentric tendency to favor vision" ("Echo of the Otherwise: Ethics of Transcendence and the Lure of Theolatry," in *Encountering the Medieval in Modern Jewish Thought*, ed. James A. Diamond and Aaron W. Hughes [Leiden: Brill, 2012], 300). Wolfson observes that the nexus of

eros, secrecy, modesty, and feminine motifs within Levinas's thought indicates a likelihood that he may have been influenced by the interrelatedness of these motifs in kabbalistic lore. The feminine for Levinas is secretive and flees from sight, veiled in its unveiling, similar to the kabbalistic hermeneutic of the secret as that which is disclosed in its hiddenness and concealed in its disclosure. Unlike the Husserlian phenomenological approach, in which intentionality is based on vision, in Levinas's phenomenology the experience of the other cannot be reduced to intentionality, and the feminine is "an apt metaphorical signifier of what eludes signification" (Elliot R. Wolfson, "Secrecy, Modesty, and the Feminine: Kabbalistic Traces in the Thought of Levinas," *Journal of Jewish Thought and Philosophy* 14 [2006]: 209).

13. Levinas, *Totality and Infinity*, 254–5.

14. Plato, *Symposium*, trans. Alexander Nehamas and Paul Woodruff (Indianapolis, IN: Hackett, 1989), 203D.

15. Levinas, *Totality and Infinity*, 264–5. In "The Builders," Rosenzweig makes a similar observation on erotic love: "love is not social." In this essay, Rosenzweig distinguishes between learning and teaching and discusses the importance of putting into practice the texts of a religious tradition in social life ("The Builders," 80).

16. Levinas, *Totality and Infinity*, 266. In the original: "Si aimer, c'est aimer l'amour que l'Aimée me porte, aimer est aussi s'aimer dans l'amour et retourner ainsi à soi" (*Totalité et Infini*, 244).

17. Jean-Luc Nancy addresses this phenomenon of love as self-love: "Nothing leads us more surely back to ourselves (to the Occident, to philosophy, to the dialectic, to literature) than love" (*A Finite Thinking*, ed. Simon Sparks [Stanford, CA: Stanford University Press, 2003], 256–9). Nancy cites Levinas's statement in discussing the economy of love as a recuperation of the self.

18. Levinas, *Totality and Infinity*, 265.

19. Claire Elise Katz, "Levinas between Agape and Eros," *Symposium: Canadian Journal of Continental Philosophy/Revue canadienne de philosophie continentale* 11, no. 2 (2007): 333.

20. See Katz, "Levinas between Agape and Eros," 335: "The alterity of the other thus prohibits a reciprocal relation. It is not simply that the relationship with the other, as Levinas conceives it, is impossible if the two participants are symmetrical to each other. The relationship is impossible because there is no other; they are the same, they could each be other."

21. Levinas, *Totality and Infinity*, 267. In the original: "Or, il faut la rencontre d'Autrui en tant que féminin, pour qu'advienne l'avenir de l'enfant d'au-delà du possible" (Levinas, *Totalité et Infini*, 299).

22. Levinas, *Totality and Infinity*, 258. Katz observes that this term, "the *not yet*," which Levinas uses repeatedly on this point, is clearly borrowed from

Rosenzweig (*Levinas, Judaism, and the Feminine*, 64). Benjamin explains the importance of this idea for Rosenzweig: "The perpetual deferral of any sort of climax, erotic or narrative, in the Song of Songs—its constant 'not yet'—has a clear theological parallel that makes it an ideal text for Rosenzweig: the distance between God-as-lover and soul-as-beloved corresponds to the crucial theological distance interposed between God and humanity" (*Rosenzweig's Bible*, 59–60). In Staehler's view, the "not yet" is initially indefinite but becomes restricted in its futural project of the child, "and it is not clear how the step from the 'not yet' to fecundity is accomplished in Levinas's examination" (*Plato and Levinas*, 85). Staehler finds this inevitability "plausible as well as disappointing. It is plausible because a child indeed exceeds and crosses out all expectations. . . . At the same time, the response is somewhat disappointing because it narrows the analysis down to one specific option when the most intriguing part of the temporal character of Eros is that it aims at something which is neither possibility nor projection" (85).

23. Levinas, *Totality and Infinity*, 257; in the original, "non-signifiance" (*Totalité et Infini*, 234). The feminine can equivocate and transcend the realm of the possible, allowing her to be "at the same time interlocutor, collaborator and master superiorly intelligent" (*Totality and Infinity*, 264).

24. For an alternative interpretation of these roles, see Katz, "From Eros to Maternity: Love, Death, and 'the Feminine' in the Philosophy of Emmanuel Levinas," in *Women and Gender in Jewish Philosophy*, 160).

25. Levinas, *Totality and Infinity*, 258–63.

26. In the original, "Les relations avec autrui se jouent—on joue avec autrui comme avec un jeune animal" (Levinas, *Totalité et Infini*, 241).

27. Tamra Wright, Peter Hughes, and Alison Ainley, "The Paradox of Morality: An Interview with Emmanuel Levinas," in *The Provocation of Levinas*, ed. Robert Bernasconi and David Wood, trans. Andre Benjamin and Tamra Wright, 169. Levinas goes on to relate animals to children, suggesting we often love both animality in children and childlike behavior in animals (172).

28. Levinas presents a more expansive view of animal ethics in "The Name of a Dog, or Natural Rights," in *Difficult Freedom*. He describes the experience of being "stripped . . . of our human skin" when he was imprisoned as a French Jewish prisoner of war (153). To those who were not imprisoned, the interned group were "subhuman, a gang of apes. . . . We were beings entrapped in their species; despite all their vocabulary, beings without language" (153). It was only a wandering dog who was able to see the prisoners' humanity: "we called him Bobby, an exotic name, as one does with a cherished dog. He would appear at morning assembly and was waiting for us as we returned, jumping up and down and barking in delight. For him, there was no doubt that we were men. Perhaps the dog that recognized Ulysses beneath his disguise on his return from

the Odyssey was a forebear of our own" (153). Because of the dog's "friendly growling" and "animal faith," Levinas calls Bobby "the last Kantian in Nazi Germany, without the brain needed to universalize maxims and drives" (153). There have been a number of studies on Levinas and animal others. See, for example, John Llewelyn, "Am I Obsessed by Bobby? (Humanism of the Other Animal)," in *Re-Reading Levinas*, 234–45; Diane Perpich, *The Ethics of Emmanuel Levinas* (Redwood City, CA: Stanford University Press, 2008), 150–76; Cynthia D. Coe, *Levinas and the Trauma of Responsibility: The Ethical Significance of Time* (Bloomington: Indiana University Press, 2018), 187–217; and Peter Atterton, "Levinas's Humanism and Anthropocentrism," in *The Oxford Handbook of Levinas*, ed. Michael L. Morgan (Oxford: Oxford University Press, 2019), 709–30.

29. Martin Buber, *I and Thou*, trans. Ronald Gregor Smith (New York: Scribner Classics, 1958), 96. Buber offers a nonanthropocentric understanding of language, in contrast to Heidegger. "In his condemnation of Heidegger, Levinas accepts the latter's anthropocentric demarcation of language as something distinctively human, a position that has been roundly criticized in more contemporary animal studies and discussions of the posthuman" (Wolfson, *The Duplicity*, 205n50).

30. Buber, *I and Thou*, 97.

31. Jacques Derrida, *The Animal That Therefore I Am*, ed. Marie-Louise Mallet, trans. David Wills (New York: Fordham University Press, 2008), 7–9: "How can an animal look you in the face? . . . my cat, the cat that looks at me in my bedroom or bathroom, this cat that is perhaps not 'my cat' or 'my pussycat,' does not appear here to represent, like an ambassador, the immense symbolic responsibility with which our culture has always charged the feline race." Derrida explains that to speak of "the animal" elides difference and particularity, and it makes us forget there is no "animal," only animals. Human self-conception is dependent on the perception of animal others.

32. As Kelly Oliver explains, Derrida "sees a moment in Levinas's writings that subverts the priority of man over woman, but it, too, is still based on the opposition between man and animal" (*Animal Lessons: How They Teach Us to Be Human* [New York: Columbia University Press, 2009], 142). Derrida challenges Heidegger and Levinas, suggesting that both, "in the very moments when their thinking promises to take us beyond the sexual binary, fall back into a dialectical logic of opposition, human versus animal" (142).

33. Peter Atterton, "Face-to-Face with the Other Animal?" in *Levinas and Buber: Dialogue and Difference*, ed. Peter Atterton, Matthew Calarco, and Maurice Friedman (Pittsburgh, PA: Duquesne University Press, 2004), 263.

34. Katz makes the following observation about this passage: "The erotic is not asymmetrical or serious; rather it is fun-loving, consuming, and light. . . . Love is consuming and silly, and often wild and animal-like. It is precisely in love that we

forget ourselves, not ourselves as the ego, but the converse. We forget ourselves as the ethical *I*" ("From Eros to Maternity," 161).

35. Sherryl Vint, *Animal Alterity: Science Fiction and the Question of the Animal* (Liverpool: Liverpool University Press, 2010), 18. Similarly, drawing on the feminist thought of Carol J. Adams's *The Sexual Politics of Meat: A Feminist-Vegetarian Critical Theory*, Aaron Gross observes, "the human/animal binary is so often paired with the male/female binary and usually in ways that are good for neither women nor animals. . . . What does considering such diverse examples together tell us about the potentially oppressive mechanisms of dividing the world into human/animal and male/female in the process of imagining humanity?" ("Animal Others and Animal Studies," in *Animals and the Human Imagination: A Companion to Animal Studies*, ed. Aaron Gross and Anne Vallely [New York: Columbia University Press, 2012], 5–6). As Oliver argues, the association with animality excludes the feminine from the social realm: "The woman's animality protects the man from his own animality. By absorbing animality, the woman allows the man to escape from animality and nature in order to enter the social" ("Paternal Election and the Absent Father," in *Feminist Interpretations of Emmanuel Levinas*, 237–8). Oliver shows that, beginning with the creation narratives in Genesis, animal difference and sexual difference have long been intimately associated (*Animal Lessons*, 143).

36. Kecia Ali, "Muslims and Meat-Eating: Vegetarianism, Gender, and Identity," *Journal of Religious Ethics* 43, no. 2 (2015): 268–9.

37. Sandford, "Levinas, Feminism and the Feminine," 147. Chanter discusses two possible responses to Levinas and the feminine: "To give a charitable reading of how Levinas's rigorously sexualized language functions would be to credit him with having seen the radical potentiality of the feminine to break up the categories of being, and to create the possibility of ethics. A less generous reading would consist of recalling that Levinas reiterates the most traditional stereotypes when he characterizes the feminine as a dimension of silence, mystery, hiding, modesty, withdrawal, domesticity, and maternity" ("Introduction," in *Feminist Interpretations of Emmanuel Levinas*, 17). Of these two possibilities, Derrida writes, "Need one choose here between two incompatible readings, between an androcentric hyperbole and a feminist one? Is there any place for such a choice in ethics? And in justice? In law? In politics? Nothing is less certain" (*Adieu to Emmanuel Levinas*, trans. Pascale-Ann Brault and Michael Naas [Stanford, CA: Stanford University Press, 1999], 44). Chanter suggests, following Derrida, that both readings can be sustained (Chanter, "Introduction," 23).

38. Levinas, *Totality and Infinity*, 267–69.

39. "Paternity remains a self-identification, but also a distinction without identification—a structure unforeseeable in formal logic" (Levinas, *Totality and Infinity*, 267).

40. Levinas, *Totality and Infinity*, 267; in the original, "Mon enfant est un étranger (Isaïe 49), mais qui n'est pas seulement à moi, car il est moi. C'est moi estranger à soi" (*Totalité et infini*, 299).

41. Levinas, *Totality and Infinity*, 277. Cohen maintains that this shifting is "natural (and occurs whenever the topic is intersubjectivity), insofar as Levinas is describing a relationship within which he is himself implicated, or, more precisely, regarding paternity and filiality, by which he is himself conditioned" (*Elevations*, 213).

42. Allen, *The Philosophical Sense of Transcendence*, 231. In Levinas's earlier works and in *Totality and Infinity*, fecundity is defined as paternity—"the engendering and loving relation from father to son" (234).

43. Allen, *The Philosophical Sense of Transcendence*, 241–2.

44. Irigaray, "The Fecundity of the Caress," 197.

45. Levinas intentionally published his two bodies of work separately. When asked how he reconciled the phenomenological and religious dimensions of his thinking, Levinas responded, "I always make a clear distinction, in what I write, between philosophical and confessional texts. I do not deny that they may ultimately have a common source of inspiration. I simply state that it is necessary to draw a line of demarcation between them as distinct methods of exegesis, as separate languages" (Levinas and Richard Kearney, "Dialogue with Emmanuel Levinas," in *Face to Face with Levinas*, ed. Richard A. Cohen [Albany: State University of New York Press, 1986], 18). I follow Katz's view that we can productively read his two sets of writing alongside one another, despite his attempts to demarcate them, and that this is especially useful when reading him on the question of the feminine (*Levinas, Judaism, and the Feminine*, 4). See also Michael Fagenblat, *A Covenant of Creatures: Levinas's Philosophy of Judaism* (Stanford, CA: Stanford University Press, 2010); Fagenblat discusses Levinas's ethics in terms of a philosophy of Judaism, considering Levinas's phenomenological thought alongside Jewish texts.

Rosenzweig similarly resisted what he viewed as a limiting designation of his work within an exclusively Judaic context. He saw the *Star*'s reception as a "Jewish book" to be a form of "social confusion," because rather than dealing with only Judaism or a philosophy of religion, it is "merely a system of philosophy" (Rosenzweig, "The New Thinking," 110). Later on, Rosenzweig offered a qualifying agreement with this description of the work: "And yet this is, to be sure, a Jewish book: not one that deals with 'Jewish things' . . . but rather one for which, to say what it has to say, especially the new thing it has to say, the old Jewish words come. Like things in general, Jewish things have always passed away; yet Jewish words, even when old, share the eternal youth of the word, and if the world is opened up to them, they will renew the world" (Rosenzweig, "The New Thinking," 131). See Peter Eli Gordon: "The denial that the Star was a

'Jewish book' must naturally be taken with a grain of salt" ("Rosenzweig Redux,"
16). In Levinas's view, "This book of general philosophy [*The Star of Redemption*]
is a Jewish book, which founds Judaism in a new way" ("'Between Two Worlds'
[The Way of Franz Rosenzweig]," 183).

46. On the slippage between the feminine and the female, see Chanter's
observation: "Although it is clear by now that Levinas does not intend his use of
the term feminine to designate in any straightforward way empirical women, and
thus can hardly be taken to be subordinating one sex to another in any simple
way, it remains the case that Levinas sometimes drops his guard and resorts to
language that invokes the actual empirical women that at other places in his texts
he assures us he does not have in mind" ("Introduction," *Feminist Interpretations
of Emmanuel Levinas*, 16.) See also Katz: "Levinas often vacillates in several of
his writings between using 'le féminin' and 'la femme,' further complicating
its referent. In both *Totality and Infinity* and 'Judaism and the Feminine,' for
example, he interchanges 'le féminin' and 'la femme.' Whether the feminine
functions simply as a metaphor, referring to the stereotypical feminine traits that
may be shared by all people, or whether it refers to empirical women is unclear"
(*Levinas, Judaism, and the Feminine*, 2). Katz maintains that "the feminine does
indeed play a dual role as both metaphor and as referent to empirical women,
and that in this dual role the feminine serves as both the interruption of virility
and the model for the ethical" (3). Sandford observes that in Levinas's texts, in
the time period up to and including *Totality and Infinity*, the feminine "appears
consistently, operating as a *philosophical* category which Levinas increasingly
tries to distance from any empirical referent. Discussion of it requires an
investigation of the origin and the implications of its use, especially given the
tendency, notable in *Totality and Infinity,* to use the phrase interchangeably with
la Femme" (*The Metaphysics of Love*, 3).

47. Emmanuel Levinas, "Judaism and the Feminine," in *Difficult Freedom:
Essays on Judaism*, 31.

48. Levinas, "Judaism and the Feminine," 31.

49. Levinas, 32–3.

50. Levinas, 33.

51. Levinas, 34.

52. Levinas," 35. See Chanter's analysis of this passage in "Feminism and
the Other," 49. See also Daniel Boyarin's discussion of the dominant rabbinic
interpretation, which insisted that the first human had both male and female
characteristics: "Far from gender (and woman) being a secondary creation,
we have in the second creation of humanity an Aristophanic separation of an
androgynous pair of joined twins, physically sexed from the very beginning"
("Gender," in *Critical Terms for Religious Studies*, ed. Mark C. Taylor [Chicago:
University of Chicago Press, 1998], 128).

53. "The idea of a love that would be a confusion between two beings is a false romantic idea. The pathos of the erotic relationship is the fact of being two, and that the other is absolutely other" (Emmanuel Levinas, "Love and Filiation," in *Ethics and Infinity: Conversations with Phillippe Nemo*, trans. Richard A. Cohen [Pittsburgh, PA: Duquesne University Press, 1985], 66).

54. Levinas, *Totality and Infinity*, 265.

55. See Staehler, *Plato and Levinas*, 85. As Claudia Welz explains, "In contrast to Aristophanes' myth in Plato's *Symposium*, which speaks about love reuniting the two halves of one sole being, Levinas underlines that the lovers are not to become one, as if the one were incomplete without the other. The desired comes close in love, but it does not merge completely with the other. Each of the two remains a being on its own" ("Keeping the Secret of Subjectivity: Kierkegaard and Levinas on Conscience, Love and the Limits of Self-Understanding," in *Despite Oneself: Subjectivity and Its Secret in Kierkegaard and Levinas*, ed. Claudia Welz and Karl Verstrynge [London: Turnshare, 2008], 203). Levinas writes, "If woman completes man, she does not complete him as a part completes another into a whole but, as it were, as two totalities complete one another—which is, after all, the miracle of social relations" (Levinas, "Judaism and the Feminine," 35). See also Katz, "Levinas between Agape and Eros," 336.

56. Levinas, "Judaism and the Feminine," 35.

57. Levinas, 36.

58. Levinas, 36.

59. Levinas, "And God Created Woman," in *Nine Talmudic Readings*, 167. On Levinas's characterization of biblical women, see Catherine Chalier, *Figures du féminin: Lecture d'Emmanuel Lévinas* (Paris: Nuit surveillée, 1982); and Chalier, "Ethics and the Feminine," in *Re-Reading Levinas*, 123.

60. Levinas, "And God Created Woman," 167–8. Compare Levinas's interpretation with Phyllis Trible, *God and the Rhetoric of Sexuality*:

> After God operates on this earth creature, to produce a companion, its identity becomes sexual. The surgery is radical, for it results in two creatures where before there was only one. The new creature, built from the material of *ha-'adam*, is female, receiving her identity in a word that is altogether new to the story, the word *issa*. The old creature transformed is male, similarly receiving identity in a word that is new to the story, *is*. . . . Their creation is simultaneous, not sequential. One does not precede the other. . . . Moreover, one is not the opposite of the other. In the very act of distinguishing female from male, the earth creature describes her as "bone of my bones and flesh of my flesh" (2: 23). These words speak unity, solidarity, mutuality, and equality. Accordingly, in this poem the man does not depict himself as either prior to or superior to the woman. His sexual identity depends upon her

even as hers depends upon him. For both of them sexuality originates in the one flesh of humanity. Differentiation, then, implies neither derivation nor subordination. . . . No opposite sex, no second sex, no derived sex—in short, no "Adam's rib." Instead, woman is the culmination of creation, fulfilling humanity in sexuality. Equal in creation with the man. (98–102)

See also Mieke Bal, *Lethal Love: Feminist Literary Readings of Biblical Love Stories* (Bloomington: Indiana University Press, 1987), 116: "[Yahweh] brings her to *ha'adam*, who, by the recognition of the other, assumes his own sexual identity . . . this is a joyful celebration of their common nature, their brother- and sisterhood. The man is, then, not the parent from whom the woman is born, as another obvious reading would have it, but, if we stick to these inappropriate family metaphors, rather, her brother. He is the son of *ha'adam*, she, the daughter." On the differentiation of *issa* and *is*, Bal writes, "The phrase 'taken from' does not mean 'made out of' but 'taken away from'" in the sense of 'differentiated from.' The man, then, is right. Out of *ha'adam* Yahweh made *issa* and *is* by separating the one from the other" (117). For a discussion of feminist criticism of this biblical passage, see Ilana Pardes, *Countertraditions in the Bible: A Feminist Approach* (Cambridge, MA: Harvard University Press, 1992), 13–38. Pardes discusses feminist readings of the creation stories that all share "an ideological critique of patriarchy" (37).

61. Levinas, "And God Created Woman," 170.

62. Levinas, 177.

63. Levinas, 174–5.

64. Levinas, 173.

65. Susan Shapiro, "'And God Created Woman': Reading the Bible Otherwise," in *Levinas and Biblical Studies*, ed. Tamara Cohn Eskenazi, Gary A. Phillips, and David Jobling (Atlanta, GA: Society of Biblical Literature, 2003), 170.

66. Shapiro, "'And God Created Woman,'" 171.

67. Shapiro, 174.

68. Katz, *Levinas, Judaism, and the Feminine*, 6.

69. See Elizabeth Grosz: "Derrida deals with the question of sexual difference largely indirectly, through his readings of various texts in which woman, femininity, or sexual difference function either as invisible but traceable supports (Heidegger) or as the explicit objects of secondarization or derision in a philosophical system (Levinas, Nietzsche)" (*Space, Time, and Perversion* [New York: Routledge, 1995], 70.)

70. Jacques Derrida, "*Geschlecht*: Sexual Difference, Ontological Difference," *Research in Phenomenology* 13 (1983): 66–7.

71. Jacques Derrida, "Choreographies: Jacques Derrida and Christie V. McDonald," *Diacritics* 12, no. 2 (1982): 73.

72. Derrida, "Choreographies," 73.

73. Derrida, "At This Very Moment, 40.

74. See Critchley, "'Bois'—Derrida's Final Word on Levinas," 186: "The faulty text has been buried. . . . Above, a woman's voice weaves and effaces itself. The gift has been given, the text for E.L. has been returned to 'Elle' and buried."

75. Derrida, "At This Very Moment," 47; the editors include the original French of the concluding passage to account for "undecidable ambiguities which the English cannot capture; see the final words, '*POUR LUI DONNER* ≈ *BOIS*,' in which it is not clear whether the pronoun refers to him or her" (Derrida, "At This Very Moment," 48). Derrida's essay ends with the term "*bois*" (drink), evoking the always-embodied ethical subject for Levinas that heeds the call of the other through sensibility, proximity, and contact. For Levinas, the Rebecca of Genesis who gives drink to the stranger is the model for the ethical act of giving sustenance to the other. See Simon Critchley: "To utter the imperative 'bois' [drink] is to give to the other . . . to nourish the hunger of the other" ("'Bois'—Derrida's Final Word on Levinas," 163.)

76. Critchley, *The Problem with Levinas*, 99.

77. Irigaray takes issue with Levinas's subjugation of sexual difference to ethics, and her critique reveals that "eros permits a patrilineal, a pater-familial, order of succession. Levinas' radical discourse on eros nevertheless clings to the rock of patriarchy" (Critchley, *The Problem with Levinas*, 97). Critchley elaborates Irigaray's critique:

> The term *fils* always has a relationship to the filial and to filiality, to the thread, to continuation. The son is that which continues, that which ensures succession. The enfant is un *fils*. The question is, why is the enfant not une *fille*, a daughter? Eros is a moment of discontinuity through the medium of the feminine, and the feminine is always conceived, as it were, classically, as a medium, as material mediation, and media. That's why you need women, so men can continue the immaterial life of form. Unfortunately, the continuation of formal, male existence needs to pass through the feminine medium of materiality (97).

78. Luce Irigaray, "The Fecundity of the Caress," 197. Kelly Oliver also asks if the future in Levinas could, instead, be a daughter: "For Levinas, it seems to go without saying that the father chooses a son rather than a daughter. The fact that he is a son is not what makes him unique; he is unique because he is this son chosen from among brothers. All children are brothers, but only this one is my son. Could the transubstantiation of the father take place in relation to a daughter? Would the father discover himself in his daughter's substance,

gestures, and uniqueness? . . . For Levinas, the future that paternity engenders is masculine. Insofar as it is masculine, it is limited. Insofar as it is limited, it is not open to radical alterity. And, insofar as it is not open to radical alterity, the future is finite and must come to an end. If there are no daughters, then there will be no more sons" ("Paternal Election and the Absent Father," 239).

79. Levinas, "Love and Filiation," 68–9. Many feminist scholars have commented on this passage in Genesis. See in particular Trible, *God and the Rhetoric of Sexuality*, 13–23; Bal, *Lethal Love*, 104–14; and Adler, *Engendering Judaism: An Inclusive Theology and Ethics* (Boston, MA: Beacon, 1998), 117–25. More recently, see Joy Ladin, *The Soul of the Stranger: Reading God and Torah from a Transgender Perspective* (Waltham, MA: Brandeis University Press, 2018), 16–34.

80. Staehler, *Plato and Levinas*, 250n9.

81. Sandford, *The Metaphysics of Love*, 5. We have seen that Sandford does not find Levinas's thought to be fertile ground for feminist readings, and she maintains that Plato's Diotima is not a feminist figure *avant la lettre*: "Despite feminist and other attempts to laud the female figure of Diotima and her metaphors of gestation and birth, the argument of the *Symposium* testifies to the subordination of the maternal-physical to the paternal-spiritual, a transcendence of the feminine by the masculine" (*The Metaphysics of Love*, 5).

82. Allen, *The Philosophical Sense of Transcendence*, 226.

83. "Let us dispense with the flute-girl who just made her entrance; let her play for herself or, if she prefers, for the women in the house. Let us instead spend our evening in conversation" (Plato, *Symposium*, 176E). On the absence/presence of the female flute player, "that fleeting figure who serves wine to the men in the symposium and who then disappears from the scene of the dialogue," see Susan E. Shapiro, "Toward a Postmodern Judaism: A Response," in *Reasoning After Revelation: Dialogues in Postmodern Jewish Philosophy*, ed. Steven Kepnes, Peter Ochs, and Robert Gibbs (Boulder, CO: Westview Press, 1998), 79.

84. Another flute girl makes her entrance toward the end of the text, heralding a bawdy group of drinkers, but only once the speeches have finished (Plato, *Symposium*, 212D). Like the *Symposium*, Plato's *Phaedo* must also evacuate the female figure before the text can get down to its business. In the *Phaedo*, the weeping, uncontrollable body of Socrates's wife must be expelled in order for philosophizing and talking about death (here, one and the same endeavor) to take place (Plato, *Phaedo*, trans. David Gallop [Oxford: Oxford University Press, 1993], 60A-B). See Katz, *Levinas, Judaism, and the Feminine*, 150.

85. On the role of Diotima in the *Symposium*, see David M. Halperin, "Why Is Diotima a Woman?," in *One Hundred Years of Homosexuality: And Other Essays on Greek Love*, 113–51 (New York: Routledge, 1990).

86. Plato, *Symposium*, 211A.

87. Plato, 211A.

88. Plato, 211E.

89. Plato, 206E.

90. Plato, 209A.

91. Plato, 209D. Sandford observes, "the only maternity that concerns Plato here is that which can be appropriated for the male" ("Masculine Mothers? Maternity in Levinas and Plato," in *Feminist Interpretations of Emmanuel Levinas*, 195).

92. Plato, *Symposium*, 209A.

93. Luce Irigaray, *An Ethics of Sexual Difference*, 21. According to Chanter, Irigaray "gives back to Diotima her own words" by referring in her commentary to the speaker as neither Plato nor Socrates but as Diotima (*Ethics of Eros: Irigaray's Rewriting of the Philosophers* [New York: Routledge, 1995], 161).

94. Socrates suggests that "everyone knows" Eros is a great god. Diotima questions him: "'Only those who don't know?' . . . 'Is that how you mean 'everyone'? Or do you include those who do know?'" Socrates responds, "'Oh, everyone together.' And she laughed. 'Socrates, how could those who say that he's not a god at all agree that he's a great god?'" (Plato, *Symposium*, 202C).

95. Irigaray, *An Ethics of Sexual Difference*, 22.

96. "Beauty of body and of soul are hierarchized, and the love of women becomes the lot of those who, incapable of being creators in soul, are fecund of body and expect the immortality of their name to be perpetuated through their offspring" (Irigaray, *An Ethics of Sexual Difference*, 29).

97. Diotima explains that when the lover is "turned to the great sea of beauty . . . he gives birth to many gloriously beautiful ideas and theories" (Plato, *Symposium*, 210E). As Rhoda Hadassah Kotzin puts it, "The imagery deployed by Plato appropriates the vocabulary of female reproductive powers to the (male) philosopher" ("Ancient Greek Philosophy," in *A Companion to Feminist Philosophy*, ed. Alison M. Jaggar and Iris Marion Young [Malden, MA: Blackwell, 1998], 18). Adriana Cavarero sees in Plato's works a distinct desire for female experience, a mimesis of pregnancy and maternal imagery: "Femininity itself belongs structurally to Socrates' and Plato's philosophy. . . . The pregnant, birth-giving male . . . stands as the emblematic figure of true philosophy" (*In Spite of Plato: A Feminist Rewriting of Ancient Philosophy*, trans. Serena Anderlini-D'Onofrio and Áine O'Healy [Cambridge, UK: Polity, 1995], 92). In my reading of Rosenzweig's *Star*, discussed in the previous chapter, the reference to God as maternal operates along similar gender registers (Rosenzweig, *Star*, 185). I suggest Rosenzweig tropes the mother as masculine—another illustration of the active divine lover. Rosenzweig's appropriation of the Song of Song's female voice at the center of his work may also mirror Plato's central appropriation of Diotima. As Braiterman writes on Rosenzweig's appropriation of the Song's

Shulamite figure, "Perhaps, after all, she's not even a woman. . . . An extra-
ordinary female figure, she assumes a major place, mid-point in the entire book.
As a centrally located persona, she masks the author's own presence, speaks his
desire, not her own" ("Revelation Camp," 60).

98. I do not intend to reify an oversimplified binary between cisgender,
biologically reproductive women and cisgender, intellectually reproductive men;
rather, I seek to emphasize that Plato here configures this restrictive binary.

99. Sandford observes, "Like Aeschylus's Athena, then, Diotima is a woman
made to renounce or denounce the female, and the exquisite irony of Diotima
is that she does so through the use of a feminine vocabulary of pregnancy and
parturition" ("Masculine Mothers?" 194.)

100. Irigaray, *An Ethics of Sexual Difference*, 27.

101. For Irigaray, the defining trait of love is its intermediary position between
a series of oppositions. Chanter explains that in Irigaray's reading, Plato has
both "caught sight of love as some kind of '*intermediary*' and lost sight of love's
intermediate character" (*Ethics of Eros*, 159). Andrea Nye argues that Irigaray
"sees in Diotima's philosophy another attempt to deprive women of their specific
sexual pleasure. . . . The maternity so important for Diotima in the lives of both
men and women is, for Irigaray, only a trap from which sexual pleasure, or
'jouissance,' must deliver us"; in contrast to Diotimean love, "Irigaray's feminine
pleasure involves a free, sensuous play of bodies and texts, engaged in for its own
sake, opposed to the establishment of any doctrine, politics, or commitment"
("Irigaray and Diotima at Plato's Symposium," in *Feminist Interpretations of Plato*,
ed. Nancy Tuana [University Park: Pennsylvania State University Press, 1994],
209–10).

102. Irigaray, *An Ethics of Sexual Difference*, 33.

103. See Janet Martin Soskice, *The Kindness of God: Metaphor, Gender, and
Religious Language* (Oxford: Oxford University Press, 2007), 106.

104. Similarly, immediately following the unwilling removal of Xanthippe
in the *Phaedo*, Socrates begins rubbing his sore leg, freed from its chain, and
launches into a lecture on the subjective perceptions of pain versus pleasure
(Plato, *Phaedo*, 60B).

105. Plato, *Symposium*, 176E.

106. Catherine Pickstock points out that "Plato advocates not simply a
leaving behind of the material, but much more a zig-zagging play between
leaving-behind, returning, and remaining" ("The Problem of Reported
Speech: Friendship and Philosophy in Plato's *Lysis* and *Symposium*," *Telos* 123
[2002]: 49). For Plato, the disclosure of the forms themselves is often limited to
particular circumstances, and they are not ultimately seen "once and for all"; the
philosopher-king is able to present the truths of the forms only "through analogy
with the material realm" (49).

107. Plato, *Symposium*, 220A.

108. Plato, 220A.

109. Plato, 216E. Socrates is "crazy about beautiful boys," and yet "it couldn't matter less to him whether a boy is beautiful. . . . In public, I tell you, his whole life is one big game—a game of irony."

110. Plato, *Symposium*, 223D.

111. As Alcibiades points out, "when Socrates is around, nobody else can even get close to a good-looking man. Look how smoothly and plausibly he found a reason for Agathon to lie down next to him!" (Plato, *Symposium*, 223B).

112. "There was noise everywhere, and everyone was made to start drinking again in no particular order" (Plato, *Symposium*, 223B).

113. Cavarero focuses on the subversive role of laughter in another Platonic female figure, the unnamed Thracian maidservant in *Theaetetus* 174A, ch. 2. The maidservant laughs at the philosopher Thales for falling into a well while absorbed in contemplating the stars above and neglecting the ground in front of him. Her laughter has traditionally been interpreted as the characteristic response of an uncomprehending simpleton confronted with a contrastingly lofty philosopher. Cavarero argues that although the servant's laughter is considered a mark of ignorance, the "ancient female laughter of the maidservant . . . becomes the figure of a female symbolic order that has the power to expose a philosophical discourse whose mendacious structure renders it liable to outrageous lapses" (*In Spite of Plato*, 56). Similarly, Simon Critchley notes that "Philosophy is an activity of self-mastery that requires the extensive regulation of affects like grief and laughter" (*The Problem with Levinas*, 12).

114. Katz suggests that while Levinas's phenomenology of eros may be indebted to Plato, his image of maternity is drawn from the Hebrew Bible ("From Eros to Maternity," 165). She highlights several narratives in the Hebrew Bible "where eros is intimately tied to fecundity, to the birth of a child and specifically to the future of the Jews" ("Levinas between Agape and Eros," 345).

115. Genesis 17:17.

116. Genesis 18:11–12. See Anne Norton, *Bloodrites of the Post-Structuralists: Word, Flesh and Revolution* (New York: Routledge, 2002), 164: "Sarah's laughter is associated in the text with her desire, pleasure in a woman's body, and a certain skepticism regarding both the word of the Lord and the power of the phallus. The Lord rebukes her laughter, and 'she was afraid.' In this text, the word overcomes the body, men overcome women, fear overcomes laughter, and faith overcomes a reasoned skepticism." See also Avital Ronell's interpretation of this incidence of biblical laughter as a scene of sexual difference in *Loser Sons* (Urbana-Champaign: University of Illinois Press, 2012), 178–9.

117. ויצחק (*vayitzḥak*), Genesis 17:17.

118. ותצחק (*vatitzḥak*), Genesis 18:12.

119. See Wilda C. Gafney: "From within the tent Sarah laughs to herself, as Abraham had previously laughed in God's face. After telling us that the eighty-nine- or ninety-year-old woman is indeed menopausal, God demands that Abraham explain Sarah's laughter, although he is never called to account for his own. Sarah denies laughing, and someone—the lack of an explicit subject makes it impossible to know if God or Abraham is speaking—rebuts her denial" (*Womanist Midrash: A Reintroduction to the Women of the Torah and the Throne* [Louisville, KY: Westminster John Knox Press, 2017], 36).

120. On Sarah's laughter of pleasure, see Catherine Conybeare, *The Laughter of Sarah: Biblical Exegesis, Feminist Theory, and the Concept of Delight* (New York: Palgrave Macmillan, 2013); and see Gafney: "Sarah asks a fascinating intimate, explicit question: 'After I have been completely dried out, will there yet be for me, wetness?' The text offers a surprising acknowledgment and affirmation of women's sexual pleasure even as it supposes that at some age—perhaps with menopause—women are past the age for intimate moisture and its pleasures" (*Womanist Midrash*, 36). See also Katz's explanation of how Sarah's laughter provides a biblical model for erotic motherhood that can illustrate the intersection of eros and ethics in "Levinas between Agape and Eros," 345; and *Levinas, Judaism, and the Feminine*, 145–7.

121. Katz, *Levinas, Judaism, and the Feminine*, 146.

122. See the interpretation of this scene by Vanessa L. Ochs:

> When Sarah laughed, God responded with anger. How dare Sarah doubt the words of the prophetic angel! After all, was anything too hard for God? God was angrier still when Sarah denied her laughter. Yet God did not take the issue up directly with Sarah. God went to Abraham and asked: 'Why did Sarah laugh?' It was not a question, an expression of curiosity. It was an accusation, which the commentators used to suggest that Sarah's laughter was distinct from Abraham's. Hers was a sign of disbelief, mistrust, lack of faith in God, who had the power to do anything, including allowing a very old woman to give birth. At this point, God misquoted Sarah to Abraham, so as not (according to legend) to bring about marital discord. . . . Although God was not speaking directly to Sarah, she spoke to God, frustrated that her laughter was misread as disbelief and not the astonishment it was. . . . I think she was saying that while she may have in fact laughed, God has misread its meaning (*Sarah Laughed: Modern Lessons from the Wisdom and Stories of Biblical Women* [Philadelphia: The Jewish Publication Society, 2005], 114).

123. Yael S. Feldman observes that Sarah's laugh has gained literary and cultural prominence: "Sarah's laughter has recently become the Jewish equivalent of 'the laugh of the Medusa,' Hélène Cixous's emblem of feminine subversiveness" (*Glory and Agony: Isaac's Sacrifice and National Narrative*

[Stanford, CA: Stanford University Press, 2010], 334n102). Ronell reads Sarah's laughter as "that of a she-devil, breaking and entering into the house of limits, bursting and busting (she bursts into laughter) the steeliness of man's calculative grid. . . . The trope of ridiculousness subverts the gravity of biblical patriarchy or shows what was always there, left untouched" (*Stupidity* [Urbana-Champaign: University of Illinois Press, 2002], 289–90).

124. Rachel Adler, *Engendering Judaism*, 105. Adler explains that when the visitor asks why she has laughed, Sarah responds with silence because his attention is focused upon the divine plan of Sarah bearing Abraham a son, and the mechanics are of no interest to him. Sarah does not attempt to explain to him why she has laughed, instead denying her laughter and listening to his "theology lecture" (106). Laughter is a "physical spasm" as mysterious to the visitor as sexuality (106). The male sages who comment on the text align themselves with the male figure, aiming to control laughter and sexuality; and yet, "[l]aughter is erotic, spontaneous, and anarchic, a powerful disturber of plans and no respecter of persons" (106). See Avivah Gottlieb Zornberg on the "essentially ambiguous" atmosphere of laughter at Isaac's birth in *The Beginning of Desire: Reflections on Genesis* (New York: Doubleday, 1995), 99; and see the analysis of Adler and Zornberg in Katz, *Levinas, Judaism, and the Feminine*, 146–7. Sarah does not laugh only about the possibility of impossibility, of birth from barrenness, but at the possibility and anticipation of pleasure. Her laughter issues not only from reproductive wonder but from the expectation of sexual enjoyment.

125. מצחק (*mitzahek*), Genesis 21:9. In *Bereishit Rabbah* 53:11, Ishmael's actions are compared to Genesis 39:17, in reference to Potiphar's wife, to suggest "sexual immorality." Rashi also interprets Ishmael's actions negatively, comparing this verse to Exodus 32:6 (לצחק), to mean that Ishmael was "worshipping idols"; to Genesis 39:17 (לצחק), to mean "immoral conduct"; and to 2 Samuel 2:14, to mean killing in war (וישחקו). Joshua Schwartz views the rabbinic portrayal as an attempt to defend Sarah's actions: "It is not surprising that post-biblical Jewish tradition as well as Christian tradition began to vindicate Sarah and to make the expulsion of Ishmael and Hagar more palatable. All of this, of course, revolved around a re-evaluation of מצחק. No longer could this word be explained as 'play' or 'laughter' with possible subtle hints of competition and rivalry . . . in order to defend Sarah, Ishmael's actions had to be as reprehensible as possible" ("Ishmael at Play: On Exegesis and Jewish Society," *Hebrew Union College Annual* 66 [1995], 205). See also Phyllis Trible, *Texts of Terror: Literary-Feminist Readings of Biblical Narratives* (Minneapolis, MN: Fortress, 1984), 33n44: "The Greek Bible says that he was 'playing with Isaac.' This reading has prompted different interpretations, e.g. that Ishmael was physically abusing Isaac; that the social equality implied between the two children was unacceptable to Sarah. When the phrase 'with Isaac' is omitted, other interpretations follow: e.g. that Ishmael

was masturbating; that his joyous demeanor aroused Sarah's maternal jealousy (Jubilees 17:4)."

126. Genesis 24:67. On this passage, see Wendy Zierler, "In Search of a Feminist Reading of the Akedah," *Nashim* 9, no. 1 (2005), 19: "Isaac's adulthood and marriage bear the imprint of this traumatic event [Abraham's attempted sacrifice of Isaac in Genesis 22], leading him to seek solace not in detachment, but rather in love and connection. The model for it, of course, is not his father, Abraham, but his mother, Sarah."

127. מצחק (*mitzaḥek*), Genesis 26:8. See Feldman's discussion of this passage in "'And Rebecca Loved Jacob,' but Freud Did Not," in *Freud and Forbidden Knowledge*, ed. Peter L. Rudnytsky and Ellen Handler Spitz (New York: New York University Press, 1994), 19. On the association between laughter and sex in this passage, Adler writes, "The king of the Philistines sees Isaac *mitzaḥek*, 'playing' with his wife (Gen. 8)," and in Exodus 32:6, during the feast for the Golden Calf, the people "'sat down to eat and drink and then rose לצחק (*l'tzaḥek*), 'to make merry,'" interpreted as an orgy by classical commentators (*Engendering Judaism*, 106–7).

128. See Ochs, *Sarah Laughed*, 112: "Though the story of Sarah's laughter in the face of God's prediction that a son would come to her in old age is the better known one, in fact, it was Abraham who, quite literally, had the first laugh." See also Phyllis Trible: "And so, at long last, it comes to pass. 'Yhwh visited Sarah . . . and did to Sarah as Yhwh had promised' (21:1). She bears a son to Abraham in his old age. Abraham names him Laughter (*Yishaq*) but Sarah interprets its meaning. . . . If Laughter (Isaac) is special to Abraham, how much more to Sarah! She claims the child for herself, 'for-me.' After all, he is her, not Abraham's, one and only son" ("Genesis 22: The Sacrifice of Sarah," in *Women in the Hebrew Bible*, ed. Alice Bach [New York: Routledge, 1999], 284).

129. יצחק (*Yizhaq*), Genesis 17:19. See Jacques Derrida, "Sarah Kofman," in *The Work of Mourning*, ed. Pascale-Anne Brault and Michael Naas (Chicago: University of Chicago Press, 2001), 187: "*Yiskhak*: he laughs: Isaac, the coming of Isaac, makes them both shake with laughter, one after the other; Isaac is the name of the one who comes to make them laugh, to laugh about his coming, at his very coming, as if laughter should greet a birth, the coming of a happy event, a coming of laughter, a coming to laugh: come-laugh-with-me." Yvonne Sherwood discusses how in this essay, "the ghost of the biblical Sarah finds her way into a work of mourning" for philosopher Sarah Kofman ("And Sarah Died," in *Derrida's Bible [Reading a Page of Scripture with a Little Help from Derrida]*, ed. Yvonne Sherwood [New York: Palgrave Macmillan, 2004], 264).

130. Sandford, *The Metaphysics of Love*, 5.

131. Allen, *The Philosophical Sense of Transcendence*, 160.

132. Tanja Staehler points out that in Plato, "Eros is intimately bound up with philosophy; it guides us into philosophical dialogues. Levinas, by contrast, marginalized Eros," a move that she finds "unfortunate" (*Plato and Levinas*, 94). Sarah Allen links Levinas's move away from erotic love with a distancing from the Greek philosophical approach: "If erotic love is the traditional way (and particularly the Greek philosophical way) of speaking of an affectivity that links thought to the Good and inspires transcendence through that which transcends thought, then in moving away from eros in his later works, Levinas is also moving further away from a *Greek* philosophical conception of transcendence (in any case) and perhaps also away from philosophy altogether as source of his conception of transcendence" (*The Philosophical Sense of Transcendence*, 261).

133. Sandford, "Masculine Mothers?" 199.

THREE

—ɷ—

FILIAL AND FRATERNAL FRIENDS

SO FAR WE HAVE SEEN that Rosenzweig emphasizes fraternity in his reading of the Song of Songs, effacing the text's celebration of sexually differentiated lovers, while Levinas's *Totality and Infinity* concludes with the paternal-son relation, and its correlative end in social fraternity, as the essential link to the future. For Levinas, human society is extrapolated from the family, and the possibility for social life depends on the brotherly bond. In this chapter, I consider Levinas's thought on the feminine alongside Rosenzweig's writing on marriage as a move beyond erotic love toward community. Existing critical theoretical readings of Levinas's phenomenology of erotic love, I argue, can be fruitfully applied to reading Rosenzweig: the father-son relationship is the focus, to the detriment of other familial models. We can conceive of these works as a genealogy of brotherhood.

Who participates in the fratriarchy, and who is excluded from it? As these foundational texts move from the familial to the social level, they construe the ideal society as a relationship of brothers in which every self is commanded to enact ethical relations with others because of shared kinship. The possibility of moving from ethics to politics is therefore predicated on the fraternal. For both thinkers, the erotic and the ethical/communal are at best in tension, more typically in opposition. Levinas's phenomenology of eros, meanwhile, reflects Rosenzweig's theory that marriage exceeds carnal relationships as lovers enter the public community and become eternal through male offspring. I question Levinas's insistence that the way forward, once erotic love is left behind, is in the communal sphere of fraternity. While "brotherhood" may seem to be an admirable aim, beyond the closed circle of the erotic, I argue, it comes at a high price, since it requires dissolving the particularities of any nonmale identity.

Levinas comes to emphasize a neighborly love purified of carnal eros, and embodied maternity will become the ethical relationship par excellence in his later work. Despite this, the fraternal sphere continues to be valorized throughout his oeuvre, as the maternal emphasis is pervaded by the filial-fraternal model.

My critique of fraternity is especially informed by Jacques Derrida's *Politics of Friendship*, an examination of the "fraternal" nature of friendship and political community. Derrida asks if there can be a society based on fraternity that is not exclusionary: "Is this incommensurable friendship, this friendship of the incommensurable, indeed the one we are here attempting to separate from its fraternal adherence, from its inclination to take on the economic, genealogical, ethnocentric, androcentric features of fraternity? Or is it still a fraternity, but a fraternity divided in its concept, a fraternity ranging infinitely beyond all literal figures of the brother, a fraternity that would no longer exclude anyone?"[1] Derrida explains that the figure of friendship shares key features with brotherhood: "the figure of the friend, so regularly coming back on stage with the features of the *brother*—who is critically at stake in this analysis—seems spontaneously to belong to a *familial, fraternalist* and thus *androcentric* configuration of politics."[2]

In the classical politics of friendship, explored by Derrida through Aristotle, Montaigne, and Nietzsche, brotherhood is crystallized in the communal bond. The ethical relation is figured as a friendship inseparable from fraternity: Platonic, free equals taking part in a homosocial compact.[3] Any relation of solidarity among nonbrothers is then thinkable only within the model of fraternization. As Derrida notes, "the fratriarchy may *include* cousins and sisters but, as we will see, including may also come to mean neutralizing."[4] The sister is included only by being rendered docile. In the second part of this chapter, I bring Hannah Arendt into conversation with Derrida to pry open the unifying concept of brotherhood, arguing that this model simultaneously eclipses and usurps the feminine on the one hand and becomes the basis for politics on the other. Arendt also draws our attention back to the specificity of these texts and concepts, which, if attended to, allows us to see the unmarked post-Christian nature of so much contemporary philosophical discourse on the "brotherhood of man."

MORE THAN LOVE?

In the first chapter, we saw that in Rosenzweig's exegesis of the Song of Songs, while man and woman may attempt to transcend their rigid biological roles, "the roots of their sexuality always re-establish the unambiguous relationship of nature," in which the male is actively demanding and the female passive.[5] By characterizing sexuality as the "subterranean roots" of love, Rosenzweig suggests gender can temporarily transcend sex but will always be drawn back to it in love. Rosenzweig's antiquated gender constructions are often discussed in terms of representing the more traditional times in which he wrote or as indicative of the grammatical construction of the original Hebrew text. I have argued that a grammatical locus for gender terminology may explain its origin but does not dissolve its harmful application. Although he allows for flexibility in that, in theory, both men and women may take on the roles of lover and beloved, Rosenzweig nevertheless stakes out an essentialist position, adhering to the binaries of the passively receiving female as beloved and the actively bestowing male as lover. While a woman can *act* as lover, she can become active only if she is gendered masculine. If she is to remain feminine, she will inescapably be drawn back by her sexuality to her natural position as the passive beloved.

In the second chapter, we saw that in *Totality and Infinity*, Levinas echoes these theoretically flexible yet practically rigid gender roles in his illustration of the feminine as passive beloved to the active male lover. The feminine functions as the preethical opening to the ethical, the condition for the ethical relation, while remaining apart from it. The feminine allows the masculine subject's access to the ethical, without participating in this relation, as the subject reaches toward the future in fecundity. For both thinkers, the subordination of the sexual to the fraternal-filial correlates to a movement in which the feminine is subordinated to the masculine, the female beloved to the male lover, the mother to the father, and the daughter to the son.

In her reading of Levinas, Luce Irigaray criticizes his relegation of the feminine to the object-like status of "beloved woman" while the man is provided with the active term "lover."[6] In the embodied erotic encounter, Irigaray writes, both partners should be referred to as lovers of one another. Interestingly, in her critique, Irigaray, like Rosenzweig, turns to the Song of Songs as an ideal model for the erotic relation, but in her exegesis the female and the male lovers share in activity, jointly giving and receiving sensual pleasure and enjoyment. The Song of Songs, then, "tells of the complexity of the nuptials between the two lovers (*l'amante et l'amant*), the two beloveds (*l'aimée et l'aimé*), who are born of different mothers and so do not belong to the same traditions, to the same genealogies, or to the same gods."[7] She therefore proposes a relation of equals: in place of the feminine as beloved (*aimée*), she suggests the term "woman lover" (*amante*) who participates in the erotic relation with the masculine lover.[8]

Irigaray focuses on the disparity between the two lovers in the Song; they do not share familial ties—they come from different traditions and backgrounds and hence are a primary model for the relation of sexual difference. She does

not, however, explain how this can be reconciled with both lovers' calls of longing to blur the lines of difference and to fuse into a relation of shared family
lines so they can announce their love to the world. The Song may be a ques-
tionable model for sexual difference; after all, the lovers apparently wish to
convert their secret, private erotic relation into a sibling relationship that can
be proclaimed to the masses, a point cannily addressed by Rosenzweig in the
Star's movement from love to community.

Levinas makes an oblique reference to the Song of Songs in *Otherwise Than
Being*: "There is an assignation to an identity for the response of responsibility,
where one cannot have oneself be replaced without fault. To this command
continually put forth only a 'here I am' (*me voici*) can answer, where the pronoun 'I' is in the accusative, declined before any declension, possessed by the
other, sick, identical."[9] In a footnote, he clarifies that he has in mind the Song
of Songs 5:8: "'I am sick with love.'"[10] In an essay on Levinas and the feminine,
Derrida points out that this phrase "is torn from the mouth of a woman, so as
to be given to the other. Why doesn't he clarify that in this work?"[11] Levinas's
reference to this passage from the Song discusses the self's response and yet
obscures the fact that this "I" is gendered in the Song as female. Derrida places
Levinas in the hermeneutic tradition that has often attempted to erase the trace
of the female lover in the Song: "Isn't it 'she' in the Song of Songs? And who
would 'she' be? Does it matter?"[12] In other words, Derrida argues that Levinas's
unmarked use of this phrase obscures the femininity of the original voice—and
that move, he suggests, does matter.

The ethics of textual appropriation are a major subject for all these thinkers
and for our considerations of them. In this essay, Derrida ironically suggests the
gesture of giving back the text to the author by showing gratitude for Levinas's
work would betray Levinasian ethics of the absolute gift: "Beyond any possible
restitution, there would be need for my gesture to operate without debt, in
absolute ingratitude."[13] Derrida's observation might provide an explanation
for Levinas's decision to cite Rosenzweig in *Totality and Infinity* not by citing
him but rather through prefatory recognition, a gesture acknowledging an
inexhaustible debt.[14] The absence of further citation may express a gesture of
grateful ingratitude, the resistance of returning the work of the other back to
the other.[15] Derrida proceeds to interrogate Levinas's work by returning the
work not to the author, to "him" (E. L., as he refers to Levinas by his initials),
but to the vocalization of these initials, to "*elle*," to *she*, to the feminine.[16] In
returning the work to E. L. rather than to "Levinas," Derrida avoids the recuperation and appropriation of the other that Levinas cautions against. In the
serious wordplay of E. L./*elle*, Derrida resists returning the work to its origin; at

the same time, he shows how the feminine is absent in its presence in Levinas's signature and in Levinas's own work. "*She*" is already there but is unseen.

In *Totality and Infinity*, Levinas moves from the erotic toward the ethical sphere, locating the possibility of eternity in a relation of paternity-filiality. For Levinas the erotic relation does not allow for externalization but can break out of its self-contained totality toward infinity through the son. This movement makes possible, in his words, "the strange conjuncture of the family."[17] Levinas indicates the central place of family in his thinking in the conclusion: "The situation in which the I thus posits itself before truth in placing its subjective morality in the infinite time of its fecundity—a situation in which the instant of eroticism and the infinity of paternity are conjoined—is concretized in the marvel of the family."[18]

For Rosenzweig, meanwhile, the lovers in the Song long to share their love in the public realm, tied to the entire community, taking the collective path toward redemption. We can productively compare Rosenzweig's expression "more than love" (*mehr als Liebe*) with Levinas's emphasis on "love without Eros" (*amour sans Eros*) in his later work. Levinas articulates this point in a 1982 interview: "From the start, the encounter with the Other is my responsibility for him. That is the responsibility for my neighbor, which is, no doubt, the harsh name for what we call love of one's neighbor; love without Eros, charity, love in which the ethical aspect dominates the passionate aspect, love without concupiscence."[19] What happens when erotic love is set aside on the way toward a fraternal community? These movements away from and exceeding erotic love resonate with one another and have implications for the roles of gender, fecundity, and embodiment.

There are certainly nuanced differences between the two, but we can locate points of convergence between these thinkers in their approaches to family and eros. For Rosenzweig, in reading the Song, erotic love can become redemptive only through a marriage represented by an expression of fraternity. The themes that conclude Levinas's *Totality and Infinity*—fecundity, filiality, and fraternity—all can be found in the central section of the *Star*, in both cases representing a communal bond that leads to eternal time. In the movement in the *Star* from revelation to redemption, the erotic relationship must be externalized and exceeded in marriage, branching out toward eternity in the relation of filiality with the son. For Levinas, the child exceeds the self's possibilities, forming a bridge toward infinity. The goal of erotic love is the production of the child, who is other than the self but remains part of the self. The child can bring the lover outside of himself toward an external being, allowing the possibility for an ethical relation brought forth out of the erotic encounter. Throughout his discussion of fecundity, Levinas elucidates the relation of filiality-paternity: "The I breaks free from itself in paternity without thereby ceasing to be an I, for the I *is* its son. The converse of paternity, filiality, the father-son relationship, designates a relation of rupture and a recourse at the same time."[20] The movement from totality to infinity concludes with filiality, the essential link to the future, and its correlative end in fraternity.

Rosenzweig's discussion of revelation in the *Star* celebrates the erotic energies of differentiated, private lovers who yearn to become amalgamated, public siblings. While Rosenzweig provides an evocative reading of the Song that homes in on the lovers' aspirations, he finally emphasizes their aims toward fraternity, rather than to differently gendered siblinghood. The communal realm is united in fraternal kinship. Levinas similarly moves through the drama of erotic love only to end up at the possibility of social life in fraternity. In *Totality and Infinity*, the encounter with the "face" leads the individual to ethical and ontological challenges according to a "philosophical anthropology": eros, love, friendship, and family.[21] Here, human society is extrapolated from the family, and the possibility for social life depends on the brotherly bond: "The relation with the face in fraternity, where in his turn the Other appears in solidarity with all the others, constitutes the social order... which encompasses the structure of the family itself."[22] In *Totality and Infinity*, the section "Beyond the Face" ends with a revealing account of fraternity that accords with a classical idea of brotherhood. This is a masculine community of brothers, "that apparently neutral and universal community of 'the human fraternity.'"[23] In Simon Critchley's view, Levinas's vision of human solidarity centers on a "silent substitution": "fraternity is always—literally—a relationship between brothers, and brothers are sons. Relations of solidarity amongst women are only conceivable though the model of fraternity."[24] According to this limited conception of solidarity, then, sorority would be nothing more than a modification of fraternity.

The gradual eclipse of feminine-gendered eros in Levinas's work is linked directly to the elision of the feminine from the production of the son-brother. Erotic love holds prominence in Levinas's early works, mainly in *Time and the Other*. *Totality and Infinity* maintains a link with erotic love while pointing to its transcendence in fecundity. Finally, in *Otherwise Than Being*, love ends up eros-free.[25] Sexual eros is transcended in fecundity and ultimately purified in a love without eroticism, as Levinas comes to emphasize a neighborly love beyond carnal eros.[26]

The body in *Otherwise Than Being* is instead alternately suffering, hungry, maternal, vulnerable, and invaded, but not erotic. Embodiment and maternity are taken up as exemplary ethical relationships, which offer many illuminating possibilities but come with their own sets of ambiguities.[27] Stella Sandford observes that once the "masculine community of brothers" makes an appearance in *Otherwise Than Being*, "maternity is not spoken of again," a familiar pattern she finds repeated from the "human fraternity" in *Totality and Infinity*.[28] Indeed, in *Otherwise Than Being*, Levinas explicitly describes the relationship with the neighbor, characterized by proximity, as a fraternal kinship relation:

> The neighbor concerns me before all assumption, all commitment consented to or refused. I am bound to him, him who is, however, the first one on the scene, not signaled, unparalleled; I am bound to him before any liaison contracted. He orders me before being recognized. Here there is a relation of kinship outside of all biology, "against all logic." It is not because the neighbor would be recognized as belonging to the same genus as me that he concerns me. He is precisely *other*. The community with him begins in my obligation to him. The neighbor is a brother. A fraternity that cannot be abrogated, an unimpeachable assignation, proximity is an impossibility to move away without the torsion of a complex, without "alienation" or fault.[29]

The neighbor (*le prochain*) in kinship (*relation de parenté*) is a brother whose relationship allows community to be possible. The fraternity leads to the possibility for ethical universality, which Levinas gives the name of illeity. Maternity is overcome in fraternity through the model of illeity.

We can view this in continuation with the move from the erotic relation to fecundity in Levinas's earlier work. Maternity is a relationship of proximity bound up in the dyad, so, as Sandford explains, "maternity by itself seems to harbor the same problem previously located in eros: a tendency to exclusivity."[30] In *Totality and Infinity*, the third party risks being excluded from eros, closely related to the feminine; in *Otherwise Than Being*, the third party may be excluded from maternity. What is lacking in both cases, Sandford astutely observes, "will then be elaborated as masculine: *illéité*. The 'trace' of *le tiers* [the third], from the alleged neutrality of the pronoun *il* (he/it), it is illeity that makes possible the 'ethical universality' of fraternity not fraught with the danger of (maternal) exclusivity."[31] Sandford argues that paternity, the central relationship in *Totality and Infinity*, actually survives covertly in the fraternal community in the conclusion of *Otherwise Than Being*. In considering the relationship between the two works, she asks, "Is it possible that the necessity to overcome the duality of erotic coupling, in *Totality and Infinity*, has become, in *Otherwise Than Being*, the necessity to overcome the duality of the asymmetrical ethical relation, epitomized in maternity?"[32] In both cases, the relationship characterized by femininity, even if it is not exclusively female, is ultimately overcome in the fraternal community. "In *Otherwise Than Being*, physicality and proximity—the maternal-feminine—must give way to the distance necessary for the abstract relation of fraternity. The universality inherent in the patrilineal genealogy must correct the asymmetry of maternal proximity if that relation is not to be the end of the line."[33]

A similar move beyond the maternal takes place in the *Star* as well. In the *Star*'s first part, Rosenzweig refers to the maternal realm in *Faust*, which in Goethe's play is called the "descent to the Mothers": "We have broken the All to pieces. . . . Since we are immersed in this imperfect work of our knowledge, we are, in our wandering into the realm of the Mothers, still the servants of the first commandment: the commandment to drown. The ascent, and the growing together in it of the imperfect work to the perfection of the new All, will come only later."[34] Rosenzweig's reference to this scene in *Faust* represents a primordial state of fragmentation, following the breaking apart of the original state of totality, the All.[35] In this scene, the masculine creativity personified by Faust draws upon the feminine creativity-fertility of the mother figure.[36] Faust's journey to the netherworld and back is paralleled by the move from the primordial world of part I of the *Star* through the world of part II to the supra world of part III.[37] Rosenzweig's reference suggests this movement is enabled by passing into and emerging from a haunted realm of mothers. The mothers must be left behind in order to embark on the journey forward.

Notably, the scene in which Faust journeys to the realm of the Mothers also sparks Levinas's interest. Levinas cites this very scene from *Faust* II in the original German as the epigraph to the final chapter of *Otherwise Than Being*, titled "Outside": "'Mephistopheles: Willst du nur hören was du schon gehört?/ Dich störe nichts, wie es auch weiter klinge/ Schon längst gewohnt der wunderbarsten Dinge. Faust: Doc im Erstarren such ich nicht mein Heil/ Das Schaudern ist der Menschheit bester Teil.'"[38] These lines directly precede Faust's descent, and his shudder results from Mephistopheles's invocation of the word *"Mütter"* (Mothers). In his epigraph Levinas directs these lines from *Faust* to the reader, who is enjoined to not only hear what has already been heard but to embrace the shuddering human response to the unknown and not yet heard, and to welcome foreign sounds. It is not incidental that the words Levinas cites from *Faust* are followed in Goethe's narrative by the descent into the maternal realm, since the figure of the maternal body is central to Levinas's *Otherwise Than Being*.

But the maternal emphasis is, in the end, pervaded by the filial-fraternal model: "The other is from the first the brother of all the other men."[39] The ethical relation of maternity is overcome in the universality of brotherhood in the social realm. The face-to-face relation, or the dialogical, opens up to the "third party"—the political: "The others concern me from the first. Here fraternity precedes the commonness of a genus. My relationship with the other as neighbor gives meaning to my relations with all the others."[40] This passage arrives in a discussion on the state and justice: the egalitarian and just state cannot do without "friendship and faces."[41] The possibility of moving from ethics to politics is predicated precisely on the fraternal.

Ultimately, Rosenzweig's articulation of marriage as infinitely more than love in the *Star*, "Ehe ist unendlich mehr als Liebe,"[42] resonates with Levinas's search for "amour sans Eros,"[43] a non-erotic, or rather post-erotic, love. It is possible that these understandings of love align with the classic Christian theological privileging of agape (love not tied to an object) over eros (the more contingent love that desires a particular object).[44] In my view, however, the post-erotic love Levinas and Rosenzweig espouse finds more resonance with the rabbinic sense of brotherly love. Mara Benjamin helpfully explains this type of love:

> Agape, in Anders Nygren's classic definition, is "spontaneous and unmotivated" by the desire for the love-object or any deficiency in the lover; it is "indifferent" to the inherent value of the love-object but creates value in that object. A rabbinic maxim expresses a similar preference for love that is "independent" of transitory qualities: "Any love that is dependent on something, when that thing perishes, the love perishes. But [a love] that is not dependent on something does not ever perish. What is a love that is dependent on something? The love of Amnon and Tamar. And a love that is not dependent on something? The love of David and Jonathan" (Pirke Avot 5:16). The rabbinic version of the hierarchy, invoking scriptural narratives rather than qualities, suggests that selfless devotion to another person is superior to erotic or sexual desire.[45]

This rabbinic model of nondependent, non-erotic love is striking for many reasons. We read in 1 Samuel 18:3 that "Jonathan made a covenant with David, because he loved him as his own soul." The love between David and Jonathan in particular has been interpreted as challenging the bounds of heteronormative and gender-normative love.[46]

Even if we accept a nonhomoerotic reading of their relationship, which seems to be implied in *Pirkei Avot* 5:16, we find in David and Jonathan an example of male-male (non-erotic) friendship being contrasted with a relationship of half siblings (Amnon and Tamar) characterized by sexual violence. These are both nonnormative relationships in their representations of same-sex intimacy in one case and opposite-sex abuse in the other. Fully analyzing the rabbinic interpretation of these relationships is beyond the purview of the current discussion, but for the purposes of the framing of ideal, brotherly love versus erotic desire, the example is illuminating. Heteroerotic desire is presented as transgressive, dangerously crossing kinship lines, and potentially leading to unsanctioned acts of violence that demand revenge. In this example, erotic love is threatening and must be contained, whereas eternal post-erotic devotion is the ultimate goal. Male friendship is privileged.[47] The nondependent, elevated love of *Pirkei Avot* is echoed in Levinas's discussion of the neighbor in the penultimate section of *Otherwise Than Being*.[48] We end up at a similar place to the homosocial fraternity illustrated in the *Star* and suggested as the end point of Levinas's major philosophical works.

BROTHERLY LOVE AND ITS LIMITS

In the philosophical canon in which Rosenzweig and Levinas both intervene, the erotic is often subordinated not only to the blood-bonded fraternal or to the disinterested heights of agape but to the philial—the powerful relationship of brotherly friendship. As with the parent-child or sibling relationship, friendship is theoretically capable of encompassing varying combinations of men and women, and yet it is consistently figured as the province of men alone, of metaphorical brothers.

In his own study of friendship, Derrida concentrates on another well-known pair whose friendship has echoes of David and Jonathan's unique connection: Michel de Montaigne and Étienne de La Boétie. Derrida arrives at Montaigne by way of classical views on friendship—Plato, Aristotle, and Cicero—thereby inscribing the philosophical tradition in an arc of friendship-as-fraternity. He asks, "Since when—whether we know it or not—have we ceased to be Aristotle's heirs?"[49] Aristotle's account of friendship makes central the virtues of similarity and likeness. This raises questions not only about the treatment of the stranger outside the political community but also the role of difference within the political group.[50] From Aristotle's *Nichomachean Ethics* onward, Derrida seeks to address "a question awaiting us, precisely the question of the brother, in the canonical—that is, androcentric—structure of friendship."[51]

Derrida begins his chapter "He Who Accompanies Me" with an epigraph on "brotherly love" from La Boétie, who writes about recognizing fellow beings as brothers: "our good mother nature . . . has given us all the great gift of speech so that we could come to a still deeper acquaintance and brotherhood . . . and has striven by every possible means to bind us together in the tight embrace of kinship and companionship."[52] Derrida reads La Boétie alongside Montaigne's famous essay "On Friendship," comparing Montaigne's views on male-male friendship with the (according to Montaigne) significantly less elevated knot of male-female marriage. For Montaigne, woman is incapable of and excluded from the friendship bond while marriage "bears only an 'imaginary resemblance' to this 'holy bond' of sovereign friendship."[53]

This argument stretches all the way back to Augustine. In *The Literal Meaning of Genesis*, Augustine asks why Eve was made as a helper for Adam if not for reproductive reasons, since they do not procreate until after they are banished from the garden of Eden: "Now, if the woman was not made for the man to be his helper in begetting children, in what was she to help him? She was not to till the earth with him, for there was not yet any toil to make help necessary. If there were any such need, a male helper would be better, and the same could be said of the comfort of another's presence if Adam were perhaps weary of solitude. How much more agreeably could two male friends, rather than a man and a woman, enjoy companionship and conversation in a life shared together."[54] Augustine concludes, therefore, that the woman could have been made as a helper only for the sake of bearing children, because if it had been for the purpose of companionship, God would have surely made a man instead. For Montaigne, the problem is the incapacity of the female person who makes up half of that bond: "the fault lies less with marriage than in woman, in her sex."[55] As Derrida points out, Montaigne therefore "silently dismisses heterosexual friendship" as well as female-female friendship, "excluding a holy bond that would unite anyone other than two men, two male 'companions,' in the figure and the oath of friendship, if not in so-called natural fraternity."[56]

Derrida's reading of Nietzsche's *Thus Spoke Zarathustra* reveals that here too (unsurprisingly) the woman is incapable of friendship, since she can know only (erotic) love, which is clearly inferior to friendship. In consequence of her incapacity for friendship, woman is necessarily and naturally excluded from the public realm: "Feminine love causes only 'injustice' and 'blindness' to be seen in all that is not loved. In other words, woman remains incapable of respecting the enemy, of honouring what she does not love."[57] The political implications are apparent:

> Incapable of friendship, enmity, justice, war, respect for the other, whether friend or enemy, woman is not man; she is not even part of humanity. Still addressing his friend as a brother . . . Zarathustra declares here that woman is the outlaw of humanity—in any case as regards the question of loving, if not that of childbirth and suckling; the nurturing mother is perhaps human (like a "cow") but not the lover that woman can be—woman, to whom friendship still remains inaccessible: "Woman is not yet capable of friendship: women are still cats and birds. Or, at best, cows."[58]

"Woman" is not "human." Her proximity to childbirth means she is infantilized, animalized, and depoliticized.

Men, for Nietzsche, are often not capable of friendship, seeing each other as merely comrades. But if women are stuck in love, figured only as enslaved or tyrannical, men have the future potential for or promise of friendship; only men can attempt to achieve freedom, equality, and fraternity. For Nietzsche, the man must strive toward a Christian spiritual fraternity: "One becomes a brother, in Christianity, one is worthy of the eternal father, only by loving one's enemy as one's neighbour or as oneself."[59] Derrida reads Nietzsche and Montaigne, along with Carl Schmitt and Hegel, on friendship as political brotherhood, asking his interlocutors to define their genealogies. In the filiation of the brother, he observes, we find two lineages: biblical and Greek. "Which brother are we talking about? . . . And which one is their father? Where were they born? On biblical or Hellenic ground? In a finite family or an infinite one?"[60]

Derrida's reading of fraternal politics/political brotherhood would have benefited from including the intervention of Hannah Arendt. Indeed, Derrida writes himself into the history of fraternity precisely by neglecting women's writing on the subject in *Politics of Friendship*, most notably Arendt.[61] In her essay "On Humanity in Dark Times: Thoughts about Lessing," first delivered as a speech upon receiving the Lessing Prize in 1959, Arendt offers a critique of "brotherhood" and its classical exclusion of Jewish politics. Arendt's essay makes clear her ambivalence upon receiving this prize in Germany only fifteen years after the war. She demarcates brotherhood and friendship on the basis of politics. "Brotherhood" exists only in dark times between persecuted peoples; as such, it cannot be political. It is friendship, rather, that should be the basis of the political realm.

Arendt focuses on the leitmotif of friendship in Gotthold Ephraim Lessing's 1779 play *Nathan the Wise*, inspired by his own friend Moses Mendelssohn.[62] Arendt compares Lessing to Rousseau, whose view of *fraternité* as the fulfillment of humanity inspired the French Revolution. Lessing, instead, considered friendship to be the central phenomenon concerning humanity. Lessing's concept of friendship had a different political valence from the eighteenth-century understanding of fraternity, in which brotherly attachment to other humans leads people to despise inhumane treatment of others. Arendt understands brotherhood differently:

> For our purposes, however, it is important that humanity manifests itself in such brotherhood most frequently in "dark times." This kind of humanity actually becomes inevitable when the times become so extremely dark for certain groups of people that it is no longer up to them, their insight or choice,

to withdraw from the world. Humanity in the form of fraternity invariably appears historically among persecuted peoples and enslaved groups; and in eighteenth-century Europe it must have been quite natural to detect it among the Jews, who then were newcomers in literary circles. This kind of humanity is the great privilege of pariah peoples; it is the advantage that the pariahs of this world always and in all circumstances can have over others. The privilege is dearly bought.[63]

Arendt points out that the French Revolution added fraternity to the liberty and equality that have always been political categories. She finds that compassion is central to the experience of fraternity in allowing for the discovery of a common human nature, for "fraternity has its natural place among the repressed and persecuted, the exploited and humiliated."[64]

Arendt explains why compassion cannot be relied upon, however, for founding human solidarity:

Now compassion is unquestionably a natural, creature affect which involuntarily touches every normal person at the sight of suffering, however alien the sufferer may be, and would therefore seem an ideal basis for a feeling that reaching out to all mankind would establish a society in which men might really become brothers. Through compassion the revolutionary-minded humanitarian of the eighteenth century sought to achieve solidarity with the unfortunate and the miserable—an effort tantamount to penetrating the very domain of brotherhood. But it soon became evident that this kind of humanitarianism, whose purest form is a privilege of the pariah, is not transmissible and cannot be easily acquired by those who do not belong among the pariahs. Neither compassion nor actual sharing of suffering is enough.[65]

Here Arendt is both rebuking a German society that lacked compassion and a sense of fellow-creaturely suffering during the Second World War and making a case for why relying on compassion as a basis for humanitarianism is not enough.[66] This compassion is limited to those who are suffering and as such cannot be counted upon to influence bystanders of that suffering to humanitarian action: "the humanitarianism of brotherhood scarcely befits those who do not belong among the insulted and the injured and can share in it only through their compassion . . . this 'human nature' and the feelings of fraternity that accompany it manifest themselves only in darkness, and hence cannot be identified in the world."[67] Brotherhood, therefore, is "irrelevant" in political terms.[68]

Here Arendt comes to speak on her own specific experience of brotherhood garnered from belonging to a pariah people: "I so explicitly stress my membership in the group of Jews expelled from Germany at a relatively early age because I wish to anticipate certain misunderstandings which can arise only too easily when one speaks of humanity. In this connection I cannot gloss over the fact that for many years I considered the only adequate reply to the question, Who are you? to be: A Jew. That answer alone took into account the reality of persecution."[69] In this declaration, Lisa J. Disch sees Arendt performing how to acknowledge her Jewish identity as a political fact while, at the same time, refuting it.[70] Arendt's address allows her to accept the prize of Lessing's legacy on her own terms, using the opportunity to question the foundationalist tradition of German Enlightenment humanism that the prize committee had hoped to reinstantiate by installing her as its intellectual heir.[71]

Arendt's reflections on identity in the context of Lessing's legacy lead her to compare brotherhood, an experience shared only by the persecuted, with the classical conception of *philia*, friendship among citizens. Arendt locates the key role of discourse and dialogue in Aristotle and classical Greek friendship. Only in the continual interchange of talk could citizens in a *polis* find the political importance of friendship. It is this classical approach to friendship that Arendt sees precisely in Lessing's play: "that humanity is exemplified not in fraternity but in friendship; that friendship is not intimately personal but makes political demands and preserves reference to the world—all this seems to us so exclusively characteristic of classical antiquity that it rather perplexes us when we find quite kindred features in *Nathan the Wise*."[72] In Arendt's view, Lessing had a sense of common humanity derived from friendship, not from compassion or brotherhood, that allowed him to enter into the discourse of friendship with "a pious Jew" such as Mendelssohn.[73] Lessing would have rejected any doctrine that prevented friendship between two human beings. In "dark times," men have a need to become closer to one another in shared brotherhood with those they resemble and with whom they will not find conflict. Arendt criticizes Enlightenment thinking by illustrating that Lessing was himself an anti-foundationalist living in darkness.[74] Lessing "could no more endure loneliness than the excessive closeness of a brotherliness that obliterated all distinctions . . . he was concerned solely with humanizing the world by incessant and continual discourse about its affairs and the things in it. He wanted to be the friend of many men, but no man's brother."[75]

Arendt highlights in the example of Lessing the limitations with an aim for shared brotherhood. This intimacy is sought out between those who closely resemble one another, and this closeness erases all distinctions between them that should instead be preserved. She shows why universal brotherhood is not ultimately a desirable aim. Friendship, in the classic sense, allows for discourse and difference. Because brotherliness is premised on sameness, it obliterates the difference that makes true dialogue possible. For Arendt, friendship is sustained not by "a common moral framework of identity, but distance," a state of betweenness characterized by plurality.[76]

Arendt's approach resonates with the evocative exploration of friendship offered more recently by Ashon Crawley, who meditates upon Foucault's reference to friendship as susceptibility to pleasure:[77]

> Susceptibility implies a kind of vulnerability, an openness, a belief in existence as radically undone, unhinged, unruly. And to be susceptible means a kind of porosity and that makes me think of air and breath and movements of inhalation and exhalation. One has to relax. Susceptibility and vulnerability together underscore the idea of existence as interstitial, as a circuit always waiting to be closed. This closure comes through friendship, which is another way to say sociality, another way to think vibration. The inventive impulse of friendship emerges from the fact that it is not institutionally informed or produced or protected. It's not like marriage where there are ceremonies and rituals that people perform in order to enter into it, it's not like marriage where there are institutions that give or withhold people's capacities for engaging the practice. Friendship is anti-institutional.[78]

Crawley links this conception of friendship to an "otherwise possibility," which is "a mode of constituting otherwise ways of being in the world."[79] Like Arendt, Crawley rejects the Enlightenment humanist tradition of the liberal subject that attempts to delineate a normative "modern Man" and, in so doing, relinquishes the "otherwise as possible."[80] But Crawley takes this further, providing an important corrective to Arendt's account. Drawing upon Sylvia Wynter's concept of the overrepresentation of Man, Crawley demonstrates how this normatizing project is always linked to one particular kind of raced, classed, and gendered human.[81]

Arendt's refusal of an externally conferred identity in the Lessing address can, in Disch's view, be a resource for the project of rewriting her position on intersectional feminist subjectivity, which is otherwise lacking in her work.[82] Although Arendt helpfully rejects "brotherhood" as the ideal relationship on political grounds, the exclusionary gendered logic of brotherhood is left unmentioned in her account. This is not, of course, unique to Arendt. In each example of exemplary brothers that preoccupy the thinkers in Derrida's work, the figure of the sister is continually obscured in a kind of repetition-compulsion: "Will it be said once again, in conclusion, that the sister is altogether mute in this interminable and eloquent dialectic of inimical brothers?"[83] It becomes clear that it is not possible to speak of universal brotherhood without rendering the sister mute and invisible.

Liliane Weissberg cannily points out that the sister nevertheless is implicated in Arendt's reading of Lessing. Arendt calls *Nathan the Wise* "the classical drama of friendship," highlighting the words "'We must, must be friends,' with which Nathan turns to the Templar."[84] Here, Weissberg observes the forgotten figure of the sister in Arendt's appreciation for the play: "for Arendt, it is important that the Romantic love between Recha and the templar remains unfulfilled, and that it is replaced by friendship, which makes for the happy ending. Arendt does not comment on the fact that Recha and the templar prove to be siblings, that the templar is able to turn into a true 'brother' for Recha, that Romantic love is prevented by genealogical bonds."[85] Katja Garloff reads the Recha-Templar relationship as a Freudian sublimation of erotic passion into sibling affection, the "transformation of interfaith romance into brotherly love."[86] Because interfaith marriage remained prohibited by church and state and by Jewish and Christian communities, Lessing cleverly invented a different reason to avoid the forbidden marriage: "In depicting incest as the obstacle to marriage ... *Nathan the Wise* retroactively changes the nature of the transgression: the problem was not that the Templar loved a Jewess but that he loved his sister."[87] Lessing imaginatively replaces the interfaith marriage prohibition with the incest taboo as the reason Recha and the Templar must be separated. "If the dramatization of the budding love between Recha and the Templar teaches the reader about the difficulties faced by a Christian-Jewish couple, the transformation of erotic passion into sibling affection demonstrates how a socially unacceptable attraction turns into a socially acceptable one."[88] Lessing thus makes the choice to dramatize desire rather than fulfillment.[89]

Recha and the Templar bring us back to the lovers in the Song of Songs who long to be siblings; in *Nathan the Wise*, rather, we find would-be lovers who end up having a shared bloodline, which allows their erotic love to be channeled into friendship. In this narrative, the budding incestuous relationship is dissolved before it can become scandalous. Ironically, Rosenzweig criticized the play precisely because of this particular familial ending. In "Lessing's Nathan," written in 1919, he refers to the "sentimentality" of the conclusion, which he finds "Not Jewish."[90] He observes of the concluding scene, "the archetypal difference of man and woman is denied in favor of the cool, fish-blooded brotherliness and sisterliness."[91] He dislikes the "flatness" of the final scene, especially the "messianic prospect" of the end, which is notably sterile: "No children."[92] In this essay, Rosenzweig's preference for reproduction as a philosophical and narrative end is consistent with the framework in the *Star*. His dislike of the play's representation of the sibling relationship as desire-free also suggests his preference for the treatment of this relationship alongside its erotic registers. In contrast to Lessing's "fish-blooded" vision of the sibling bond, the potentially erotic nuances of the brother-sister relationship will in turn be discussed in the next chapter in relation to Rosenzweig's thought and letters.

For her part, Arendt may forget about the sister's role in the play, but her critique nevertheless highlights the forgotten place of Jewish politics in the philosophical genealogy of brotherhood discussed by Derrida. Arendt's and Derrida's readings of fraternity's philosophical lineage allow us to see that, although Levinas's and Rosenzweig's ideas are structured by fratriarchal logic, they stand out within the philosophical frat club because their positionality is evident. Katz convincingly makes the case that we should read Levinas's work on the feminine with his Jewish sources in mind, because he draws upon Jewish texts.[93] Jewish philosophers can therefore provide a stark contrast with the standard subject of modern Western philosophy: "that subject has typically been white, male, and Protestant—the last part of which is typically overlooked, even by feminist philosophers, thereby overlooking the way that religion has also figured the subject in the history of philosophy . . . the examination of this subject might be put in productive tension with the subject as normally envisaged in Western philosophy."[94]

Batnitzky maintains that there are consequences to Rosenzweig's and Levinas's uncritical use of gendered terms and language that we must explore, including that they do not account for differences that are in fact different. Without excusing them, though, "we see that their use of gendered categories adds to our understanding of the complexity of the ways in which identities are constructed philosophically."[95] They make explicit how certain philosophical approaches "remain entrenched (often unconsciously) in a kind of post-Christian rhetoric that aspects of Jewish philosophy can call into question."[96]

In this regard, feminist approaches in Jewish philosophy that account for difference can contribute to the field of intersectionality studies, which considers how individuals and societies are mutually constituted by structures of power including race, class, sexuality, gender, and ability.[97] Sarah Imhoff notes that the vector of religion has largely been left out of the study of intersectionality.[98] Marla Brettschneider convincingly argues that "intersectionality theorists will do well to include Jewish views and critiques of Christian privilege and Christian hegemony within the purview of analysis in the field."[99] Although intersectionality literature is a growing field that includes a variety of viewpoints, it "virtually excludes examination of Jewish experience and perspectives," which could expand its scope.[100] Recently, religious studies scholars like Crawley have shown how the modern category of religion "colluded with the making of modern Man and its overrepresentation" in Western thought.[101] As Crawley clearly puts it, "To be normative in terms of race, gender, and class was to *also* be normative in terms of religion, it was to *have* religion, it was to be Christian."[102]

As an essential component to our reading, then, we are enjoined to examine how Rosenzweig and Levinas's thought is explicitly marked as male and Jewish, forcing the reader to confront the usually invisible assumptions underlying Western thought that attempt to implicitly shore up a masculine and Christian norm. We might even say that at times, they subversively account for their own positionality. Jewish philosophers may also offer an alternative to the classical male Christian subject by presenting a more permeable masculinity that is open to alterity. But this potentially capacious subjectivity requires the reader to see masculinity as gendered *in the first place*. These Jewish philosophers describe a male, cisgender, and heterosexual subject. Only when it is examined *as gendered* can the study of men, maleness, and masculinity be an extension of feminist critique.[103] Otherwise, we fall into the trap of assuming masculinity as normative instead of recognizing it as one particular and contingent identity among others. In order to reveal power relations at work in these texts, it is incumbent upon readers to emphasize the positionality of canonical authors rather than to reflexively assign them a normative neutrality. For Jewish philosophy to contribute to intersectionality, readers must first pay attention to the contingency and specificity of its established thinkers and aim to incorporate a wider multiplicity of identities and voices.

NOTES

1. Derrida, *Politics of Friendship*, 236–7.
2. Derrida, viii.
3. The homoerotic dimension of brotherly friendship will be discussed further in the next chapter.
4. Derrida, *Politics of Friendship*, viii.
5. Rosenzweig, *Star*, 183.
6. Irigaray, *An Ethics of Sexual Difference*, 194.
7. Luce Irigaray, "Questions to Emmanuel Levinas: On the Divinity of Love," trans. Margaret Whitford, in *Re-Reading Levinas*, 110.
8. Irigaray, "Questions to Emmanuel Levinas," 115. Claire Katz points out that Irigaray does not take into account the central role of Jewish sources in Levinas's thought and exegesis: see *An Introduction to Modern Jewish Philosophy*,

132; *Levinas, Judaism, and the Feminine*, 70; and "For Love Is as Strong as Death: Taking Another Look at Levinas on Love," *Philosophy Today* 45 (2001): 127.

9. Levinas, *Otherwise Than Being*, 142.

10. Levinas, *Otherwise Than Being*, 198n5; in the original, "Je suis malade d'amour," *Cantique des Cantiques*, 5:8, quoted in Levinas, *Autrement qu'être*, 222n1. (The translation mistakenly cites Song of Songs 6:8). The original Hebrew, *cholat ahava ani* (חולת אהבה אני), suggests the English expression *lovesick*.

11. Derrida, "At This Very Moment," 19.

12. Derrida, 18.

13. Derrida, 13.

14. "Franz Rosenzweig's *Stern der Erlösung*, a work too often present in this book to be cited" (Levinas, *Totality and Infinity*, 28.)

15. Levinas discusses the necessity of this absence of return in his essay "The Trace of the Other:" "A work conceived in its ultimate nature requires a radical generosity of the same who in the work goes unto the other. It then requires an *ingratitude* of the other. Gratitude would in fact be the *return* of the movement to its origin" ("The Trace of the Other," in *Deconstruction in Context*, trans. Alphonso Lingis, ed. Mark Taylor [Chicago: University of Chicago Press, 1986], 349).

16. Derrida, "At This Very Moment," 20: "the presumed signatory, E. L., does not directly say *I* in the text."

17. Levinas, *Totality and Infinity*, 279.

18. Levinas, 306.

19. Emmanuel Levinas, "Philosophy, Justice, and Love," in *Entre Nous: On Thinking-of-the-Other*, trans. Michael B. Smith and Barbara Harshaw (New York: Columbia University Press, 1998), 103; in the original, "La rencontre d'Autrui est d'emblée ma responsabilité pour lui. La responsabilité pour le prochain qui est, sans doute, le nom sévère de ce qu'on appelle l'amour du prochain, amour sans Eros, charité, amour ou le moment éthique domine le moment passionnel, amour sans concupiscence" (Levinas, "Philosophie, Justice et Amour," in *Entre Nous: Essais sur le penser-à-l'autre* [Paris: Bernard Grasset, 1991], 121). Katz rightly points out that we must take into consideration the medium of the interview in citing it: "the status of an interview in a philosophical argument is unclear to me. Philosophers say many things, even in interviews. But what they say in an interview does not change the fact that the writing in the project to which they refer might say something other than what they had hoped or believed it to say" (*Levinas, Judaism, and the Feminine*, 158n3). In this case, I find that Levinas's articulation of "amour sans Eros" in the interview echoes the move from the dyad to the social sphere in his philosophical work.

20. Levinas, *Totality and Infinity*, 278.

21. "The entirety of human existence, philosophical anthropology, endlessly paraphrases this abstract thought by insisting, with pathos, on finitude. In reality what is at issue is an order where the very notion of the Good first takes on meaning; what is at issue is society" (Levinas, *Totality and Infinity*, 103).

22. Levinas, *Totality and Infinity*, 280.

23. Sandford, "Masculine Mothers?" 197, referring to Levinas, *Totality and Infinity*, 215.

24. Critchley, *The Problem with Levinas*, 107.

25. See Allen, *The Philosophical Sense of Transcendence*, 10–11. Tanja Staehler comments, "In *Otherwise Than Being or Beyond Essence*, Eros plays no role anymore" (*Plato and Levinas*, 252n24).

26. On the comparison between the neighborly models in Rosenzweig and Levinas, see Martin Kavka:

> Undoubtedly, both Rosenzweig and Levinas are concerned with how humankind can engender the preconditions for eternal truth (in Rosenzweig) or messianic triumph (in Levinas) through love of neighbor. However, I will argue that Rosenzweig's nonembodied thinking of the neighbor causes a severe ethical problem and that the fourth section of *Totality and Infinity* (specifically the phenomenology of eros) and the analysis of sensibility in *Otherwise than Being* can be understood to serve as a corrective to the ethical danger that undergirds Rosenzweig's eschatology. For Rosenzweig sees the neighbor only as an alter ego . . . one can claim that in the system of the *Star*, the neighbor serves only as a means to the end of the praying chorus of the Jewish community. My love of neighbor has nothing to do with the neighbor him- or herself; I am simply interested in making the voice of my congregation louder" (*Jewish Messianism*, 133–4.)

27. The model of maternal embodiment will be discussed in more detail in chapter 5.

28. Sandford, "Masculine Mothers?" 197.

29. Levinas, *Otherwise Than Being*, 87; in the original, "Le prochain est frère. Fraternité irrécusable, assignation irrécusable, la proximité est une impossibilité de s'éloigner sans la torsion du complexe—sans 'aliénation' ou sans faute" (Levinas, *Autrement qu'être*, 138).

30. Sandford, "Masculine Mothers?" 197, referring to Levinas, *Totality and Infinity*, 215.

31. Sandford, "Masculine Mothers?" 197–8.

32. Sandford, 198–9.

33. Sandford, 198–9.

34. Rosenzweig, *Star*, 34.

35. Rosenzweig offers other analyses of Goethe in the *Star*. The introduction to part three includes discussions of Goethe's life and his relation to Christianity and to Nietzsche. In the *Star*, Rosenzweig outlines Goethe's limitations as a lack of eternal time: "temporality is not eternity. The purely temporally lived life of Goethe, the most alive of the children of men, was already in the pure temporality only a single moment, only an imitating one, dangerous to life. The temporal needs the support of the eternal" (Rosenzweig, *Star*, 306). For an assessment of Rosenzweig's admiration of Goethe, see Robert Gibbs, *Correlations in Rosenzweig and Levinas*, 126.

36. In *Faust*, Mephistopheles ominously hints that the realm of the Mothers can be reached by a twofold journey—one downward, to the hell of the pagans, and the other deep within the self: "MEPHISTOPHELES: These are higher mysteries./ I do so reluctantly./ Goddesses are enthroned in sublime solitude,/ Outside time,/ Outside space—/ Even to speak of them embarrasses me./ They are the Mothers! FAUST: (*Startled.*) The Mothers! MEPHISTOPHELES: What's that? Afraid? FAUST: The Mothers! The Mothers!/ It sounds so strange. MEPHISTOPHELES: And so it is./ Goddesses unknown to you mortals,/ And reluctantly named by us./ You'll need to dig deep to reach them./ It's your fault we're having to do this" (Johann Wolfgang von Goethe, *Faust: Part One and Two*, trans. Carl R. Mueller [Hanover, NH: Smith and Kraus, 2004], 255–6). For more on the mythical background to this scene, see Harold Jantz, *The Mothers in Faust: The Myth of Time and Creativity* (Baltimore, MD: Johns Hopkins University Press, 1969). Jantz argues that the realm of Mothers is central to the drama of *Faust* as a whole and should be read within this context: "The Mothers are not only an essential element in the dramatic action, they are also an indispensable link in a vital symbolic series" (37).

37. Amy Hill Shevitz, "Mother, Wife, and Lover: A Preliminary Study of the Three Women Who Most Influenced Rosenzweig's Philosophy of Love," *Franz Rosenzweig Congress, Gebot, Gesetz, Gebet: Love, Law, Life*, University of Toronto, September 3, 2012. I am grateful to Shevitz for sharing her paper with me. She discusses the symbolism of the realm of the mothers: "The Faust theme also appears in Rosenzweig's letters to his mother. . . . *The Star*'s linkage of the Mothers with the move from protocosmos to hypercosmos is deepened by Rosenzweig's theological commitment to the physical inheritance of Judaism. At the very least, biological Jewishness was [his mother's] gift to him."

38. Levinas, *Otherwise Than Being*, 175, citing *Faust* II, 6268–72: "Are you so narrow-minded? Only comfortable with what you've heard before?/ Whatever comes, whatever its sounds,/ let nothing disturb you./ You're well accustomed now to strange happenings. FAUST: What do you want of me,/ to turn to stone?/ That's not where my salvation lies./ Shuddering awe is the greatest part of Man" (Goethe, *Faust*, 258). For analyses of Levinas alongside Goethe, see Silvia Benso, "Missing the Encounter with the Other: Goethe's *Sufferings of Young Werther* in Light

of Levinas," in *In Proximity: Emmanuel Levinas and the Eighteenth Century*, ed. Melvyn New, Robert Bernasconi, and Richard A. Cohen, 197–214 (Lubbock: Texas Tech University Press, 2001); and Donald R. Wehrs, "Levinas, Goethe's *Wilhelm Meisters Lehrjahre*, and the Compulsion of the Good," in *In Proximity*, 215–42.

39. Levinas, *Otherwise Than Being*, 158; in the original, "Autrui est d'emblée le frère de tous les autres hommes" (*Autrement qu'être*, 246).

40. Levinas, *Otherwise Than Being*, 159. Note the original emphasis on community in the French: "La fraternité précède ici la communauté de genre" (*Autrement qu'être*, 247). The slippage between genre and gender is also more explicit in the original.

41. Levinas, *Otherwise Than Being*, 160.

42. Rosenzweig, *Der Stern der Erlösung* (Heidelberg: L. Schneider, 1954), 150.

43. Levinas, "*Philosophie, Justice et Amour*," 121.

44. John Davenport compares Levinas's ethics to agape, offering a critique of both; see "Levinas's Agapeistic Metaphysics of Morals: Absolute Passivity and the Other as Eschatological Hierophany," *The Journal of Religious Ethics* 26, no. 2 (fall 1998): 331–66. Katz maintains that Levinas's eros cannot be mapped onto Christian agape; see "Levinas Between Agape and Eros."

45. Benjamin, *The Obligated Self*, 30.

46. For a genderqueer reading of the relationship between David and Jonathan, see Yaron Peleg, "Love at First Sight? David, Jonathan, and the Biblical Politics of Gender," *Journal for the Study of the Old Testament* 30, no. 2 (2005): 171–89.

47. American philosopher Horace Kallen compared his friendship with the writer and philosopher Alain Locke to the model he saw represented in David and Jonathan. In a eulogy to Locke, Kallen wrote that he preferred "friendship" to the locution of "brothers":

> Men come and go but Man goes on forever, and it is in their eternal and universal Manhood that all men are brothers. That this brotherhood involves the blood rivalry of Cain and Abel perhaps much more commonly than the relationship between David and Jonathan seems not to affect this monist creed, nor the cliché regarding the fatherhood of God and the brotherhood of Man, which is one of its commoner expressions. A better word for what is intended by "brotherhood" is the word "friendship." For this word carries no implication of an identical beginning and common end that are to be attributed to the event that two persons or two peoples or a thousand peoples who are different from each other and must perforce live together with each other, seek such ways of togetherness as shall be ways of peace and freedom ("Alain Locke and Cultural Pluralism," *The Journal of Philosophy* 54, no. 5 [February 28, 1957]: 120).

I thank David Weinfeld for pointing out this reference to me.

48. Levinas, *Otherwise Than Being*, 159.

49. Derrida, *Politics of Friendship*, 7.

50. See Hunt-Hendrix, "The Ethics of Solidarity," 32–3: "The emphasis on similarity as a key factor in friendships raises questions about the extent to which diversity has a place in this modern scheme. . . . But if the friend is simply another self, what room is there for difference? Derrida argues that the impulse to claim the other as the self is colonizing . . . while this insinuation of fraternity and friendship has established a principle of cohesion, it is also a source of exclusion and domination."

51. Derrida, *Politics of Friendship*, 13.

52. La Boétie, *Slaves by Choice*, trans. Malcolm Smith (Egham: Runnymede Books, 1988), 48; quoted in Derrida, *Politics of Friendship*, 171.

53. Derrida, *Politics of Friendship*, 180, quoting Michel de Montaigne, *Essays*, trans. M. A. Screech and Allen Lane (London: Penguin Press, 1991).

54. Augustine, *The Literal Meaning of Genesis*, trans. John Hammond Taylor, S.J. Vol. II. (New York: Newman Press, 1982), 75.

55. Derrida, *Politics of Friendship*, 190n6.

56. Derrida, 180.

57. Derrida, 282, quoting Nietzsche, *Thus Spoke Zarathustra*, 87–8.

58. Derrida, *Politics of Friendship*, 283.

59. Derrida, 286.

60. Derrida, 164.

61. Of course, Derrida might respond that he purposefully focuses on the canonical (male) narratives of friendship to highlight their limitations. See *Politics of Friendship*, 229:

> We have not privileged the great discourses on friendship so as to submit to their authority or to confirm a hierarchy, but, on the contrary, as it were, to question the process and the logic of a canonization which has established these discourses in a position of exemplary authority. The history of friendship cannot be reduced to these discourses, still less to these *great* discourses of a *philosophical* genre. But precisely to begin the analysis of the forces and procedures that have placed the *majority* of these *major* discourses in the *major* position they have acquired, all the while covering over, reducing, or marginalizing the others, one must begin by paying attention to what they say and what they do.

Nevertheless, he ends up reproducing this very canon in his analysis.

62. Katja Garloff notes that Lessing and Mendellsohn "ultimately call for brotherly love as the appropriate affect between members of different religions" in their writings about religious toleration and Jewish emancipation (*Mixed Feelings*, 21–2). For more on the friendship of Lessing and Mendelssohn, which

began in the 1750s, see Leo Strauss, *Leo Strauss on Moses Mendelssohn*, ed. Martin
Yaffe (Chicago: University of Chicago Press, 2012); and Hannah Arendt, "The
Enlightenment and the Jewish Question," in *The Jewish Writings*, ed. Jerome
Kohn and Ron H. Feldman (New York: Schocken Books, 2007). Peter Svare
Valeur notes that Rosenzweig saw this relationship

> less as an opening for German–Jewish understanding than as the beginning
> of a fateful process of Jewish assimilation, a process whereby German
> Jews would forsake their own history, tradition and religious creed for an
> Enlightenment mantra of secularized reason. For Franz Rosenzweig, who
> himself entertained a highly complex intellectual relationship with the
> Catholic Eugen Rosenstock-Huessy, the friendship between Lessing and
> Mendelssohn was, as he put it, "too messianic" in its cult of humanism and
> tolerance, and he saw Lessing's *Nathan der Weise*, where that friendship was
> implicitly celebrated, as "anaemically" lacking in "das Blut der Gegenwart."
> For Rosenzweig and others of his generation, the eighteenth century
> ideology—under whose banner friendship, alongside other values such as
> secularization and the humanity of the "naked being" ranked as the highest
> political forces—had clearly outlived its rightful historical role ("Notes on
> Friendship: Moses Mendelssohn and Gotthold Ephraim Lessing," *Oxford
> German Studies* 45, no. 2 [2016], 142–43.)

63. Hannah Arendt, "On Humanity in Dark Times: Thoughts about Lessing,"
trans. Clara and Richard Winston, in *Men in Dark Times* (New York: Harcourt
Brace, 1993), 12–13.

64. Arendt, "On Humanity in Dark Times," 14.

65. Arendt, "On Humanity in Dark Times," 14. Liliane Weissberg comments,
"The 'brotherhood' that manifests itself in dark times—and manifests itself most
obviously among persecuted people—does and cannot hold; it does not orient
itself within the context of the political present, and indicates worldlessness"
("Humanity and Its Limits: Hannah Arendt Reads Lessing," in *Practicing
Progress: The Promise and Limitations of Enlightenment*, ed. Richard E. Schade and
Dieter Sevin [Amsterdam: Brill, 2007], 194.)

66. Arendt goes on to compare muteness with true dialogue: "pleasure and
pain, like everything instinctual, tend to muteness, and while they may well
produce sound, they do not produce speech and certainly not dialogue....
Gladness, not sadness, is talkative, and truly human dialogue differs from mere
talk or even discussion in that it is entirely permeated by pleasure in the other
person and what he says. It is tuned to the key of gladness, we might say" ("On
Humanity in Dark Times," 15–16). Avital Ronell comments, "Hannah had every
reason to scrap modulations of muteness from her registry, for she is mistrustful
of those who went silent in the night of need, retreating to the relative safety of

an 'inner emigration.' Thus, Germans who practiced some form of muteness, barely squeaking out protest, fell short of the creditable bar. . . . Dialogue tutors political practicability; it's the way of showing that you count yourself in. Too many contemporaries faded out and ducked into muted refuge" ("Hannah Arendt Swallows the Lessing-Prize," *MLN* 131, no. 5 [December 2016]: 1165).

67. Arendt, "On Humanity in Dark Times," 16.

68. Arendt, 17.

69. Arendt, 17–8.

70. Lisa J. Disch, "On Friendship in 'Dark Times,'" in *Feminist Interpretations of Hannah Arendt*, ed. Bonnie Honig (University Park: Pennsylvania State University Press, 1995), 286.

71. Disch, "On Friendship in 'Dark Times,'" 289–91.

72. Arendt, "On Humanity in Dark Times," 25. Weissberg provides further context to this passage: "A term like 'brotherhood' was popular during the time of the Enlightenment and gained significance for the French Revolution, but during the Third Reich, it would have seemed to be vacuous and dangerous, too. A philosopher such as Jean-Jacques Rousseau would still propagate a general 'brotherhood,' but it is Lessing's achievement to go beyond it. A critic such as Lessing searches not for brotherhood but for critical friendship, one that is rooted in the Here and Now" ("Humanity and Its Limits," 194).

73. Arendt, "On Humanity in Dark Times," 29.

74. Arendt, 30. See Weissberg:

> To be no brother, but a friend—so Arendt views Lessing's own ambitions, and the goal of his critique. His criticism helped establish a public sphere that allowed for plurality, for many different individual voices. But in drawing a picture of Lessing's exceptional position, Arendt also writes a scathing critique of Enlightenment thought that finally separates Lessing from Kant. . . . The Enlightenment itself turns out to be a dark time. . . . There is no doubt that the Hamburg prize committee had thought of the Enlightenment in different terms. Did it not invite a German Jewish thinker to return to Germany so that the spirit of the Enlightenment could be confirmed there once again? ("Humanity and Its Limits," 195).

75. Arendt, "On Humanity in Dark Times," 30.

76. Disch, "On Friendship in 'Dark Times,'" 304; "Just what does Arendt mean by friendship in this context? She does not mean to recommend a relationship based in the humanist ideal of respect for man in the abstract. But neither does she mean to recommend a communitarian vision of brotherhood. Both would deny plurality, the first by grounding itself in an abstract universalist sameness, and the second by depending upon a compassion that destroys the space that is the very condition of plurality. Instead, Arendt moves to the inter-est, or 'between them,' to sustain the kind of friendship she has in mind" (304).

77. Michel Foucault, "Friendship as a Way of Life," in *Ethics: Subjectivity and Truth*, ed. Paul Rabinow, trans. Robert Hurley (New York: New Press, 1997), 136; cited in Ashon T. Crawley, *The Lonely Letters* (Durham, NC: Duke University Press, 2020), 29.

78. Crawley, *The Lonely Letters*, 29.

79. Crawley, 30.

80. Crawley, 28–9.

81. See Crawley:

> The overrepresentation of Man is because this particular kind of human, this genre of human, is represented as the only way to be human and also the normative way to practice humanity. If one does not think, dress, eat, behave, relate to others in ways that this particular kind of raced, gendered, classed human does, one is not human at all according to this particular logic of what it means to be human and be Man. What is the normative race, gender, and class? In the sixteenth, seventeenth, and eighteenth centuries, it was (and still is today) white, landed gentry, which is to say, cisgender men that owned property, who claim whiteness as property. This owning of property in the so-called New World would necessitate the violence of genocidal practices, called colonization, that is still ongoing (*The Lonely Letters*, 28; referring to Sylvia Wynter, "Unsettling the Coloniality of Being/Power/Truth/Freedom: Towards the Human, After Man, Its Overrepresentation—An Argument," *CR: The New Centennial Review* 3, no. 3 [2003]: 257–337).

82. See Disch: "Arendt's refusal to acknowledge the public relevance of her womanhood is no model for feminist subjectivity. . . . such a refusal is nothing less than an affirmation of the class, ethnic, and heterosexual privileges with which gender is complicit. By contrast, Arendt's 'vigilant partisanship' toward the 'political fact' of her Jewish identity in the Lessing address suggests a strategy for negotiating the 'slippery ambiguities' of confirming one's identity as a woman, without also claiming either an authentic or abstract universal standpoint on womanhood" ("On Friendship in 'Dark Times,'" 305).

83. Derrida, *Politics of Friendship*, 165.

84. Arendt, "On Humanity in Dark Times," 25.

85. Weissberg, "Humanity and Its Limits," 195.

86. Garloff, *Mixed Feelings*, 24.

87. Garloff, 35. See Gillian Rose:

> "Fraternity," captured by Lessing's play *Nathan the Wise*, 1769, ostensibly a paean of praise to the brotherhood of man, is seen to imply evasions which cannot be contained even though—or precisely because—fraternity is figured between brother and sister, man and woman. At the end of the play, Recha, adopted daughter of the wise Jew Nathan, and the Christian Knight

Templar renounce their great passion for each other on coming to learn that they are brother and sister, and in turn closely related to the Muslim Sultan. The play celebrates the transformation of erotic love into love of humanity in spite of the evident reluctance of the lovers to participate in this transformation. The apparently smooth resolution of the play simply moves the guiding taboo from miscegenation to incest in a way which is most unconvincing, for it unveils "fraternity" as sacrifice and loss shored up by prohibition and intrinsically unstable (*The Broken Middle: Out of Our Ancient Society* [Oxford, UK: Blackwell, 1992], 186–87).

88. Garloff, 37.

89. Garloff, 44.

90. Franz Rosenzweig, "Lessing's Nathan," in *Cultural Writings of Franz Rosenzweig*, ed. and trans. Barbara E. Galli (Syracuse, NY: Syracuse University Press, 2000), 106.

91. Rosenzweig, "Lessing's Nathan," 108.

92. Rosenzweig, 111. See Garloff: "Franz Rosenzweig once deplored the lack of children at the end of *Nathan the Wise*, which he read as a sign of the 'bloodlessness' of the idea of emancipation" (*Mixed Feelings*, 32). Leora Batnitzky notes that Rosenzweig was critical of Lessing's "generic universalism" ("Foreword," in *Cultural Writings of Franz Rosenzweig*, xvii–xviii).

93. "Levinas's reading and use of the feminine seems clearly rooted in Jewish texts, and his view of love and the erotic also appears to have a Jewish orientation, even if one allows that there is no such thing as one Jewish orientation but multiple views. . . . At the very least, Levinas's use of the feminine is provocative. It asks us to consider how women, and the feminine, have been portrayed historically in the philosophical canon. In what ways has Levinas, in spite of his insistence to offer a new view of subjectivity, reinscribed a traditional view of women in the service of that project?" (Katz, *An Introduction to Modern Jewish Philosophy*, 132–3).

94. Katz, *An Introduction to Modern Jewish Philosophy*, 109–10. See also Katz, "Philosophy, the Academy, and the Future of Jewish Learning," 157.

95. Batnitzky, "Dependency and Vulnerability," 144.

96. Batnitzky, 145.

97. For a helpful definition of intersectionality, see Patricia Hill Collins and Sirma Bilge:

Intersectionality is a way of understanding and analyzing the complexity in the world, in people, and in human experiences. The events and conditions of social and political life and the self can seldom be understood as shaped by one factor. They are generally shaped by many factors in diverse and mutually influencing ways. When it comes to social inequality, people's lives and the organization of power in a given society are better understood as being shaped not by a single axis of social division, be it race or gender or class, but by many axes that work together and influence each other. Intersectionality as an analytic tool gives people better access to the complexity of the world and of themselves. (*Intersectionality*, 2)

Critical legal scholar Kimberlé Crenshaw coined the term *intersectionality* in "Demarginalizing the Intersection of Race and Sex: A Black Feminist Critique of Antidiscrimination Doctrine, Feminist Theory and Antiracist Politics," *University of Chicago Legal Forum* (1989): 139–67.

98. Imhoff, *Masculinity and the Making of American Judaism*, 5: "scholars who work with the theory of intersectionality have emphasized race, class, gender, and ability as co-constitutive social processes of identification, but rarely include religion."

99. Brettschneider, *Jewish Feminism and Intersectionality*, 146.

100. Brettschneider, 10.

101. Crawley, *The Lonely Letters*, 29.

102. Crawley, 28.

103. Imhoff, *Masculinity and the Making of American Judaism*, 20.

FOUR

—ᛉ—

SCANDALOUS SIBLINGS

IN THE FIRST CHAPTER, I read Rosenzweig's interpretation of the Song of Songs through his focus on fraternity. This chapter revisits Rosenzweig's preoccupation with the brother-sister relationship in his life, letters, and thought, considering what is at stake when we read for biography in a philosophical work. His exegesis of the Song in the *Star* especially calls for this kind of comparative reading, because it was written via letters to Margrit Rosenstock-Huessy, whom he called his "sister-bride"—a term lifted from the Song. These letters, and what other biographical traces reveal about his relationships with "Gritli," her husband, Eugen, and Rosenzweig's own wife, Edith, raise complex questions about the ethical tensions arising from attempts to resolve the seemingly competing claims of blood ties and erotic desire in "siblinghood." If marriage in the *Star* was "more than love,"[1] then his real-life marriage was also, perhaps, less than the bond he felt with his intellectual and emotional kin. In this chapter, I examine the scandal of the biographical trace in philosophical writing, the regulations of kinship in both life and thought, and the tension between erotic love and family obligations.

Cultural critics of the period immediately preceding Rosenzweig's composition of the *Star* have observed that in a number of spheres, the brother-sister relationship was a cultural touchstone. To help examine the meaning and symbolism of this sibling relationship for Rosenzweig, I turn first to Hegel's famous celebration of Sophocles's *Antigone*. The brother-sister relationship was a focal point for Romantic rhetoric of the late eighteenth and nineteenth centuries, animating the works of Musil, Wordsworth, Shelley, Hegel, Byron, and Wagner, and Antigone incarnated ideal sisterhood for this tradition.[2] Perhaps unsurprisingly, the focus on ideal brother-sister relationships also led to a fixation on brother-sister incest in the long nineteenth century. The Freudian Oedipal paradigm later intervened, replacing the horizontal lines of radical kinship with an inescapable vertical construct, and so Antigone was replaced by Oedipus.[3] In my view, however, we can better understand Rosenzweig's idealization of the brother-sister relationship in both his philosophical work and his life if we look back to the reception history of *Antigone*, which became the urtext of the brother-sister relationship following Hegel, who obsessively returned to Antigone—specifically, her relationship to her brother, Polyneices.

Hegel and Rosenzweig both focused on an ancient poetic source to illustrate their philosophical emphasis on the brother-sister relationship. I find the two thinkers' interpretations both idiosyncratic and illuminating of their own preoccupations. While they chose texts on sibling relationships with expansive dynamics, they each ultimately subsumed the sister into a fraternal relation. As a result, some responses to Hegel's philosophy of kinship and gender difference can be fruitfully applied to Rosenzweig's ideas on love, eros, and marriage as they played out in both his thought and, in related ways, his own life. Inspired by Derrida's reading of Hegel alongside his letters to loved ones, this chapter's second section investigates the biographical circumstances surrounding Rosenzweig's writing of *The Star of Redemption*. I argue that Rosenzweig's text and its production history mutually illuminate each other when it comes to the troubling gender dynamics that subsume the sister-wife in both philosophy and life.

KINSHIP AND DESIRE IN HEGEL'S *ANTIGONE*

The *Star*'s focus on the brother-sister relationship in the Song of Songs echoes Hegel's valorization of this particular family bond, perhaps unsurprisingly, since Rosenzweig was a Hegel scholar—making an extended consideration of Hegel's reading useful for understanding Rosenzweig's context and concerns.[4] Hegel discusses the unique connection of brothers and sisters in his *Phenomenology of Spirit*. In his view, the family relationships of husband and wife, children and parents are limited by the disparities and inequalities inherent to their dynamics; wives are unequal to their husbands, and children are unequal to their parents.[5] But the relationship between brothers and sisters "in its unmixed form" stands out: "They are the same blood which has in them reached a state of rest and equilibrium. Therefore, they do not desire one another, nor have they given to, or received from, one another this independent being-for-self; on the contrary, they are free individualities in regard to each other."[6]

In Hegel's reading, the relationship of the brother and sister is an ideal bond of "identity-in-difference" that cannot be found in other relationships.[7] The brother-sister relation is universal, transcending particularity and ethical contingency. In other family relationships, the woman does not know her own "being-for-self" in the other partner.[8] "The brother, however, is for the sister a passive, similar being in general; the recognition of herself in him is pure and unmixed with any natural desire."[9] The daughter feels great emotion when her parents pass away but can achieve self-actualization only once this occurs. She likewise has affection for her husband and children, but "as mother and wife there is something natural and replaceable about her"; because she is not equal to her husband, having "duties where he mainly has pleasures," she cannot gain self-recognition in her relationship with him.[10] Rather, Hegel writes, "in brother and sister there are none of the inequalities due to desire nor any possibility of replacement: the loss of a brother is irreparable to a sister, and her duty to him is the highest."[11] Hegel invokes Sophocles's *Antigone* in his references to human and divine law, man and woman, and the family's role in death and burial.[12] He refers to the play's protagonist, who claims that the only irreplaceable family relationship she has is with her brother.

Here, a brief summary of the play's kinship dynamics will be useful for understanding how Hegel interprets them. Antigone's genealogy is fraught. In the play's opening lines, Antigone refers to "all the evils that stem from Oedipus," her father, that have plagued the lives of herself and her unfortunate siblings.[13] The protagonist's sister, Ismene, recounts the tale of the sisters' cursed origins: their parents, Jocasta and Oedipus, were mother and son, and their brothers killed one another, "by their hands dealing mutual death."[14] The offspring of this tragic coupling are doomed due to their unnatural origins.[15] Polyneices fought against his city, bringing enemies to attack it, and his brother, Eteocles, defended it. After they killed one another, their uncle Creon, Jocasta's brother, took power and brought peace to the city. At the play's opening he gives burial rights to the honorable brother, Eteocles, but denies them to the traitor Polyneices, in punishment for his attempts to harm the city and its inhabitants. Creon sentences Antigone to death for carrying out the burial rites. The family bonds in this narrative are continually perverted and broken; Oedipus unknowingly kills his father, Laius, and marries his mother, then their two sons go on to kill one another. Ultimately Jocasta's brother leaves his nephew's body to rot and condemns his niece, Antigone, to death.

Hegel refers to *Antigone* in both *Philosophy of Right* and *Aesthetics*. In the former, he introduces a note on the play during a discussion of the differences between the sexes, locating the husband in the political sphere and the wife in the domestic sphere of familial piety: "Hence Piety is in the 'Antigone' of Sophocles most superbly presented as the law of the woman, the law of the nature, which realizes itself subjectively and intuitively, the law of an inner life, which has not yet attained complete realization, the law of the ancient gods, and of the under-world, the eternal law, of whose origin no one knows, in opposition to the public law of the state. This opposition is in the highest sense ethical, and hence also tragic; it is individualized in the opposing natures of man and woman."[16] In the ensuing discussion, he goes on to enumerate the ways women differ from men: in education, character, and ability. He summarizes his argument in a statement that the man is like the animal and the woman like the plant, more inclined to nature than government.[17]

Hegel uses his reading of the play to describe the woman as the unique site of familial ethical responsibility in his philosophical system.[18] Slavoj Žižek notes that Hegel oddly slides from praising Antigone in particular to critically appraising womanhood in general.[19] The only discussion of woman in the *Philosophy of Right*, as in the *Phenomenology*, comes within the context of the ethical life of the family.[20] Nevertheless, Patricia Jagentowicz Mills points out, Hegel scholars generally ignore the "woman question" and thus miss the critical significance of woman's role, "which not only limits woman but limits Hegel's philosophy."[21] Seyla Benhabib takes this further, arguing that Hegel relegates women's place to the family despite living in a revolutionary time in which he encountered accomplished and nonconformist women in his social circle. This viewpoint extended to his reading of the play: "Hegel's Antigone is one without a future; her tragedy is also the grave of utopian, revolutionary thinking about gender relations. Hegel, it turns out, is women's gravedigger."[22] For Hegel, Antigone evidently represents one of two competing ethical systems: the divine law of the family, rather than the human law of the state. This pairing has effects beyond the family. Stefani Engelstein notes that "the free and nonerotic recognition between brother-sister pairs provides a bridge to the political sphere."[23] But the same gender asymmetry "that allows this mirroring to reinforce subjectivity rather than collapsing" restricts the sister to the role of bridge, enabling only the brother to cross into the greater political realm.[24]

In his *Aesthetics*, Hegel pits the play's two protagonists, Antigone and Creon, against one another, demonstrating that they both commit wrongs and suffer consequent losses. Because Antigone has royal lineage and, moreover, is about to be married to the sovereign's son, she should obey any royal decree. Creon, for his part, "should have respected the sacred tie of blood and not ordered anything against its pious observance. So there is immanent in both Antigone and Creon something that in their own way they attack, so that they are gripped and shattered by something intrinsic to their own actual being."[25] Antigone dies before becoming a bride, but Creon is punished for committing her to death by the suicides of his son and his wife that result from it.

Hegel contends that this play knows no peer in its genre: "Of all the masterpieces of the classical and the modern world—and I know nearly all of them and you should and can—the *Antigone* seems to me to be the most magnificent and satisfying work of art of this kind."[26] Hegel elevates *Antigone* as the best portrayal within the specific genre of tragic conflict because both parties, Antigone and Creon, have no choice but to transgress equally valid laws in both instances.[27] In this sense, Hegel valorizes the play because the two main figures have competing claims that the audience can see are both right and wrong. Neither choice is unequivocally correct, for both have disastrous consequences. The tragic nature of this play stems from a conflict between two competing values, whether understood as familial or civic, religious or political, with the woman representing the familial/religious sphere and the man representing the state. Ultimately, Creon regrets his actions, but the play would not be as tragic if his had been an easy or obvious choice to make.[28] Creon and Antigone are arguing in entirely different terms, with no middle ground on which to meet. Antigone states that the gods demand burial rights for both brothers, but Creon maintains that the just and evil man cannot have an equal share or treatment. The play's dramatic engine is the impossibility of adjudicating between them. In the world beyond, her piety constitutes the true virtue, even if she is being impious to Creon's laws on earth.[29] The essence of this tragedy, and of its appeal to Hegel, is this impossibility.

In the play, Creon has been breaking the law of the gods by leaving Polyneices outside when he is meant to be in the earth, and by committing Antigone to be buried when she should remain aboveground. He has not respected the laws of the living and the laws of the dead but has confused them. Antigone's efforts to bury her brother in the public realm further muddle the rigid social structures that exclude mourning from the public sphere, containing it within the proper site of female domesticity. Funeral rites were meant to be confined to the household realm of womanhood in ancient Greek society, and thus mourning conducted publicly interjects the feminine into the masculine space of the polis.[30] As women, Antigone and Ismene have a very limited sense of power in the religious sphere once Creon has edged his way into it. The chorus acknowledges this new divide: "in our new contingencies with the gods, he is our new ruler."[31] The women represent the ancient religious obligation to bury the dead, which is pitted against a newer idea of civic responsibility, personified by Creon.

Hegel's exclamation on the excellence of the play is strange, because he is fixated on the figure of a woman who is "inadmissible" in his system.[32] Antigone is both exemplary of and excluded from the ethical system he espouses. For Hegel, Antigone is the bearer and defender of familial ethics. She faces off against Creon, who upholds the universal law of the state. But Antigone, because she is representative of womanhood, is simultaneously the "eternal enemy" and "everlasting irony" in the life of the community, external to the life of the polis.[33]

In *Glas*, a side-by-side reading of both Hegel and the writer Jean Genet,[34] Derrida identifies the aspect of the brother-sister relationship that so intrigues Hegel in his work—the focal point of desire or, more importantly, the lack thereof. Derrida writes that for Hegel, the brother-sister relationship raises itself hierarchically above the relations of husband and wife, parent and child, "by appeasing, verily by annulling strictly sexual desire."[35] In the play, Antigone regrets that her only marriage will be to Hades, and she calls her tomb her "bridal chamber."[36] Antigone never becomes wife or mother, which makes her ideal for Hegel's purposes.[37] Derrida notes that Hegel's analysis "is fascinated by the essential figure of this sister who never becomes citizen, or wife, or mother. Dead before being able to get married, she fixes, grasps, transfixes, transfigures herself in this character of eternal sister taking away with her her womanly, wifely desire."[38]

Judith Butler explains that Hegel's criteria for recognition and its possibilities for kinship are based on a required absence of desire:

> Hegel does not tell us why, precisely, the ostensible lack of desire between
> brother and sister qualifies them for recognition within the terms of
> kinship, but his view implies that incest would constitute the impossibility
> of recognition, that the very scheme of cultural intelligibility, of *Sittlichkeit*,
> of the sphere in which reciprocal recognition is possible, presupposes the
> prepolitical stability of kinship. Implicitly, Hegel appears to understand
> that the prohibition against incest supports kinship, but this is not what
> he explicitly says. He claims, rather, that the "blood" relation makes desire
> impossible between sister and brother, and so it is the blood that stabilizes
> kinship and its internal dynamics of recognition. Thus Antigone does not
> desire her brother, according to Hegel, and so the *Phenomenology* becomes
> the textual instrument of the prohibition against incest, effecting what it
> cannot name, what it subsequently misnames through the figure of blood.[39]

According to Hegel, outside of her relationship with her brother, Antigone is incapable of acquiring recognition within the ethical order. It is the relationship with Polyneices that allows her to give and receive recognition, and she can have recognition with her brother only as long as no desire exists between them.

Derrida asks if Hegel has mistakenly "transformed into structural and para-digmatic legality" one particular family situation illustrated in one particular drama.[40] Hegel has structured his concept of the family on Antigone—a very suspect model who, it must be remembered, is a product of incestuous relations. Hegel never refers to the generation that precedes Antigone, "as if it were foreign to the elementary structures of kinship," rather than a structure of the unconscious.[41]

It is deeply ironic that Hegel should choose a story whose genealogy is based on the fundamental perversion and confusion of kinship (in the actions of Oedipus and Jocasta) as the paradigmatic text of proper kinship relations. A daughter born of a mother who is also her grandmother is for Hegel the ethical subject par excellence. Only in relating to her dead brother, whom she never desired (because incest is foreign to Greek drama?!), can she gain recogni-tion and enter the ethical realm. Or perhaps because their biological legacy is so tragic and muddled, they would be the most likely to avoid interfamilial desire at all costs, because they, more than most, have seen the miseries it can bring to each successive generation. In any case, Hegel has built his model for non-incestuous kinship on (for psychoanalytic purposes, at least) the urtext of incestuous relationships.

When Hegel refers to the brother's irreplaceability for the sister, he explicitly refers to the protagonist's words. On the way to her entombment, Antigone explains why she has gone against the will of the state to bury her brother: "If my husband were dead, I might have had another, and child from another man, if I lost the first. But when father and mother both were hidden in death, no brother's life would bloom for me again."[42] Hegel's observation that the brother is irreplaceable to the sister works in the specific empirical case of Antigone, whose parents have indeed already passed. But how does this condition trans-late to universal situations?

Many readers of the play find this speech peculiar. Commentators from Goethe to Jacques Lacan have been perplexed by Antigone's ranking of her brother over a possible future husband or child.[43] Antigone's words are viewed as scandalous because she elevates her mother's natal family over her (still hypothetical) conjugal family. But when readers like Hegel make the mistake of extending Antigone's argument to apply to all brothers and sisters, observes Mary Beth Mader, they forget that the play itself treats Antigone's family re-lationships as singularly aberrant. It makes no sense to take an aberrant rela-tionship as exemplary of universal relations. In the speech where she says her brother is irreplaceable, she cannot be offering a generally recommendable rationale for her actions, because by the play's own standards, the nature of her family is exceptional and monstrous. It is the source of her suffering.

Even more than that, though, Antigone's speech has to be read within the particular case of her family, because in this statement she is attempting to right the wrongs inaugurated by her parents' incestuous union. Antigone is "sister, aunt, and niece to Polyneices," and by insisting on performing burial rites for her brother *as* her brother (and not as all the other kinship relations he is to her as well), she "attempts to bring a lost generational order back to the family."[44] She makes this speech to claim him as her brother, not her nephew or uncle (which he also is).[45] "Her insistence on her parents being the unique source of a brother is obviously significant in her task to efface the family crime."[46] Within the kinship order that both Antigone and the play take to be normative, she *should* not procure a sibling for herself, even though she *could*, if her father were still alive. Antigone aims to "undouble her overwritten kin," and that is the reason her brother *as* brother must be ranked over husband and child in the particular and unique case of *this* family.[47]

Engelstein reads the specter of incest in the play's reception as evidence of what readers were and were not willing to see. The play was the most pervasive literary touchstone of the nineteenth century, a narrative framed around a "consummate sister who, for the sake of burying her brother Polyneices, would consummate nothing else."[48] In the twentieth century, the play became a theoretical touchstone but focused more on Antigone's relationship to Creon and the state, eliding her relationship to her siblings. "In particular, the incestuous passion of Ismene for Antigone, which echoes that of Antigone for Polyneices, has been obscured by presuppositions about gender and sexuality."[49] Societal assumptions and prohibitions on incest work to instill norms of heterosexuality, and Mader suggests that the focus on one potentially incestuous relationship over another tells us more about the reader's assumptions of sexual normativity than about the play's actual framing of these relationships. The commentators who class the brother-sister love as incestuous instead of other potential sites of incest in the play "may simply express a preponderant anxiety about specifically heterosexual incest or perhaps reproductive incest. Of course, in some cases, this preponderance may actually be an incapacity to suspect incestuous potential in such relationships for the reason that same-sex relations have not registered as potentially amorous or erotic at all."[50] The choice to view desire or its absence in a particular relationship speaks to the reader's ability to *see* certain relationships as viable in the first place.

Similarly, Butler notes that multiple "blindnesses" afflict both the text of the play and its proliferating interpretations, beginning with Hegel's reading.[51] These readings cast the play's protagonists, Antigone and Creon, in an oppositional encounter between the forces of kinship and state power, dynamics that are entrenched within a logic of gender opposition. As Butler points out, such interpretations do not see the fluid boundaries of gender appropriation at work in the narrative. Hegel fails to see the expansiveness in the character of Antigone, in the category of "woman" that he rigidly delimits, and in the role of the sister.

Efforts to read the play as a conflict between sharply delineated male and female characters ignore how the play challenges gender norms. Antigone takes on Creon's "masculine" language and power in her actions, and Creon himself says Antigone poses a grave threat to him by "unmanning" him: "I swear I am no man and she the man if she can win this and not pay for it."[52] What would happen if Antigone were to become "the man"? Claims to gender are at stake here, and they are literally a matter of life and death.[53] There are other instances in which Creon sets the play up as a wrestling match between woman and man, demonstrating that the play's entire action threatens this divide.[54] Creon finds fault with his son Haemon for taking on "womanly" characteristics: "It seems this boy is on the woman's side. . . . Your nature is vile, in yielding to a woman. . . . You woman's slave."[55] The play is continually unsettled by women who act like "men" and by men who act like "women."

Creon, and the play itself, is able to find resolution only with the arrival of the blind prophet Tiresias, who is ultimately able to change Creon's mind, even if it is too late. Creon laments, "The mistakes of a blinded man are themselves rigid and laden with death. . . . Oh, the awful blindness of those plans of mine."[56] The prophet also embodies two other sets of opposites that can seemingly never be resolved: male and female. Sophocles's audience would have known the backstory to this liminal figure: while walking one day, Tiresias saw two snakes enjoined and proceeded to strike them with a staff. Tiresias was then metamorphosed into a woman; coming upon the snakes again years later, Tiresias repeated this act of striking them and was turned back into a man.[57] Tiresias thus represents mediation itself—between blindness and sight, between male and female.[58] Only one who has been both sexes can address the issue of conflict in this play, representing the embodiment and melding of the two opposites. It should be noted, however, that Tiresias turns up to fix the problems of the play as a man. Tiresias has taken on a woman's body in the past but in both original and final states is ultimately, and significantly, embodied as male.[59]

It may be the play's commentary on the nature of gender roles that Hegel seeks to amplify. According to Molly Farneth, Hegel reads these scenes as a lesson on the construction and maintenance of social norms. He wants to show that norms and laws are not fixed nor given, as Antigone and Creon mistakenly think, but rather must be worked out in communities. Hegel seeks to offer an account of how ethical conflicts emerged in the specific sociopolitical conditions of ancient Greece and how they might be confronted and overcome. In Farneth's analysis, Hegel is not presenting his own views. It is thus not Hegel who identifies Antigone as a woman who is limited to the spheres of human kinship and divine law but the Greek ethical system, which then ignores her complex genealogy and role as a social and political agent.[60] Butler asks why Hegel dismisses the possibility of sexual desire between brothers and sisters using the case of Antigone as a prime example, since she is the product of an incestuous relationship. Farneth thinks Butler's reading misses the point; it is not Hegel but the Greek sphere of ethical life (*Sittlichkeit*) that ignores Antigone's particularity. Hegel finds in Greek tragedy the paradigmatic example of Greek *Sittlichkeit*'s inconsistencies and inadequacies.

When Butler accuses Hegel of gender essentialism, according to Farneth, she is confusing Hegel's description of a system that is organized around strictly divided gender roles with an endorsement of that system. "Hegel shows that identities and obligations must not be taken as fixed and given—or generalized and transhistorical—and that ethical conflict can only be overcome in a community that acknowledges gender and other identities as normative commitments, open to revision."[61] When socially constructed norms, including gender norms, are taken to be natural and shielded from critique, the outcome is disastrous. Antigone's and Creon's fates are tragic because they see their identities and responsibilities as fixed. Woman is then not the "internal enemy" for Hegel himself but for a system he is implicitly criticizing. Farneth views Hegel's reading of the play as "amenable to the development of a feminist ethics"[62] while acknowledging that he himself was not a feminist: "Despite his criticism of the naturalization of gender roles in the *Phenomenology of Spirit*, he expresses patriarchal and misogynistic views elsewhere in his work."[63] Nevertheless, Farneth maintains that Hegel, in his reading of *Antigone*, offers a critique of norms, including gender norms, that have been taken to be natural and given.

I find Farneth's explanation largely convincing. I wonder, though, if she gives Hegel too much credit as a clear-eyed reader of *Antigone*. To my mind, Hegel misses certain dimensions in the play, and in this regard I agree with Mader, who argues that his reading "imposes much too readily on the play Hegel's own assumptions about family relations, gender roles, and customs pertaining to death."[64] Of course, Farneth is not claiming that Hegel is an ideal reader but rather that we should understand his claims from the perspective of his argument about Greek social and ethical life.

It can be equally helpful to see what Hegel does not see in the play, or refuses to see. Hegel's reading of *Antigone* centers on the mutual recognition crystallized in the brother-sister relationship. But in *Antigone,* other sibling relationships are central to the play as well; after all, the conflict between same-sex siblings frames the play's narrative—between the brothers who have destroyed one another in battle, and between their surviving sisters, Antigone and Ismene, whose burdened dialogue opens the play.[65] In the troubled and bloody genealogy of *Antigone,* brothers are both rivals and doubles, dealing mutual death blows.[66] The fraternal strife occurs offstage, setting up the sequence of events even as it stands outside them. But the play opens with another set of doubles, as the two sisters, Antigone and Ismene, meet in front of the palace gates in Thebes. Notably, the immediate action is initiated not with the brothers at war but with the two sisters in conversation.

Neither of these sets of relationships, these doublings, interests Hegel as much as the relationship between Antigone and Polyneices, the brother whose body is left to rot by the sovereign. What about the two sisters whose words open the play?[67] One can perhaps assume why Hegel would overlook sisterly relationships in his discussion of the family in the *Phenomenology,* given his meager views on womanhood, but why not consider the fraternal relation? After all, both same-sex sibling relationships are central to the play, driving the drama forward. Perhaps Hegel seeks to focus on Antigone and Polyneices because they represent the only untroubled sibling relationship in the play; the brothers are fratricidal, and the sisters cannot seem to get along or come to any agreement, but the titular sister is willing to die to support her dead brother's honor. Hegel praises Antigone for prioritizing her role as a sister and ethical agent over concerns of physical welfare or obedience to the state. But the latter are seemingly rational goals, which are upheld and articulated by her sister, Ismene. Antigone is entirely aware that in doing her sisterly duties, she places her own life in peril.[68]

The best relationship for Hegel must be between brother and sister, and not between same-sex brothers or sisters, because, as Derrida observes, "in truth a sexual difference is still necessary, a sexual difference posited as such and yet without desire."[69] Hegel, as have so many other readers, misses the sister relationship in the play in favor of focusing on the brother and sister. To help explain this interpretive phenomenon, George Steiner locates the theme of sorority at the center of Romantic rhetoric of the late eighteenth and nineteenth centuries. Because many biographies and fictions from this period are pervaded by themes of incest, "the exaltation of sisterliness has been seen in this pathological perspective."[70] So since accounts of sisters were so often about incest, they were pathologized. While Steiner gives an influential account of nineteenth-century views of sisterliness, in all the examples he gives, from

Hegel to Byron, the relation is described from the brother's perspective. So it is no surprise that this relationship colors how these Romantic readers, and Steiner himself, understand the play. It is striking that in all these accounts of the supposed relation of sisterliness, there are no examples of sisters in relation to one another.

The play begins when "Antigone rejects Ismene's offer of sisterly solidarity."[71] Hegel totally overlooks this central relationship. While it is true that Antigone valorizes her commitment to her brother, Ismene's primary attachment is to her sister. By abandoning her living sister in favor of her dead brother, Antigone serves the fraternal economy that ties woman "to the particularity of the body and blood relationship" and keeps her from the political realm.[72] According to Mary C. Rawlinson, feminist political readings that characterize Antigone as a heroic ideal fail to appreciate how "Antigone's action turns away from life and sisterly solidarity in favor of fraternity and its assignment of women to the care of the [dead] body."[73]

Bonnie Honig takes this one step further. In *Antigone, Interrupted*, Honig maps the play's complex theoretical and philosophical reception history, ever since Hegel canonized the play in the early nineteenth century. Honig seeks to stage a dramaturgical interruption of the play's reception for new political and feminist interpretative possibilities. "Perhaps no element of Antigone's reception history is more settled than the belief that Antigone's sister, Ismene, is an anti-political character who lacks the courage or imagination to act when called upon to do so."[74] Like Rawlinson, Honig turns to the forgotten Ismene and her focus on survival. But while Rawlinson rehabilitates Ismene by elevating her this-worldly orientation over her sister's sacrificial desire, Honig sees the sisters operating not in conflict with one another but in sororal solidarity.[75] Honig argues that Sophocles's readers and spectators, from Hegel to Lacan and Butler, have failed to detect this central dimension, overlooking an Antigone who is equally committed to her sister and therefore equally committed to life, not just to death. While most critics view Antigone as disdainful of her sister, Honig reveals the "sororal collusion at the play's center" and Antigone's loyalty to the last living member of her immediate family.[76] Antigone dies not only for her dead brother but for her living sister.[77] Antigone's motivation becomes the desire to protect Ismene from Creon's wrath. In performing "a sororal enmity that is as false as it is convincing to Creon, Antigone saves her sister's life and leaves alive a remnant of the natal family."[78] In this account of sororal power, "It matters that there are two of them, not just one, for as they act in agonistic concert they hint at an alternative politics, and an alternative to Hegel's dialectic."[79]

LIFE, LOVE, AND LETTERS

In Irigaray's view, Hegel's reading "is already the effect of a dialectic produced by the discourse of patriarchy."[80] For Hegel, "Woman is the guardian of the blood," and Irigaray reads the circulatory logic of Hegel's *Antigone* in the imagery of liquid, clots, and fluid. Blood figures prominently in the readings of both Hegel and Rosenzweig on the brother-sister relationship, but it is at work in differing ways. For Hegel, shared blood serves to ensure the precondition for recognition between brother and sister—that is, the absolute suspension of desire, allowing for reciprocal engagement and self-actualization. In *Philosophy of Right*, Hegel expands on the criteria for marriage within society: it must be monogamous, and it must take place between "families that are unconnected, and between persons who are distinct in their origin. Between persons related by blood, therefore, marriage is contrary to the conception of it. . . . Consanguineous marriages find opposition. . . . What is already united cannot be first of all united by marriage. . . . What is to be joined ought to be at first distinct and separate."[81] Brothers and sisters are "already united" by their blood. For Rosenzweig, on the other hand, shared blood is not the precondition for the ideal relationship between a man and a woman but the goal that they are striving to attain. While Hegel would stay away from the suggestive dimension of sibling relationships, Rosenzweig has no difficulty with the potentially ambiguous nature of this kinship relation.

Why do both thinkers fixate on the relationship of brothers and sisters? These relationships can certainly be found in the texts they are reading—such a relationship forms the heart of the conflict in *Antigone*, and it is exemplified by a call of longing in the Song of Songs. But as I've elucidated, other sibling and family relationships are central to the play and are overlooked in Hegel's analysis. Similarly, Rosenzweig focuses on a yearning for fraternal feeling between the lovers despite their explicit desire to be brother and sister. He recasts the different-gendered siblings of the Song of Songs as brothers. Both thinkers bend and mold their poetic sources of inspiration to their own philosophical goals.

Rosenzweig and Hegel draw on these source texts, one biblical, the other Greek, to tell the reader where their philosophical investment lies. Notably, in both texts chosen by the philosophers to explicate this relationship, the male figure has other options for self-recognition while the female figure is limited. In the Song of Songs, Rosenzweig's source material, the male lover has no difficulty calling his beloved sister; we hear this motif repeated again and again—"my sister, my bride." But the female figure can only wish to call her lover brother—"oh, that you were as my brother"—and although she can long for it, she cannot seem to attain it. Likewise, in Hegel's analysis, the brother Polyneices can certainly find self-recognition through other avenues, such as citizenship and the participation in the community of statehood.[82] But the sister Antigone has access to her being-for-self only in and through her relationship with her brother.

Derrida finds Hegel's exclamation on the excellence of the play to be an "odd declaration ... in the tone of a personal confidence. That is rather rare; the statements in the first person, the allusions to personal readings, the pieces of advice, the various 'it seems to me,' can all be counted. What is happening?"[83] By paying attention to the rhetorical deviations Hegel makes when writing about the play, Derrida shows that the play is linked to the personal for Hegel. Talking about the play leads Hegel to talk inadvertently about himself. Derrida will suggest something scandalous for a traditional philosophical reading: we can better understand why these thinkers focused on these particular relationships in their source texts by reading the biographical traces in their philosophical exegeses.

In his reading of Hegel, Derrida questions the supposedly desire-free relationship of brother and sister by turning to the philosopher's letters. In *Glas*, Derrida makes a textual break to insert letters written by Hegel to his sister and female loved ones.[84] He includes Hegel's correspondences with his sister Christiane, his lover/friend Nanette Endel, and his fiancée/wife Marie von Tucker.[85] By interrupting his commentary on Hegel's *Phenomenology of Spirit* with this biographical meditation on Hegel's life, Derrida implies that "Hegel's repressed desire for his sister dictates his insistence on portraying the brother-sister relationship as one of purity in his philosophical tracts."[86] As Tina Chanter explains, for Hegel the brother-sister relationship "must be the purest of all, because Hegel's own relationship to his own sister—an imperative that operates as a fiat—must remain unmixed with desire."[87] Hegel's own life seems to have transgressed the law that his philosophy enacts.

Derrida further explores the reading of biography in his essay "Otobiographies: The Teaching of Nietzsche and the Politics of the Proper Name." Derrida questions "the only kind of reading held to be philosophically legitimate," in which the life, signature, and name of the philosopher is expelled from the practice of reading.[88] When the philosopher's biography is considered no more than a "corpus of empirical accidents," the demands of the textual corpus are ignored.[89] Derrida plays on this notion of corpus to insist on the role of the (philosopher's) body in the body of work. "How can one avoid taking all this [the philosophy and the life] into account when reading these texts? One reads only by taking it into account."[90] I would argue that this framework applies to Rosenzweig as well, especially considering the corpus of writing he left behind with both philosophical and autobiographical signatures. As Benjamin Pollock explains, there are philosophical stakes to intellectual biography, particularly in the case of a thinker like Rosenzweig: "a proper understanding of a key moment in a philosopher's life can indeed illuminate his philosophy. But in Rosenzweig's case this is so largely because Rosenzweig himself appears to have lived and experienced the key events in his life in metaphysical terms. . . . The harmony between Rosenzweig's life and his thought is compelling."[91]

Derrida's reading of Hegel in *Glas* highlights the unique nature of the brother-sister relationship, the place of the poetic source interjected into the philosophical work, and the letters sent by the philosopher to female loved ones—all themes that resonate with Rosenzweig's reading of the Song of Songs. Derrida's reading complicates Hegel's notion of the brother-sister relationship as the most ideal because it is free from desire. Hegel seemingly dismisses this dimension, yet it is brought up lyrically in the Song of Songs, and it is further emphasized in Rosenzweig's exegesis. As we will see, the sister-bride motif of the *Song* permeates the sphere of letter-writing for Rosenzweig as well.

Letter writing has come in for significant analysis as an activity and a genre. Janet Gurkin Altman highlights the seemingly contradictory impulses of the letter writer: although a letter generally has a deeply personal nature, it betrays the letter writer's inherent desire for a reader and for dialogic discourse. Altman distinguishes the letter from other textual forms. Whereas diary keeping is not concerned with any eventual reader—in fact, it is instead concerned with keeping itself shielded from a reader's eyes—the epistle is "the result of a union of writer and reader."[92] Behind all epistolary writing is the fundamental desire for exchange. While the letter, "as a reflection of self, of the self's relationships, connotes privacy and intimacy," as a document addressed to another, it nevertheless "reflects the need for an audience, an audience that may suddenly expand when that document is confiscated, shared, or published."[93] Rosenzweig's *Star*, significantly, began in epistolary form, as elements of what would later become his great work were composed on military postcards sent home to his mother from the Balkan front.[94] When asked to describe her son's profession, Rosenzweig's mother described him, notably, as a letter writer.[95]

Unlike a conversation, a letter is not, by its very nature, ephemeral. It can be retained, and its future privacy or distribution is dependent on the receiver, or on other unpredictable circumstances that can occur posthumously. The written letter can be both intimately personal and intended for the eyes of another. Within its very own epistolary status, it carries the possibility of eventual public dissemination in publication. This all resonates with the textual beginnings of the *Star*. Rosenzweig's letters to his lover Margrit Rosenstock echo aspects of his theological and philosophical interpretation of the Song of Songs, and he began writing this chapter shortly after their affair began. Katja Garloff maintains that it is valid to read his life alongside his work through the letters and that reading the *Star* in conjunction with these letters "does not reduce philosophy to autobiography."[96] This reading practice is more than just a question of genre, whether epistolary or philosophical; it is a question of animating the sociopolitical stakes of Rosenzweig's thought.

The letters to Margrit primarily span the years from 1917 to 1922 and were collected and published in 2002 as *Die 'Gritli'-Briefe: Briefe an Margrit Rosenstock-Huessy*. Rosenzweig employed the conflating term "sister-bride" in his letters to Gritli (as he referred to her).[97] She was the wife of Rosenzweig's close friend, the philosopher Eugen Rosenstock-Huessy, who profoundly influenced Rosenzweig's theological development.[98] Rosenzweig and Margrit began a passionate affair in 1918, a year after they met. While writing the *Star* from 1918 to 1919, Rosenzweig wrote to Margrit almost every day. The letters address key philosophical issues in Rosenzweig's work—particularly, his notion that love can never be purely human.[99] His letters illuminate how events in his life shaped and were shaped by his philosophical thought.

Scholars have addressed the philosophical importance of Rosenzweig's letters, pointing out that the activities of philosophy and letter writing are not mutually exclusive.[100] Rivka Horwitz argues that the letters in the *Gritli-Briefe* allow for a new understanding of the *Star*: "The thousands of pages that make up the Gritli and Eugen letters are intimately connected with the writing of the *Star* and belong together."[101] Myriam Bienenstock suggests that Rosenzweig's "new" thinking is actually reminiscent of the oldest way of doing philosophy in the dialogical mode, contrasted with the more modern nineteenth-century approach to philosophy.[102] Rosenzweig himself insisted on preserving his letters because they testified to a dialogue beyond the time and place in which they were written and sent.

Rosenzweig wrote to Margrit of the *Star*, "basically it is all one long letter to you."[103] Rosenzweig's correspondence to Margrit contains numerous echoes of the Song of Songs.[104] In a 1918 letter, Rosenzweig wrote that since their relationship could never become official, as she was married to Eugen, "the best metaphor he could imagine for their bond came from the Song of Songs 4–5: 'what the loved one in the Song of Songs is called: 'my sister, my bride'—in which one term contradicts the other and the heart, undecided between them, knows simply that it loves.'"[105] Rosenzweig began writing the chapter on "Revelation" shortly after their affair began. Later on, in 1918, he evoked the Song again: "Dear Heart, what a year of death this is—but not just of death but of what is as strong as death. My soul encircles you and loves you. This Book II 2 that I am now writing belongs to you. . . . It is not 'for you' but—yours. Yours—as I am."[106] The chapter contained "as much from you as from me."[107] When he sent her the chapter upon its completion, "he described it as 'the seal' and 'symbol' of the formal bond that life denied them and therefore like the ring she 'should have worn.'"[108] He wrote to her that although the chapter was not difficult, it was "nevertheless sealed up seven times for most readers and 'all seals open up only through you.'"[109] In referring to his chapter on revelation as the "seal" of his bond with Margrit, and in writing "all seals open up only through you," Rosenzweig communicates the convergence of absence and presence intrinsic to the allegorical interpretation of the Song. The seal marks the trace of the loved one who will always be absent, even in her presence. Even when he possesses her, he is aware that she is not entirely his.[110]

The life events surrounding the writing of both the *Star* and the letters with Margrit indicate a dimension that expands the rigidly heteronormative schema in the *Star*'s section on revelation. In many ways, the relationship with Margrit was a triad. Eugen knew about the affair between his wife and best friend, and "after initial bouts of jealousy, seems to have approved and in some sense felt a part of it."[111] Scholars have noted the queer horizon of the relationship both in implicit and explicit terms. In discussing interreligious models of love, Garloff reads Rosenzweig's letters and refers to "the triangle of himself and the Rosenstock-Huessys . . . his Christian friends and lover(s)."[112] In pointing to the triad bond, Garloff is careful not to impose a framework of dyadic heterosexuality on the three. By referring to Franz, Eugen, and Margrit as a "triangle," Garloff follows Michael Zank, who calls the "Rosenzweig-Rosenstock Triangle" a "community of love."[113] Zank notes that Rosenstock himself later referred to their dynamic as a "'trialogue'" and a "'bodily trinity' that renders all 'individualistic analyses a primitivization that would block comprehension.'"[114]

The important dates in the respective relationships offer even more evidence of the overlapping intimacies in the triad. Rosenzweig recorded February 24, 1918, as the climactic date of his relationship with Margrit, while the anniversary of Margrit and Eugen Rosenstock's Christian wedding ceremony in 1915 was also February 24.[115] Rosenzweig decided, then, that his "anniversary" with Margrit was the same as her anniversary with her husband. In a 1918 letter, Rosenzweig wrote to Margrit, "Eugen must know that he is the lord of our love, that it falls into an abyss if he turns away."[116] The triad was a "virtual exchangeability" of individuals characterized by "an interwovenness that blurs the boundaries among the selves."[117] The throuple, as I'll call it, is queer in the sense that it exceeds normative erotic structures.[118] Their "trialogue" and "bodily trinity" was united by romantic, intellectual, and spiritual elements, and it is evidence that Rosenzweig experimented with other models of imagining love beyond the opposite-sex twosome. Furthermore, the relationship between Rosenzweig and Eugen suggests an erotic dimension of male friendship. Braiterman observes of the homoeroticism in the *Star* and in the letters, "The real tensions occur, not between men and women, but between men."[119] The letters between the three "testify to Eugen's magnetic power over Rosenzweig," and even in the letters to Margrit, Eugen is the dominating presence.[120] The bond between the men, ultimately, outlasted the affair with Margrit.[121]

Evidently, Rosenzweig hoped his love for Rosenstock-Huessy(s) would translate to his love for a more appropriate partner. Garloff writes that he searches for "a female 'neighbor' with whom he can contract a marriage and create a Jewish home—and finds her in Edith Hahn. . . . Rosenzweig hopes that his love for Rosenstock-Huessy, whom he cannot marry, both because she is married to someone else and because she is a Christian, will inspire his affection for his soon-to-be Jewish wife."[122] Before their marriage, Rosenzweig wrote in an optimistic tenor to Edith, using the terms of love and dialogue that are echoed in the *Star*, "Believe me, a person who loves will no longer tolerate anything dead around him. And since love teaches him 'not to run away,' there's nothing left him, whether for good or ill, but to love. . . . We never awaken for our own sakes; but love brings to life whatever is dead around us."[123] At Rosenzweig's 1920 wedding to Hahn, Margrit sang a Bach aria, "Mein Freund ist Mein" ("My Beloved Is Mine"), from Bach's cantata "Wachet Auf," which includes passages from the Song of Songs. Rosenzweig wrote to Margrit the following week, "'Is not the Song of Songs our, your-my song? And did not you sing it to us, Edith and me, at our wedding? . . . and I am yours.'"[124] On the eve of their wedding, Rosenzweig wrote of the day's social activities, "'It was really like shortly before one's death when, as they say, one's entire life passes before one's eyes. . . . I sat next to Edith and I felt as I really do most of the time: I had nothing, absolutely *nothing* to say to her. . . . I certainly know why I call it a death.'"[125] On April 23, 1920, he wrote to Margrit, "I know quite well that Edith's and my living together cannot be called a marriage. But saying it makes it even worse."[126] Tellingly, Rosenzweig felt that the love he had for Margrit was sisterly, whereas he did not feel sufficient sisterly feelings toward Edith.[127]

Given the importance of letters to the development of Rosenzweig's thinking, one could borrow Derrida's experimental method from *Glas* and imagine side-by-side visual treatments of his letters alongside his published philosophical works. Adhering to Derrida's intertextual model, an excerpt from Rosenzweig's chapter on the Song of Songs in the *Star* would be situated beside the letters he wrote to Margrit Rosenstock-Huessy, in which he referred to her as his "sister-bride:"

May 21, 1918:

"What the loved one in the Song of Songs is called: 'my sister, my bride'—in which one term contradicts the other and the heart, undecided between them, knows simply that it loves."[128]

November 2, 1918:

"Dear Heart, what a year of death this is—but not just of death but of what is as strong as death. My soul encircles you and loves you. This Book II 2 that I am now writing belongs to you. . . . It is not 'for you' but—yours. Yours—as I am."[129]

April 4, 1920:

"Is not the Song of Songs our, (your-my) song? And did not you sing it to us, Edith and me, at our wedding?
and I am yours."[130]

BOOK TWO, PART TWO

The sob of the beloved sobs toward a beyond of love, toward a future of its present revelation; it sighs toward an eternal love . . . a becoming external of the love that no longer grows in the I and You, but demands to be grounded in view of the entire earth. The beloved implores the lover to tear open the heavens of his eternal presence, which resist her longing for an eternal love, and to come down to her so that she can set herself like a seal upon his ever-throbbing heart and like a ring that sits firmly on his never-resting arm. Marriage is not love. Marriage is infinitely more than love; marriage is the fulfillment on the outside, in it love comes out from its blissful inner completeness and stretches out its hand, in a helpless and unquenchable longing—"Oh, would that you were my brother . . ."

This fulfillment will no longer take place for the soul in its being over. To its cry, no answer comes echoing from the mouth of the lover. The soul aspires to this realm of the brotherliness.[131]

The illustration of the letters alongside the philosophical work emphasizes the role of the human epistolary exchange in Rosenzweig's notion of intersubjectivity more generally and "speech-thinking" (sprachdenken) more specifically, in which monologue is surpassed in the spontaneity of dialogue, which is rooted in the possibility of the divine other. In this mode of speaking, there is an inseparable connection between human-divine and human-human speech. Unlike the monologue, dialogue has the character of spontaneity, in which it is impossible to anticipate what the other will say. Thinking knows its thoughts in advance, whereas the speech-thinker, or "language-thinker," depends on the temporal dimension. "To need time means: being able to anticipate nothing, having to wait for everything, being dependent on the other for one's own."[132] Rosenzweig proposes a new mode of thinking based "on needing the other and, what amounts to the same, on taking time seriously."[133]

During the period in which Rosenzweig developed the project of the *Star*, he sought to achieve a "synthesis of Goethe and Kant, of poetry and philosophy, of history and philosophy, of revelation and reason."[134] In his essay "The New Thinking," Rosenzweig argues that in most philosophical dialogues, no real dialogue is taking place, for "even then, the other merely raises objections which I myself would really have to raise—which is the reason why most philosophical dialogues, including most of Plato's, are so boring."[135] Rosenzweig's new thinking is a poeticizing of philosophy, an appeal to the poet to rectify the shortcomings of philosophical dialogue. Unlike philosophy, poetry is not beholden to a universal ideal of totality. The method of Rosenzweig's "New Thinking" seeks to infuse classical dialogue with living speech—to inject philosophy with poetry.

In 1922, a year after the *Star* was published, Rosenzweig was diagnosed with amyotrophic lateral sclerosis. In the period following his diagnosis, from 1922 to 1924, he turned to poetry, translating and writing commentary on the medieval Jewish poet Judah Halevi.[136] According to Rosenzweig, his translations of and notes on Halevi's poems "contain instructive examples of the practical application of the new thinking" and may thus be read as a way to apply the theories of the *Star* to life.[137] Rosenzweig wrote during this later period that "all speech is translation."[138] Speaking to the other is true dialogue, and spontaneous conversation that cannot be anticipated already involves translation. The poem itself is already engaged in speech, in an act of translation. Rosenzweig wrote that all speaking is translation as he was engaged in the project of translating poetry while his own speech was eluding him. As he lost all physical capacity for speech, Rosenzweig turned to poetry and translation and bore a hope for dialogical speech-thinking.

In referring to his inclusion of Hegel's letters, Derrida explains that the epistolary and biographical gestures should not be conflated: "The citation of letters is not to be confused with the diverse operations called 'biographical' that are related to 'the author's life.' The letters have a status apart, not only because their stuff is writing, but because they engage what we are tracking here interminably under the name signatory."[139] In the case of Rosenzweig, how do the letters relate to the philosophy? Is Rosenzweig's articulation of love in his philosophical work consistent or at odds with the sense of love from the letters? In the *Star*, there is continuity between love and its externalization in matrimony. The move from revelation to redemption is enabled by the neighborly love arrived at through marriage. In the *Star*'s reading of the Song, the goal and attainment of marriage are symbolized by lovers seeking to become siblings in order to make their love public. Drawing on the Song of Songs, Rosenzweig states in the *Star* that marriage is not love—it exceeds love, tying the community together through the perpetuation of common blood.[140] But in the real-life letters, there is a marked disjunction between love and marriage, and these terms are conflated in lovers who will never be married for numerous reasons. There is a contradiction between sibling love as the underpinning of the ideal masculine society in the *Star* and Rosenzweig's use of the term *sister-bride* in correspondence with Margrit.

But one model need not be reduced to the other. The philosophical and the biographical, the formal and the epistolary, can resonate with one another along with their apparent contradictions. This is apparent in Derrida's reading of Hegel alongside his letters. The disconnect between both the public and private spheres for Rosenzweig, and furthermore between the disparate forms that these spheres take in writing—between the published and the unpublished (or yet to be published)—need not be easily resolved, and the intertextual model offered by Derrida allows us to view the epistolary alongside the philosophical. It is notable that the term *sister-bride* is taken up both in the *Star* and in the letters, and not surprisingly, given the textual origins of the philosophical work. It makes sense that the question of love in these works cannot be easily explained or solved and that each runs up against the other in both conflicting and mutually illuminating ways.

Although Rosenzweig wrote his chapter on revelation before his marriage to Edith, he wrote it in the knowledge that he would never be able to marry Margrit. As Horwitz notes, even while writing love letters to her, Rosenzweig never forgot that "Gritli was the wife of his friend and that they would never marry."[141] Horwitz discusses a letter to Margrit in the context of the emphasis on Jewish community in the *Star*: "There is a sense of melancholy and depression in the letters of that period. He knows that if he married out of his religion, he would be acting contrary to the hope that he had expressed in the *Star*. His children, then, would not have a Jewish future."[142] Rosenzweig comments on the propagation of Judaism in the *Star*: "is not the woman through whom, according to an old axiom of rights, Jewish blood is propagated? Not only the child of two Jewish parents, already the child of a Jewish mother is Jewish by birth."[143] Reading the biographical along with the philosophical allows for the possibility that Rosenzweig may be expressing an anxious awareness of Jewish legal status being decided through matrilineal descent. If marriage is meant to carry on the Jewish people united by blood, as Rosenzweig explicitly states in the *Star*, then Margrit, as a Christian, would presumably be all the more impossible to marry. In Rosenzweig's *Star of Redemption*, and perhaps also in his life, marriage must go beyond love. As Garloff observes, "In Rosenzweig's letters to Rosenstock-Huessy . . . he insists on the separation between Jews and Christians and believes that Jewish endogamy is crucial to this end."[144] Rosenzweig promotes endogamous marriage in both the *Star* and in life.

The issue of endogamy brings us back to *Antigone*. In an illuminating reading, Chanter shows that the Oedipal cycle was conceived against the background of a recent shift in marriage practices "away from exogamy and toward endogamy."[145] Oedipus's marriage to Jocasta is an extreme extension of this endogamous logic in the collapse of kinship distinctions. Oedipus unknowingly enacts "an extreme, hyperbolic form of the recent Athenian turn toward endogamy."[146] The play acts as a warning against this social turn. Antigone rejects this trend, refusing to marry her kin Haemon and thereby removing herself from a system that relies on the traffic in women.[147] "Her refusal points out the impossibility of a system that looks exclusively inward, threatening to become ever more incestuous, ever more exclusionary, ever more allergic to outsiders, ever more protective of its borders—a system that is in danger, we might say, of autoimmunity."[148] Reading Chanter's *Antigone* alongside Rosenzweig's blood community, we see what is at stake in the endogamous economy: the status of women as objects of exchange.

Women may be the key to this system, but they are often written out of its history. Scholars have noted the irony that Rosenzweig elucidated a philosophy of speech-thinking while himself losing the physical capacity for speech. Similarly, much scholarship on Rosenzweig's life, letters, and thought notes the process by which he communicated his prolific work after he became paralyzed by ALS: his wife, Edith, recited the alphabet until he blinked his eyes to indicate she had arrived at the first letter of the word he wanted, and again until she reached the next letter, and the next. Often, Edith's role is not mentioned at all, and Rosenzweig is memorialized as a courageous sufferer of ALS "who translated the Bible with Martin Buber even as he lost all voluntary muscle control and the capacity of speech."[149] The narrative that erases her role from the translation has gone largely untroubled. In the reception of this biographical account, the mechanics of *how* that translation work was done—*who* the apparatus, or more-than-apparatus, was—is omitted. Amy Hill Shevitz observes that this remarkable and time-consuming process "has become a central trope in the legend of Rosenzweig, an emblem of his intellectual and spiritual strength in the face of adversity."[150] Yet as Shevitz importantly illustrates, this story is presented as a legend in which Rosenzweig is the producer of thoughts and his wife is only a physical conduit for his brilliance:

> When describing Edith's activity, the language used by her contemporaries reinforces her secondary status in a very particular way: by literally subsuming her into her husband's body and self. It is a trope that Franz himself cultivated ... the dominant image is of a sort of spirit-possession: as his body gradually fades away, his senses and faculties move in to take over her body. ... In this view, there was one body and one mind, and the body was Edith's and the mind, Franz's. Even when she was carrying the conversations, and despite occasional recognition of her "unusual perception," it was assumed that it was solely he who was speaking.[151]

Edith herself, however, was a trained educator who had advanced command of Hebrew.[152] In addition to providing her husband's physical care, she substituted for him as an instructor at the Frankfurt *Lehrhaus* where he had previously taught.[153] She had a central role in the Rosenzweig-Buber Bible translation, yet when Buber mentioned her part in passing, it was only as "'seine Frau,' her entire being subsumed in her marital status."[154] As Shevitz writes, "because the men viewed her as a wife providing wifely support—and not as a scholar—they had no compunction about slighting her involvement."[155] If we willfully forget that Edith almost assuredly did more than passively transpose Rosenzweig's thoughts, we erase her from the narrative, and we tell an incomplete story.

Furthermore, we have the letters today not only because of the Rosenstock-Huessys' efforts to preserve them but "thanks to the [unnamed] maidservant who shipped across the Atlantic what her masters had left behind."[156] The mechanisms of writing, translation, and transmission—in this case the *women* who painstakingly translated, secured, and conducted the work—are obscured. Chanter's reading of *Antigone* demonstrates that the play's evocation of endogamous family relationships raises important questions about the mutual implications of gender, class, and enslavement. Only once we see identity categories as implicated in one another can we resist the tendency to reify them: "the fluidity and mutual implication of marriage practices, their impact on lines of genealogy, on legitimating political alliances and determining who had political rights and who were excluded from them, who were slaves and who were citizens, makes it imperative not to isolate questions of gender or sexual difference in interrogating Antigone."[157] The need to think about gender in the context of mutually constitutive categories such as sexuality, race, class, and ability extends to our reading of philosophical biography.

Reading the scandal of biography allows us to consider the struggle between erotic love and family obligation, and to see that this tension informs Rosenzweig's philosophical/ biographical regulation of kinship and bloodlines. There is good reason to avoid reducing the philosophical text to the philosopher's life. But there are risks to this approach. If we stay safely removed from the biographical sphere, then we risk effacing and forgetting the women who were central to the work, and we reify the patriarchal structures that, especially in Rosenzweig's case, allowed the work of philosophy to be done.

NOTES

1. Rosenzweig, *Star*, 219.
2. George Steiner, *Antigones* (Oxford: Oxford University Press, 1986), 12–3.
3. Steiner, *Antigones*, 18. See John E. Seery, "Acclaim for *Antigone's Claim* Reclaimed (or, Steiner contra Butler)," in *Judith Butler's Precarious Politics. Critical Encounters*, ed. Terrell Carver and Samuel A. Chambers (New York: Routledge, 2008), 72: "between the eighteenth and twentieth centuries, radical depictions of incest shift from horizontal (inter-sibling) tales to vertical (parent–child) tales, from one kind of incest to another." See also Davidoff, *Thicker Than Water*; and Engelstein, *Sibling Action*, 1: "the *long nineteenth century*—the period from about 1770 to 1915—developed a set of theories and practices that placed the sibling—envisioned as relation, structure, and *action*—at the foundation of epistemological systems on which subjectivity, civic organization, economic networks, and scientific methodologies were grounded."
4. Rosenzweig's doctoral dissertation was entitled "Hegel and the State." Hegel was one of Rosenzweig's main philosophical influences, although Rosenzweig subsequently argued against the idealist subsuming of the particular under the mark of the "All," the universal. See Benjamin Pollock, *Franz Rosenzweig and the Systematic Task of Philosophy* (Cambridge, UK: Cambridge University Press, 2009). Pollock explains that Hegel has an important place in the development of Rosenzweig's philosophical approach, in which the concept of system has lasting significance for contemporary philosophy (52). On the role of Hegel in Rosenzweig's thought, see also Wayne Cristaudo, *Religion, Redemption, and Revolution: The New Speech Thinking of Franz Rosenzweig and Eugen Rosenstock-Huessy*, 292–309; and Bruce Rosenstock, *Philosophy and the Jewish Question: Mendelssohn, Rosenzweig, and Beyond* (New York: Fordham University Press, 2009), 4: "Opposed, then, to the pagan forces of Hegelian philosophy and the state, according to Rosenzweig, stands the messianic hopefulness associated with revelation."
5. For Hegel, the relationship of husband and wife "has its actual existence not in itself but in the child—an 'other'" (G. F. Hegel, *Phenomenology of Spirit*,

trans. Arnold V. Miller [Oxford: Oxford University Press, 1979], 273). This relationship is characterized by emotion and is based in nature. It is dependent on an external other for its own "return-into-self" (273).

6. Hegel, *Phenomenology of Spirit*, 274. Hegel elaborates on the special status of the brother-sister relationship: "A relationship unmixed with transience or inequality of status is that of brother and sister. In them identity of blood has come to tranquility and equilibrium. As sister, a woman has the highest intimations of ethical essence, not yet brought out into actuality or full consciousness: she manifests internal feeling and the divinity that is raised above the actual" (553, note to paragraph 457). Engelstein comments that for Hegel, "the sibling is a mirror in which one becomes conscious of oneself through becoming conscious of an other to which one is not linked as cause or effect, as parent or as child" (*Sibling Action*, 52).

7. Patricia Jagentowicz Mills, "Hegel's Antigone," in *Feminist Interpretations of G. W. F. Hegel*, ed. Patricia Jagentowicz Mills (University Park: Pennsylvania State University Press, 1996), 61.

8. Hegel, *Phenomenology of Spirit*, 275.

9. Hegel, 275.

10. Hegel, 553, note to paragraph 4.

11. Hegel, 553, note to paragraph 457.

12. In his analysis of family, Hegel explains that spirit, as consciousness, divides itself into the distinct ethical substances of human and divine law. The family, the site of blood relations, stands outside the community of law and coincides with the sphere of death. Death is "the fulfillment and the supreme 'work' which the individual as such undertakes on its behalf. . . . Blood-relationship supplements, then, the abstract natural process by adding to it the movement of consciousness, interrupting the work of Nature and rescuing the blood-relation from destruction" (*Phenomenology of Spirit*, 271). It is the family's responsibility to rescue the dead from dishonor by placing loved ones in the earth. This duty is the "perfect *divine* law, or the positive *ethical* action towards the individual" (271).

13. Sophocles, "Antigone," in *Greek Tragedies*, ed. David Grene and Richmond Lattimore, trans. David Grene (Chicago: University of Chicago Press, 1991), l.3.

14. Sophocles, "Antigone," l.16.

15. As Luce Irigaray notes, "Blood is no longer pure" in *Antigone* (*Speculum of the Other Woman*, trans. Gillian C. Gill [Ithaca, NY: Cornell University Press, 1985], 217).

16. G. F. Hegel, *Philosophy of Right*, trans. S. W. Dyde (Kitchener, Ontario: Batoche Books, 2001), 144, paragraph 166.

17. Hegel, *Philosophy of Right*, 144, paragraph 166. Rosenzweig also uses vegetative imagery; he likens the lover in the Song to a tree that "bursts forth

its branches from out of itself, and just as each limb breaks out from the trunk, no longer remembering it, and denying it; but the tree stands there, adorned with the branches which belong to it" (*Star*, 175). He employs the palm tree to illustrate the possibilities in love for transcending rigid gender characteristics, which are nevertheless rooted in nature-ordained sex roles (183). Rosenzweig may be evoking the rabbinic conception of the palm tree as androgynous; see the discussion in chapter 1 on this passage.

18. See Mills, "Hegel's *Antigone*," 59.

19. "Hegel, after celebrating the sublime beauty of Antigone, her unique 'naïve' identification with the ethical substance . . . all of a sudden passes into *general* considerations about the role of 'womankind' in society and history, and, with this passage, the pendulum swings into the opposite extreme: woman stands for the pathological—even criminal—perversion of the public Law" (Slavoj Žižek, "From Antigone to Joan of Arc," *Helios* 31, no. 1–2 [2004]: 56).

20. Žižek, "From Antigone to Joan of Arc," 78.

21. Patricia Jagentowicz Mills, *Woman, Nature, and Psyche* (New Haven, CT: Yale University Press, 1987), 26: "Alexandre Kojève, for example, finds it 'curious' that woman is the agent of destruction in the pagan world, and Charles Taylor writes off woman's role by saying that the ethical spirit goes under, 'in any case, by whatever steps.'" See Alexandre Kojève, *Introduction to the Reading of Hegel*, ed. Allen Bloom, trans. James H. Nichols, Jr. (Ithaca, NY: Cornell University Press, 1980), 62: the destruction of the pagan world is brought about by woman, "for it is the Woman who represents the family principle—i.e., that principle of *Particularity* which is hostile to Society as such and whose victory signifies the ruin of the State, of the Universal properly so-called." In Charles Taylor's reading of Hegel, the family, and more particularly woman, is the agent of the state's dissolution as a result of being repressed by the state: "Women induce their menfolk to exercise power for the dynasty rather than for the public weal, they turn the heads of youth away from the wisdom of the elders; and since this youth in turn must be exalted by the state as its defenders, their corruption has disastrous effects. In any case, by whatever exact steps, the ethical spirit goes under and gives way to an age of alienation" (*Hegel* [Cambridge, UK: Cambridge University Press, 1977], 177).

22. Seyla Benhabib, "*On Hegel, Women, and Irony*," in *Feminist Interpretations of G. W. F. Hegel*, 41; "Hegel saw the future, and he did not like it" (38).

23. Engelstein, *Sibling Action*, 101.

24. Engelstein, *Sibling Action*, 101–2. "For Hegel, the sister serves as the bridge that enables the brother to cross—as she cannot—from the sphere of divine law to that of human law, moving from nature to spirit, from family to the political" (52–3).

25. G. F. Hegel, *Aesthetics: Lectures on Fine Art, Volume II*, trans. T. M. Knox (Oxford: Clarendon, 1975), 1217–18.

26. Hegel, *Aesthetics*, 1218. Engelstein explains the appeal of the play in the late eighteenth century context: "Sophocles's *Antigone* became a touchstone for theory and literature because it scrutinizes interconnections that had again become relevant—between subject, family, community, place, the kinship of a population, the definition of the foreign, and the effects of colonialization" (*Sibling Action*, 28).

27. Hegel, *Aesthetics*, 1218n1.

28. According to Creon's judgment, which appears politically sound, a former citizen who leads an attack against a city's peace cannot be treated with respect by that city and must consequently be punished. Polyneices betrayed the citizens of the city, so he cannot be given an honorable burial by those he had attempted to gravely harm. He cannot be honored as a just man when he committed wicked crimes (Sophocles, "Antigone," l.217–25). Creon's judgment has a purpose beyond merely punishing the traitor. The threat of punishment is a method with which to maintain peace in the city by instilling fear that those who betray the city will be met with harsh consequences.

29. Antigone acknowledges this difficulty to Ismene: "You were right in the eyes of one party, I in the other" (Sophocles, "Antigone," l.612). Tina Chanter points out that while critics have generally read these passages in Hegel as viewing Antigone solely on the side of divine law and Creon on the side of the state, each law contains within it its opposite: "The individual act of Antigone is not only based upon the divine, it also reflects a political meaning in the sphere of human law. Similarly, while Creon's decree may be based on the political authority of the state, it is not divorced from the divine law" ("Antigone's Dilemma," in *Re-Reading Levinas*, 136).

30. Nicole Loraux observes that "feminine sorrow should be hermetically sealed inside the house, especially when the mourning woman is a bereaved mother who weeps over her son," such as Eurydice's silent exit following the death of her son Haemon, who is Antigone's betrothed (*Mothers in Mourning: With the Essay 'Of Amnesty and Its Opposite,'* trans. Corinne Pache [Ithaca, NY: Cornell University Press, 1998], 25).

31. Sophocles, "Antigone," l.173–4.

32. Derrida, *Glas*, trans. John P. Leavey, Jr., and Richard Ran (Lincoln: University of Nebraska Press, 1990), 151.

33. Hegel, *Phenomenology of Spirit*, 288. See Gillian Rose: "What is the meaning of these acts? Do they represent the transgression of the law of the city—women as the irony of the political community, as its ruination? Do they bring to representation an immediate ethical experience, 'women's experience,' silenced and suppressed by the law of the city, and hence expelled outside its walls? No. In these delegitimate acts of tending the dead, these acts of justice, against the current will of the city, women reinvent the political life of

the community" (*Mourning Becomes the Law: Philosophy and Representation* [Cambridge, UK: Cambridge University Press, 1996], 35).

34. Simon Critchley elucidates Derrida's method of reading in *Glas*: "When he wishes to offer a parenthetical remark or a quotation from a different source, he uses the formal device of the judas, a marginal window in the main text, which acts as a commentary upon his commentary and should not be judged to be of subordinate importance to the main text" ("Derrida's Reading of Hegel in *Glas*," in *Ethics-Politics-Subjectivity: Essays on Derrida, Levinas and Contemporary French Thought* [London: Verso, 1999], 1).

35. Derrida, *Glas*, 147–48.

36. Sophocles, "Antigone," l.945; "I have known nothing of marriage songs nor the chant that brings the bride to bed. My husband is to be the Lord of Death" (l.875–77).

37. Juliet Mitchell points out that "Antigone is a heroic ideal. To be this she has had to renounce marriage and motherhood. For neither girls nor boys does the heroic self involve reproduction—becoming mothers and fathers" (*Siblings: Sex and Violence* [Cambridge, UK: Polity, 2003], 30).

38. Derrida, *Glas*, 150. Antigone exemplifies the essence of ethical life, marking an impossible place within the Hegelian system in which ethics is irreducible to dialectics. Derrida shows that the relationship between Antigone and Polyneices cannot be contained within the limits of this system. See Critchley, "Derrida's Reading of Hegel in *Glas*," 14.

39. Judith Butler, *Antigone's Claim: Kinship between Life and Death* (New York: Columbia University Press, 2002), 13.

40. Derrida, *Glas*, 165.

41. Derrida, 165.

42. Sophocles, "Antigone," l.966–69. On this point, Derrida notes, "So the brother is irreplaceable—not the mother, the only family member *naturally* subtracted from every substitution" (*Glas*, 165). Engelstein comments, "Hegel reads Antigone into an ethical narrative that is bound up with the political, but he did so in such a way as to exclude her as a woman, and to exclude women as such from a public sphere envisioned as universal" (*Sibling Action*, 52).

43. Mary Beth Mader, "Antigone's Line," in *Feminist Readings of Antigone*, ed. Fanny Söderbäck (Albany: State University of New York Press, 2010), 156–7. Jacques Lacan notes that Antigone's speech has the "suggestion of a scandal" (*The Ethics of Psychoanalysis, 1959–1960* [New York: Norton, 1992], 256). See also Bonnie Honig, *Antigone, Interrupted* (New York: Cambridge University Press, 2013), 131.

44. Mader, "Antigone's Line," 164–5.

45. "Antigone stresses that Polyneices is her brother (rather than her nephew or uncle) precisely by stressing that Oedipus is their father (rather than their

brother). She is trying to disambiguate the dual status of brother-father in the case of Oedipus and the multiple status of brother-nephew-uncle in the case of Polyneices and of herself as sister-daughter relative to Oedipus and sister-niece-aunt relative to Polyneices. She is trying to insist on one of these positions—father for Oedipus and brother for Polyneices—in an essentially restorative effort, that is, an effort to reestablish a family tree with less horrifying articulations" (Mader, "Antigone's Line," 165). From the play's own perspective on kinship, the generational order of this family is "incestuously compressed, generatively overlapping, or relationally congested" (167).

46. Mader, "Antigone's Line," 166.

47. Mader, 169–70. Chanter points out that although much commentary on the play focuses on the brother's irreplaceability, there is a lack of critical literature on another foundational demarcation Antigone draws: "Antigone's discrimination of her brother Polynices from a slave is part of a larger complex of themes concerning the status of outsiders, foreigners, and slaves that informs the Oedipal cycle, the significance of which has been largely neglected by the philosophical and psychoanalytic traditions" (*Whose Antigone?: The Tragic Marginalization of Slavery* [Albany: State University of New York Press, 2011], x). Chanter maintains that a "European, colonialist framework continues to drive Western, philosophically and psychoanalytically inspired readings of the Oedipal cycle" (ix). When critics privilege theories of sexual difference and incest at the expense of other issues raised by the play, she argues, they obfuscate the problems of slavery and citizenship.

48. Engelstein, *Sibling Action*, 23.

49. Engelstein, 28. See Mader, "Antigone's Line," 161: "Ismene professes her love for Antigone in tones that resemble Antigone's passionate pleas for her brother's priority."

50. Mader, "Antigone's Line," 162.

51. "The blindnesses in the text—of the sentry, of Teiresias—seem invariably repeated in the partially blind readings of the text" (Butler, *Antigone's Claim*, 6). Seery responds to what he sees as Butler's blindnesses in the very act of drawing attention to other interpreters' blind spots: "for all the merits of Butler's spirited intervention, she is nonetheless the person constructing the very attributions and evasions in Hegel's text that she assigns so adamantly to Hegel. . . . Surprisingly, for someone who claims that she is reprising (or discovering) an incestuous reading of Antigone against those who ignore it or insist otherwise, Butler doesn't really explore the nature of the incest, and in fact pays little heed to it ("Acclaim for *Antigone's Claim* Reclaimed," 67–8). To these categorizations of blindnesses, I would add the legacy that initiates the play's narrative—the self-induced blindness of the incestuous father, Oedipus, who puts out his own eyes with the fastenings of his dead mother's robes once he finally discovers the

truth about his background ("He tore the brooches—/ the gold chased brooches fastening her robe—/ away from her and lifting them up high/ dashed them on his own eyeballs, shrieking out/ such things as: they will never see the crime/ I have committed or had done upon me!)" (Sophocles, "Oedipus the King," *Sophocles I*, ed. David Grene and Richmond Lattimore, trans. David Grene [Chicago: University of Chicago Press, 1991], l.1268–73.)

52. Sophocles, "Antigone," l.528–9.

53. Chanter explains, "In *taking on* her brother's death, in performing the burial rights denied him by the polis, Antigone is precisely taking on a male role. In so far as she puts his honor before her fulfillment as a woman, she is not acting as a woman, but in the courage that it takes to defy the king's command, she acts as if she were a man. She may be remaining true to her feminine role as guardian of the family, but at the same time she is subverting the relationship between family and polis" ("Antigone's Dilemma," 140).

54. "When I am alive no woman shall rule" (Sophocles, "Antigone," l.578); "from this time forth, these must be women, and not free to roam" (l.636–7); "we cannot give victory to a woman./ If we must accept defeat, let it be from a man" (l.732–3).

55. Sophocles, "Antigone," l.802–20.

56. Sophocles, l.1340–44.

57. In this canonical version of the story, Tiresias was then blinded for intervening in a dispute between Hera and Zeus on the intensity of female versus male pleasure. See Luc Brisson, *Le Mythe de Tirésias: Essai d'analyse structurale* (Leiden: Brill, 1976), 55–6. Alternately, Nicole Loraux discusses the less prominent myth of Tiresias. Rather than seeing the coupling of two snakes, Tiresias was blinded after seeing Athena's nude body as she was bathing (*The Experiences of Tiresias: The Feminine and the Greek Man*, trans. Paula Wissig [Princeton, NJ: Princeton University Press, 1995], 211–12).

58. On Tiresias's refusal of sexual difference, see Georges Leroux, "'Communal Blood, Fraternal Blood . . .' The Space of *Antigone* and the Aporias of Difference," in *The Returns of Antigone*, 157.

59. In this regard, Tiresias is akin to a male androgyne, whose androgyny is expressive of being a male female. On the male androgyne, see Wolfson, *Language, Eros, Being*, 142–89.

60. Molly Farneth, *Hegel's Social Ethics: Religion, Conflict, and Rituals of Reconciliation* (Princeton, NJ: Princeton University Press, 2017), 17.

61. Farneth, *Hegel's Social Ethics*, 31.

62. Farneth, 28.

63. Farneth, 31.

64. Mader, "Antigone's Line," 166.

65. The Hebrew Bible is similarly occupied with rivalry between same-sex siblings; the first family assassin in the Bible, Cain, sets out to kill his brother.

Similarly, the drama of Israel's history springs from a literal struggle of twins in the womb, culminating in Jacob's fleeing from Esau's wrath. Jacob's betrayal of his brother inaugurates a narrative of biblical forefathers and tribes, themselves the product of marked sisterly rivalry in the form of Jacob's wives. Yael Feldman observes that in contrast to the Freudian Oedipal model based on the conflicting father-son relationship, the family relationships driving the narrative forward in the Hebrew Bible tend to be sibling rivalries. The horizontal struggles in the Bible are insufficient for Freud's intergenerational psychoanalytic purposes: "Greek mythology, with its constant 'vertical' generational struggle, with its potential and actual infanticides and patricides, offered a better fit" ("'And Rebecca Loved Jacob,' but Freud Did Not," in *Freud and Forbidden Knowledge*, ed. P. Rudnytsky and E. Handler Spitz [New York: New York University Press, 1994], 9). See also Feldman, "Why Didn't Freud Like Jacob? Biblical Siblings and Jewish Gender," in *Intertextuality in Literature and Culture: Festschrift for Ziva Ben Porat*, ed. Michael Gluzman and Orly Lubin (Tel Aviv: Hakibbutz Hameuchad and Porter Institute at Tel Aviv University, 2012), 353–76.

66. As Creon says, "They met their double fate upon one day,/ striking and stricken, defiled each by a brother's murder" (Sophocles, "Antigone," l.189–90). See Irigaray, *Speculum of the Other Woman*, 217: "each sister and brother has a double."

67. Derrida notes that without question, Hegel does not attend to the sister-sister relationship: "Hegel supposes that she would not have any sexual relationship with her sister; with her brother either; but with her sister, nondesire is not the without-desire of a nonsexual relationship, it is a desire suspended in the sexual difference" (*Glas*, 163).

68. David V. Ciavatta explains that by completing the burial rites and going against Creon's injunction, Antigone "implicitly declares that, for her, bare, natural life is not worth living, for it is only on the condition that she can live in such as a way as to continue to affirm her intersubjectively determined identity as sister—and, with it, the intersubjective system of relational identities that constitutes her brother *as brother*, rather than leaving him as a decomposing bit of nature—that she experiences her life as worthwhile" (*Spirit, the Family, and the Unconscious in Hegel's Philosophy* [Albany: State University of New York Press, 2009], 76). For Hegel, "Antigone stands as an ethical hero insofar as she refutes even the natural impulse toward self-preservation" (76).

69. "The fact that she is of the same blood as her brother seems to suffice to exclude desire" for Hegel (Derrida, *Glas*, 149). Elsewhere, Derrida refers to Hegel's analysis of Antigone when he discusses the genealogical, ethnocentric, and androcentric features of fraternity: "What happens when, in taking up the case of the sister, the woman is made a sister? And a sister a case of the brother? This could be one of our most insistent questions, even if, having done so too

often elsewhere, we will here avoid convoking Antigone, here again the long line of history's Antigones, docile or not, to this history of brothers that has been told to us for thousands of years" (*Politics of Friendship*, vii–ix).

70. Steiner, *Antigones*, 13.

71. Mills, "Hegel's Antigone," 72.

72. Mary C. Rawlinson, "Beyond Antigone: Ismene, Gender, and the Right to Life," in *The Returns of Antigone*, 106.

73. Rawlinson, "Beyond Antigone," 103.

74. Honig, *Antigone, Interrupted*, 151.

75. Honig, 154. See also Simon Goldhill, "Antigone and the Politics of Sisterhood," in *Laughing with Medusa: Classical Myth and Feminist Thought*, ed. Vanda Zajko and Miriam Leonard (Oxford: Oxford University Press, 2006), 141–62.

76. Honig, *Antigone, Interrupted*, 156.

77. Honig, 133. "Antigone avows the sacrifice when she tells Ismene to go on living and says, 'My death will be enough.' And Ismene subtly acknowledges her sister's gift by ceasing at that point to remonstrate with her and accepting her own fate. The idea that political action is heroic has blinded us to the sisters' actions in concert and perhaps also to conspiratorial and even sororal powers in the world around us. Such limited views of political agency are well tested by rereading the very play that has to some extent undergirded them and whose conventional interpretation is undergirded by them."

78. Honig, 169; "If this sororal conspiracy has been almost invisible until now, that may be because readers and spectators do not admire conspiracy as a mode of action and they have trouble imagining a female agency that is agonistically and solidaristically sororal and not merely subject to male exchange. . . . To see this, we must set aside the Creonic framing that has become hegemonic, in which heroic action alone, solitary and disruptive, counts as action" (170).

79. Honig, 182.

80. Irigaray, *Speculum of the Other Woman*, 217.

81. Hegel, *Philosophy of Right*, paragraph 168; 145.

82. See Isabelle Torrance, "Antigone and Her Brother: What Sort of Special Relationship?" in *Interrogating Antigone in Postmodern Philosophy and Criticism*, ed. S. E. Wilmer and Audrone Zukauskaite (Oxford: Oxford University Press, 2010), 240: for Hegel, "The male, the brother, must leave the sphere of the family in order to fulfil his role in society, associated with law-making and the state, while the female, the sister, remains in the sphere of the family and is a guardian of divine law."

83. Derrida, *Glas*, 150–1.

84. The text of Derrida's *Glas* is frequently staggered without warning, requiring active work on the reader's part to find where a discussion is

interrupted, sometimes mid-word. See, for example, the discussion of Hegel's *Aesthetics*, which leaves off abruptly on 152 and is taken up again ten pages later, interjected with Hegel's letters. Critchley refers to the text's "graphic complexity": "this is a book that seeks to escape linearity and circularity, the metaphorics of speculative dialectics. . . . By repeating the Hegelian system, largely in the manner of a commentary, and by letting Hegel speak for—and against—himself, the system somehow begins to decompose, morsels fall off and remain outside the grasp of the dialectic" ("Derrida's Reading of Hegel in *Glas*," 26).

85. Derrida, *Glas*, 151–2. Critchley notes that by homing in on Hegel's reading of the brother-sister relation, Derrida "focuses on a seemingly minor point in a text, a point that one might easily overlook in a casual reading, and then shows how this point is the text's blind spot from which its entire conceptual edifice can be deconstructed" ("Derrida's Reading of Hegel in *Glas*," 12–3). Derrida returns to Hegel's Antigone in *The Postcard*, this time evoking also the Shakespearean brother-sister bond in *Hamlet*. In the penultimate letter of the section "Envois," Derrida references Laertes's recrimination to the Priest over his sister Ophelia's grave: "'*A ministering angel shall my sister be, when thou liest howling.*' And libido, said Christiane Hegel's brother, never comes to disturb the peace between brother and sister, for this is a relation 'without desire'" (*The Postcard: From Socrates to Freud and Beyond*, trans. Alan Bass [Chicago: University of Chicago Press, 1987], 255; emphasis original). As in *Glas*, in *The Postcard* Derrida inserts letters into the philosophical text. But rather than including letters written by the philosopher under discussion and interspersing them within the philosophical argument, as with Hegel's letters in *Glas*, in *The Postcard* Derrida includes an entire section of his own letters written to unnamed loved ones.

86. Chanter, "Whose Antigone?," 23.

87. Chanter, 24.

88. Jacques Derrida, "Otobiographies: The Teaching of Nietzsche and the Politics of the Proper Name," trans. Avital Ronell, in *The Ear of the Other: Otobiography, Transference, Translation*, ed. Christie McDonald (Lincoln: University of Nebraska Press, 1985), 5.

89. Derrida, "Otobiographies," 5.

90. Derrida, 6.

91. Pollock, *Franz Rosenzweig's Conversions*, 218–9. On the topic of biography, it is noteworthy that despite his emphasis on fraternity in the *Star* and his use of the sibling terminology from the Song of Songs, Rosenzweig was in fact an only child.

92. Janet Gurkin Altman, *Epistolarity: Approaches to a Form* (Columbus: Ohio State University Press, 1982), 88.

93. Altman, *Epistolarity*, 186–7.

94. Derrida refers to the scene of writing this work: "Rosenzweig himself, in an eruptive manner, like a series of brief volcanic tremors, writes *The Star of Redemption* on postcards, so it is said, while serving at the front" (Jacques Derrida, "Interpretations at War: Kant, the Jew, the German," in *Acts of Religion*, trans. Moshe Ron, ed. Gil Anidjar [New York: Routledge, 2002], 143). Harold Stahmer stresses the centrality of letters to Rosenzweig's thought: "Rosenzweig's practice of exchanging letters, and then circulating certain ones among his 'Kreis,' his 'group,' his small circle of close friends, was essential to the shaping of the *Star* at every stage in its development" ("The Letters of Franz Rosenzweig to Margrit Rosenstock-Huessy: 'Franz,' 'Gritli,' 'Eugen' and *The Star of Redemption*," in *Der Philosoph Franz Rosenzweig [1886–1929] Internationaler Kongress—Kassel 1986: Band I: Die Herausforderung jüdischen Lernens*, ed. Wolfdietrich Schmied-Kowarzik [Freiburg: Verlag Karl Alber, 1988], 129). Stahmer notes that the inner circle consisted of Eugen and Margrit Rosenstock-Huessy and Rudolf and Hans Ehrenberg, while the outer group consisted of Gertrud Oppenheim, Adele Rosenzweig, and Viktor von Weizsäcker. He emphasizes the importance of the entire circle's correspondence, not just those letters between Rosenzweig and Margrit. On the topic of the *Star*'s section on Revelation, Stahmer acknowledges, "If any portion of the *Star* could be singled out to reflect the direct influence of Gritli on Rosenzweig's thinking, based on Rosenzweig's own testimony, then 'Part Two, Book 2' is unquestionably the strongest statement" (131).

95. Rosenzweig recalled this description in a 1919 letter to Margrit Rosenstock-Huessy, in which he acknowledged that his mother's pronouncement of his profession was proving quite accurate as of late: "Mutter sagt von mir: Beruf: Briefschreiber. In der letzten Zeit stimmst wirklich" (*Die 'Gritli'-Briefe*, 472); cited in translation by Myriam Bienenstock as "Profession: épistolier . . . ces derniers temps, c'est vraiment le cas" ("'*Le règne des mères:*' Les '*Lettres à sa mère*' de Franz Rosenzweig," *Les Cahiers du Judaïsme* 33 [December 2011]: 33). Bienenstock notes that Rosenzweig's admission to Margrit that his mother views his profession as a letter writer is meant ironically ("*Le règne des mères*," 33). Rosenzweig was born three years after Franz Kafka in similarly assimilated milieus, and so Bienenstock suggests that Rosenzweig's letters to his mother should be given consideration alongside Kafka's Letter to His Father (30–32). See also Gesine Palmer: "Rosenzweig was proud of being called by his mother, Adele, 'profession: writer of letters'" ("'Dying for Love'—Making Sense of an (Unwitting?) Inversion in Franz Rosenzweig's *Star of Redemption*," *Bamidbar* 4, no. 2 [2019]: 28).

96. Garloff, *Mixed Feelings*, 146.

97. For another series of letters in which the intimacy is framed as siblings, albeit without the corresponding term wife/husband, see Paul Celan and Nelly Sachs: "Paul beloved brother—away now with other forms of address" (*Paul*

Celan, Nelly Sachs: Correspondence, ed. Barbara Wiedemann, trans. Christopher Clark [Riverdale-on-Hudson, NY: Sheep Meadow, 1995], 22.) As John Felstiner's introduction to their letters observes, "'Sister Nelly' and 'Brother Paul,' they called each other, during a sixteen-year exchange of letters unlike any other we have—an exchange that bonded them with more-than-familial intensity . . . they found in each other the sibling they'd always craved and an unquestioning need for poetry" (vii).

98. Rosenzweig was influenced by Eugen Rosenstock-Huessy's concept of orientation, in which the super-historical entry into the historical provides an orientation point in history. Pollock discusses Rosenstock's influence on Rosenzweig's thought in detail in *Franz Rosenzweig's Conversions*; William Young discusses the intellectual friendship between Rosenzweig and Rosenstock in *Uncommon Friendships: An Amicable History of Modern Religious Thought* (Eugene, OR: Cascade Books, 2009), 19–117.

99. Paul Mendes-Flohr notes that the correspondence between Rosenzweig and Gritli "indicates that there was a strong autobiographical moment" to Rosenzweig's thesis that both human and divine love is markedly sensual ("Between Sensual and Heavenly Love," 312). Myriam Bienenstock argues that the *Gritli Briefe* illustrate that theology was not necessarily the main context within which Rosenzweig elaborated his theory of love, a central concept of the *Star*, but rather that the purely human sensuous context was central. She maintains that the *Briefe* can address philosophical issues for Rosenzweig concerning the suprasensuous divine aspects of human love and the reasons that love can never be purely human ("How to do Philosophy by Writing Letters: Rosenzweig as a Letter-Writer," paper presented at the Franz Rosenzweig Congress, *Gebot, Gesetz, Gebet: Love, Law, Life*, University of Toronto, September 2, 2012). William Hallo addresses the significance of the letters for Rosenzweig's thought in "'Gibt Es So Etwas Wie Autoexegese? Franz Rosenzweigs Gritli-Briefe und der Stern,'" in *Franz Rosenzweigs "neues Denken." Band II: Erfahrene Offenbarung—in theologos*, ed. Wolfdietrich Schmied-Kowarzik (Munchen: Verlag Karl Alber Freiburg, 2004).

100. Bienenstock, "How to Do Philosophy by Writing Letters." See also Bienenstock, "'*Le règne des meres*,'" 30–9.

101. Rivka Horwitz, "The Shaping of Rosenzweig's Identity According to the Gritli Letters," in *Rosenzweig als Leser: kontextuelle Kommentare zum 'Stern der Erlösung*,' ed. Martin Brasser (Tübingen: Max Niemeyer, 2004), 11. Horwitz maintains that "Gritli was his inspiration. His love for her enabled him to free himself and to thrive and write with such intensity" (13).

102. Bienenstock notes that his letters have not yet been published exhaustively as an exchange and questions why the intimacy and presumed voyeurism of

Rosenzweig's published letters would prevent them from being considered as a philosophical edition ("How to Do Philosophy by Writing Letters)."

103. Horwitz, "The Shaping of Rosenzweig's Identity," 11, citing Franz Rosenzweig, *Die 'Gritli'-Briefe: Briefe an Margrit Rosenstock-Huessy*, ed. Inken Rühle and Reinhold Mayer (Tübingen: Bilam, 2002), 182: "im Grunde schreibe ich dir ja nur einen einzigen langen Brief."

104. As Horwitz observes, "In the light of the letters, is it any wonder that love and *The Song of Songs* played such a central role in Rosenzweig's *Star of Redemption*?" ("The Shaping of Rosenzweig's Identity," 42).

105. Rosenzweig, *Gritli-Briefe*, 99, cited in Moyn, "Divine and Human Love," 196; in the original, "den Liebenden im Hohen Lied sagen: 'du meine Schwester Braut'—dass ein Name den andern verneint und das Herz, zwischen beiden in der Schwebe, nur weiss dass es liebt."

106. Rosenzweig, *Gritli-Briefe*, 177, cited in Michael Zank, "The Rosenzweig-Rosenstock Triangle, Or, What Can We Learn From *Letters to Gritli*?: A Review Essay," *Modern Judaism* 23, no. 1 (2003): 86.

107. Rosenzweig, *Gritli-Briefe*, 190, cited in Ephraim Meir, *Letters of Love: Franz Rosenzweig's Spiritual Biography and Oeuvre in Light of the Gritli Letters* (New York: Peter Lang, 2006), 68.

108. Moyn, *Origins of the Other*, 146, citing Rosenzweig, *Gritli-Briefe*, 691.

109. Meir, *Letters of Love*, 98, citing *Gritli-Briefe*, 186. This may be an allusion to the Book of Revelation 5:1, which describes a book sealed on the back with seven seals.

110. See Yudit Kornberg Greenberg: "The love depicted in the Song is contextualized in a romantic relationship and celebrates a series of spontaneous and passionate moments that produce joy and ecstasy, however fleeting. Fulfillment of this love relationship is yearned for, yet never fully obtained. . . . Erotic desire and the vicissitudes of separation and union permeate the Song's poetry. . . . The lovers' frequent separation generates the longing for sustained intimacy" ("Erotic Representations of the Divine," 5). See also Wolfson, "Suffering Eros and Textual Incarnation," 351–62; and Fishbane, "The Song of Songs and Ancient Jewish Religiosity," 74–5. Garloff discusses this dynamic in the letters: "In his correspondence with his Christian lover [Margrit], Franz Rosenzweig develops an intricate theory of how their love affair ultimately enhances the distance between them and anchors each of them more firmly in their respective religious tradition" (*Mixed Feelings*, 13); "Over the course of the correspondence, the irreducible distance between the lovers becomes the hallmark of revelatory love, and in fact of all love" (154).

111. Garloff, *Mixed Feelings*, 151.

112. Garloff, 151.

113. Zank, "The Rosenzweig-Rosenstock Triangle," 89. By contrast, Gisele Palmer calls Rosenzweig's relationship with Eugen and Gritli "auto-destructive" ("Dying for Love," 37).

114. Zank, "The Rosenzweig-Rosenstock Triangle," 94n24; referring to a 1960 letter by Rosenstock in Stahmer, "Franz Rosenzweig's Letters to Margrit Rosenstock-Huessy," 397–8.

115. Zank, "The Rosenzweig-Rosenstock Triangle," 96n41.

116. Rosenzweig, *Gritli-Briefe*, 106; cited in translation in Zank, "The Rosenzweig-Rosenstock Triangle," 82.

117. Zank, "The Rosenzweig-Rosenstock Triangle," 80; "Some letters are addressed to one but switch their address in the middle to address the other. Some letters are addressed to Gritli, but Rosenzweig really meant Eugen. Some of the letters are addressed to one but then are signed off to both."

118. See Moore, "The Song of Songs in the History of Sexuality," 328: queer theory maintains "that neither heterosexuality nor homosexuality are transhistorical essences, but are historical formations of relatively recent vintage instead. . . . So long as heterosexuality, in particular, is assumed to be natural, neutral, universal, or God-given, it remains the ultimate ideological formation." See also Larisa Reznik, "This Power Which Is Not One: Queer Temporality, Jewish Difference, and the Concept of Religion in Mendelssohn's *Jerusalem*," *Journal of Jewish Identities* 11, no. 1 (January 2018): 146: "Queer theory is one discipline offering us a way of registering 'difference' as a kind of record of dominant norms trying and failing to take hold exhaustively. Queer theory also helps us appreciate how power works by combining and coordinating distinct concepts and practices to appear as commonsensically, inevitably belonging together (or, conversely, not belonging together)."

119. "The relative place of men and women in Rosenzweig's life and thought was itself fraught. A woman's presence means nothing in either *The Star of Redemption* or the recently published letters sent by Rosenzweig to his lover Margarit (Gritli) Rosenstock-Huessy and to her husband, Rosenzweig's beloved friend Eugen Rosenstock. . . . What Rosenzweig came to call 'my Judaism' was a homoerotic compact marked by four features that are basic to fin de siècle homoeroticism: intensive homosocial circles, overwhelming male authority, open erotic discourse, and self-conscious devotion to beauty" (Braiterman, *The Shape of Revelation*, 229). "Strongly drawn to the image of men, Rosenzweig advanced a Judaism that was openly erotic and intensely homosocial, the precise combination that constitutes the homoerotic element to his thinking" (235). See Young, *Uncommon Friendships*, 21: "Braiterman has challenged the prevailing focus on Gritli, arguing that the homoerotic, masculinist conception of religion that Rosenzweig develops in his correspondence with Rosenstock—and, even in the discussion of revelation in the *Star*—objectifies and excludes Gritli, rather than making her central."

120. Braiterman, *The Shape of Revelation*, 233.

121. Zank, "The Rosenzweig-Rosenstock Triangle," 80.

122. Garloff, *Mixed Feelings*, 151.

123. Amy Hill Shevitz, "Silence and Translation: Franz Rosenzweig's Paralysis and Edith Rosenzweig's Life," *Modern Judaism* 35, no. 3 (October 2015): 282–3, citing *Franz Rosenzweig: His Life and Thought*, ed. Nahum Glatzer (Indianapolis, IN: Hackett, 1998), 90. The original German letter of January 16, 1920, can be found in Franz Rosenzweig, *Briefe und Tagebücher*, ed. Rachel Rosenzweig and Edith Rosenzweig-Scheinmann (The Hague: Springer, 1979), 2:663. Shevitz notes, "He was clear to her that he viewed their coming together as the next step in his Jewish development, which was now the main concern in his life."

124. Rosenzweig, *Gritli-Briefe*, 576: "Ist nicht das Lied der Lieder unser, (dein-mein) Lied? Und hast du es uns, Edith und mir, nicht zur Hochzeit gesungen? . . . [Notenauszug 140 Kantate von Bach] Und ich bin Dein."

125. In the original, "es war ein Tag wirklich wie kurz vor dem Sterben, es heisst doch dass da das ganze Leben an einem rasch vorüberzieht . . . ich sass neben Edith und es ging mir wie eigentlich meist: ich hatte nichts, aber auch nichts mit ihr zu reden . . . Ich weiss ja wohl, weshalb ich es sterben nenne" (Rosenzweig, *Gritli-Briefe*, 574; cited in translation in Zank, "The Rosenzweig-Rosenstock Triangle," 77).

126. In the original, "Ich weiss wohl, dass das keine Ehe ist, worin ich mit Edith lebe. Aber gesagt wird es noch schlimmer als es schon so ist" (Rosenzweig, *Gritli-Briefe*, 582, cited in translation in Zank, "The Rosenzweig-Rosenstock Triangle, 77).

127. Braiterman, *The Shape of Revelation*, 234; referring to Rosenzweig, *Gritli-Briefe*, 524.

128. Rosenzweig, *Gritli-Briefe*, 99.

129. Rosenzweig, 177.

130. Rosenzweig, 576.

131. Rosenzweig, *Star*, 219.

132. Rosenzweig, "The New Thinking," 126.

133. Rosenzweig, 127.

134. Paul W. Franks and Michael L. Morgan, "From 1914 to 1917," in Rosenzweig, *Philosophical and Theological Writings*, 32.

135. Rosenzweig, "The New Thinking," 126.

136. Paul W. Franks and Michael L. Morgan, "From 1917 to 1925," in *Philosophical and Theological Writings*, 84.

137. Rosenzweig, "The New Thinking," 128, cited by Barbara Galli, *Franz Rosenzweig and Jehuda Halevi*, 289.

138. Franz Rosenzweig, *Franz Rosenzweig: His Life and Thought*, ed. Nahum Glatzer (Indianapolis, IN: Hackett, 1988), 255.

139. Derrida, *Glas*, 152. Mara Benjamin observes that the publication of the "Gritli" letters has exacerbated the "hagiographic impulse in Rosenzweig

scholarship," which she deems "pervasive and unfortunate" (*Rosenzweig's Bible*, 6n9.)

140. "Marriage is not love. Marriage is infinitely more than love; marriage is the fulfillment on the outside, in it love comes out from its blissful inner completeness and stretches out its hand, in a helpless and unquenchable longing—Oh, would that you were my brother" (Rosenzweig, *Star*, 218–9).

141. Horwitz, "The Shaping of Rosenzweig's Identity," 13.

142. Horwitz, 38; referring to Rosenzweig, *Gritli-Briefe*, 508.

143. Rosenzweig, *Star*, 346; in the original, "ist doch nach altem Rechtssatz sie es, durch die sich das jüdische Blut fortpflanzt; nicht erst das Kind zweier jüdischer Eltern, schon das Kind einer jüdischen Mutter ist durch seine Geburt Jude" (*Stern*, 84).

144. Garloff, *Mixed Feelings*, 151.

145. Chanter, "Whose Antigone?," ix.

146. Chanter, 8.

147. See Gayle Rubin, "The Traffic in Women: Notes on the 'Political Economy' of Sex," in *Toward an Anthropology of Women*, ed. Rayna R. Reiter (New York: Monthly Review Press, 1975).

148. Chanter, "Whose Antigone?," 5.

149. Zank, "The Rosenzweig-Rosenstock Triangle," 74.

150. Shevitz, "Silence and Translation," 285.

151. Shevitz, 285–8.

152. "When she finished high school, she enrolled in a communal training program for teachers of Hebrew and Judaica in Berlin, as the best way for a woman to obtain a systematic Jewish education. Her instructors were unable to accommodate the level of learning she desired, which included Talmud, but she finished the program with a diploma following an examination written about theodicy in the work of Philo of Alexandria" (Shevitz, "Silence and Translation," 282). "Minimally, Edith could not have assisted adequately with the Bible translation had she not been sufficiently competent in Hebrew to navigate dictionaries" (289). "It is entirely plausible that Edith could have pursued an intellectual career on her own had she wished" (292).

153. Shevitz, "Silence and Translation," 284.

154. Shevitz, 289.

155. Shevitz, 289; "The Buber-Rosenzweig translation, then, includes within it a second level of translation" that was carried out by Edith (289–90).

156. Zank, "The Rosenzweig-Rosenstock Triangle," 90.

157. Chanter, "Whose Antigone?," 21.

FIVE

—ᴍ—

SACRIFICIAL MOTHERS, SACRIFICIAL SISTERS

IN HER REREADING OF SOPHOCLES'S *Antigone*, discussed in the previous chapter, Bonnie Honig highlights the blind spot of sorority in the play's reception history. Beginning with Hegel, readers have been so focused on the brother-sister relationship and the Creonic framing of the characters that they have ignored the play's central sisterly bond. The sororal solidarity of Antigone and her sister Ismene compels us to ask, "What assumptions about sacrifice, heroism, and agency may perhaps blind us to sororal and other solidaristic forms of agency and their powers, both in the play and possibly in the world around us?"[1] This question frames the concerns of the present chapter. Honig argues that Ismene's transgressive activities invite "a new consideration of sororal action in concert, largely elided or dismissed by critics in spite of the text's hospitality to it."[2] The possibility of sisterly sacrifice—in which one sister, Antigone, offers herself in place of another, Ismene—allows readers to envision sororal solidarity "as an alternative and potentially promising kinship resource."[3] This chapter extends the critique of Levinas's gender economy from previous chapters while also suggesting Levinas's maternal ethics can help point toward such alternative and potentially promising structures of collectivity. Here, I intend to demonstrate my contention, made throughout this book, that a gendered reading of modern Jewish philosophers can expose their limitations in a way that simultaneously makes their approaches available as we seek a way forward.

In his later work, Levinas develops an account of embodied maternity, which may reflect a corrective to his previous focus on the father-son relationship. He describes an ethics of substitution and sacrifice that becomes exemplified in the phenomenology of the maternal body. In this chapter, I read his work on substitution and maternity alongside his response to the *Aqedah* (the binding of Isaac) in Genesis 22. By reading these accounts together, I will suggest that Levinas can offer resources for imagining less patriarchal kinship frameworks, even if (as I have argued) his own ethics remain within the fraternal system. Ultimately, as we have seen, Levinas's ethical relationship of maternity is overcome in the social realm through the ideal of universal brotherhood. Although there are helpful elements to Levinas's idea of embodied maternity, then, I will argue that there are also drawbacks to his approach. He slips between pregnant bodies and figural ethical gestation, much as he tended to slip in his earlier work between actual women and the symbolic feminine. He plainly states that the body is not merely a metaphor in his work, and I take this assertion seriously. If it is not merely figural, we have to be especially cautious when an ethical relationship of embodied maternity is characterized as self-sacrificial.

While the Levinasian model of maternal self-sacrifice does not take us far enough, it can point to new possibilities for imagining gender, kinship, and embodied responsibility, and it can illuminate both the risks and the positive potential of familial language for describing ethical and communal relationships. In this chapter, I turn first to cultural intertexts, from classical Greek drama and the Hebrew Bible, that interrogate the ethics of fathers' real or potential sacrifices of their children. This reading allows me to show how Levinas's maternal model functions to critique the patriarchal mode. Finally, I consider how interventions in twenty-first century popular narrative and culture both recapitulate and subvert traditional models of Greek and biblical paternal sacrifice, exposing a continued interest in and worry over the ethics of sacrifice, of either self or the other. I will close where I began, by arguing that sororal power represents an interruption to patriarchal models of kinship and the most promising way forward as we explore how to break out of the fratriarchal bind in which many of our foundational texts remain caught.

BIBLICAL AND CLASSICAL SACRIFICIAL FATHERS

The incident of attempted human sacrifice in Genesis 22 is remarkably succinct, considering both its controversial subject matter and how much subsequent commentary and interpretation it has generated.[4] Over the span of only a few verses, God calls upon Abraham to offer up his favored son, and Abraham responds dutifully by raising his knife, only to be stopped at the last moment by an angelic voice. Some commenters, like Søren Kierkegaard, have admired Abraham's willingness to shed his son's blood. In *Fear and Trembling*, Kierkegaard views Abraham's willingness to sacrifice his son in obedience to

God's command as the ultimate act of faith. Levinas, however, takes a radically different stance. Directly rebuking Kierkegaard, Levinas writes, "Abraham's attentiveness to the voice that led him back to the ethical order, in forbidding him to perform a human sacrifice, is the highest point in the drama. That he obeyed the first voice is astonishing: that he has sufficient distance with respect to that obedience to hear the second voice—that is the essential."[5]

For Levinas, the drama of Abraham and Isaac is a scandal in which one human fails to open up to the other. As Edith Wyschogrod explains, ethics involves a radical giving of the self, "total self-donation."[6] Abraham personifies this ethical responsibility when he stands up to God's fury and speaks on behalf of the lives of the just in Sodom and Gomorrah in Genesis 18.[7] Similarly, in the *Aqedah* episode, the notable moment is not Abraham's unwavering agreement to sacrifice his son but his listening and responding to the transcendent ethical call *not* to kill, despite the temptation to do so. The central element of the narrative becomes, for Levinas, the ethical priority of obedience to the other person. As Claire Katz observes, "Abraham realizes that to be irresponsible to God and responsible to Isaac, is precisely to be responsible to God."[8] Wyschogrod explains how Levinas reinterprets the story to be one of "radical sacrifice of the self."[9] Levinas does not reject sacrifice outright but instead reverses the order of Abraham's sacrifice, "contending that it is the self that must be willing to surrender in the interest of the other."[10]

Wyschogrod explains that, paradoxically, Kierkegaard's interpretation allows Levinas to arrive at this reversal: "Levinas credits Kierkegaard with bringing to the fore what Levinas calls persecuted truth in contrast to truth triumphant, the former opening the way for sacrifice not *of* the other, but of the self *for* the other."[11] This sacrifice is not in response to a heavenly voice but is rather "in the prosaic interest of responsibility."[12] Levinas clearly rejects Kierkegaard's account of Abraham's attempted sacrifice, yet it is Kierkegaard's challenge and close reading of the narrative that allows Levinas to arrive at his own counterapproach of sacrificing the self for the other. It is this order reversal, I will argue, that allows Levinas to shift from the biblical archetype of paternal sacrifice to the ethical model of maternal self-sacrifice. In what follows, I will compare Levinas's interpretation of biblical paternal sacrifice with the archetypal sacrificial father of Greek drama to underline both the potential and the problems with a model of ethically substitutive maternity.

Levinas's reading of the *Aqedah* reflects on its relationship to Greek philosophy and myth. In his essay "The Trace of the Other," Levinas argues that philosophy has been characterized by a return to itself; each movement outward is defined by an odyssey homeward. He suggests, however, that there can be an encounter with the other that does not depend on a return to origins: "To the myth of Ulysses returning to Ithaca, we wish to oppose the story of Abraham who leaves his fatherland forever for a yet unknown land, and forbids his servant to even bring back his son to the point of departure."[13] For Levinas, the move from ontology to ethics is related to the challenge Judaism poses to Greek thought, which can be seen in Ulysses's opposition to Abraham: "The itinerary of philosophy remains that of Ulysses, whose adventure in the world was only a return to his native island—a complacency in the Same, an unrecognition of the Other."[14]

Levinas presents Ulysses as an opposing figure to Abraham, the former homebound and the latter exiled. But from the perspective of the *Aqedah,* it is another Greek figure, Agamemnon, who provides a useful contrast to Abraham. The repercussions of a father's controversial sacrifice of his daughter resonate throughout Aeschylus's *Oresteia* trilogy. While Agamemnon freely gives up his daughter, Iphigenia, for the greater good of the state, Abraham's attempted sacrifice of his son serves no political end. In contrasting the narratives of sacrifice in the Greek and Hebrew traditions, the question of gender is brought to the forefront.[15] Over the course of the *Oresteia* plays, a varied judgment of familial sacrifice is offered as the line between what makes sacrifice justifiable or condemnable becomes ambiguous.

In *Agamemnon,* the chorus's position on the titular character's violent maltreatment of his daughter is unequivocal: Iphigenia's sacrifice was a regrettable murder. Agamemnon is described at first as conflicted about the task ahead, but once his mind is set, he engages in a relentless flurry of action to complete what he sees as a necessary sacrifice. Along with the other kings setting out to battle, he passionately calls for his daughter's blood. She does not submit to her death and attempts to enlist the kings' pity, to no avail.[16] By contrast, in Euripides's account, *Iphigenia at Aulis,* the act is retold to Clytemnestra, the girl's mother, as a joyous event that she welcomed. Iphigenia, meanwhile, is saved at the last moment by the gods, who put a doe in her place (although the audience speculates if this is merely a device to placate the mourning mother).

While Aeschylus's Iphigenia is passive, treated as an inert body, Nicole Loraux points out that Euripides chooses to grant her "the courage and free choice that, in the untragic conditions of real life, were denied to the young Greek girl by society."[17] For the sacrifice to be legitimate, the victim had to be willingly sacrificed; in an animal sacrifice, for example, the animal could not be hunted but should come of its own accord. Euripides emphasizes Iphigenia going by her own wishes because "a victim's voluntary participation was an important part of Greek sacrificial ideology."[18] Only in Aeschylus's *Agamemnon* is Iphigenia presented as unwilling. Since murder victims in Greek tragedy were typically male, and the type of death characteristic of females was either suicide or sacrifice, the possibility of categorizing Iphigenia's death as unjustifiable murder threatens to blur the line between masculinity and femininity.[19]

The maiden who goes willingly to her death in *Agamemnon* is the Trojan prophetess Cassandra, "serene . . . to the altar like a driven ox of God."[20] She recognizes her imminent demise as a sacrifice, the result of her father's war.[21] Just as Agamemnon sacrifices his daughter for political ends, so too does Priam ultimately, albeit indirectly, sacrifice his daughter, Cassandra, in war. In both cases, the father must eschew responsibility for his daughter's life in order to wage battle on a communal scale; the general good (politics) is upheld over the particular (family).

In Aeschylus's play, Iphigenia goes to the sacrifice unwillingly. The playwright thus sets the audience against Agamemnon, allied with Clytemnestra—a stance that nevertheless is contradicted in the following two plays' treatments of his death. Clytemnestra explains the killing of her husband as an act of justified vengeance: "when with no thought more than as if a beast had died,/ when his ranged pastures swarmed with the deep fleece of flocks,/ he slaughtered like a victim his own child, my pain/ grown into love, to charm away the winds of Thrace."[22] The killing of Agamemnon is warranted as a sacrificial act.[23] Agamemnon validates his act of infanticide as a sacrifice, for which his wife castigates him. She kills him in return—an act she deems ritualistic and necessary.

In the next play, *The Libation Bearers*, the line between just and unjust slaughter seems more clearly drawn. The chorus deems the killing of females necessary and retributive, and the killing of males unholy and evil.[24] The chorus speaks of Althaea, "who maimed her child," and Scylla, "a girl/ of blood, figure of hate/ who, for the enemy's/ sake killed one near in blood," yet no longer mention the horrific slaughter of Iphigenia or characterize the upcoming killing of Clytemnestra as anything but necessary.[25] But male acts of killing women (such as a father who kills his daughter, or a son who kills his mother), become in the course of the two plays following *Agamemnon* justified and ultimately required in order to achieve narrative resolution.

Orestes eventually avenges his father's murder by Clytemnestra and her lover, Aegisthus. He is then, however, pursued by the Furies, female deities who avenge matricide. In the last play of the trilogy, *The Eumenides*, the law of men is pitted against feminine chaos. The play represents the triumph of male order over female disorder, as Apollo, the god of light, stands against the Furies, the "gloomy children of the night."[26] The judge is Athena, the female warrior god born from Zeus's head, the feminine characteristic of fecundity having been appropriated by male potency. As a warrior Athena has decidedly masculine traits, and she is not sexualized. She is a virgin not born of a mother's sexual activity, who is herself nonmaternal and unmarried: "It is my task to render final judgment here./ This is a ballot for Orestes I shall cast./ There is no mother anywhere who gave me birth,/ and, but for marriage, I am always for the male/ with all my heart, and strongly on my father's side."[27] The play's conclusion suggests that only one who is not born from a womb can break away from the female desire for vengeance.[28] By ruling in favor of Orestes, Athena assuages the mother's deadly fury and brings the cycle of female violence to a close.[29]

The *Oresteia* begins with the assumption of the audience's previous knowledge of the characters' genealogy, which is framed by the horizon of sibling violence. In the legend with which Aeschylus and his audience would have been familiar, Agamemnon's father, Atreus, is involved in a conflict with his brother, Thyestes, possibly due to Thyestes's affair with Atreus's wife. As a result, Atreus tricks his brother into eating all of his children save for one, Aegisthus. Thyestes places a curse on the line of Atreus, and his sons, Agamemnon and Menelaus, seek to do battle in Troy but must first sacrifice Agamemnon's daughter. Thyestes's son Aegisthus, replicating his father's pattern, ends up as the consort of Agamemnon's wife, Clytemnestra, leading to the death of Agamemnon at his return. The genealogy of the plays is thus rife with infanticide and cannibalism, and the sacrifice of Agamemnon's child is prefaced by his father's killing of his cousins. Thyestes has his children served up to him by his brother, Atreus, as fraternal and paternal ties are devoured and destroyed.[30] The play's characters lay claim to a heritage of child murder/sacrifice. Agamemnon, who is able to kill his own daughter, descends from a father who sees fit to kill his own brother's children.

In the *Oresteia*, the dangerous female wrath of the Furies is pacified by male reason. The mother demands retribution for her young, leading to a cycle of violence that can be ended only by the court. The path toward civilization achieved at the end of *The Eumenides* begins with a father sacrificing a daughter, and before that, with Agamemnon's father, Atreus, slaying the children of his brother and feeding them to him. And yet, the blood feud is attributed to women who demand retribution for slain young and must be overcome by masculine order. The crime at this point in the narrative is put on the mother's head, and it is Clytemnestra's act that must be avenged by Orestes, for whom the trilogy is named. The plays struggle with the problem paternal sacrifice poses to ethics, unsure whether to deem it sacrifice or murder, but the resolution offered in the *Oresteia* is in a male court of justice.[31]

As biblical narratives and commentaries make clear, questions about the line between (justified) sacrifice and (unjustified) murder were pervasive in the ancient world. The *Aqedah* is perhaps the most famous example, but it is far from alone. Like Agamemnon, in Judges 11 Jephthah sacrifices his daughter to the divine for the political good of his people.[32] Both fathers give their progeny—significantly, only their female offspring—for their country. But although in the Bible Jephthah is depicted as a hero of faith sacrificing his daughter for the good of his people, Pseudo-Philo later portrays this act in a negative light in the pseudepigraphic work *The Book of Biblical Antiquities*. Jephthah's actions are no longer courageous but rather ill-motivated and ignorant. God, in this retelling, will help Jephthah's people *despite* his offer of sacrifice.[33] While Jephthah, like Agamemnon, freely gives up his daughter for the greater good of the state and for his own benefit, Abraham's sacrifice of his son will serve no political end. Jephthah initiates the sacrifice of his daughter, whereas God initiates the sacrifice of Isaac.[34]

In *Fear and Trembling* (1843), Søren Kierkegaard, writing as Johannes de Silentio, compares the figures of Agamemnon, Jephthah, and Junius Brutus to Abraham. Kierkegaard views the sacrificial father of the young daughter as a tragic hero of the pagan tradition, to be contrasted with Abraham: "When an enterprise of concern to a whole nation is impeded . . . when the soothsayer carries out his sad task and announces that the deity demands a young girl as sacrifice—then the father must heroically bring this sacrifice."[35] Kierkegaard elucidates the difference between the tragic hero and Abraham: "The tragic hero is still within the ethical. He allows an expression of the ethical to have its τέλος in a higher expression of the ethical. . . . Abraham's situation is different. By his act he transgressed the ethical altogether and had a higher τέλος outside it, in relation to which he suspended it."[36] According to this explanation, unlike Abraham, the tragic hero Agamemnon does not enter into a private relationship with the divine.

How can God, the originator of the moral code, demand that which ethically constitutes a murder? For Kierkegaard, Abraham is able to forsake the general ethical sphere due to this paradox of faith, as God demands a teleological suspension of the ethical in the relationship of singularity with the human. Abraham, as the "knight of faith," stands alone in absolute duty to God in his movement from the ethical to the religious sphere.[37] Through his belief in the absurd, Abraham relinquishes the attempt to understand the situation; the divine command goes against the ethical universal and God's own promise to Abraham regarding his son. But the impossible might become possible, and God might return what has been taken from him. The religious sphere must exceed the ethical, and Abraham will transcend ethics in sacrificing Isaac to the divine. The individual, likewise, cannot be subsumed under the universal. The individual is thus able to stand in relation to the absolute while remaining an individual: "Faith is namely this paradox that the single individual is higher than the universal. . . . After having been in the universal he as the single individual isolates himself as higher than the universal."[38]

Writing a century after Kierkegaard, Martin Buber responds to the notion of a suspension of the ethical for a higher purpose. He questions how, in its association with the divine, an act of murder that was considered immoral can become moral, and that which was purely evil can be transformed into the purely good. In moving beyond the universal to a singular relation between man and God, the value of universal ethics becomes dangerously relativized: "that which is a duty in the sphere of the ethical possesses no absoluteness as soon as it is confronted with the absolute duty toward God. . . . God establishes the order of good and evil, and breaks through it where he wishes" based on the particular individual with whom God shares a personal relation.[39] Abraham's act has no greater universal purpose and thus crosses over from ethics to faith. Buber poses a critical question: "Who is it whose voice one hears? . . . Are you really addressed by the Absolute or by one of his apes?"[40]

Jean-Paul Sartre echoes this skepticism in his 1946 *Existentialism and Humanism*, as he discusses the subject of anguish in Kierkegaard's account of Abraham. If an angel did in fact appear and order Abraham to sacrifice his son, then obedience would be obligatory: "But anyone in such a case would wonder, first, whether it was indeed an angel and, secondly, whether I am really Abraham. Where are the proofs?"[41] Sartre compares this event to the hallucinations experienced by a woman who believes she is receiving orders via telephone. When questioned by her doctor, she replies that the voice claimed to be God. "And what, indeed, could prove to her that it was God? If an angel appears to me, what is the proof that it is an angel; or, if I hear voices, who can prove that they proceed from heaven and not from hell, or from my own subconsciousness or some pathological condition? Who can prove that they are really addressed to me?"[42]

Buber similarly argues that it is not apparent that the voice demanding the sacrifice is God's and not Satan's. One should never suspend the ethical for the religious if it is at all unclear whose voice is making that demand. Buber points out the problem of extricating religion from ethics, arguing that suspending the ethical would be an irreligious move. Both Buber and Levinas respond to Kierkegaard's account from a post-Shoah perspective and are deeply concerned about the dangerous moment in which ethics is transcended.[43]

Like Buber, Levinas takes issue with Kierkegaard's conclusions, arguing that a religion that praises murder as sacrifice and obedience over morality cannot be considered ethical. Levinas points out that Kierkegaard's thought remains too far entrenched within a subjectivity of egoism. The only way to venture forth from the self for Kierkegaard is in a "solitary *tête-à-tête*" with God.[44] This action "does not open man to other men but to God, in solitude," whereas one should instead become open to God by being open to others.[45] In Kierkegaard's interpretation ethics is disdained, as the ethical stage is subverted to the religious domain: "The ethical means the general to Kierkegaard. The singularity of the *I* would be lost under the rule that is valid for all."[46] But the relation to the other person does not need entail "that entering into, and disappearing within, generality."[47]

Kierkegaard calls for a turning away from the external because subjectivity is threatened by generality. But instead of turning away from the exterior toward the subjective self, Levinas argues that the totality of the self must be shattered; relating to the external, to other people, is an ethically necessary move. Subjectivity, instead of being threatened by the encounter with the external world, is founded on this encounter, and on responsibility to the other. Levinas offers a counterinterpretation of the event: Kierkegaard "describes the encounter with God as a subjectivity rising to the religious level: God above the ethical order! His interpretation of this story can doubtless be given a different orientation. Perhaps Abraham's ear for hearing the voice that brought him back to the ethical order was the highest moment in this drama."[48]

In Genesis 22, the three moments in which Abraham utters "here I am" are essential to the story of the binding of Isaac. Abraham responds with these words first to God, who orders the sacrifice; then to Isaac, who only once questions his father and then remains silent; and finally, in the defining moment for Levinas, to the voice ordering him to stop. For Kierkegaard, it would seem that the "here I am" constituting Abraham's subjectivity is, in the first response to God, in obedience; but for Levinas, the remarkable moment of the "here I am" is in the third response, in which Abraham halts and responds. This key response in the *Aqedah* episode is echoed by Levinas in *Otherwise Than Being or Beyond Essence*. Here he invokes Abraham's response to the call of the other, the second response to the ethical command: "The word *I* means *here I am*, answering for everything and for everyone."[49] In the response to the ethical command, the subject responds, "'Here I am' which is obedience to the glory of the Infinite that orders me to the other."[50] As he sees it, in the response "here I am" (*me voici* or *hineni* הנני), the speaker bears witness to the infinite in the other person.

For Levinas, the other places the command not to kill in me, and I respond before even hearing this command, which exists beyond language, discourse, and content. The demand, or call, comes from elsewhere. It is in my response that I find the other's ethical command: "I find the order in my response itself... as a sign given to the neighbor, as a 'here I am.'"[51] Following this observation, we can hear in this response Abraham attending to the human other whose command precedes speech; Isaac is strangely silent while his father binds him.[52] Accordingly, Abraham would be responding "here I am" not to God, but to the silent call issued by his son, finding himself already responding before Isaac has even spoken, recognizing the call of the other ordering him not to kill.

MATERNAL SACRIFICE AND EMBODIMENT

In Aeschylus's *Oresteia*, Athena is the appropriate arbiter within a male court of justice, because she manages to entirely avoid the relation of maternity. She is born from her father, and she never becomes a mother herself. The resolution to the tale of Agamemnon's sacrifice is achieved as far removed from the maternal experience as possible. The way out of the cyclical maternal vengeance of Clytemnestra is through the masculine court, subverting female violence with male order.

Levinas suggests an alternative: the way out of the ethical paradox in the *Aqedah*, out of paternal violence, can be offered by the paradigmatic maternal ethical relation to the other. The maternal relation may provide the framework by which Abraham spares his son, the defining moment occurring as he recognizes the call of the ethical and sets down the knife. With this reframing, we can see how Levinas views the necessary interruption of ontology by feminine ethics.[53] Along these lines, Isaac's mother, Sarah, may have known that the way to God was through the ethical, the ability to substitute the self for other. Not only must she not sacrifice Isaac, but she may even go so far as to put herself in his place. After all, in the biblical narrative, she dies immediately following the *Aqedah*.[54] Katz explains that when we read this in Levinasian terms, "we might even say that she substituted herself for him."[55] Indeed, in *Midrash Rabbah*, the rabbis speculate that Sarah dies because Isaac tells her how closely he escaped death by his father's hands.[56] In another midrashic source, *Tanhuma*, the rabbis imagine that Abraham gives Sarah an excuse for Isaac's impending absence, telling her that he is taking their son away to be educated, because Abraham worries that if he takes Isaac without informing her, she will kill herself.[57] In both of these sources, the rabbis link Sarah's death or potential demise to the *Aqedah*.

Levinas does not discuss Sarah's absence or role in the *Aqedah* narrative.[58] Like Levinas, Derrida reads Genesis 22 through the lens of Kierkegaard's influential interpretation, but Derrida explicitly refers to the absence of Sarah from the "monstrous" story: "It is difficult not to be struck by the absence of woman. . . . It is a story of father and son, of masculine figures, of hierarchies among men (God the father, Abraham, Isaac; the woman, Sarah, is she to whom nothing is said, not to mention Hagar)."[59] Derrida observes that the woman's place is central only in the accounts of tragic heroes like Agamemnon, insofar as the female victim is required for the sacrifice to take place. In fact, he suggests that the "logic of sacrificial responsibility" would most likely be "altered, inflected, attenuated or displaced, if a woman were to intervene in some consequential manner."[60] He poses a rhetorical question: "Does the system of this sacrificial responsibility and of the double 'gift of death' imply at its very basis an exclusion or sacrifice of woman?"[61] In the French, this doubling is more apparent. The French title, "*Donner la mort*," plays on the ordinary meaning of *donner*, "to give," and the idiomatic expression "to put to death," or to put oneself to death, as in *se donner la mort*.[62] This dually understood gift of death/putting (oneself) to death implies a double sacrifice of woman, both in the sense of leaving women out of the sacrificial economy and in sacrificing women to that very economy by literally putting them to death, or by requiring that they give up their own lives.

We can see, then, how the figure of Sarah hovers on the margins of Levinas's maternal ethics of sacrifice, which I will now explore. Maternity is the specific corporeal metaphor ascribed to the experience of ethical interruption in Levinas's later work, and his maternal ethics is radical. According to this model, the self is passive as a result of an attachment to another that has already been made. The maternal relation becomes the model for ethics, as the mother's body encompasses the other within her but not absorbed into her, allowing the other to remain other. The mother is claimed by another being and is responsible for this other prior to choice, for she must feed the fetus inside her in her own act of ingestion.[63] The importance of substituting and sacrificing oneself for the other becomes epitomized in the phenomenology of the maternal body, the "gestation of the other in the same."[64]

Levinas phenomenologically situates subjectivity and the ethical relationship in sensibility and embodied exposure. He describes responsibility in decidedly physical terms. The ethical subject is vulnerable and open to the pangs of hunger and the joys of eating.[65] There are numerous references throughout his work to bread, soup, clothing, and vulnerable contact.[66] In Levinas's writings on substitution, the ethical relationship involves trauma, obsession, sensibility, and proximity. His essay "Substitution" (1968) was revised for the later publication of *Otherwise Than Being or Beyond Essence* (1974), in which it is situated as the central chapter. What is striking about the shift between the essays is the way that embodiment is figured. In the earlier essay, the relationship is primarily epidermal, not maternal. Levinas uses the expression "in one's skin," which is "not simply a metaphor," and he describes this further with vascular imagery: "the diastole and systole of the heart beating softly against the lining of one's own skin."[67] Levinas clarifies that "the body is not merely an image or a figure," and in a note he adds, "The body is neither an obstacle opposed to the soul nor a tomb that imprisons it. It is the very susceptibility of the Self, a susceptibility to wounding and sacrifice."[68] He reiterates this epidermal relation: the self is "in itself as one is in one's skin (and this incarnation is not metaphorical, since to be in one's skin is an extreme way of being exposed, different from things)."[69] The subject is exposed to wounding and immolation, and this is emphatically not metaphorical. The relational subject literally has a thin skin.

In the later version of this essay, the language of the epidermal subject remains, recurring like a refrain. The subject is "twisted over itself in its skin, too tight in its skin ... accused in its skin, too tight for its skin ... like one is in one's skin, that is, already tight, ill at ease in one's own skin.... In its own skin ... tight in its skin."[70] The language is intentionally repetitive. It becomes impossible to escape from, much like the experience of being involuntarily responsible. What has changed, though, is that here the sensitive-skinned subject becomes embodied in a kind of parasitic maternity. This is experienced "in the form of incarnation, as being-in-one's-skin, having-the-other-in-one's-skin."[71] The other is within and yet apart. "Maternity in the complete being 'for the other'" becomes the primary form of this materiality.[72] These experiences are relational; the self is bound in responsibility for the other person through physical awareness of the other's pain. This does not merely involve a relation of empathy, of suffering *with* or *by* the other. In substitution, rather, is "the possibility of putting oneself in the place of the other, which refers to the transference from the 'by the other' into a 'for the other.'"[73] Levinas uses the language of persecution to describe the bearing of the gestational other.[74] It can bring about pain within the self, residing beneath the skin while remaining its own entity.

The experience of having an other within the self, with all its physical and symbolic residues, is explored alternately in philosopher Jean-Luc Nancy's account of receiving a heart transplant.[75] This sense of strangeness residing within the body converts the self into something both intimately known and impossibly foreign: "A gradual slippage was separating me from myself."[76] The experience threatens the divide between inside and outside: "My heart was becoming my own foreigner—a stranger precisely because it was inside. Yet this strangeness could only come from outside for having first emerged inside."[77] Nancy's depiction of this transplantation, which is always both corporeal and representational, resonates with Levinas's portrayal of a subject who must take the other within the self's own body.

We have seen that in the earlier account of substitution, Levinas makes use of cardiac and epidermal imagery in illustrating the incarnated subject. In the later account, those emphases remain, but the subject becomes pulmonary and gestational. If Nancy provides us with an evocative lived example of the other-within-the-self in the organ transplant, then what does maternity offer Levinas that these other examples do not?

The answer, I suggest, is sacrifice, which is substitution carried through to its most extreme manifestation. Levinas writes that in substituting for the other person, the self has no choice in experiencing the trauma of responsibility. To be responsible for one who causes me suffering is the utmost ethical response. The key is that "it is as *my own* that substitution for the neighbor is produced.... No one can substitute himself for me, who substitutes myself for all."[78] That is, I cannot require someone else to substitute themselves for me, because "to say that the other has to sacrifice himself to the others would be to preach human sacrifice!"[79] Levinas is not advocating human sacrifice. Rather, he is observing that the ethical relationship involves substitution for the other. This occurs on the physical level and involves the comparably quotidian act of giving bread to the other as well as the most extreme act of giving life for another.[80] He is not prescribing that people sacrifice themselves but rather making an experiential and philosophical observation that this does happen. Humans do not merely respond to the will to live, but instead, in some cases, they give up their own lives so that others may live.

Levinas is here offering a rejoinder to Heidegger, arguing that in the latter's approach the sacrifice of self for other would be impossible. In *Being and Time*, death remains in the sphere of the individual, for whom it is impossible to authentically experience the death of others. As Heidegger writes, "*No one can take the Other's dying away from him*. Of course someone can 'go to his death for another'. But that always means to sacrifice oneself for the Other *in some definite affair*.... By its very essence, death is in every case mine."[81] For Heidegger, the authentic relation toward death is ultimately a solitary endeavor, one I must anticipate alone. When I stand alone before death, all my relations to other people become undone.[82] The experience of the deaths of others is merely secondhand. Death cuts off all relations with others and is not an intersubjective affair.[83] Heidegger stresses that each person should take on a relation to death not as a future event but as an ever-present possibility. "Being-towards-death" is an attitude constant in each person's ontological structure. Instead of losing the self in inauthenticity, in what he terms "Das Man" ("the they," or the public), the self can become authentic by anticipating death.

While for Heidegger, I am towards-death in a principally individual relation, Levinas emphasizes that meaning continues beyond my death.[84] In Levinas's view, Heidegger lacks an ethics of sacrifice, and his account results in the privileging of the individual's own death. The possibility of dying is then isolating and "cuts all my ties with other men."[85] Levinas takes issue with Heidegger's notion of death that cannot draw meaning from the encounter with others' deaths, objecting to Heidegger's insistence that the existential experience of death can come only from the self.

Heidegger does note that one can sacrifice oneself for another, but death will always be that of the individual. Heidegger's argument that I cannot experience the death of another as if I were that person is a sound one; the death of another will never allow me to experience death as I do when I am encountering my own death, and while I might be able to postpone another's death for the time being, they will, nevertheless, eventually die.[86] Nevertheless, Levinas argues that it is indeed possible, in fact ethically necessary, to be able to substitute yourself for another. At its most extreme, this can involve being responsible for the other's life to the point of death: "the sacrifice for another [autrui] would create an other relation with the death of the other: a responsibility that would perhaps answer the question of why we can die. In the guiltiness of the survivor, the death of the other [l'autre] is my affair."[87] The Heideggerian anxiety toward death is recast by Levinas as "a responsibility stronger than death."[88]

This brings us back to the maternal relation in *Otherwise Than Being*. By living for the child, the mother breaks out of the ego toward another and toward the future. As an ethical structure based on the role of maternity, sacrifice "is not a losing of oneself; rather, it is a giving of oneself in the other."[89] Katz points out that Levinas's ethics of sacrifice is descriptive rather than prescriptive. It is not a prescription that maternity is a sacrifice but rather a matter of fact that mothers risk their own lives in the process of pregnancy and childbirth, since the threat of maternal death persists even today. Maternal gestation and birth, then, necessarily inhabit the sphere of potential sacrifice. In this view, Levinas is not advocating death in childbirth but rather acknowledging its real-life dangers.[90]

In *Otherwise Than Being*, Levinas refers continually to empirical breathing, hungry, exhausted, and invaded bodies, and the pregnant body is central to the text's preoccupation with embodiment. Levinas's description of maternity can be useful for thinking about the ethical relationship as primarily embodied. But it is not apparent whether maternity functions as a metaphor, an ethical relation applying to all, or as a specifically corporeal reference. Are these pregnant bodies figural or material, or is such a dichotomy even possible for him?

Here it will be helpful to look closely at the rhetorical language Levinas uses in reference to maternity. When discussing sensibility and proximity, he notably uses a simile linked with "comme" rather than a metaphor (in the original, "psychisme sous les espèces d'une main qui donne jusqu'au pain arraché à sa bouche. Psychisme comme un corps maternel)."[91] In the translation, the simile is turned into metaphor: "psyche in the form of a hand that gives even the bread taken from its own mouth. Here the psyche is the maternal body."[92] This is significant, because Levinas wrote something closer to "the psyche like a maternal body," in which the difference between object and referent are not collapsed. Later, the simile is preserved in the translation, when Levinas refers to a neighbor "who could not leave me indifferent ... as the maternal milk was able to inscribe the movements of sucking in the instincts of the newly born"[93] (in the original, "comme le lait maternel.")[94]

When discussing vulnerability and contact, he writes evocatively about maternity, gestation, and internal pain, and here he does not use a simile:

> Sensibility ... is maternity, gestation of the other in the same [la sensibilité est ... maternité, gestation de l'autre dans le même.] Is not the restlessness of someone persecuted but a modification of maternity, the groaning of the wounded entrails by those it will bear or has borne [qu'elles porteront ou qu'elles portaient]? In maternity what signifies is a responsibility for others [Dans la maternité signifie la responsabilité pour les autres], to the point of substitution for others and suffering both from the effect of persecution and from the persecuting itself in which the persecutor sinks [s'abîme]. Maternity, which is bearing par excellence [La maternité—le porter par excellence], bears [porte] even responsibility for the persecuting by the persecutor.[95]

Here, we can see that it is more than a question of being *like* the maternal body; sensibility *is* maternity. In the central section on substitution, Levinas clearly identifies maternity as a metaphor: "The evocation of maternity in this metaphor suggests to us the proper sense of the oneself."[96]

I am dwelling on the language he uses because here, as in the earlier version of the essay, Levinas asserts that allusions to skin and heartbeat are not to be interpreted only figuratively—"the body is not only an image or figure here."[97] I take this assertion seriously. As we have seen, his language reflects the all-encompassing way he is treating maternity, and we can assume that references to the maternal body are also not merely figurative. My concern is what this means for actual people. While all human bodies can be pulmonary and shivering—as we have seen, he offers many evocative and effective examples of embodied vulnerability throughout—only some of those bodies can empirically become pregnant. The slippage between actual woman and the symbolic feminine that occurs in his earlier work is extended here between actual and figurative embodiment, between real pregnant bodies and figural ethical gestation.[98] It is possible for an ethics of maternity to not be essentialist. Perhaps all, regardless of gender or parental status, can become analogous to a maternal body in relations with others. But while Levinas's movement from paternity to maternity remedies his previous focus on father-son relations, the function of maternity in this work is not straightforward, and his preoccupation with maternal sacrifice calls for critical engagement. If it is not merely figural, we have to be especially cautious when an ethical relationship of embodied maternity is characterized as self-sacrificial.

Furthermore, as we've seen, Levinas uses both the terms *maternity* and *gestation*, and he seems to refer to them interchangeably: "It is maternity, gestation of the other in the same."[99] But maternity involves far more than gestation, and the relation of the self to the other outside the pregnant body is not explicitly discussed (beyond the passing reference to the newborn being suckled, which I referred to above). Levinas's phenomenology of maternity is limited in its focus on *prenatal* maternity. What would his ethics of maternity look like if it took into account birth and beyond?[100] Of course, this might lead his approach back to the place where Derrida and Irigaray criticized it, when Levinas referred in *Totality and Infinity* to father-son relationships and the relationship of fecundity with the child. Perhaps he resists referring to postnatal maternity later on because he seeks to rectify the limitations of his earlier work, and he sees gestational maternity as the best way to respond to these criticisms.

What would an alternative look like? Julia Kristeva also explains how the experience of maternity can provide a paradigm for the encounter with the other, and her intervention suggests a possible corrective to Levinas's approach by including in detail what happens with the child after birth. Kristeva illustrates her own experience of pregnancy, referring to blood, pain, tearing, bodily fibers, veins, placenta, marrow, and wonder. As Kristeva explains, the arrival of the child "extracts woman out of her oneness and gives her the possibility—but not the certainty—of reaching out to the other, the ethical."[101] Like Levinas, Kristeva writes that the pregnant body experiences the other as an invasion into the self, an interruption of the ego: "My body is no longer mine."[102] But while Levinas's ethical structure remains within the state of pregnancy, Kristeva goes on to describe the process of birth as the paradigmatic encounter with the other: "There is him, however, his own flesh, which was mine yesterday.... What connection is there between myself, or even more unassumingly between my body and this internal graft and fold, which, once the umbilical cord has been severed, is an inaccessible other? My body and ... him ... the abyss between what was mine and is henceforth but irreparably alien."[103]

For Kristeva, the sacrifice for the son occurs at the very moment of birth, at which point the mother is forced to let her child into the world, to give up the connection between them to an irrevocable separation. The mother relinquishes that utter intimacy of the other-within-the-same to allow the child to enter society, which must invariably mean breaking away from the child. In so doing, she gains a unique interpersonal experience: "The arrival of the child ... leads the mother into the labyrinths of an experience that, without the child, she would only rarely encounter: love for an other."[104] More recently, Mara Benjamin has put maternal experience into conversation with central themes in Jewish thought, showing that the relationship with the child is fruitful terrain for theological and ethical models of intersubjectivity.[105]

Kristeva refers to self-sacrifice in losing closeness with the child by turning it toward the external world. Interestingly, Kierkegaard describes the method of weaning and turning the child away as an allegory for Abraham's actions at Moriah: "When the child is to be weaned, the mother, too, is not without sorrow, because she and the child are more and more to be separated, because the child who first lay under her heart and later rested upon her breast will never again be so close."[106] Abraham knows that his act of faith must turn Isaac away from him. In this sense, Kierkegaard acknowledges a level of *self*-sacrifice in Abraham's relationship with his son. This sacrifice of self-for-other is illustrated by Kierkegaard with a decidedly maternal reference, casting Abraham as the "mother" to his child.

Similarly, for Levinas the maternal relation offers an alternate form of substitution in which the parent takes the place of the child on the altar, or in which any self takes the place of any other. In emphasizing the feminine as the interruption of the virile, Levinas may be arguing for the need for Abraham to be "feminized": for Levinas, "the father—the masculine—can get to the experience of the other, but only by first becoming feminine."[107] If we read Levinas's work on substitution and maternity alongside his analysis of the *Aqedah*, an alternative comes into view. We see that Abraham should effectively shift from sacrifice of the other to substitution *for* the other, transitioning from Abraham to Sarah, from father to mother. Levinas writes that the self "is bound in a knot that cannot be undone in a responsibility for others."[108] Perhaps, then,

Abraham realizes that instead of binding Isaac, he is himself already tied to Isaac and must instead bind himself to/for his son. According to this model, Levinas effectively transposes Abraham into a figurative mother. But this interruption of the virile leading to Abraham's feminization can also be seen as another masculine appropriation of the female (which we saw earlier in Plato and Rosenzweig), as the male figure takes on maternal characteristics. And even if the ideal ethical relation of the maternal body is a metaphor that is not to be taken literally, this metaphor still enforces traditional cultural norms of essentialized femininity that, in turn, restrict the value of women to their roles as mothers.

Of course, if Levinas had not focused on maternity in his later work, then he would be equally subject to criticism for ignoring this relationship. But the model of maternal self-sacrifice perpetuates a number of troubling assumptions, and there are real ethical problems with self-sacrificial models of motherhood that promote extreme self-abnegation.[109] In Levinas's work, the maternal relation's characterization as self-sacrificial becomes even more complicated when carried beyond the immediate familial link. How is substitution to the point of sacrifice mediated in the world? Levinas suggests that we can all learn from the example of the maternal body how to bear the persecuting of the persecutor. While it is one matter to conceptualize this in terms of the other-within-the-self in the case of the maternal body, it is another entirely to broaden this formula and take into account its possible social implications. Should victims take it upon themselves to be responsible for the persecuting of their persecutors in even extreme contexts? To what degree? It is not apparent how the individual relationship of the mother to the child within her translates to plural relationships with others.

Perhaps Levinas's answer to this would be that the maternal model teaches us how we are responsible to provide sustenance for others, and this responsibility is automatic, like breathing, or like feeding the body inside you through your own act of ingestion. It can involve nourishing the other or being responsible for the other even if that other causes you great pain, as in childbirth. In this relation, I would find myself "devoted to the others, without being able to resign, and thus as incarnated in order to offer itself, to suffer and to give."[110] But, as we have seen, Levinas does not only use the corporeal examples of breath and skin in the second version of this essay. He adds the maternal body, precisely because this example takes substitution to its limit. The sacrifice of self for other is the most extreme form of this relationship of utter responsibility. In this case, it is not at all clear to me how the relation of maternity as self-sacrificial can apply to every relationship with others, nor that it necessarily should.

This is what Derrida refers to as the aporia of responsibility. Abraham's approach to sacrifice teaches us that "far from ensuring responsibility, the generality of ethics incites to irresponsibility."[111] In every act of ethical responsibility, one necessarily acts irresponsibly to everyone not included in that act: "I cannot respond to the call, the request, the obligation, or even the love of another without sacrificing the other other, the other others. Every other (one) is every (bit) other [tout autre est tout autre]; everyone else is completely or wholly other."[112] In the extreme case of this, Abraham must choose to be either responsible to God and irresponsible to Isaac or vice versa. In its more quotidian manifestations, if I choose to act ethically in a Levinasian sense toward one person by giving them water or food, or I choose to adopt this one stray cat, then in that very action I am acting irresponsibly to all the other people I am not nourishing, or to all the other stray cats I am not taking in.[113] "I am responsible to any one (that is to say to any other) only by failing in my responsibilities to all the others, to the ethical or political generality."[114] All of these necessary sacrifices can never be justified, and "I must hold my peace about it."[115] The aporia of ir/responsibility is inescapable and inevitable.

By making any one ethical choice, "I am sacrificing and betraying at every moment all my other obligations: my obligations to the other others whom I know or don't know, the billions of my fellows (without mentioning the animals that are even more other others than my fellow), my fellows who are dying of starvation or sickness."[116] In Genesis 22, animals are even more other others because although one sacrifice (human) is aborted, another act of slaughter (animal) still has to take place, according to the internal substitutionary logic of the narrative. The collective human readership may breathe a sigh of relief when Abraham stays his hand, but the scape-ram is not so satisfied with the denouement. The urgent question of animal ethics in these cases of paradigmatic substitution needs to be made explicit. Isaac's life is spared, but only, and crucially, at the expense of the animal. The sacrificial economy is upheld.

The reversal of the sacrificer's gender suggested by Levinas's reading of the *Aqedah* puts forward an alternate mode of sacrifice in which substitution would not involve a doe in the place of Iphigenia or a ram instead of Isaac, as in the narratives, but the mother in place of the child. However, it must be noted that in comparing these Greek and Hebraic accounts of sacrifice, the father's act is stopped only once a male child is on the altar. Levinas illuminates a unique alternative to that sacrificial model, but until that other for whom the mother sacrifices herself can also be explicitly nonmale, and until the model of ethical self-sacrifice is not predicated on the figurative or literal body of the mother,

the androcentrism inherent in the tales persists. Moving away from metaphorical maternity may be necessary to avert the disturbingly gendered dynamic of
self-sacrifice.

ALTERNATIVE SACRIFICIAL MODELS

Levinas's provocative and problematic ethics of sacrifice has a number of
echoes in contemporary cultural artifacts, and speculative fictions provide
an experimental area in which to explore his approach. As Kathryn Lofton
has shown, the archives of popular culture can allow us to explore how cultural products provide common sites for encounter and reimagining. Popular
culture is a particularly rich site of communal participation that can suggest
how to "organize the world other than how it has been organized."[117] Injecting
popular culture into my reading productively highlights the idiosyncrasies and
potential difficulties in this ethics of maternal sacrifice and offers alternative
gender pairings in this substitutional dynamic. It also illuminates the extent to
which ancient narrative models persist, though frequently unacknowledged.

The Greek and Hebraic model of paternal sacrifice, for example, is closely
adhered to in season five of the television series *Game of Thrones*, in which the
princess Shireen is burnt alive by her father, Stannis, and his priest Melisandre.[118] Stannis's army has been deprived of their supplies by camp infiltrators.
He is advised by Melisandre that the king's blood in his daughter's veins will
appease the Lord of Light, who will change his army's fortunes. While Stannis's
wife, Selyse, initially agrees to the sacrifice, she attempts to intervene at the last
moment but is restrained while her daughter is killed. Shortly after, it appears
that she takes her own life in remorse. This narrative closely follows the events
of Genesis 22, in which a father is given a divine decree to sacrifice his child and
resolves to go through with the act without apparent hesitation, and his wife,
the child's mother, dies shortly thereafter.

Some viewers have noted that the scene intentionally mirrors Agamemnon's
sacrifice of Iphigenia in order to self-consciously update the classic tragedy
as a narrative form.[119] Others observe that the killing of Shireen emphasizes
how "the brutality of the world seems to hit the young women of Westeros
the hardest," comparing her sacrifice to the shedding of blood of the male
character Gendry, who emerges from his encounter with Melisandre relatively
unscathed.[120] In the show's following season, Stannis's former lieutenant Davos Seaworth offers a very Levinasian rejoinder to the logic of paternal sacrifice. When confronted by Davos, Melisandre admits that her interpretation of
her god's wishes was faulty, and she attempts to evince responsibility for the

murder: "I only do what my Lord commands." Davos responds, "If he commands you to burn children, your Lord is evil."[121]

If *Game of Thrones* explicitly engages the model of paternal sacrifice, a number of alternatives have also become prevalent in popular narrative and culture. The entirety of J. K. Rowling's Harry Potter series hinges on the mother's self-sacrifice for her son. Lily Evans Potter's key act is highlighted repeatedly throughout the narrative, and the author herself attests to having written the series for her own daughter. The reader eventually learns that only this very drastic act of maternal sacrifice was able to thwart the villain's success. The protagonist owes both his life and his characteristic facial scar to his mother's ultimate sacrifice for her beloved infant son. It is revealed that this sacrificial act lingers in the bodies and blood of the hero and his nemesis, linking them inextricably: "He took your blood believing it would strengthen him. . . . He took a part of your mother's sacrifice into himself. If he could only have understood the precise and terrible power of that sacrifice, he would not, perhaps, have dared to touch your blood."[122]

While Harry Potter presents the conciliatory figure of the sacrificial mother as the child's savior, other prevalent contemporary narratives are marked by the traumatic residues of maternal violence toward the child. The independent video game *The Binding of Isaac*, for example, offers a contemporary twisted take on the biblical story, substituting a homicidal mother for the Abrahamic sacrificial father.[123] Since its debut, Internet searches for "the binding of Isaac" do not primarily produce content on the biblical episode but rather on the popular video game. The archetypical biblical tale of attempted sacrifice, the object of Kierkegaard's veneration, has been entirely recast online; in fan conversations on reddit, the networking community website, many players attest to surprise that the phrase relates to a foundational biblical narrative rather than a video game.[124]

The action of the game takes place in an Oedipal underworld teeming with traumatic response and repetition compulsion. The design presents crude childlike drawings contrasted with its violent events. The game player controls a naked, crying child seeking to escape the deluded God-fearing mother's murderous impulses to cleanse him of sin. The plot offers an odd conflation of the biblical narrative with a son's matricidal wishes. In the backstory, Isaac and his mother live contentedly enough, with Isaac playing by himself while his mother watches television. The game begins after Isaac's mother hears the voice of God demanding that she sacrifice her son to prove her faith. In response, Isaac flees through a trapdoor of his room into the basement of their house.

Over the course of the game, played entirely in this hellish subterranean realm, Isaac comes into contact with enemies, dead brothers and sisters, and

eventually his mother. The player must move through the unknown space below, pursued by his now giant mother, who ultimately attempts to quash him
underfoot. This psychoanalytically overrich narrative gets around the problem
of paternal sacrifice by locating all parental wrath in the figure of the zealous
mother. If the game player attempts to quit, the Isaac avatar guilts them into
remaining by asking, "Are you sure you want me to die?" While other similar
"quest" or "rogue" type games allow the player to acquire weapons and shields
with which to fight enemies, Isaac fights for his life with nothing but his tears:
"In between levels the player is greeted with short animations of Isaac's dreams
in which he is mocked by other boys and neglected by his mother."[125]

The Binding of Isaac has enjoyed great popularity, along with its additional
content, Wrath of the Lamb, which takes its inspiration from the biblical substitution of animal-for-human, and its update, The Binding of Isaac: Rebirth, and ex-
pansions, Afterbirth and Repentance, which were released to acclaim. The game's
popularity has carried over to meme status. On twitch.tv, a popular site for video
games, writing BibleThump brings up an image of Isaac crying; it is written
multiple times a minute to express sadness online. This meme has now prolifer-
ated and is used on other sites as well, moving well beyond its original referent.

When game creator Edmund McMillen was interviewed on the symbolic origins of the game, he responded with ambivalence in reflecting on his religious
Catholic upbringing. He had originally intended to illustrate what he viewed
as the negative aspects of religion from a child's point of view but found that
drawing upon this past illuminated "the mysterious aspects of this world, the
undefined themes, which I obviously still have somewhere inside me."[126] The
game came to meditate upon self-sacrifice as the "ultimate gift to the world."[127]
Perhaps McMillen drew on the traditional Christian interpretation of Genesis
22, in which Isaac becomes a typology for Jesus's future sacrifice.[128] In that case,
though, it would have been more applicable to title the game The Sacrifice of
Isaac (which allows for a future typology of enacted sacrifice) rather than the
term used more widely in Jewish interpretations, The Binding of Isaac (which
restricts itself to the near-sacrifice in the Genesis narrative). It is also possible
that he switches to a sacrificial mother to invoke Catholic Mariology. Whatever
his inspirations, it is evident that he has created a deeply Freudian transformation of the Aqedah.

McMillen's game demonstrates that retelling archetypal sacrificial stories
through contemporary contexts has widespread appeal. This video game brings
to mind the reversal of Abraham and Sarah suggested by Levinas's reading in
substituting mother for father, and it opens itself up to sophisticated interpretations of self-sacrifice and gift-giving. But it is still limited by its reliance on

parental sacrifice that we see in the Hebraic and Greek sacrificial models. To find a more productive inversion of the narrative that would serve as a better model for human relationships, we may need to look outside the vertical parental model.

Popular dystopian literature can offer alternatives to both forms of parental sacrifice, paternal and maternal. Interestingly, given the reflexive turn to "brotherhood" (and its concomitant erasure of first the lover, then the sister) as an antihierarchical alternative that I have discussed in both Levinas and Rosenzweig, among other twentieth-century philosophers, contemporary popular culture has demonstrated a strong if undertheorized interest in the self-sacrificial ethics of the sororal relationship. For example, The Hunger Games series, published in 2008–10, and its accompanying films, are driven by the generosity of sisterly sacrifice in a plot that explicitly references the Greek myth of Theseus and the Minotaur. Each year a "reaping" occurs in which young people from outlying districts are sacrificed for the entertainment of the privileged few in the capital. These games serve as a political tool to keep the masses in check. The action begins with the heroine taking her younger sister's place in a battle to the death with other adolescents: "With one sweep of my arm, I push her behind me. 'I volunteer!' I gasp. 'I volunteer as tribute!'"[129] Her act is one of substitutional sacrifice on behalf of her younger sister.[130] In this narrative, the model of vertical intergenerational sacrifice is replaced with horizontal intragenerational sororal sacrifice.

The song that plays during the closing credits of the film of The Hunger Games explicitly links Genesis 22 with the film's narrative. In Arcade Fire's "Abraham's Daughter," Katniss is reimagined as an unnamed daughter of the patriarch who prevents the sacrifice from occurring. In a possible paratextual reference to the unnamed Jephthah's daughter in Judges 11, the protagonist of the song is asked by the angel "what her name was/ She said, I have none/ Then he asked, how can this be/ My father never gave me one."[131] In this version of the story, the angel calls for "the slaughter," and the daughter steps in with her bow raised, defying both the angel and her father: "You'd better let young Isaac go."[132] In the film, a young woman rises up against an oppressive state to save her sister; the songwriters thus align Abraham's sacrificial logic with tyranny and invent a daughter as the Aqedah's resistance fighter.

Perhaps most evocative of theoretical contributions to the study of death and sacrifice is the television series Buffy the Vampire Slayer, which aired from 1997 to 2003. This series has been critically lauded for challenging and overturning traditional constructions of gender, its subversive aims embodied in the figure of the young female warrior. Buffy predated the subsequent teen vampire craze by more than a decade, not to mention countless other media, with an exemplary depiction of allegory, myth, sexual expression, and cultural theory, and a literal expression of the symbolic truism that high school is hell. The passing years have contributed to the Buffyverse's rising status in the academy.[133]

The narrative arc of the fifth season explicitly alludes to Derrida's *The Gift of Death*. Over the course of this season, the heroine and her younger sister become more dependent on one another after losing their mother. Buffy takes a hallucinatory journey in the desert and comes into contact with the spirit of the original Slayer, who instructs her cryptically that her gift is death. At first Buffy rejects this message, refusing the sacrificial implication. In the lead-up to this revelation, she asks if her work as a demon slayer will inhibit her ability to love. The ancient figure responds, "You are full of love. . . . Love. Give. Forgive. Risk the pain. It is your nature. Love will bring you to your gift."[134] Buffy responds, incredulously, "I . . . *what*? . . . I'm full of love? . . . I'm getting a gift? Or do you mean that I have a gift to give to someone else?" The original slayer simply responds, "death is your gift." Buffy then becomes serious: "Ok—no. Death is not a gift. My mother just died; I know this. If I have to kill demons because it makes the world a better place, then I kill demons. But it is not a gift to anybody." It is only later on in the final episode of the season, entitled simply "The Gift," that Buffy realizes she must sacrifice herself to save her sister (and the world) and understands the meaning of the first slayer's words: "Death is your gift." Ultimately, Buffy's friends bring her back to life in the next season, reuniting her with her sister in the routine work of living and fighting evil.

In *The Gift of Death*, Derrida argues that dying for the other does not signify a substitution for the other. Dying in the place of the other would be impossible; "Once it is established that I cannot die *for* another (in his place) although I can die *for* him (by sacrificing myself for him or dying before his eyes), my own death becomes this irreplaceability that I must assume if I wish to have access to what is absolutely mine."[135] Sacrifice is linked to economy, as Abraham's decision is a gamble on the life or loss of his son. The impossibility of the gift lies in its defying reciprocity, opening and exceeding the circular economy of exchange in the act of giving, as the one who gives must give up all claims of ownership to the gift.

Paternal sacrifice presents a problem because it does not take into account the wishes of the sacrificed individual. Maternal self-sacrifice may resolve that issue by collapsing sacrificer and sacrificee into one, but in doing so it creates an alarming expectation of maternal self-elision. Reading *Buffy* alongside Derrida allows us to see that sacrifice as gift can be more capaciously represented with a self-sacrifice that does not involve the elision or death of the woman but instead a redemption/transformation of the sister-pair.

Buffy represents the urtext of sisterly sacrifice in a popular cult medium. The theme of sororal sacrifice was later fantastically popularized, meanwhile, in a Disney film. We learn in the film *Frozen* (2013) that "an act of true love will thaw a frozen heart." We are conditioned to assume that this must involve romantic love for a male character, but this expectation is productively disrupted in the final scenes of the film. The curse placed on the protagonist Anna is broken only with an act of self-sacrifice drawn from her true love—for her sister.

As these examples suggest, prominent modes of sacrifice in twenty-first century popular culture can offer a compelling study in contrasts with older dominant modes of paternal sacrifice. Popular fictions can provide "escape hatches from these resilient reproductions."[136] Alternate futures and realities propose rich possibilities for gender substitutions. In these narratives, both the sacrificer and sacrificed are embodied by female figures. They suggest that the unique relationship of sisters may find a way out of the problem. While still residing within the sphere of sacrifice, these and other narratives refuse the hierarchical gender operations of more traditional modes of sacrificial kinship. Popular narrative interventions demonstrate that the horizon of sacrifice, gender, and ethical substitution evoked by Levinas continues to gain cultural relevance.

Levinas's challenge to the *Aqedah* offers us a way out of the restrictive economy of paternal sacrifice. Katz argues that Levinas's evocation of the maternal bond demonstrates a shift from the philosophical focus on death to an emphasis on life. As Mary C. Rawlinson has shown in her reading of *Antigone*, refocusing on the sisters of the narrative similarly allows readers to shift from the philosophical preoccupation with death to the valorization of life. When commentators elevate Antigone's relationships to her deceased family members over the relationship with her living sister Ismene, they reinscribe the logic of the fratriarchy and become complicit "in its sacrifice of actual life to speculative abstraction."[137] The emphasis on death over life "provides infrastructure for the fraternal economy by which women are subjected."[138] Honig takes up this argument when she points out that Antigone does not only die for her dead brother; "she also, in a way perhaps less alien to contemporary readers, dies for her living sister."[139]

Levinas's ethics of maternal self-sacrifice is provocative, and his image of embodied maternity is powerful, but there are limitations to this framework.[140] While the Levinasian model of maternal self-sacrifice does not take us far enough, it can point to other ways of imagining gender, kinship, and embodied ethics. The example of sisterly sacrifice offers a potentially rich theoretical alternative to models of parental sacrifice in which the body on the altar is spared only if it is male, as in the *Aqedah*. Furthermore, the sacrificial love between sisters inverts the violence between brothers that we archetypally find in both biblical and Greek tales of sibling male rivalry. As Honig points out, though, elevating the sisterly relationship could result in a "normative effort to promote sorority as a privileged site of agency."[141] The move to sorority as a model "may turn out only to restage rather than interrupt the fraternity or phallocracy we seek to contest," and it may not be possible to break the spell of phallocracy by moving from other kinship formations to sisters.[142] But even if the model of sisterhood has limitations, as Honig writes, "surely it is a start."[143] Imagining and accounting for sororal agency can allow us to extricate ourselves from sedimented interpretations and to develop the neglected dimension of sorority in our reading.

NOTES

1. Honig, *Antigone, Interrupted*, 155. Honig addresses the view that Antigone's death was a sacrifice: "In nineteenth century Germany, philosophers from Hegel to Schelling, Goethe, and even the composer Felix Mendelssohn, approached Antigone through a sacrificial structure typical of their Christian moment" (155). Antigone was seen as paradigmatic of "the sort of uncompromising and selfless loyalty and devotion that stood as a particularly central virtue of modern Christianity and was useful to the still-new state form" (155).

2. Honig, *Antigone, Interrupted*, 268n21. Through a close reading of the two burials in the play, Honig argues that the first burial, of Polyneices, usually goes unnoticed by critics, despite the fact that Ismene claims responsibility for it. Commentators unfairly label Ismene as passive compared to her heroic sister, even though there is overwhelming textual evidence to the contrary.

3. Honig, *Antigone, Interrupted*, 15. Honig calls attention to Antigone's frantic efforts to distract Creon after he commands that Ismene be brought to justice. "The sisters then argue in front of Creon about whether Ismene should share Antigone's fate. The argument is won by Antigone, who never utters her sister's name again. Antigone is often criticized for this. It is a sign of her coldness, critics say. But what if the erasure of Ismene is Antigone's gift to her, the gift of survival to the sister who initially sought to survive?" (165). As Honig demonstrates, Antigone succeeds in convincing Creon that her sister had nothing to do with either of the burials and thus saves Ismene from a tragic fate by taking all of the blame herself.

4. For an account of classical medieval exegesis of Genesis 22, see Albert van der Heide, *"Now I Know": Five Centuries of Aqedah Exegesis* (Cham: Springer International, 2017). For a reading of the *Aqedah* as the master narrative of traditional Jewish cultural memory, see David N. Gottlieb, *Second Slayings: The Binding of Isaac and the Formation of Jewish Memory* (Piscataway, NJ: Gorgias Press, 2019).

5. Emmanuel Levinas, *Proper Names*, trans. Michael B. Smith (Stanford, CA: Stanford University Press, 1996), 77.

6. Edith Wyschogrod, "Introduction," in *The Enigma of Gift and Sacrifice*, ed. Edith Wyschogrod, Jean-Joseph Goux, and Eric Boynton (New York: Fordham University Press, 2002), 8.

7. See Tikva Frymer-Kensky, "Akeda: The View from the Bible," in *Beginning Anew: A Woman's Companion to the High Holy Days*, ed. Gail Twersky Reimer and Judith A. Kates (New York: Touchstone, 1997), 132: "Could this have been Abraham's test? Was Abraham supposed to fight for Isaac the way he had fought for Sodom and Gomorrah? Was he supposed to demand that God not demand the death of an innocent child and, in addition, that God not break God's own covenant but keep the divine promise of a future for Abraham? If so, maybe Abraham failed the test!"

8. Claire Elise Katz, "The Responsibility of Irresponsibility: Taking (Yet) Another Look at the Akedah," in *Addressing Levinas*, ed. Eric Sean Nelson, Antje Kapust, and Kent Still (Evanston, IL: Northwestern University Press, 2005), 29. "Abraham moves from faith to ethics, from sacrifice of the other to response to the other" (33n37). As Katz shows, in reading this story, Levinas emphasizes the need to respond primarily to the other person. In this respect, it is helpful to consider how he both draws on and diverges from Rosenzweig's theological approach. Benjamin explains how Levinas reimagines Rosenzweig's formulation of intersubjectivity between human and divine: "Levinas built on Rosenzweig's framework but translated his notion of existential encounter into the interhuman sphere: not God but my fellow human, in her defenseless need, shatters my illusions of self-contained, autonomous agency, interrupting and making demands on me" (*The Obligated Self*, 86). Levinas offers a counterpoint to Rosenzweig's theocentrism: "He effectively reverses Rosenzweig's account by secularizing it: the fellow human being, not God, occasions the revelation of my obligation to her. Levinas emphasizes the immanent nature of his account; it need not invoke God, being self-sufficient as a site for ethics. And yet, for Levinas, encounter with one's fellow human opens up what he calls transcendence, even as this transcendence, paradoxically, remains 'terrestrial'" (123).

9. Wyschogrod, "Introduction," 8.

10. Wyschogrod, 8.

11. Wyschogrod, 9. Indeed, Kierkegaard does bring up the possibility of self-sacrifice for Abraham, but only if Abraham had *not* had faith: "If Abraham had doubted . . . He would have cried out to God, 'Reject not this sacrifice; it is not the best that I have, that I know very well, for what is an old man compared with the child of promise, but it is the best I can give you. Let Isaac never find this out so that he may take comfort in his youth.' He would have thrust the knife into his own breast. He would have been admired in the world, and his name would never be forgotten; but it is one thing to be admired and another to become a guiding star that saves the anguished" (Søren Kierkegaard, *Fear and Trembling; Repetition*, trans. Howard V. Hong and Edna H. Hong [Princeton, NJ: Princeton University Press, 1983], 20–1). See Dorota Glowacka, "Sacrificing the Text: The Philosopher/Poet at Mount Moriah," *Animus* 2 (1997): 35–45: "Kierkegaard surmises that Abraham would actually prefer to partake of human generality; for example, he would gladly perform the heroic deed and offer his own life to spare Isaac's. Then, his actions would be intelligible to all. . . . Abraham's faith, however, ejects him from a secure abode in the universal" (36).

12. Wyschogrod, "Introduction," 9.

13. Levinas, "The Trace of the Other," 348. For discussion of this passage, see Wolfson, *The Duplicity*, 74–5. Wolfson reads Levinas's depiction of Abraham alongside Rosenzweig and Heidegger on the theme of homeland: "Levinas positions the identity of nonplace in Judaism as an alternative to the Heideggarian notion of homeland based on enrootedness in the soil." See also Ephraim Meir, "The Meaning of the Abrahamic Adventure in Levinas's Thought," in *Levinas Faces Biblical Figures*, ed. Yael Lin (Lanham, MD: Lexington, 2014), 19–34; and Glowacka, "Sacrificing the Text": "Levinas draws an analogy between the adventure of Western philosophy, the philosophy of immanence that always equates thought and being, and the journey of Ulysses. . . . This story, in which the Other emerges only as the transmutation of the same, is foiled by the Abrahamic journey, in which the promised destination is unknown" (40).

14. Emmanuel Levinas, "Meaning and Sense," in *Basic Philosophical Writings*, ed. Adriaan Peperzak, Simon Critchley, and Robert Bernasconi (Bloomington: Indiana University Press, 1996), 48. Earlier, in his wartime notebooks, Levinas had also criticized the course of philosophizing as a return to one's homeland, likened to clear-minded Ulysses tied to the mast of his ship, resisting the self's voyage outward: "retour. Philosopher, c'est retourner dans sa patrie" (*Oeuvres Complètes*, Vol. 1, ed. Rodolphe Calin and Catherine Chalier [Paris: Bernard Grasset, 2009], 344). Later, the relational experience is described as being "without recourse, without fatherland" (Levinas, *Otherwise Than Being*, 103). In Levinas's view, the Greek and Hebrew traditions need not be incompatible with one another, and he often blurs the two, using biblical

idioms in his philosophical writings. In this sense, the separation he intends between his philosophical and "confessional" writings belies a more nuanced relation between the two. For more on Levinas's use of the terms *Greek* and *Hebrew*, see Derrida, "Violence and Metaphysics," 153; Jill Robbins, *Prodigal Son/Elder Brother: Interpretation and Alterity in Augustine, Petrarch, Kafka, Levinas* (Chicago: University of Chicago Press, 1991), 103; Annette Aronowicz, "Introduction," in Emmanuel Levinas, *Nine Talmudic Readings*, xiv–xv; Gibbs, *Correlations in Rosenzweig and Levinas*, 157–8; Tamra Wright, *The Twilight of Jewish Philosophy: Emmanuel Levinas' Ethical Hermeneutics* (Amsterdam: Harwood Academic, 1999), 158; Oona Eisenstadt, "Levinas versus Levinas: Hebrew, Greek, and Linguistic Justice," *Philosophy & Rhetoric* 38, no. 2 (2005): 145–58; Michael L. Morgan, *Discovering Levinas* (Cambridge, UK: Cambridge University Press, 2007), 336; Elliot R. Wolfson, "Secrecy, Modesty, and the Feminine," 196; Leora Batnitzky, "Levinas between German Metaphysics and Christian Theology," in *The Exorbitant: Levinas between Jews and Christians*, ed. Kevin Hart and Michael A. Signer (New York: Fordham University Press, 2010), 17; Richard A. Cohen, *Levinasian Meditations: Ethics, Philosophy, and Religion* (Pittsburgh, PA: Duquesne University Press, 2010), 261; and Elliot R. Wolfson, "Apophasis and the Trace of Transcendence: Wyschogrod's Contribution to a Postmodern Jewish Immanent a/Theology," *Philosophy Today* 55 (November 2011), 329.

15. For more on this intersection, see Feldman, *Glory and Agony*, 7. Feldman addresses the ethics and gender of human sacrifice in Greek mythology and the Jewish and Christian traditions, offering a genealogy of responses to twentieth-century sacrificial tropes in Hebrew culture. She reads the primal Hebraic story of male attempted sacrifice alongside the sacrifice of Jephthah's daughter in Judges 11–2 and its own classical Greek analogues, illustrating the gender discrepancies in the tales: "How should we interpret the *gender* difference between the Hebraic archetypal sacrificial story and its many Greek variants, where the sacrificial victim is mostly a virgin daughter?" (7).

16. "Her supplications and her cries of father/ were nothing, nor the child's lamentation/ to kings passioned for battle./ The father prayed, called to his men to lift her/ with strength of hand swept in her robes aloft/ and prone above the altar, as you might lift/ a goat for sacrifice" (Aeschylus, "Agamemnon," in *Oresteia*, trans. Richmond Lattimore [Chicago: University of Chicago Press, 1953], l:227–34).

17. Nicole Loraux, *Tragic Ways of Killing a Woman*, trans. Anthony Forster (Cambridge, MA: Harvard University Press, 1987), 45.

18. Jan N. Bremmer, "Sacrificing a Child in Ancient Greece: The Case of Iphigeneia," in *The Sacrifice of Isaac: The Aqedah (Genesis 22) and Its Interpretations*, ed. Ed Noort and Eibert Tigchelaar (Leiden: Brill, 2002), 30.

19. Loraux, *Tragic Ways of Killing a Woman*, 32. Loraux points out that while Iphigenia's death is generally described with the language of throat-cutting and sacrifice, *sphazō* and *thyō*, there are passages that classify Iphigenia's death as murder, *phonos*. See also 72n22 on the variations in vocabulary describing sacrifice and murder in Greek tragedy.

20. Aeschylus, "Agamemnon," 1.1297–8.

21. "Lost are my father's altars, but the block is there/ to reek with sacrificial blood, my own" (Aeschylus, "Agamemnon," l.1277–8).

22. Aeschylus, "Agamemnon," 1.1415–8.

23. "By my child's Justice driven to fulfillment, by/ her Wrath and Fury, to whom I sacrificed this man" (Aeschylus, "Agamemnon," 1.1432–3).

24. "The female force, the desperate/ love crams its resisted way/ on marriage and the dark embrace/ of brute beasts, of mortal men" (Aeschylus, "The Libation Bearers," in *Oresteia*, l.599–602).

25. Aeschylus, "The Libation Bearers," l.605–15.

26. Aeschylus, "The Eumenides," *Oresteia*, l.416.

27. Aeschylus, "The Eumenides," l.734–38.

28. Monique Schneider views Levinas's later work as an attempt to reverse the matricidal impulses of Western thought, which are exemplified in Athena's avowal of her purely masculine parentage in Aeschylus's *Oresteia*. See Monique Schneider, "En deçà du visage," in *Emmanuel Levinas: L'éthique comme philosophie première*, ed. Jean Greisch and Jacques Rolland (Paris: Éditions du Cerf, 1993), 149; cited in Stella Sandford, "Masculine Mothers?," 185.

29. If in the *Oresteia* order is restored by the androgynous figure of Athena, a similar dynamic sees the blind prophet Tiresias resolving the action in Sophocles's *Antigone*. Tiresias mediates between prophetic vision and blindness, between the divine and the human. Tiresias also serves to mediate the play's thematic conflict between men and women because, as the audience is aware, the prophet was once a woman. In Homer's *Odyssey*, again, Athena resolves the cycle of vengeance. Odysseus is in an impossible situation, as the families of the noblemen he killed will certainly come after him in revenge. Then, suddenly, Athena, taking on the form of a man, steps in and moderates, "hand[ing] down her pacts of peace/ between both sides for all the years to come—/ the daughter of Zeus whose shield is storm and thunder,/ yes, but the goddess still kept Mentor's build and voice" (Homer, *The Odyssey*, trans. Robert Fagles [New York: Penguin Classics, 1997], book 24, l.509–602). These narratives emphasize that only one with both masculine and feminine characteristics can bring the story to a satisfying and final closure, but ultimately all three resolutions are coded male. These figures are not truly androgynous, equal parts male and female, but rather closer to Wolfson's elucidation of the male androgyne, their androgyny expressive of being a male female (see Wolfson, *Language, Eros, Being*, 142–89).

30. The scope of sibling violence similarly hangs over *Antigone*, whose action is set in motion as a result of brothers becoming political enemies.

31. See Seyla Benhabib, "On Hegel, Women, and Irony": in the *Oresteia*, Aeschylus "exposed the clash between the early and the new orders as a clash between the female power of blood and the male power of the sword and the law . . . between the maternal power of birth and the paternal power of the law" (43n41).

32. A number of scholars have examined Jephthah's sacrifice of his daughter and its implications. For representative examples, see Phyllis Trible, *Texts of Terror*, 93–116; Mieke Bal, *Death & Dissymmetry: The Politics of Coherence in the Book of Judges* (Chicago: University of Chicago Press, 1988), 41–68; and Esther Fuchs, *Sexual Politics in the Biblical Narrative: Reading the Hebrew Bible as a Woman* (London: Sheffield Academic Press, 2000), 177–99; Johanna Stiebert, *Fathers and Daughters in the Hebrew Bible* (Oxford: Oxford University Press, 2013), 72–101; and Ken Stone, "Animal Difference, Sexual Difference, and the Daughter of Jephthah," *Biblical Interpretation* 24, no. 1 (January 2016): 1–16. In comparing Jephthah's daughter to Isaac, Stone writes, "Isaac is spared when his place is taken *by* an animal, while Jephthah's daughter is sacrificed *like* an animal" (5). The sacrifice of Jephthah's daughter is echoed in 2 Kings 3:27, when the Moabite King sacrifices his son as a burnt offering for military success. But, Stone observes, "Women's greater vulnerability to animalization can't be ignored when we ask how the daughter of Jephthah, in distinction from Isaac or other male Israelite narrative characters, becomes a burnt offering given by her father to Israel's God" (8). According to Stiebert, the fact that Jephthah's daughter is sacrificed indicates not her expendability but rather her importance. Her sacrifice in Judges 11 "stresses not inconsequentiality but its opposite: the high value and possibly also love for the daughter" (*Fathers and Daughters*, 94). Furthermore, Stiebert argues that Jephthah's daughter displays more agency than Isaac in Genesis 22 because she "acts, speaks, negotiates for spending two months with her friends, and makes the decision to submit to the vow" (95).

33. "And the Lord was very wroth and said: Behold, Jepthan hath vowed that he will offer unto me that which meeteth with him first. Now therefore if a dog meet with Jepthan first, shall a dog be offered unto me? And now let the vow of Jepthan be upon his firstborn, even upon the fruit of his body, and his prayer upon his only begotten daughter. But I will verily deliver my people at this time, not for his sake, but for the prayer which Israel hath prayed" (Pseudo-Philo, *The Biblical Antiquities of Philo*, trans. M. R. James, 39:10–11; available at http://www .sacred-texts.com/bib/bap/bap55.htm). See Trible, *Texts of Terror*, 115n59: In *The Book of Biblical Antiquities*, "God criticizes Jephthah harshly for his wicked vow; his daughter, given the name Seila, dies willingly so that her sacrificial death

would not be in vain; and God decrees that she is wiser than both her father and 'the wise men of the people.'"

34. For an insightful comparative reading of the biblical sacrificial victims Isaac and Jephthah's daughter with both fictional and nonfictional narratives of lynching and the Holocaust, see Jodi Eichler-Levine, *Suffer the Little Children: Uses of the Past in Jewish and African American Children's Literature* (New York: New York University Press, 2013), 91–153.

35. Kierkegaard, *Fear and Trembling*, 57. The tragic heroes all "heroically have overcome the agony, heroically have lost the beloved, and have only to complete the task eternally" (58).

36. Kierkegaard, *Fear and Trembling*, 59.

37. In linking the *Aqedah* primarily to Abraham's faith, Kierkegaard likely echoes Hebrews 11:17: "By faith Abraham, when put to the test, offered up Isaac. He who had received the promises was ready to offer up his own son."

38. Kierkegaard, *Fear and Trembling*, 55. There are many resonances between the thought of Kierkegaard and Rosenzweig on the leap of faith and the movement from the human to the religious sphere; see Michael D. Oppenheim, *Søren Kierkegaard and Franz Rosenzweig: The Movement from Philosophy to Religion* (PhD diss., University of California—Santa Barbara, 1976), 205–39, and Welz, *Love's Transcendence*, 89–276.

39. Martin Buber, *Eclipse of God: Studies in the Relation Between Religion and Philosophy* (New York: Harper, 1957), 115.

40. Buber, "On the Suspension of the Ethical," 118–19. This doubt recalls Immanuel Kant's response to the narrative. In *The Conflict of the Faculties* (1798), Kant argues that the command could not have come from God, because God would not contradict the moral law: "in some cases man can be sure that the voice he hears is *not* God's; for if the voice commands him to do something contrary to the moral law, then no matter how majestic the apparition may be, and no matter how it may seem to surpass the whole of nature, he must consider it an illusion" (Immanuel Kant, *The Conflict of the Faculties*, trans. Mary J. Gregor [Lincoln: University of Nebraska Press, 1992], 115). Kant then refers explicitly to Genesis 22: "Abraham should have replied to this supposedly divine voice: 'That I ought not kill my good son is quite certain. But that you, this apparition, are God—of that I am not certain, and never can be, not even [if] this voice rings down to me from (visible) heaven'" (115). On Kant's reading, see Claus Westermann, *Genesis 12–36: A Commentary*, trans. John J. Scullion (Minneapolis: Augsburg, 1985), 354. Tikva Frymer-Kensky shows how both Kant's and Kierkegaard's interpretations could be drawn from the same text. Through a comparative analysis of God's statement in verse 12, *ata yadati* ("now I know"), with the same phrase in Psalm 20, Frymer-Kensky concludes,

This crucially ambiguous sentence leads to utterly different conclusions—
one, that binding Isaac for sacrifice is a mark of Abraham's special virtue
and fidelity; and the other, that binding Isaac was a failure of Abraham,
who was after all only human and who missed his opportunity to rise in
defense of justice. The first explanation places a high value on submission,
the second on God-wrestling. In modern philosophy the latter position
has been identified with Kant, who argued that the moral is the ultimate;
and the former with Kierkegaard, who proclaimed Abraham as a "knight
of faith" who operated in a realm beyond morality. The story can support
either position. . . . Part of the impact of this story lies in the fact that it
makes us aware of our own values as we read it. We cannot remain
neutral. (134–5)

41. Jean-Paul Sartre, *Existentialism and Humanism*, trans. Philip Mairet
(London: Methuen, 1970), 31.

42. Sartre, *Existentialism and Humanism*, 31. We can compare Sartre's account
with the "mistake of hearing" that Franz Kafka reads into the story. In Kafka's
"Abraham," Abraham is the worst student in the classroom, who "rose in the
expectant stillness and came forward from his dirty desk in the last row because
he had made a mistake of hearing, and the whole class burst out laughing"
("Abraham," in *The Basic Kafka*, ed. Erich Heller [New York: Pocket Books,
1979], 174). The skeptical response to the call on high is echoed in Euripides's
Electra, in which Orestes asks a similar question of the sacrifice of his sister:
"Was it not some fiend that bade it, assuming the god's likeness?" (Euripides,
"Electra," in *Ten Plays by Euripides*, trans. Moses Hadas and John McLean
[Toronto: Bantam Books, 1981], l.979).

43. As Katz explains, "the loss of the ethical in the name of duty is precisely
what Levinas fears. The *Shoah* . . . was an outcome of a view that condones the
subordination of the ethical to duty" (Katz, *Levinas, Judaism, and the Feminine*,
120). Katz refers to the post-Shoah view of the *Aqedah* shared by Buber and
Levinas: "could we not say that this distance from obedience, this sensitivity to
hearing a second voice—if there was one—is precisely what the Nazis lacked?"
(116n14). Similarly, in Stine Holte's view, Levinas takes issue with the dangerous
consequences of Kierkegaard's reading, namely a religion dissociated from
ethics: "Religion should not be spared from ethics; if it is, the consequences
might be fatal" ("Asymmetry, Testimony, and God in Levinas's Later Thinking,"
in *Despite Oneself: Subjectivity and Its Secret in Kierkegaard and Levinas*, 82). As
Frymer-Kensky puts it, in the late twentieth century, "history teaches us the
horrors that can be perpetrated by those who 'hear' God's command" ("Akeda:
The View from the Bible," 143).

44. Levinas, *Proper Names*," 70.

45. Levinas, 70. Instead of turning inward to find God, away from others, Levinas asks whether "a renunciation of self should not accompany that desire for salvation so underrated by systematic philosophy" (71).

46. Levinas, *"Proper Names,"* 72.

47. Levinas, 72.

48. Levinas, 74.

49. Levinas, *Otherwise Than Being*, 114. Rosenzweig refers to Abraham's response to God in the *Star*, in the section "The Call" (*"Der Anruf"*) (Rosenzweig, *Star*, 189; *Stern*, 113). He compares Abraham's response to God, "I am here" (*"Hier bin ich"*), with Adam's lack of response to God in Genesis 3: "The man hides, he does not answer, he remains mute, he remains the Self as we know it. . . . the woman, for her part . . . is the one who did it, and she then throws the guilt on the last It: it was the serpent" (Rosenzweig, *Star*, 190; *Stern*, 113). Adam tries to hide behind the woman and the serpent. Abraham, however, answers when called by his proper name: "To God's question: 'Where are you?' the man still remained a You, as a defiant, obstinate Self; when called by name twice, with the strongest fixity of purpose to which one cannot remain deaf, the man, totally open, totally unfolded, totally ready, totally—soul, now answers: 'I am here'" (Rosenzweig, *Star*, 190). Whereas Adam remains closed within himself, Abraham's response to his proper name involves being open to the call and "listening" (*"Das Hören"*). Katz compares Rosenzweig's depiction of the call to Levinas's reading of the *Aqedah*: Rosenzweig "describes the movement of humanity from Adam, who did not hear God, to Abraham, who did. Rosenzweig describes this movement in terms of the recognition of responsibility. Adam, upon being asked what he had done, does not reply with an 'I.' He does not say, 'I did it.' Rather, he says, 'she did it'. . . . The 'here I am' marks the moment of subjectivity" ("The Responsibility of Irresponsibility," 28). Katz situates Levinas's reading of Kierkegaard in the context of his idea of fecundity: "If we reread Levinas's work *Totality and Infinity* into this story, we could say that the father-son relationship Levinas describes is playing itself in the Akedah, as it does nowhere else. Nowhere in Judaism does fecundity mean more than it does in Abraham's relationship to Isaac, a relationship in which the son's life and the future of Israel are, literally, suspended in his father's hands" (27).

50. Levinas, *Otherwise Than Being*, 146.

51. Levinas, 150.

52. On Isaac's silence, see Yvonne Sherwood, "A Recently Discovered Letter from Isaac to Abraham (Annotated)," in *Biblical Blaspheming: Trials of the Sacred for a Secular Age* (Cambridge, UK: Cambridge University Press, 2012), 182: "And I *say* nothing. Even as you stand over me, bound and trussed up like an animal when I have surely worked out that this is no normal father-son-bonding-day-out or fishing trip I say nothing. I do not scream, squeak or whimper. The lack

of any noise or words of Isaac is unbelievable, incredible, unbearable." Notably, the son's silence is not a feature of the Qur'anic narrative. In Surah 37, the son verbally consents to the sacrifice, after he is explicitly consulted by his father. See Qur'an 37:99–111. For comparisons of the sacrifice of Abraham's son in Judaism, Christianity, and Islam, see Yvonne Sherwood, "Binding-Unbinding: Divided Responses of Judaism, Christianity, and Islam to the 'Sacrifice' of Abraham's Beloved Son," *Journal of the American Academy of Religion* 72, no. 4 (December 2004): 821–61; Jon Levenson, *Inheriting Abraham: The Legacy of the Patriarch in Judaism, Christianity, and Islam* (Princeton, NJ: Princeton University Press, 2012); Carol Bakhos, *The Family of Abraham: Jewish, Christian, and Muslim Interpretations* (Cambridge, MA: Harvard University Press, 2014); and David L. Weddle, *Sacrifice in Judaism, Christianity, and Islam* (New York: New York University Press, 2017).

53. See Katz: "The relationship between ethics and ontology that characterizes his project can also be cast as a tension between the 'feminine' and the 'masculine,' between passivity and virility" ("From Eros to Maternity," 154).

54. Genesis 23:2. For an analysis of the role of Sarah in this narrative, see Wendy Zierler, "In Search of a Feminist Reading of the Akedah." Zierler suggest that "Sarah's absence from the *Akedah* narrative allows her to endure in the story as an alternative to the Abrahamic theology of detachment" (19).

55. Katz, "Levinas Between Agape and Eros," 345. In Katz's view, Sarah's death "does not indicate a normative component showing that a mother ought to sacrifice her life. Rather, it indicates the risk one takes precisely when one loves and cares for another" ("From Eros to Maternity," 170).

56. *Midrash Leviticus Rabbah*, Genesis 23:1–2. James A. Diamond discusses the narrative of Sarah's death in the response of Kalonymous Kalman Shapira, the Piaseczner Rebbe, known as the Warsaw Ghetto Rebbe: "One of the most daring theological statements on death, or any aspect of Jewish theology, for that matter, to my mind is his reinvention of the midrashic causal link between the *akedah* and the subsequent narrative of Sarah's death. Her death, as R. Shapira recalls it, is a consciously chosen and defiant response to the perceived news of her son's death" ("Constructing a *Jewish* Philosophy of Being toward Death," in *Jewish Philosophy for the Twenty-First Century: Personal Reflections*, ed. Hava Tirosh-Samuelson and Aaron W. Hughes [Leiden: Brill, 2014], 77). R. Shapira casts Sarah's death "as the supreme expression of a dying for others, a willing death to evoke compassion and effect an end to suffering" (78). This conception of death is defined "in terms of the other rather than the self. . . . That ethic conditions the very height of humanity on a care for the other whose life and suffering takes precedence over one's own" (79).

57. *Midrash Tanhuma, Vayera* 22.

58. Elsewhere, in his essay "Judaism and the Feminine," Levinas attributes sacrifice to female biblical figures: "Biblical events would not have progressed

as they did had it not been for their watchful lucidity, the firmness of their determination, and their cunning and spirit of sacrifice" (31).

59. Jacques Derrida, *The Gift of Death*, trans. David Wills (Chicago: University of Chicago Press, 1995), 76. For an insightful womanist reading of the dynamic between Abraham, Sarah, and Hagar, see Wilda C. Gafney, *Womanist Midrash: A Reintroduction to the Women of the Torah and the Throne* (Louisville, KY: Westminster John Knox Press, 2017), 30–44, particularly Gafney's discussion of how Sarah weaponizes patriarchal norms in her exploitation of Hagar, and how "Sarah's economic and social privilege and national origin separate her from Hagar, even though they share gender peril" (38). For a reading of sisterhood and solidarity in this biblical narrative, see Renita J. Weems, *Just a Sister Away: A Womanist Vision of Women's Relationships in the Bible* (San Diego, CA: LuraMedia, 1988).

60. Derrida, *The Gift of Death*, 76.

61. Derrida, 76.

62. See David Wills, "Translator's Preface," *The Gift of Death*, vii.

63. Lisa Guenther explains that this self is responsible "even for the one who interrupts my identity and afflicts me with pain, commanding me to bear her 'like a maternal body'" (*The Gift of the Other: Levinas and the Politics of Reproduction* [Albany: State University of New York Press, 2006], 126). Alison Ainley comments, "In his attempts to address the other's appeal, Levinas has recourse to a language of pain and suffering, which is meant to mark the quintessential experience of being for another. Maternity is the mark of such an experience because it is a pain of the body, a corporeal undertaking that cannot be disregarded" ("Levinas and Kant: Maternal Morality and Illegitimate Offspring," in *Feminist Interpretations of Emmanuel Levinas*, 214.)

64. Levinas, *Otherwise Than Being*, 75.

65. As Simon Critchley observes, "In what must be the world's shortest refutation of Heidegger, Levinas complains that *Dasein* is never hungry. . . . As Levinas wittily puts it, 'The need for food does not have existence as its goal, but food'" ("Introduction," *The Cambridge Companion to Levinas*, 21; quoting Levinas, *Totality and Infinity*, 134). Jean Améry makes a similar point, asserting that only "if one is free it is possible to entertain thoughts of death that at the same time are not also thoughts of dying, fears of dying" (*At the Mind's Limits: Contemplations by a Survivor on Auschwitz and Its Realities [Jenseits von Schuld und Sühne]*, trans. Sidney Rosenfeld and Stella P. Rosenfeld [Bloomington: Indiana University Press, 1980], 17). Améry maintains that *Dasein*'s contemplative exercise can take place only if the self is already sheltered and fed. One can think on the nature of Heideggerian Being if one is nourished and clothed; otherwise, one is necessarily trapped within the realm of beings. See also Levinas, *Oeuvres Complètes*, Vol. 2, ed. Rodolphe Calin and Catherine

Chalier (Paris: Bernard Grasset, 2009), 151–72, a lecture delivered to the *College philosophique* on February 16, 1950. Here Levinas discusses Heidegger's *Sein und Zeit* as lacking the experience of enjoyment: "Jouir, c'est respirer, boire, manger, aller au musée, lire, se promener etc" (156). See also *Time and the Other*, 70–1, in which Levinas compares all-consuming physical suffering to Heidegger's notion of being-towards-death: "Death in Heidegger is an event of freedom, whereas for me the subject seems to reach the limit of the possible in suffering. It finds itself enchained, overwhelmed, and in some way passive."

66. Levinas's provocatively material and embodied phenomenology of subjectivity was likely influenced by his experience during the Second World War. The third Geneva Convention prohibited Nazis from rerouting prisoners of war; because he was a French officer, he was interned as a POW at a labor camp (see Simon Critchley, "Emmanuel Levinas: A Disparate Inventory," in *The Cambridge Companion to Levinas*, xv–xxx). In notebooks written during his captivity, Levinas discusses the experience of being drawn back from the intellect to basic animality and materiality: "L'animalité de l'homme. Non pas dans l'étude de sa physiologie et de sa psychologie. Mais dans la perception de l'homme. Le sentir. Comme un bœuf ou une vache qui [se] sont [mis à] marcher sur leurs pattes arrière . . . Tout cela apparait aussi dans les prétentions intellectuelles derrière lesquelles gît en quelque manière cette face animale, limitée par elle-même . . . Agaçant dans sa matérialité" (*Oeuvres Complètes*, Vol. 1, 65). Levinas's philosophical approach to death and the images in *Otherwise Than Being* of persecution, being a hostage and feeding the hungry are reminiscent of the Shoah (see Katz, "The Responsibility of Irresponsibility," 23). Levinas later writes that after the Shoah, "in the face of overproud metaphysical systems, man's freedom succumbs to physical suffering;" in the past, "provided that he accepted his death," a man "could call himself free. But now physical torture, cold and hunger or discipline, things stronger than death, can break this freedom" (Levinas, "The Struthof Case," in *Difficult Freedom*, 149–50).

67. Levinas, "Substitution," In *Basic Philosophical Writings*, ed. Adriaan Peperzak (Bloomington: Indiana University Press, 1996), 87. In the original: "L'expression 'dans sa peau' n'est pas une métaphore . . . la diastole et la systole du cœur battant sourdement contre la paroi de sa propre peau" (Levinas, "La Substitution," *Revue Philosophique de Louvain* 91, no. 66 [1968]: 496). This phrasing later reappears in *Otherwise Than Being* (109); *Autrement qu'être* (172).

68. Levinas, "Substitution," 87; 182n27. In the original: "Le corps n'est pas seulement l'image ou la figure" (496); "Le corps n'est ni l'obstacle opposé à l'âme, ni le tombeau qui l'emprisonne, mais ce par quoi elle est la susceptibilité même,—ce qui se blesse et s'immole,—le Soi" ("La Substitution," 496n13).

69. Levinas, "Substitution," 88–9. In the original: "en soi comme dans sa peau—et cette incarnation n'est pas métaphorique, car être dans sa peau

est une manière extrême d'être exposé qui n'advient pas aux choses" ("La Substitution," 499).

70. Levinas, *Otherwise Than Being*, 104, 106, 108, 110.

71. Levinas, 115.

72. Levinas, 108.

73. Levinas, 117–8.

74. Batnitzky explains that maternity "gives material meaning" to Levinas's statement on bearing responsibility for the persecution of the persecutor: "*Otherwise Than Being* turns directly to questions of material existence in order to describe the phenomenality of ethics as first philosophy. . . . Reference to 'maternity' is a fundamental component of Levinas's attempt at articulating the materiality of the ethical, human task" ("Dependency and Vulnerability," 134).

75. Jean-Luc Nancy, *L'Intrus*, trans. Susan Hanson (East Lansing: Michigan State University Press, 2002), 3: "the sensation was something like one breath, now pushed across a cavern, already imperceptibly half-open and strange; and, as though within a single representation, the sensation of passing over a bridge, while still remaining on it." Levinas also represents the openness to the other through breath: the subject is "forced to detach itself from itself, to breathe more deeply, all the way" (Levinas, *Otherwise Than Being*, 110); "breathing is transcendence in the form of opening up" (Levinas, 181).

76. Nancy, *L'Intrus*, 4.

77. Nancy, 4.

78. Levinas, *Otherwise Than Being*, 126.

79. Levinas, 126.

80. See Levinas, *Otherwise Than Being*, 77: "a subject is of flesh and blood, a man that is hungry and eats, entrails in a skin, and thus capable of giving the bread out of his mouth, or giving his skin." In another essay, Levinas unequivocally articulates this ethical obligation: "Responsibility for the other to the point of dying for the other!" ("Diachrony and Representation," in *Entre Nous: On Thinking-of-the-Other*, trans. Michael B. Smith and Barbara Harshaw [New York: Columbia University Press, 1998], 173). Levinas's references to substitution, sacrifice, and incarnation can be seen as echoing Christological themes. Batnitzky maintains that there are "some broad affinities between Levinas's philosophy and Christian theology, in terms of both form and content"; she suggests viewing him as neither a distinctively Jewish nor a secular thinker ("Levinas between German Metaphysics and Christian Theology," 19). For a discussion of how Christian theologians have adopted Levinas's thought, see Robyn Horner, "On Levinas's Gifts to Christian Theology," in *The Exorbitant: Levinas between Jews and Christians*, 140. See also David Brezis, *Levinas et le tournant sacrificiel* (Paris: Hermann, 2012). Brezis discusses Levinas's position on sacrifice in view of the notable emergence of a Christian

vocabulary of sacrifice, atonement, substitution, and kenosis in Levinas's later writings (254).

81. Martin Heidegger, *Being and Time*, trans. John Macquarrie and Edward Robinson (San Francisco: Harper & Row, 1962), 284.

82. Heidegger, *Being and Time*, 294–5.

83. Heidegger, 294.

84. Levinas, "Diachrony and Representation," 174.

85. Emmanuel Levinas, *God, Death and Time*, trans. Bettina Bergo, ed. Jacques Rolland (Redwood City, CA: Stanford University Press, 2000), 51.

86. On Levinas's flattening of Heidegger's analysis of death in *Being and Time*, see Elliot Wolfson, "Echo of the Otherwise: Ethics of Transcendence and the Lure of Theolatry," in *Encountering the Medieval in Modern Jewish Thought*, ed. James A. Diamond and Aaron W. Hughes (Leiden: Brill, 2012), 261–324.

87. Levinas, *God, Death and Time*, 39. Katz explains that Levinas's entire project can be seen in this light: "According to Levinas, philosophy's history as a discipline gave priority to the ontological over the ethical, and the relationship we have to our own death had priority over the ethical relationship we have to the other" ("From Eros to Maternity," 154).

88. Levinas, *Otherwise Than Being*, 195n10. Levinas refers to a central verse from the Song of Songs in responding to Heidegger: "Here, on the contrary, the meaning of death does not begin in death. This invites us to think of death as a moment of death's *signification*, which is a meaning that overflows death.... Expressions like 'love is stronger than death' (in fact, the Song of Songs says precisely: 'Love, as strong as death') have their meaning" (Levinas, *God, Death and Time*, 104). According to Robert Bernasconi, "To say that love is stronger than death is, according to Levinas, to say that the death of someone I love affects me more than my own death" ("A Love That Is Stronger Than Death: Sacrifice in the Thought of Levinas, Heidegger and Bloch," *Angelaki: Journal of Theoretical Humanities* 7, no. 2 [2002], 12). Indeed, Batnitzky explains that Rosenzweig's central reference to the Song of Songs, "love is as strong as death" (Rosenzweig, *Star*, 169), provides Levinas with "the quintessential response to Heidegger. In the context of Levinas's philosophy, Rosenzweig's formulation would describe the limitation of Heidegger's view of the self and of death" ("Levinas between German Metaphysics and Christian Theology," 21).

89. Katz, *Levinas, Judaism, and the Feminine*, 137.

90. See Katz, *Levinas, Judaism, and the Feminine*, 164n43: "Every time a woman goes to full term and gives birth she assumes a risk, a life-threatening risk.... Women risk their lives for the possibility to create a future.... That individuals, in this case women, might find the life of an other worth the sacrifice of their own lives indicates the possibility of ethics—the for-the-other." Katz here is responding to the following potentially troubling passage from an interview with

Levinas by Bracha Ettinger: "the 'dying' of a woman is certainly unacceptable. . . . I think the heart of the heart, the deepest of the feminine, is dying in giving life, in bringing life into the world. . . . I am not emphasizing dying but, on the contrary, *future*" (Bracha Lichtenberg Ettinger, *Que dirait Eurydice? What Would Eurydice Say? Bracha Lichtenberg Ettinger in Conversation with Emmanuel Levinas* (Paris: BLE Atelier, 1997), 27; cited in Katz, *Levinas, Judaism, and the Feminine*, 52.

91. Levinas, *Autrement qu'être*, 109.

92. Levinas, *Otherwise Than Being*, 67.

93. Levinas, 88.

94. Levinas, *Autrement qu'être*, 140.

95. Levinas, *Otherwise Than Being*, 75; *Autrement qu'être*, 121.

96. Levinas, *Otherwise Than Being*, 104; in the original, "l'évocation de la maternité dans cette métaphore" (*Autrement qu'être*, 165).

97. Levinas, *Otherwise Than Being*, 109; "The body is neither an obstacle opposed to the soul, nor a tomb that imprisons it, but that by which the self is susceptibility itself . . . to be exposed to sickness, suffering, death, is to be exposed to compassion" (195n12).

98. According to Stella Sandford, in Levinas's language of maternity "the distinction between the literal and the metaphorical" has been confused "almost beyond repair" ("Masculine Mothers?," 183).

99. Levinas, *Otherwise Than Being*, 75; in the original, "maternité, gestation de l'autre dans le même" (*Autrement qu'être*, 121).

100. Mara Benjamin points out the problems with maternity in Levinas's work: "The pregnant body represents the generativity and 'fecundity' of the encounter with the face of the Other. Yet pregnancy here is entirely metaphorical; Levinas excludes or marginalizes actual parent and child, even as he insists on the capacity of the vulnerable Other to command" ("Intersubjectivity Meets Maternity: Buber, Levinas, and the Eclipsed Relation," in *Thinking Jewish Culture in America*, ed. Ken Koltun-Fromm [Lanham, MD: Lexington, 2013], 267). Levinas's concept of maternity can nevertheless be productive: "Levinas' inquiry into the 'infinity' that lies within intersubjective relationships provides a framework for thinking about the theological meaning of mothering" (275).

101. Julia Kristeva, *The Kristeva Reader*, ed. Toril Moi (New York: Columbia University Press, 1981), 182.

102. Kristeva, 167.

103. Kristeva, 169–79.

104. Kristeva, 206. In referring to her experience of maternity, Kristeva discusses the encounter more specifically with a son; Levinas, too, can be criticized for retaining an emphasis on the child-as-son. Is it specifically the son who provides the unique ethical encounter with the mother? Freud would

respond in the resounding affirmative. In his lecture on "Femininity," Freud writes that the perpetual female wish for a penis is fulfilled only once she gives birth to one: "The difference in a mother's reaction to the birth of a son or a daughter shows that the old factor of lack of a penis has even now not lost its strength. A mother is only brought unlimited satisfaction by her relation to a son; this is altogether the most perfect, the most free from ambivalence of all human relationships" (Sigmund Freud, "Femininity," in *The Standard Edition of the Complete Psychological Works*, ed. and trans. J. Strachey et al. [London: Hogarth Press, 1964], 22:134). While Kristeva does mention the specific example of a son, she decidedly dismisses Freud's assessment of maternal desire for a child as resulting from penis envy: "The fact remains, as far as the complexities and pitfalls of maternal experience are involved, that Freud offers only a massive *nothing*" (*The Kristeva Reader*, 178–79). She refers as well to the mother-daughter relation, again drawing from her own experience, this time as a child. The experience of being "face to face with her daughter" causes a mother to "differentiate between same beings," offering a unique encounter in which the same confronts the other-as-same (*The Kristeva Reader*, 184). But this relation is conflicted, a "war between mother and daughter," a "passion (love or hatred)" felt for another woman to which one is exposed only after "having taken her own mother's place . . . having herself become a mother" (183–4).

105. See Mara Benjamin, *The Obligated Self*.

106. Kierkegaard, *Fear and Trembling*, 13.

107. Katz, *Levinas, Judaism, and the Feminine*, 145. See also Claire Elise Katz, "No Place for Old Women, or Young Women Either," *Bamidbar* 4, no. 2 (2019): 79: "Levinas's ethical project takes Jewish philosophy to its furthest point and declares that the most ethical posture to take is for men to become like women—to be in (ethical) drag." According to Yael Feldman, major male figures in the Bible often display "unexpected 'feminine' behavior," and this may be what allows Abraham to stay his hand, unlike his Greek paternal counterparts (Feldman, "'And Rebecca Loved Jacob,' but Freud Did Not," 73).

108. Levinas, *Otherwise Than Being*, 105; in the original, "il se noue indénouable dans une responsabilité pour les autres" (*Autrement qu'être*, 134).

109. See Benjamin: "Some of these tendencies—and the feminist rejection of them—are especially pronounced in Christian theological-ethical discourse. . . . The self-sacrificial element of maternal love here and elsewhere embodies a feminized ideal of *imitatio christi*. . . . Hence feminist Christian theologians often argue for correctives precisely on this point" (*The Obligated Self*, 35n35).

110. Levinas, *Otherwise Than Being*, 105.

111. Derrida, *The Gift of Death*, 61.

112. Derrida, 68. See Glowacka: "The aporia of responsibility lies in the paradox that ethics also calls for irresponsibility. . . . The contradiction between

responsibility in general and absolute responsibility to and for the Other cannot be overcome by appealing to a higher tribunal" ("Sacrificing the Text," 41).

113. "How would you ever justify the fact that you sacrifice all the cats in the world to the cat that you feed at home every morning for years, whereas other cats die of hunger at every instant? Not to mention other people?" (Derrida, *The Gift of Death*, 71).

114. Derrida, *The Gift of Death*, 70.

115. Derrida, 70.

116. Derrida, 69.

117. Kathryn Lofton, *Consuming Religion* (Chicago: University of Chicago Press, 2017), 4.

118. *Game of Thrones*, "The Dance of Dragons," season 5, episode 9, directed by David Nutter, written by David Benioff and D. B. Weiss, aired June 7, 2015, on HBO. The sacrifice of Shireen is unique to the television series, as it does not occur in the published books in which Shireen is still alive. See Joanna Robinson, "How Tonight's *Game of Thrones* Signaled a Brutal Departure from the Books," *Vanity Fair*, June 10, 2015, https://www.vanityfair.com/hollywood /2015/06/stannis-burns-shireen-game-of-thrones-dance-of-dragons.

119. "Shireen's murder has raised complaints from critics who protest that it was out-of-character for Stannis. But the plot might as well be based on the ancient Greek tragedy *Iphigenia in Aulis*, by Euripides. Every beat of the Greek myth is the same as Stannis's story: The troops are stuck and starving and the general, Agamemnon, must sacrifice his own daughter to turn the fates to their favor. The mother begging for mercy, the disapproving second-in-command who can do nothing to stop it, the daughter who says she will do whatever it takes to help—it's all a clear echo" (Amanda Marcotte, "Don't Be So Shocked by the Deaths on *Game of Thrones*: The Show Is a Classical Tragedy," *Slate*, June 9, 2015, https://slate.com/culture/2015/06/game-of-thrones-is-a-classical-tragedy-don't -be-so-shocked-by-the-deaths.html).

120. Robinson, "How Tonight's *Game of Thrones* Signaled a Brutal Departure from the Books."

121. *Game of Thrones*, "The Winds of Winter," season 6, episode 10, directed by Miguel Sapochnik, written by David Benioff and D. B. Weiss, aired June 26, 2016, on HBO.

122. J. K. Rowling, *Harry Potter and the Deathly Hallows* (Vancouver: Bloomsbury, 2007), 568–9.

123. Edmund McMillen and Florian Himsl, *The Binding of Isaac*, 2011, https:// store.steampowered.com/app/113200/The_Binding_of_Isaac/.

124. See, for example, the 2015 Reddit thread https://www.reddit.com/r /bindingofisaac/comments/3gpyke/compilation_of_answers_from_edmunds _recent_qa/.

125. Drew Dixon, "*The Binding of Isaac* Review," *Paste Monthly*, October 7, 2011, http://www.pastemagazine.com/articles/2011/10/the-binding-of-isaac-review-pcmac.html.

126. Edmund McMillen, "Binding of Isaac: Origins (IGTM Special Edition Extended Interview)," September 8, 2014, https://www.youtube.com/watch?v=bMqFTuMECeA.

127. McMillen, "Binding of Isaac: Origins."

128. See Carey Walsh, "Christianity: Traditional Christian Interpretations of Genesis 22," in *Interpreting Abraham: Journeys to Moriah*, ed. Bradley Beach and Matthew Powell (Minneapolis, MN: Fortress Press, 2014); for a comparison of Jewish and Christian interpretations of Genesis 22, see Edward Kessler, *Bound by the Bible: Jews, Christians and the Sacrifice of Isaac* (Cambridge, UK: Cambridge University Press, 2004).

129. Suzanne Collins, *The Hunger Games* (New York: Scholastic Press, 2008), 22.

130. As Katniss explains, "in district 12, where the word *tribute* is pretty much synonymous with the word *corpse*, volunteers are all but extinct" (Collins, *The Hunger Games*, 22).

131. Arcade Fire, "Abraham's Daughter," track 1 on *The Hunger Games: Songs from District 12 and Beyond*, Republic, 2012, compact disc.

132. Arcade Fire, "Abraham's Daughter."

133. See Katharine Schwab, "The Rise of *Buffy* Studies," *The Atlantic*, October 1, 2015, http://www.theatlantic.com/entertainment/archive/2015/10/the-rise-of-buffy-studies/407020/.

134. *Buffy the Vampire Slayer*, "The Gift," season 5, episode 22, written and directed by Joss Whedon, aired May 22, 2001, on the WB Television Network.

135. Derrida, *The Gift of Death*, 43–4. On Derrida's reading, see Oona Eisenstadt, "Preferring or not Preferring: Derrida on Bartleby as Kierkegaard's Abraham," in *Derrida's Bible*, 167–79.

136. Lofton, *Consuming Religion*, 287.

137. Rawlinson, "Beyond Antigone," 106.

138. Rawlinson, 113.

139. Honig, *Antigone, Interrupted*, 8.

140. As Katz observes, while Levinas's maternal ethics "presents itself radically . . . it is also at once the place where we see the limits of his ethical project" ("Levinas Between Agape and Eros," 346).

141. Honig, *Antigone, Interrupted*, 183.

142. Honig, 183.

143. Honig, 183.

—⁓—

EPILOGUE

Beyond the Fraternal Family

THROUGHOUT THIS BOOK, I HAVE asked how critical gender analysis can lead to a more inclusive field of study, highlighting how biographical traces can lead us into a deeper engagement with works that have been and will likely continue to be foundational. Along with reinvestigations of twentieth-century foundational works' classical sources, biography helps us see the effects of textually unmarked positionality. As I bring this exploration to a close, I will first discuss my own transformative experiences of reading Levinas and Rosenzweig, then press more firmly on how the patriarchal logic structuring their texts is situated in the context of twentieth-century Jewish concerns, and finally turn to imagining a more inclusive field.

I was introduced to Levinas as an undergraduate student by Dorota Glowacka in her classes on literature, theory, and philosophy. I was immediately drawn to Levinas's thought. I felt particularly nourished by his invocation of traditional Jewish sources, both biblical and rabbinic. Reading his work made the turn to Christian referents in other postclassical works seem more apparent and less automatically accepted. His style, too, entranced me. Although his language was strange and unfamiliar, I felt that I could sense his meaning at an instinctual level. As a reading subject, I was made to feel both cast out and drawn in. When I teach Levinas's work, I mention this experience to students, who are often understandably anxious about their lack of comprehension. Levinas wants us to be not at home when we read him. If we can immediately grasp and assimilate his meaning, then we miss his fundamental point about alterity. This is why understanding (*comprendre*) can be limiting—it tries to take and grasp (*prendre*), without letting the other be.

Particularly in Levinas's later work, the reader must enter into a repetitive, rhapsodic style of writing that aims to write against the philosophical discourse and to be rooted in this discourse while simultaneously dislocated from its language. Levinas proceeds from a position of linguistic displacement, struggling to find a home in the French language, which is forever elusive since it was not his mother tongue.[1] Likely in conversation with the voice of Derrida, Levinas struggles to write otherwise than ontology while always necessarily restricted to the pull of a more rigid line of reasoning. This becomes a fundamental question in his work: is it possible to move past the ontological framework of Western thought without having recourse to that very frame of argumentation, and without taking up the language of ontology?[2] Levinas himself encapsulates this dilemma by paraphrasing Derrida's statement in the conclusion of his essay "Violence and Metaphysics": "Not to philosophize is still to philosophize."[3]

I am particularly drawn to the ethical and poetic modes Levinas takes up as expressions of "saying," as opposed to the propositional nature of the "said." Levinas's work intriguingly oscillates between these two modes, demonstrating the eruption of the synchronic by the diachronic, the ontological by the ethical, the virile by the feminine, and the Greek by the Jewish. We can see how this aligns with temporal registers. Time is experienced through the relation to the other. Levinas contrasts a relation of synchrony, in which the self remains the same, to diachrony, in which the other, of another time, interrupts the self and disrupts its temporality and inward comportment. Levinas's distinction between the saying (le dire) and the said (le dit) relates to his concept of time. Philosophical language tends to reduce the saying to the said, but "responsibility for another is precisely a saying prior to anything said."[4] The saying effects an interruption of totality, an ethical exposure to the other that operates along diachronic registers, while the said is synchronic and involves an ontological statement or assertion with an identifiable meaning. The saying represents interruption, infinity, infection by the other, proximity and contact, while the said represents systematic thinking, totality, and self-containment.

The place of temporality is also central to the arc of Rosenzweig's Star of Redemption. My dialogical encounter with the Star began as a graduate student in a directed reading course with my doctoral advisor, Elliot Wolfson. Wolfson's elucidation of linear circularity/circular linearity has shaped my reading of the Star.[5] I began reading at the end and ended at the beginning—not back to where I had begun but to a beginning not previously reached. Revelation is situated at the core of the Star because it occurs in the present; it brings the past of creation toward the future of redemption at every moment. Rosenzweig's evocative notion of dialogical speech emphasizes time as the mode in which the eternal continually cuts across the transience of human temporality. In Rosenzweig's messianic vision, one constantly anticipates but can never expect redemption to occur at every moment.[6]

Rosenzweig's understanding of the eschatological moment as erupting the present is consonant with his notion of speech-thinking, in which the dialogical relation to the other cuts across time in the human's relationship to the divine. When I teach Rosenzweig's thought now, I ask students to imagine how speech-thinking would look and sound. We discuss how, for Rosenzweig, poetry breaks the totality of the individual realm by reaching out toward the public sphere. The poem throws open the door of the solitary individual, inviting speech with others. Monologue is surpassed in the spontaneity of dialogue, reflecting his aim to do away with the boundaries between myth and reason, poetry and philosophy. The method of his new thinking originates in its temporality. Whereas thinking is timeless and conducted in solitude, "speaking is time-bound, time-nourished. . . . it does not know in advance where it will arrive; it lets its cues be given by others. It lives in general from the life of the other."[7] In the movement toward eternity, death's finality is overcome. We see this in Rosenzweig's *Star*, which opens with the words "From death" and ends "Into Life."[8] His central chapter begins by invoking a key line from the Song of Songs: "Love is as strong as death."[9] This verse, so fruitful to Rosenzweig's enterprise, resonates in Levinas's project as well, as Levinas asserts infinity over death through fecundity.

Poetry, infinity, alterity, and time: these are captivating ideas that Rosenzweig and Levinas think through in original, breathtaking, and challenging ways. It is easy to remember why I was first pulled to these works as a reader and continue to be invested in their expansive possibilities. Twentieth-century Jewish thinkers uniquely "continue to mark out a powerful place for religion and religious thought in contemporary culture, the zone between one person and another where the human and the divine intermingle."[10] I have spent years, and now a monograph of my own, working through these texts not because I want to dismiss them as hopelessly passé and patriarchal but because I want to be able to address them as a reader, with everything that responsible addressing implies. Time and intersubjectivity are central to these thinkers. To engage with these texts in real dialogue, we must first acknowledge how in them eternity is predicated on figurative and literal procreation, how infinity points toward a homosocial, male utopia, and how encounters with the other, whether divine or terrestrial, are often expressed in normatively limiting ways. We have to come to terms with gender terminology mobilized to affirm norms of procreative marriage and, as Mara Benjamin writes, "a more general failure to render visible the hidden gender economy underneath modern Jewish think-ers' most influential texts."[11] In order to explore the possibilities that emerge from these works, then, we need to expose the narrative models that persist beneath our explicit acknowledgment.

Patriarchal structures can be seen to have defined some of the key interven-tions in modern Jewish thought, in works that implicitly and explicitly hinge on the regulation of women's bodies to perpetuate continuity. The resurgence of interest in Rosenzweig can be found both in his connection with the more widely discussed Levinas and, Peter Eli Gordon suggests, because of "the as-similationist worries endemic to North America."[12] Rosenzweig's confirmation of "communal solidarity" in his notion of Jews as a blood community in the *Star* would have appealed to this audience.[13] This was precisely the exclusive idea that "made Rosenzweig so attractive to North American readership—the idea of Jewish uniqueness."[14] Rosenzweig was not alone in this positioning. As Katja Garloff has shown in the case of Enlightenment thinker Moses Mendels-sohn, "Mendelssohn wanted to promote the cultural and political integration of Jews into German society while maintaining their religious distinctiveness, and endogamous marriage was crucial in this regard."[15] There is thus a his-tory of endogamy in German-Jewish thought and beyond. Gordon notes that the connection between the Holocaust and assimilation was made explicit by Emil Fackenheim's well-known addition to the 613 *mitzvot* (commandments), in which Jews must resolve to deny Hitler a posthumous victory by ensuring Jewish survival.[16]

In the twentieth century, Jewish communal institutions, informed by the work of Jewish sociologists, identified a "marriage crisis" as a priority to ad-dress and avoid by furthering the impetus of Jewish survival. As Lila Corwin Berman observes, "An intimate affair between Jews and sociologists was con-summated by the 1970s around their common interest in—and, for some, deep fear of—Jewish intermarriage."[17] The social researchers of the time highlighted correlations between the declining fertility and marriage rates of American Jews and growing aspirations among women for power and control over their bodies. This social research apparatus was predicated on the legislation of wom-en's bodies in the service of continuity. Marla Brettschneider convincingly makes the case that this is "a heterosexist paradigm."[18] Rosenzweig's focus on a Jewish community of blood clearly participates in the demographic panic of twentieth-century Jewish population studies, though with a philosophical rather than sociological inflection.

The continuity paradigm rests on an epistemological and political system that focuses its "normative and affective power on women and their bodies."[19]

As Lila Corwin Berman, Kate Rosenblatt, and Ronit Y. Stahl convincingly argue, discussions of Jewish continuity and communal survival have been predicated historically on restrictive sexual and gender politics. This paradigm demands women's obedience to a specific family model and holds women responsible for perpetuating (or for failing to perpetuate) Jewish family and community. The continuity narrative enforces surveillance over women's bodies, deprioritizes women's autonomy, and emphasizes the dual importance of endogamy and increased fertility as the means for securing the Jewish future. Berman, Rosenblatt, and Stahl's analysis demonstrates that this model's "assumptions about women's bodies as objects to be controlled and policed" have become integrated into Jewish scholarship, discourse, and institutional life "to validate the simple 'truth' of women's primary role in Jewish continuity: as incubators."[20] The patriarchal structures and logics of the continuity paradigm work together to "naturalize hierarchies, regimes of power, and modes of control."[21]

The assumed narrative of Jewish continuity that posits reproduction as an end in and of itself is a patriarchal symptom but not a necessary approach. By reassessing these canonical works, then, we address issues that stand at the center of contemporary conversations. Only once we have done the work of critical reading can we see how these important twentieth-century Jewish thinkers can provide valuable models and capacious language for intersubjective ethics, embodiment, and positionality.

How do these demands extend to the ways we canonically (re)construct the field of modern Jewish thought? Recent work, such as the essays collected in *Modern Middle Eastern Jewish Thought: Writings on Identity, Politics, and Culture*, have productively challenged a Eurocentric model by opening up the canon to include writings from the Arab East on topics including colonialism, secularization, and the rise of nationalism.[22] Sarah Hammerschlag shows that even among Europeans, French Jewish thought provides an avenue both to challenge the German-centric model of the field and to highlight authors and thinkers often left out of the discussion, including Sarah Kofman, Simone Weil, Albert Memmi, Jacqueline Mesnil-Amar, and Hélène Cixous.[23]

I myself have found work at the intersection of gender studies, religious studies, and philosophy to be especially fruitful, as is evident from many of my most frequent interlocutors in this study. Claire Katz includes a sustained consideration of the role of gender in the development of modern Jewish philosophy.[24] Elliot R. Wolfson reads Jacques Derrida and Edith Wyschogrod alongside prominent twentieth-century Jewish philosophers to explore transcendence and immanence in Jewish thought, postmodern negative theology, and apophasis.[25] Zachary Braiterman illustrates the central place of aesthetics in shaping modernist German Jewish thought.[26] Melissa Raphael calls into question the androcentrism of post-Holocaust Jewish theology, including women's diaries and memoirs in her "canon" in order to remedy the textual processes of exclusion that write them out of systematic discourse.[27] Mara Benjamin challenges the tendency to relegate "gender, race, and most other factors that affect social life" to the sphere of superficiality in modern Jewish theology, demonstrating instead how quotidian social realities contain religious and ethical significance.[28] These interventions show how productive it can be to expand our notion of Jewish thought to include alternate forms, affective networks, and nonsystematic, poetic, and epistolary sources.

Modern Jewish thought, as these writers have shown, has been a largely masculine discursive space, and as I have argued in this book, foundational texts that rely on fratriarchal logic are always built on androcentric frameworks. "Brotherhood" is generally accepted as a shorthand for human solidarity, without regard for the significance of its specifically gendered language and the links between that language and the exclusion of difference. Familial metaphors such as these have political, philosophical, and symbolic meaning. Fraternity *appears* universal, but its power is drawn from an exclusive structural bond that "draws its affective strength from the exclusivity of family," another social form frequently assumed to be universal and stable.[29] Whether invoked against or as foundational to the state, as Kathryn Lofton comments, imagining particular forms of "family" as a human universal leads us into "new kinds of orthodoxy."[30] The family persists as an irreducible social and metaphorical unit. "However much the family might be reorganized or queered, it endures as the story within every story."[31] The broader category of kinship "captures the system of social organization based on real or putative family ties."[32] As we have seen, in Jewish studies concepts of kinship have been overinvested in biblical models of normativity.[33] To find alternative ways of thinking about connections while retaining the power of familial metaphors, we might instead emphasize chosen family structures, conceiving of family as not restricted to biological lineage, and exploring genealogy with more expansive definitions.

Queering kinship in Jewish studies can highlight not only how traditional Jewish masculinity and femininity are constructed but also the ways that homosocial spheres have served as erotically charged sites of identity formation. Naomi Seidman, for example, effectively shows how "Jewish homosociality contributed to and was often the affective basis for the formation of Jewish kinship bonds."[34] Queer perspectives "have allowed us to see with ever greater clarity that kinship is necessarily an 'invention.'"[35] Seidman demonstrates how even Jewish heteronormativity and traditional kinship patterns "are also queer, if by queer we mean the specificity, contingency, distinction, unnaturalness, and even oddity of all sex-gender systems, including heteronormative ones."[36] Queer theory as a discipline can unveil the attempts of dominant norms to persevere, making explicit "how power works by combining and coordinating distinct concepts and practices to appear as commonsensically, inevitably belonging together (or, conversely, not belonging together)."[37]

Another theoretically rich site from which to challenge normative kinship has arisen from the fields of posthumanities and critical animal studies. Donna Haraway demonstrates how "companion species" can show us how to live intersectionally.[38] Haraway contends that each subject develops alongside other species: "I am who I become with companion species, who and which make a mess out of categories in the making of kin and kind."[39] Theorists of critical animal studies observe that the human/animal binary has been constructed alongside other hierarchical and damaging boundaries such as male/female, civilized/primitive, and body/mind. Thinking with animal others can challenge normative formations of kinship, universal brotherhood, and sexual difference. As Kelly Oliver observes, "Phrases like the 'brotherhood of man' and 'fraternity' do not grate on the ears just because they exclude animals but also because they exclude sisterhood, woman, and sorority . . . within the patriarchal imaginary, woman and maternity are closely related to animal and animality; women's bodies have been imagined as subject to, and determined by, natural processes that make them closer to animals than to men."[40] Critical animal studies opens kinship up beyond the sphere of the human and beyond a patriarchal lineage of blood.

In the previous chapter, I suggested sororal solidarity as a way to move beyond the network of fraternal reproduction. My turn to sorority has been influenced by my desire to find more expansive kinship language that matches my own lived experiences, so it makes sense that I find sisterhood to be a welcome alternative, given my close relationship to my own sister. It is likewise not surprising that the other framework I find useful is the relationship with companion species. I have lived with and loved six dogs in my life, and these relationships have led me to confront and be confronted by ethical interruption, responsibility, and a radical stepping outside myself that I can refer to only in the language of alterity. With them, I experience time diachronically. This is not a symmetrical relationship, because they are dependent on me in so many ways, and I am called upon to respond. Haraway's description of the human-canine relationship shows how capacious it can be for thinking alternatively about what Levinas calls alterity: "we inhabit not just different genera and divergent families but altogether different orders. . . . Who knows where my chemical receptors carried her messages or what she took from my cellular system for distinguishing self from other and binding outside to inside? . . . We are training each other in acts of communication we barely understand."[41] These companion species are, significantly, "other to each other, in specific difference," constituting each other as "beings-in-encounter."[42]

Living with and loving canine others has made me more aware of why, in Haraway's view, we have never been human. But Haraway shows how, even for those who do not live with companion species, "To be one is always to *become with* many."[43] To inhabit a human body is to be one with many non-human organic entities. "I am vastly outnumbered by my tiny companions" of bacteria, fungi, and protists, and "I become an adult human being in company with these tiny messmates."[44] To be embodied is to already have the other-within-the-self, in the Levinasian sense—or, more accurately, to have multiple others-within-the-self. There is no embodied self that is not already constituted with and alongside others.

Beyond the biological family, and beyond the human family, we can push at the limits of the canon. The radically embodied subject we find in Levinas can lead us to confront assumptions about ability in philosophical subjectivity. Reading crip theory alongside Rosenzweig's thought on speech and his biographical circumstances would allow us to interrogate what Robert McRuer calls compulsory ablebodiedness in philosophical reception and how "compulsory heterosexuality is contingent on compulsory ablebodiedness, and vice versa."[45] The concepts of alterity, speech-thinking, and diachrony can call us to embrace productive anachronistic and thematic frameworks. In applying these approaches pedagogically, and in critically examining the sources, syllabi, and edited volumes from which we teach, we then become more aware of overlooked methods. In a class on Spinoza, we might assign a contemporary essay on bodies and affect, or alongside Levinas an article highlighting the blind spot of sexual difference. We can play with categories by admitting letter writing, memoir, and testimony to the philosophical corpus. By emphasizing the positionality of the Great Male Thinkers, we can explicitly acknowledge how all identities are culturally and socially constructed. We can make visible the systems of power involved in canon formation and the metaphorical structures that are reproduced in many of these works. In doing so, we will begin to move the field beyond the fratriarchy.

NOTES

1. Levinas's first language was Russian, which explains the frequent relation of his work to Russian sources, such as Tolstoy and Dostoevsky, which he read

in his youth. His parents spoke Yiddish to one another. As a child, he studied the Hebrew Bible with tutors. See Simon Critchley, "Emmanuel Levinas: A Disparate Inventory," in *The Cambridge Companion to Levinas*, xv–xxx.

2. As Elliot Wolfson puts it, "The paradoxical language embraced by Levinas . . . is meant to forge a path that inceptually emerges from but ultimately circumvents philosophical reasoning," but the path of thought Levinas marks as otherwise-than-being is liable to succumb to the very same ontological taxonomy it is meant to undermine ("Imagination and the Theolatrous Impulse: Configuring God in Modern Jewish Thought," in *The Cambridge History of Jewish Philosophy: Volume 2: The Modern Era*, ed. Martin Kavka, Zachary Braiterman, and David Novak (Cambridge, UK: Cambridge University Press, 2012), 668. As Dorota Glowacka observes, "For Levinas, the mediating, representational character of language transforms every written text into an accomplice of appropriative totality" ("Sacrificing the Text: The Philosopher/Poet at Mount Moriah," *Animus* 2 [1997]: 35–45, 44).

3. Levinas, "God and Philosophy," *Basic Philosophical Writings*, 129; citing Derrida: "It was a Greek who said, 'If one has to philosophize, one has to philosophize, if one does not have to philosophize (to say it and think it.) One always has to philosophize'" ("Violence and Metaphysics: An Essay on the Thought of Emmanuel Levinas," in *Writing and Difference*, 152).

4. Levinas, *Otherwise Than Being*, 43.

5. As Wolfson writes, "That the end validates the beginning does not mean that the beginning is simply repeated in the end. On the contrary, the end is foretold by the beginning that cannot preview the end just as the beginning is previewed by an end that cannot foretell the beginning" (*Giving Beyond the Gift*, 44).

6. On the themes of time and messianism in Rosenzweig, see Dana Hollander, *Exemplarity and Chosenness*, 159–83.

7. Rosenzweig, "The New Thinking," 125–6.

8. Rosenzweig, *Star*, 9; 447.

9. Rosenzweig, *Star*, 169.

10. Braiterman, *The Shape of Revelation*, 260.

11. Mara H. Benjamin, "Agency as Quest and Question," 11. See also Mara Benjamin, "What Do We Owe Rosenzweig?" *Bamidbar* 4, no. 2 (2019): 99.

12. Gordon, "Rosenzweig Redux," 18.

13. Gordon, 37.

14. Gordon, 36.

15. Garloff, *Mixed Feelings*, 26. As Garloff explains, "Mendelssohn rejects interfaith marriage as a model of integration and suggests brotherly love as an alternative" (26).

16. "Jews are forbidden to hand Hitler posthumous victories. They are commanded to survive as Jews, lest the Jewish people perish. . . . A Jew may

not respond to Hitler's attempt to destroy Judaism by himself cooperating in its destruction" (Emil Fackenheim, "The Commanding Voice of Auschwitz," in *God's Presence in History: Jewish Affirmations and Philosophical Reflections* [New York: Harper & Row, 1970], 84). See Gordon: "Of course, to 'deny Hitler a posthumous victory' was a highly polemical injunction; it threatened to collapse the distinction between acculturation and genocide. But in the minds of many American Jews, the appeal to follow Rosenzweig's example found great resonance. In the wake of the Holocaust, many in the Jewish community were especially anxious that genuineness be restored and assimilation reversed" ("Rosenzweig Redux," 18). As Martin Kavka notes, Rosenzweig was "hagiographically constructed to be exemplary for the American Jews in the immediate aftermath of World War II" ("Annulling Theocentrism," *Bamidbar* 4, no. 2 [2019]: 85). On the post-Holocaust discourse of Jewish communal survival and endogamy and its link to concerns about assimilation and intermarriage, see Lila Corwin Berman, *Speaking of Jews: Rabbis, Intellectuals, and the Creation of an American Public Identity* (Berkeley: University of California Press, 2008), 69–72.

17. Lila Corwin Berman, "Sociology, Jews, and Intermarriage in Twentieth-Century America," *Jewish Social Studies* 14, no. 2 (winter, 2008): 33. The efforts to provide statistically based descriptions of Jewish life, marriage, and childbearing were undertaken by social scientists prior to the Shoah, beginning in the late nineteenth century. As Mitchell B. Hart argues, the collection and utilization of this work on sex and statistics in Jewish life was ideologically motivated from the beginning (*Social Science and the Politics of Modern Jewish Identity* [Stanford, CA: Stanford University Press, 2000], 74–95). For research on interfaith marriage that challenges the continuity crisis narrative, see Keren R. McGinity, *Still Jewish: A History of Women and Intermarriage in America* (New York: New York University Press, 2012); Jennifer A. Thompson, *Jewish on Their Own Terms: How Intermarried Couples are Changing American Judaism* (New Brunswick, NJ: Rutgers University Press, 2013); Helen Kiyong Kim and Noah Samuel Leavitt, *JewAsian: Race, Religion, and Identity for America's Newest Jews* (Lincoln: University of Nebraska Press, 2016); and Samira K. Mehta, *Beyond Chrismukkah: The Christian-Jewish Interfaith Family in the United States* (Chapel Hill: University of North Carolina Press, 2018).

18. Brettschneider, *Jewish Feminism and Intersectionality*, 133.

19. Lila Corwin Berman, Kate Rosenblatt, and Ronit Y. Stahl, "Continuity Crisis: The History and Sexual Politics of an American Jewish Communal Project," *American Jewish History* 104, no. 2/3 (April/July 2020): 168–69.

20. Berman, Rosenblatt, and Stahl, "Continuity Crisis," 189.

21. Berman, Rosenblatt, and Stahl, 189–90.

22. Moshe Behar and Zvi Ben-Dor Benite, eds., *Modern Middle Eastern Jewish Thought: Writings on Identity, Politics, and Culture, 1893–1958* (Waltham, MA: Brandeis University Press, 2013).

23. Sarah Hammerschlag, ed., *Modern French Jewish Thought: Writings on Religion and Politics* (Waltham, MA: Brandeis University Press, 2018).

24. Katz, *An Introduction to Modern Jewish Philosophy.*

25. Wolfson, *Giving Beyond the Gift.*

26. Braiterman, *The Shape of Revelation.*

27. Melissa Raphael, *The Female Face of God in Auschwitz: A Jewish Feminist Theology of the Holocaust* (London: Routledge, 2003).

28. Benjamin, *The Obligated Self,* 122.

29. Engelstein, *Sibling Action,* 100.

30. Lofton, *Consuming Religion,* 8.

31. Lofton, 284; "Either way you define it, family is a claim of differentiating dependency: this *us* exists in part by how it distinguishes itself from all the other *they.* . . . it seems as if the family is the organizational imperative nobody can shake. Is there nothing that exceeds its grasp?" (285).

32. Lofton, *Consuming Religion,* 184.

33. In many of these models, "fathers give birth to sons" in genealogies that are strung together by a "curious male umbilical cord" (Sherwood, "A Recently Discovered Letter from Isaac to Abraham [Annotated]," 183n8; 183).

34. Naomi Seidman, *The Marriage Plot: Or, How Jews Fell in Love with Love, and with Literature* (Redwood City, CA: Stanford University Press, 2016), 18.

35. Seidman, *The Marriage Plot,* 299.

36. Seidman, 300.

37. Reznik, "This Power Which Is Not One," 146.

38. Donna Haraway, *When Species Meet* (Minneapolis: University of Minnesota Press, 2007), 18.

39. Haraway, *When Species Meet,* 19.

40. Kelly Oliver, *Animal Lessons,* 17. Derrida suggests the animal can be a site of resistance to the political fraternity: "we shall have to ask ourselves, inevitably, what happens to the fraternity of brothers when an animal appears on the scene. . . . What happens to animals, surrogate or not, to the ass and ram on Mount Moriah? . . . In looking at the gaze of the other, Levinas says, one must forget the color of his eyes. . . . he is speaking of man, of one's neighbor as man, kindred, brother; he thinks of the other human and this, for us, will later be revealed as a matter for serious concern" (*The Animal That Therefore I Am,* 12).

41. Donna Haraway, *When Species Meet,* 15–6.

42. Haraway, *When Species Meet,* 16; 5. For an illuminating discussion of refiguring "trans-species correspondence, rather than oppositional difference" in asymmetrical ethical relations between human and nonhuman animals, see Zakiyyah Iman Jackson, *Becoming Human: Matter and Meaning in an Antiblack World* (New York: New York University Press, 2020), 73.

43. Haraway, 4.

44. Haraway, 4. See also Denise Kimber Buell: "Attention to bacteria, viruses, protists, and other microbes from the vantage point of relational ontologies can help formulate positions on agency and ethics to evaluate afresh ancient views and practices" ("The Microbes and Pneuma That Therefore I Am," in *Divinanimality: Animal Theory, Creaturely Theology*, ed. Stephen Moore [New York: Fordham University Press, 2014], 66).

45. Robert McRuer, *Crip Theory: Cultural Signs of Queerness and Disability* (New York: New York University Press, 2006), 2. See also Tobin Siebers, *Disability Theory* (Ann Arbor: The University of Michigan Press, 2008), 4: "To call disability an identity is to recognize that it is not a biological or natural property but an elastic social category both subject to social control and capable of effecting social change"; Jasbir K. Puar, *The Right to Maim: Debility, Capacity, Disability* (Durham, NC: Duke University Press, 2017), xiv: "Disability is not a fixed state or attribute but exists in relation to assemblages of capacity and debility, modulated across historical time, geopolitical space, institutional mandates, and discursive regimes. . . . The non-disabled/disabled binary traverses social, geographic, and political spaces"; and Julia Watts Belser, "Judaism and Disability," in *Disability and World Religions: An Introduction*, ed. Darla Schumm and Michael Stoltzfus (Waco, TX: Baylor University Press, 2016), 97: "One of the signal contributions of disability studies has been to challenge the idea of the 'naturalness' of disability as a stable and easily recognizable category. While popular notions commonly assume that disability is rooted in the 'obvious' deficiency of certain human bodies, disability studies insists on a social and political understanding of disability."

BIBLIOGRAPHY

Adler, Rachel. *Engendering Judaism: An Inclusive Theology and Ethics*. Boston: Beacon, 1998.

Aeschylus. "Agamemnon." In *Oresteia*, translated by Richmond Lattimore, 33–90. Chicago: University of Chicago Press, 1953.

———. "The Eumenides." In *Oresteia*, translated by Richmond Lattimore, 133–171. Chicago: University of Chicago Press, 1953.

———. "The Libation Bearers." In *Oresteia*, translated by Richmond Lattimore, 91–132. Chicago: University of Chicago Press, 1953.

Ainley, Alison. "Levinas and Kant: Maternal Morality and Illegitimate Offspring." In *Feminist Interpretations of Emmanuel Levinas*, edited by Tina Chanter, 203–23. University Park: Pennsylvania State University Press, 2001.

Ali, Kecia. "Muslims and Meat-Eating: Vegetarianism, Gender, and Identity." *Journal of Religious Ethics* 43, no. 2 (2015): 268–88.

Alighieri, Dante. *Vita Nuova*. Translated by Dino S. Cervigni and Edward Vasta. Notre Dame, IN: University of Notre Dame Press, 1995.

Allen, Sarah. *The Philosophical Sense of Transcendence: Levinas and Plato on Loving beyond Being*. Pittsburgh, PA: Duquesne University Press, 2009.

Altman, Janet Gurkin. *Epistolarity: Approaches to a Form*. Columbus: Ohio State University Press, 1982.

Améry, Jean. *At the Mind's Limits: Contemplations by a Survivor on Auschwitz and Its Realities*. Translated by Sidney Rosenfeld and Stella P. Rosenfeld. Bloomington: Indiana University Press, 1980.

Anidjar, Gil. *Blood: A Critique of Christianity*. New York: Columbia University Press, 2014.

Arcade Fire. "Abraham's Daughter." Track 1 on *The Hunger Games: Songs from District 12 and Beyond*. Republic, 2012, compact disc.

Arendt, Hannah. "The Enlightenment and the Jewish Question." In *The Jewish Writings*, edited by Jerome Kohn and Ron H. Feldman, 3–18. New York: Schocken Books, 2007.

———. "On Humanity in Dark Times: Thoughts about Lessing." In *Men in Dark Times*, translated by Clara Winston and Richard Winston, 3–32. New York: Harcourt Brace, 1993.

Aronowicz, Annette. "Introduction." In *Nine Talmudic Readings*, by Emmanuel Levinas, xiv–xv. Bloomington: Indiana University Press, 1994.

Atterton, Peter. "Face-to-Face with the Other Animal?" In *Levinas and Buber: Dialogue and Difference*, edited by Peter Atterton, Matthew Calarco, and Maurice Friedman, 262–81. Pittsburgh, PA: Duquesne University Press, 2004.

———. "Levinas's Humanism and Anthropocentrism." In *The Oxford Handbook of Levinas*, edited by Michael L. Morgan. Oxford: Oxford University Press, 2019, 709–30.

Augustine. *The Literal Meaning of Genesis*. Translated by John Hammond Taylor, S. J. Vol. II. New York: Newman, 1982.

Bakhos, Carol. *The Family of Abraham: Jewish, Christian, and Muslim Interpretations*. Cambridge, MA: Harvard University Press, 2014.

Bal, Mieke. *Death & Dissymmetry: The Politics of Coherence in the Book of Judges*. Chicago: University of Chicago Press, 1988.

———. *Lethal Love: Feminist Literary Readings of Biblical Love Stories*. Bloomington: Indiana University Press, 1987.

Batnizky, Leora. "Dependency and Vulnerability: Jewish and Feminist Existentialist Constructions of the Human." In *Women and Gender in Jewish Philosophy*, edited by Hava Tirosh-Samuelson, 127–52. Bloomington: Indiana University Press, 2004.

———. "Foreword." In *Cultural Writings of Franz Rosenzweig*. By Franz Rosenzweig. Edited and translated by Barbara E. Galli, ix–xix. Syracuse, NY: Syracuse University Press, 2000.

———. *Idolatry and Representation: The Philosophy of Franz Rosenzweig Reconsidered*. Princeton, NJ: Princeton University Press, 2000.

———. "Levinas between German Metaphysics and Christian Theology." In *The Exorbitant: Levinas Between Jews and Christians*, edited by Kevin Hart and Michael A. Signer, 17–31. New York: Fordham University Press, 2010.

Bauer, Nancy. *Simone de Beauvoir, Philosophy, and Feminism*. New York: Columbia University Press, 2001.

Behar, Moshe, and Zvi Ben-Dor Benite, eds. *Modern Middle Eastern Jewish Thought: Writings on Identity, Politics, and Culture, 1893–1958*. Waltham, MA: Brandeis University Press, 2013.

Benhabib, Seyla. "On Hegel, Women, and Irony." In *Feminist Interpretations of G. W. F. Hegel*, edited by Patricia Jagentowicz Mills, 25–43. University Park: Pennsylvania State University Press, 1996.

Benjamin, Mara. "Agency as Quest and Question: Feminism, Religious Studies, and Modern Jewish Thought." *Jewish Social Studies* 24, no. 2 (winter 2019): 7–16.

———. "Intersubjectivity Meets Maternity: Buber, Levinas, and the Eclipsed Relation." In *Thinking Jewish Culture in America*, edited by Ken Koltun-Fromm, 261–84. Lanham, MD: Lexington, 2013.

———. "Love in the *Star*? A Feminist Challenge." *Bamidbar* 4, no. 2 (2019): 10–27.

———. *The Obligated Self: Maternal Subjectivity and Jewish Thought*. Bloomington: Indiana University Press, 2018.

———. *Rosenzweig's Bible: Reinventing Scripture for Jewish Modernity*. Cambridge, UK: Cambridge University Press, 2009.

———. "What Do We Owe Rosenzweig?" *Bamidbar* 4, no. 2 (2019): 97–99.

Benso, Silvia. "Missing the Encounter with the Other: Goethe's *Sufferings of Young Werther* in Light of Levinas." In New, Bernasconi, and Cohen, eds., *In Proximity: Emmanuel Levinas and the Eighteenth Century*, 197–214.

Bernasconi, Robert. "A Love That Is Stronger Than Death: Sacrifice in the Thought of Levinas, Heidegger and Bloch." *Angelaki: Journal of Theoretical Humanities* 7, no. 2 (2002): 9–16.

Bernasconi, Robert, and Simon Critchley, eds. *The Cambridge Companion to Levinas*. Cambridge, UK: Cambridge University Press, 2002.

———. *Re-Reading Levinas*. Bloomington: Indiana University Press, 1991.

Biale, David. *Blood and Belief: The Circulation of a Symbol between Jews and Christians*. Berkeley: University of California Press, 2007.

———. *Eros and the Jews: From Biblical Israel to Contemporary America*. New York: Basic Books, 1992.

Bienenstock, Myriam. "How to Do Philosophy by Writing Letters: Rosenzweig as a Letter-Writer." *Franz Rosenzweig Congress, Gebot, Gesetz, Gebet: Love, Law, Life*, University of Toronto, September 2, 2012.

———. "'Le règne des mères:' Les 'Lettres à sa mère' de Franz Rosenzweig." *Les Cahiers du Judaïsme* 33 (December 2011): 30–39.

Boyarin, Daniel. *Carnal Israel: Reading Sex in Talmudic Culture*. Berkeley: University of California Press, 1995.

———. "Gender." In *Critical Terms for Religious Studies*, edited by Mark C. Taylor, 117–35. Chicago: University of Chicago Press, 1998.

Boyarin, Daniel, Daniel Itzkovitz, and Ann Pellegrini. "Strange Bedfellows: An Introduction." In *Queer Theory and the Jewish Question*, edited by Daniel Boyarin, Daniel Itzkovitz, and Ann Pellegrini, 1–18. New York: Columbia University Press, 2003.

Braiterman, Zachary. "After Germany: An American Jewish Philosophical Manifesto." In *Jewish Philosophy for the Twenty-First Century: Personal Reflections*, edited by Hava Tirosh-Samuelson and Aaron W. Hughes, 42–60. Leiden: Brill, 2014.

———. "Revelation Camp: Gender, Franz Rosenzweig, and the Con-fusion of Concepts." *Bamidbar* 4, no. 2 (2019): 53–73.

————. *The Shape of Revelation: Aesthetics and Modern Jewish Thought*. Redwood City, CA: Stanford University Press, 2007.

Bremmer, Jan N. "Sacrificing a Child in Ancient Greece: The Case of Iphigeneia." In *The Sacrifice of Isaac: The Aqedah (Genesis 22) and Its Interpretations*, edited by Ed Noort and Eibert Tigchelaar, 21–43. Leiden: Brill, 2002.

Brettschneider, Marla. *Jewish Feminism and Intersectionality*. Albany: State University of New York Press, 2016.

Brezis, David. *Levinas et le tournant sacrificial*. Paris: Hermann, 2012.

Brisson, Luc. *Le mythe de Tirésias: Essai d'analyse structurale*. Leiden: Brill, 1976.

Buber, Martin. *Drei Reden über das Judentum*. Frankfurt am Main: Rütten and Loening, 1920.

————. *Eclipse of God: Studies in the Relation between Religion and Philosophy*. New York: Harper, 1957.

————. *I and Thou*. Translated by Ronald Gregor Smith. New York: Scribner Classics, 1958.

————. *On Judaism*. Translated by Eva Jospe. Edited by Nahum N. Glatzer. New York: Schocken Books, 1967.

Buell, Denise Kimber. "The Microbes and Pneuma That Therefore I Am." In *Divinanimality: Animal Theory, Creaturely Theology*, edited by Stephen Moore, 63–87. New York: Fordham University Press, 2014.

Butler, Judith. *Antigone's Claim: Kinship between Life and Death*. New York: Columbia University Press, 2002.

————. *Gender Trouble: Feminism and the Subversion of Identity*. New York: Routledge, 1999.

————. *Parting Ways: Jewishness and the Critique of Zionism*. New York: Columbia University Press, 2012.

Burton, Joan B. "Themes of Female Desire and Self-Assertion in the Song of Songs and Hellenistic Poetry." In *Perspectives on the Song of Songs*, edited by Anselm C. Hagedorn, 180–205. Berlin: Walter de Gruyter, 2005.

Carsten, Janet. *After Kinship*. Cambridge, UK: Cambridge University Press, 2003.

Cavarero, Adriana. *In Spite of Plato: A Feminist Rewriting of Ancient Philosophy*. Translated by Serena Anderlini-D'Onofrio and Áine O'Healy. Cambridge, UK: Polity, 1995.

Chalier, Catherine. "Ethics and the Feminine." In *Re-Reading Levinas*, edited by Robert Bernasconi and Simon Critchley, 119–129. Bloomington: Indiana University Press, 1991.

————. *Figures du féminin: Lecture d'Emmanuel Lévinas*. Paris: Nuit surveillée, 1982.

Chanter, Tina. "Antigone's Dilemma." In Bernasconi and Critchley, eds., *Re-Reading Levinas*, 130–47.

————. *Ethics of Eros: Irigaray's Rewriting of the Philosophers*. New York: Routledge, 1995.

———. "Feminism and the Other." In *The Provocation of Levinas: Rethinking the Other*, edited by Robert Bernasconi and David Wood, 32–56. London: Routledge, 1988.

———, ed. *Feminist Interpretations of Emmanuel Levinas*. University Park: Pennsylvania State University Press, 2001.

———. "Introduction." In Chanter, ed., *Feminist Interpretations of Emmanuel Levinas*, 1–27.

———. *Whose Antigone?: The Tragic Marginalization of Slavery*. Albany: State University of New York Press, 2011.

Ciavatta, David V. *Spirit, the Family, and the Unconscious in Hegel's Philosophy*. Albany: State University of New York Press, 2009.

Coe, Cynthia D. *Levinas and the Trauma of Responsibility: The Ethical Significance of Time*. Bloomington: Indiana University Press, 2018.

Cohen, Richard A. *Elevations: The Height of the Good in Rosenzweig and Levinas*. Chicago: University of Chicago Press, 1994.

———. *Levinasian Meditations: Ethics, Philosophy, and Religion*. Pittsburgh, PA: Duquesne University Press, 2010.

Collins, Patricia Hill, and Sirma Bilge. *Intersectionality*. Cambridge, UK: Polity, 2016.

Collins, Suzanne. *The Hunger Games*. New York: Scholastic Press, 2008.

Conybeare, Catherine. *The Laughter of Sarah: Biblical Exegesis, Feminist Theory, and the Concept of Delight*. New York: Palgrave Macmillan, 2013.

Cooper, Andrea Dara. "From Sister-Wife to Brother-Neighbor: Rosenzweig Reads the Song of Songs." *Journal of Jewish Thought and Philosophy* 28, no. 2 (2020): 228–58.

———. "Gender and Modern Jewish Thought." In *Oxford Bibliographies in Jewish Studies*. Edited by Naomi Seidman. New York: Oxford University Press, 2021.

Corwin Berman, Lila. "Jewish History Beyond the Jewish People." *AJS Review* 42, no. 2 (November 2018): 269–92.

———. "Sociology, Jews, and Intermarriage in Twentieth-Century America." *Jewish Social Studies* 14, no. 2 (winter, 2008): 32–60.

———. *Speaking of Jews: Rabbis, Intellectuals, and the Creation of an American Public Identity*. Berkeley: University of California Press, 2008.

Corwin Berman, Lila, Kate Rosenblatt, and Ronit Y. Stahl. "Continuity Crisis: The History and Sexual Politics of an American Jewish Communal Project." *American Jewish History* 104, no. 2/3 (April/July, 2020): 167–194.

Crawley, Ashon T. *The Lonely Letters*. Durham, NC: Duke University Press, 2020.

Crenshaw, Kimberlé. "Demarginalizing the Intersection of Race and Sex: A Black Feminist Critique of Antidiscrimination Doctrine, Feminist Theory and Antiracist Politics." *University of Chicago Legal Forum* (1989): 139–67.

Cristaudo, Wayne. *Religion, Redemption, and Revolution: The New Speech Thinking of Franz Rosenzweig and Eugen Rosenstock-Huessy.* Toronto: University of Toronto Press, 2012.

Critchley, Simon. "'Bois'—Derrida's Final Word on Levinas." In Bernasconi and Critchley, eds., *Re-Reading Levinas*, 162–89.

———. "Derrida's Reading of Hegel in *Glas.*" In *Ethics-Politics-Subjectivity: Essays on Derrida, Levinas and Contemporary French Thought*, 1–29. London: Verso, 1999.

———. "Introduction." In Bernasconi and Critchley, eds., *The Cambridge Companion to Levinas*, 1–32.

———. "Emmanuel Levinas: A Disparate Inventory." In Bernasconi and Critchley, eds., *The Cambridge Companion to Levinas*, xv–xxx.

———. *The Problem with Levinas.* Oxford: Oxford University Press, 2015.

Dagan, Haggai. "The Motif of Blood and Procreation in Franz Rosenzweig." *AJS Review* 26, no. 2 (2002): 241–49.

"The Dance of Dragons." *Game of Thrones.* Season 5, Episode 9, directed by David Nutter, written by David Benioff and D. B. Weiss. Aired June 7, 2015, on HBO.

Davenport, John. "Levinas's Agapeistic Metaphysics of Morals: Absolute Passivity and the Other as Eschatological Hierophany." *The Journal of Religious Ethics* 26, no. 2 (fall 1998): 331–66.

Davidoff, Leonore. *Thicker Than Water: Siblings and Their Relations, 1780–1920.* Oxford: Oxford University Press, 2012.

De Beauvoir, Simone. *The Second Sex.* Translated and edited by H. M. Parshley. New York: Vintage Books, 1989.

Delaney, Carol. "Cutting the Ties That Bind: The Sacrifice of Abraham and Patriarchal Kinship." In *Relative Values: Reconfiguring Kinship Studies*, edited by Sarah Franklin and Susan McKinnon, 445–67. Durham, NC: Duke University Press, 2001.

Derrida, Jacques. *Adieu to Emmanuel Levinas.* Translated by Pascale-Ann Brault and Michael Naas. Stanford, CA: Stanford University Press, 1999.

———. *The Animal That Therefore I Am.* Edited by Marie-Louise Mallet. Translated by David Wills. New York: Fordham University Press, 2008.

———. "At This Very Moment in This Work Here I Am." Translated by Ruben Berezdivin. In Bernasconi and Critchley, eds., *Re-Reading Levinas*, 11–49.

———. "Choreographies: Jacques Derrida and Christie V. McDonald." *Diacritics* 12, no. 2 (1982): 66–76.

———. "*Geschlecht*: Sexual Difference, Ontological Difference." *Research in Phenomenology* 13 (1983): 65–83.

———. *The Gift of Death.* Translated by David Wills. Chicago: University of Chicago Press, 1995.

———. *Glas*. Translated by John P. Leavey Jr. and Richard Ran. Lincoln: University of Nebraska Press, 1990.

———. "Interpretations at War: Kant, the Jew, the German." Translated by Moshe Ron. In *Acts of Religion*, edited by Gil Anidjar, 135–88. New York: Routledge, 2002.

———. *Monolingualism of the Other: Or, the Prosthesis of Origin*. Translated by Patrick Mensah. Redwood City, CA: Stanford University Press, 1998.

———. "Otobiographies: The Teaching of Nietzsche and the Politics of the Proper Name." Translated by Avital Ronell. In *The Ear of the Other: Otobiography, Transference, Translation*, edited by Christie McDonald, 1–38. Lincoln: University of Nebraska Press, 1985.

———. *Politics of Friendship*. Translated by George Collins. London: Verso, 2005.

———. *The Postcard: From Socrates to Freud and Beyond*. Translated by Alan Bass. Chicago: University of Chicago Press, 1987.

———. "Sarah Kofman." In *The Work of Mourning*, edited by Pascale-Anne Brault and Michael Naas, 165–88. Chicago: University of Chicago Press, 2001.

———. "Violence and Metaphysics: An Essay on the Thought of Emmanuel Levinas." In *Writing and Difference*, translated by Alan Bass, 79–133. Chicago: University of Chicago Press, 1978.

Diamond, James A. "Constructing a Jewish Philosophy of Being toward Death." In *Jewish Philosophy for the Twenty-First Century: Personal Reflections*, edited by Hava Tirosh-Samuelson and Aaron W. Hughes, 61–80. Leiden: Brill, 2014.

Disch, Lisa J. "On Friendship in 'Dark Times.'" In *Feminist Interpretations of Hannah Arendt*, edited by Bonnie Honig, 285–311. University Park: Pennsylvania State University Press, 1995.

Dixon, Drew. "*The Binding of Isaac* Review." *Paste Monthly*. October 7, 2011. http://www.pastemagazine.com/articles/2011/10/the-binding-of-isaac-review-pcmac.html.

Eichler-Levine, Jodi. *Suffer the Little Children: Uses of the Past in Jewish and African American Children's Literature*. New York: New York University Press, 2013.

Eilberg-Schwartz, Howard. "Introduction: People of the Body." In *People of the Body: Jews and Judaism from an Embodied Perspective*, edited by Howard Eilberg-Schwartz, 1–15. Albany: State University of New York Press, 1992.

Eisenstadt, Oona. "Levinas versus Levinas: Hebrew, Greek, and Linguistic Justice." *Philosophy & Rhetoric* 38, no. 2 (2005): 145–58.

———. "Preferring or not Preferring: Derrida on Bartleby as Kierkegaard's Abraham." In *Derrida's Bible (Reading a Page of Scripture with a Little Help from Derrida)*, edited by Yvonne Sherwood, 167–80. New York: Palgrave Macmillan, 2004.

Engelstein, Stefanie. *Sibling Action: The Genealogical Structure of Modernity*. New York: Columbia University Press, 2017.

Erlewine, Robert. *Judaism and the West: From Hermann Cohen to Joseph Soloveitchik*. Bloomington: Indiana University Press, 2016.

Ettinger, Bracha Lichtenberg. *Que dirait Eurydice? What Would Eurydice Say? Bracha Lichtenberg Ettinger in Conversation with Emmanuel Levinas*. Paris: BLE Atelier, 1997.

Euripides. "Electra." In *Ten Plays by Euripides*, translated by Moses Hadas and John McLean, 233–72. Toronto: Bantam Books, 1981.

Fackenheim, Emil. "The Commanding Voice of Auschwitz." In *God's Presence in History: Jewish Affirmations and Philosophical Reflections*, 84–92. New York: Harper & Row, 1970.

Fagenblat, Michael. *A Covenant of Creatures: Levinas's Philosophy of Judaism*. Stanford, CA: Stanford University Press, 2010.

Farneth, Molly. *Hegel's Social Ethics: Religion, Conflict, and Rituals of Reconciliation*. Princeton, NJ: Princeton University Press, 2017.

Feldman, Yael. "'And Rebecca Loved Jacob,' but Freud Did Not." In *Freud and Forbidden Knowledge*, edited by Peter L. Rudnytsky and Ellen Handler Spitz, 7–25. New York: New York University Press, 1994.

———. *Glory and Agony: Isaac's Sacrifice and National Narrative*. Stanford, CA: Stanford University Press, 2010.

———. *No Room of Their Own: Gender and Nation in Israeli Women's Fiction*. New York: Columbia University Press, 1999.

———. "Why Didn't Freud Like Jacob? Biblical Siblings and Jewish Gender." In *Intertextuality in Literature and Culture: Festschrift for Ziva Ben Porat*, edited by Michael Gluzman and Orly Lubin, 353–76. Tel Aviv: Hakibbutz Hameuchad and Porter Institute at Tel Aviv University, 2012.

Fishbane, Michael. *The Garments of Torah: Essays in Biblical Hermeneutics*. Bloomington: Indiana University Press, 1989.

———. "Introduction to the Commentary: Song of Songs." In *Song of Songs: The Traditional Hebrew Text with the New JPS Translation*. Philadelphia: The Jewish Publication Society, 2015.

———. "The Song of Songs and Ancient Jewish Religiosity: Between Eros and History." In *Von Enoch bis Kafka: Festschrift für Karl E. Grözinger*, edited by Manfred Voights, 69–81. Wiesbaden: Harrassowitz, 2002.

Foucault, Michel. *Ethics: Subjectivity and Truth*. Edited by Paul Rabinow. Translated by Robert Hurley. New York: New Press, 1997.

Fraade, Steven D. "Ascetical Aspects of Ancient Judaism." In *Jewish Spirituality: From the Bible through the Middle Ages*, edited by Arthur Green, 253–88. New York: Crossroad, 1986.

Franks, Paul W., and Michael L. Morgan. "From 1914 to 1917" and "From 1917 to 1925." In Franz Rosenzweig, *Philosophical and Theological Writings*, edited

and translated by Paul W. Franks and Michael L. Morgan, 25–47; 84–94.
Indianapolis, IN: Hackett, 2000.

Freud, Sigmund. "Femininity." In *The Standard Edition of the Complete Psychological Works*. Vol XXII. Edited and translated by J. Strachey et al. London: Hogarth Press, 1964.

Frymer-Kensky, Tikva. "*Akeda*: The View from the Bible." In *Beginning Anew: A Woman's Companion to the High Holy Days*, edited by Gail Twersky Reimer and Judith A. Kates, 127–44. New York: Touchstone, 1997.

Fuchs, Esther. *Sexual Politics in the Biblical Narrative: Reading the Hebrew Bible as a Woman*. London: Sheffield Academic Press, 2000.

Gafney, Wilda C. *Womanist Midrash: A Reintroduction to the Women of the Torah and the Throne*. Louisville, KY: Westminster John Knox Press, 2017.

Galli, Barbara. *Franz Rosenzweig and Jehuda Halevi: Translating, Translations, and Translators*. Montreal: McGill-Queen's University Press, 1995.

Garloff, Katja. *Mixed Feelings: Tropes of Love in German Jewish Culture*. Ithaca, NY: Cornell University Press, 2016.

Gibbs, Robert. *Correlations in Rosenzweig and Levinas*. Princeton, NJ: Princeton University Press, 1992.

"The Gift." *Buffy the Vampire Slayer*. Season 5, Episode 22, written and directed by Joss Whedon. Aired May 22, 2001, on the WB Television Network.

Glowacka, Dorota. *Disappearing Traces: Holocaust Testimonials, Ethics, and Aesthetics*. Seattle: University of Washington Press, 2012.

———. "Sacrificing the Text: The Philosopher/Poet at Mount Moriah." *Animus* 2 (1997): 35–45.

———. "The Trace of the Untranslatable: Emmanuel Levinas and the Ethics of Translation." *PhaenEx* 7, no. 1 (spring/summer 2012): 1–29.

Goldhill, Simon. "Antigone and the Politics of Sisterhood." In *Laughing with Medusa: Classical Myth and Feminist Thought*, edited by Vanda Zajko and Miriam Leonard, 141–62. Oxford: Oxford University Press, 2006.

Gordon, Peter Eli. "Rosenzweig and the Philosophy of Jewish Existence." In *The Cambridge Companion to Modern Jewish Philosophy*, edited by Michael L. Morgan and Peter Gordon, 122–46. Cambridge, UK: Cambridge University Press, 2007.

———. "Rosenzweig Redux: The Reception of German-Jewish Thought." *Jewish Social Studies* 8, no. 1 (fall 2001): 1–57.

Gottlieb, David N. *Second Slayings: The Binding of Isaac and the Formation of Jewish Memory*. Piscataway, NJ: Gorgias, 2019.

Gottlieb Zornberg, Avivah. *The Beginning of Desire: Reflections on Genesis*. New York: Doubleday, 1995.

Greenberg, Yudit Kornberg. *Better Than Wine: Love, Poetry, and Prayer in the Thought of Franz Rosenzweig*. Atlanta, GA: Scholars Press, 1996.

———. "Erotic Representations of the Divine." *Oxford Research Encyclopedia of Religion* (December 22, 2016). https://doi.org/10.1093/acrefore/9780199340378 .013.120" https://doi.org/10.1093/acrefore/9780199340378.013.120.

Gross, Aaron. "Animal Others and Animal Studies." In *Animals and the Human Imagination: A Companion to Animal Studies,* edited by Aaron Gross and Anne Vallely, 1–24. New York: Columbia University Press, 2012.

Grosz, Elizabeth. *Space, Time, and Perversion.* New York: Routledge, 1995.

Guenther, Lisa. *The Gift of the Other: Levinas and the Politics of Reproduction.* Albany: State University of New York Press, 2006.

Hallo, William. "Gibt Es So Etwas Wie Autoexegese? Franz Rosenzweigs Gritli-Briefe und der Stern." In *Franz Rosenzweigs "neues Denken." Band II: Erfahrene Offenbarung—in theologos,* edited by Wolfdietrich Schmied-Kowarzik. Munchen: Verlag Karl Alber Freiburg, 2004.

Hammerschlag, Sarah, ed. *Modern French Jewish Thought: Writings on Religion and Politics.* Waltham, MA: Brandeis University Press, 2018.

Haraway, Donna. *When Species Meet.* Minneapolis: University of Minnesota Press, 2007.

Hart, Kevin, and Michael A. Signer. *The Exorbitant: Levinas between Jews and Christians.* New York: Fordham University Press, 2010.

Hart, Mitchell B. *Social Science and the Politics of Modern Jewish Identity.* Stanford, CA: Stanford University Press, 2000.

Hegel, G. F. *Aesthetics: Lectures on Fine Art.* Translated by T. M. Knox. Oxford: Clarendon, 1975.

———. *Phenomenology of Spirit.* Translated by Arnold V. Miller. Oxford: Oxford University Press, 1979.

———. *Philosophy of Right.* Translated by S. W. Dyde. Kitchener. Ontario: Batoche Books, 2001.

Heidegger, Martin. *Being and Time.* Translated by John Macquarrie and Edward Robinson. San Francisco: Harper & Row, 1962.

Hill Shevitz, Amy. "Mother, Wife, and Lover: A Preliminary Study of the Three Women Who Most Influenced Rosenzweig's Philosophy of Love." *Franz Rosenzweig Congress, Gebot, Gesetz, Gebet: Love, Law, Life,* University of Toronto, September 3, 2012.

———. "Silence and Translation: Franz Rosenzweig's Paralysis and Edith Rosenzweig's Life." *Modern Judaism* 35, no. 3 (October 2015): 281–301.

Hollander, Dana. *Exemplarity and Chosenness: Rosenzweig and Derrida on the Nation of Philosophy.* Redwood City, CA: Stanford University Press, 2008.

Holte, Stine. "Asymmetry, Testimony, and God in Levinas's Later Thinking." In *Despite Oneself: Subjectivity and Its Secret in Kierkegaard and Levinas,* edited by Claudia Welz and Karl Verstrynge, 81–91. London: Turnshare, 2008.

Homer. *The Odyssey.* Translated by Robert Fagles. New York: Penguin Classics, 1997.

Honig, Bonnie. *Antigone, Interrupted.* New York: Cambridge University Press, 2013.

Horner, Robyn. "On Levinas's Gifts to Christian Theology." In Hart and Signer, eds., *The Exorbitant: Levinas between Jews and Christians,* 130–49.

Horwitz, Rivka. "From Hegelianism to a Revolutionary Understanding of Judaism: Franz Rosenzweig's Attitude toward Kabbala and Myth." *Modern Judaism* 2, no. 1 (2006): 31–54.

———. "The Shaping of Rosenzweig's Identity According to the Gritli Letters." In *Rosenzweig als Leser: kontextuelle Kommentare zum 'Stern der Erlösung,'* edited by Martin Brasser, 11–42. Tübingen: Max Niemeyer, 2004.

Hughes, Aaron W. *Rethinking Jewish Philosophy: Beyond Particularism and Universalism.* Oxford: Oxford University Press, 2014.

Hunt-Hendrix, Leah. "The Ethics of Solidarity: Republican, Marxist, and Anarchist Interpretations." PhD diss., Princeton University, 2014.

Hutchings, Kimberly. *Hegel and Feminist Philosophy.* Cambridge, UK: Polity, 2003.

Hyman, Paula E. *Gender and Assimilation in Modern Jewish History.* Seattle: University of Washington Press, 1995.

Imhoff, Sarah. *Masculinity and the Making of American Judaism.* Bloomington: Indiana University Press, 2017.

———. "Women and Gender, Past and Present: A Jewish Studies Story." *Jewish Social Studies* 24, no. 2 (winter 2019): 74–81.

Irigaray, Luce. *An Ethics of Sexual Difference.* Translated by Carolyn Burke and Gillian C. Gill. Ithaca, NY: Cornell University Press, 1993.

———. "Questions to Emmanuel Levinas: On the Divinity of Love." Translated by Margaret Whitford. In Bernasconi and Critchley, eds., *Re-Reading Levinas,* 109–18.

———. *Speculum of the Other Woman.* Translated by Gillian C. Gill. Ithaca, NY: Cornell University Press, 1985.

Jackson, Zakiyyah Iman. *Becoming Human: Matter and Meaning in an Antiblack World.* New York: New York University Press, 2020.

Jakobsen, Janet, and Ann Pellegrini. *Love the Sin: Sexual Regulations and the Limits of Religious Tolerance.* Boston: Beacon, 2004.

James, Elaine T. *Landscapes of the Song of Songs: Poetry and Place.* Oxford: Oxford University Press, 2017.

Jantz, Harold. *The Mothers in Faust: The Myth of Time and Creativity.* Baltimore, MD: Johns Hopkins University Press, 1969.

Kafka, Franz. "Abraham." In *The Basic Kafka,* edited by Erich Heller, 172–74. New York: Pocket Books, 1979.

Kallen, Horace. "Alain Locke and Cultural Pluralism." *The Journal of Philosophy* 54, no. 5 (February 1957): 119–27.

Kant, Immanuel. *The Conflict of the Faculties*. Translated by Mary J. Gregor. Lincoln: University of Nebraska Press, 1992.

Kaplan, Marion A. *The Making of the Jewish Middle Class: Women, Family, and Identity in Imperial Germany*. Oxford: Oxford University Press, 1991.

Katz, Claire Elise. "For Love Is as Strong as Death: Taking Another Look at Levinas on Love." *Philosophy Today* 45 (2001): 124–32.

———. "From Eros to Maternity: Love, Death, and 'the Feminine' in the Philosophy of Emmanuel Levinas." In *Women and Gender in Jewish Philosophy*, edited by Hava Tirosh-Samuelson, 153–78. Bloomington: Indiana University Press, 2004

———. *An Introduction to Modern Jewish Philosophy*. London: I.B. Tauris, 2014.

———. "Levinas between Agape and Eros." *Symposium: Canadian Journal of Continental Philosophy/Revue canadienne de philosophie continentale* 11, no. 2 (2007): 333–50.

———. *Levinas, Judaism, and the Feminine: The Silent Footsteps of Rebecca*. Bloomington: Indiana University Press, 2003.

———. "No Place for Old Women, or Young Women Either." *Bamidbar* 4, no. 2 (2019): 74–82.

———. "Philosophy, the Academy, and the Future of Jewish Learning." In *Jewish Philosophy for the Twenty-First Century: Personal Reflections*, edited by Hava Tirosh-Samuelson and Aaron W. Hughes. Leiden: Brill, 2014.

———. "Reinhabiting the House of Ruth: Exceeding the Limits of the Feminine in Levinas." In Chanter, ed., *Feminist Interpretations of Emmanuel Levinas*, 145–70.

———. "The Responsibility of Irresponsibility: Taking (Yet) Another Look at the Akedah." In *Addressing Levinas*, edited by Eric Sean Nelson, Antje Kapust, and Kent Still, 17–33. Evanston, IL: Northwestern University Press, 2005.

Kavka, Martin. "Annulling Theocentrism." *Bamidbar* 4, no. 2 (2019): 83–96.

———. *Jewish Messianism and the History of Philosophy*. Cambridge, UK: Cambridge University Press, 2004.

———. "Screening the Canon: Levinas and Medieval Jewish Philosophy." In *New Directions in Jewish Philosophy*, edited by Aaron W. Hughes and Elliot R. Wolfson, 17–51. Bloomington: Indiana University Press, 2010.

Kessler, Edward. *Bound by the Bible: Jews, Christians and the Sacrifice of Isaac*. Cambridge, UK: Cambridge University Press, 2004.

Kierkegaard, Søren. *Fear and Trembling; Repetition*. Translated by Howard V. Hong and Edna H. Hong. Princeton, NJ: Princeton University Press, 1983.

Kim, Helen Kiyong, and Noah Samuel Leavitt. *JewAsian: Race, Religion, and Identity for America's Newest Jews*. Lincoln: University of Nebraska Press, 2016.

Kojève, Alexandre. *Introduction to the Reading of Hegel.* Edited by Allen Bloom. Translated by James H. Nichols, Jr. Ithaca, NY: Cornell University Press, 1980.

Koltun-Fromm, Ken. *Imagining Jewish Authenticity: Vision and Text in American Jewish Thought.* Bloomington: Indiana University Press, 2015.

Kotzin, Rhoda Hadassah. "Ancient Greek Philosophy." In *A Companion to Feminist Philosophy,* edited by Alison M. Jaggar and Iris Marion Young, 9–20. Malden, MA: Blackwell, 1998.

Kristeva, Julia. "A Holy Madness: She and He." In *Tales of Love,* translated by Leon S. Roudiez, 82–100. New York: Columbia University Press, 1987.

———. *The Kristeva Reader.* Edited by Toril Moi. New York: Columbia University Press, 1981.

Kuper, Adam. *The Reinvention of Primitive Society: Transformations of a Myth.* London: Routledge, 2005.

Lacan, Jacques. *The Ethics of Psychoanalysis, 1959–1960.* New York: Norton, 1992.

Ladin, Joy. *The Soul of the Stranger: Reading God and Torah from a Transgender Perspective.* Waltham, MA: Brandeis University Press, 2018.

Leroux, Georges. "'Communal Blood, Fraternal Blood . . .' The Space of *Antigone* and the Aporias of Difference." In *The Returns of Antigone: Interdisciplinary Essays,* edited by Tina Chanter and Sean D. Kirkland, 155–71. Albany: State University of New York Press, 2014.

Levenson, Jon. *Inheriting Abraham: The Legacy of the Patriarch in Judaism, Christianity, and Islam.* Princeton NJ: Princeton University Press, 2012.

Levinas, Emmanuel. "And God Created Woman." In *Nine Talmudic Readings,* translated by Annette Aronowicz, 161–77. Bloomington: Indiana University Press, 1994.

———. "'Between Two Worlds' (The Way of Franz Rosenzweig)." In *Difficult Freedom: Essays on Judaism,* translated by Seán Hand, 181–201. Baltimore, MD: Johns Hopkins University Press, 1997.

———. "Diachrony and Representation." In *Entre Nous: On Thinking-of-the-Other,* translated by Michael B. Smith and Barbara Harshaw, 159–78. New York: Columbia University Press, 1998.

———. *Existence and Existents.* Translated by Alphonso Lingis. The Hague: Martinus Nijhoff, 1978.

———. "Foreword." In Mosès, *System and Revelation: The Philosophy of Franz Rosenzweig,* translated by Catherine Tihanyi, 13–22. Detroit, MI: Wayne State University Press, 1992.

———. "Franz Rosenzweig: A Modern Jewish Thinker." In *Outside the Subject,* translated by Michael B. Smith, 49–66. Stanford, CA: Stanford University Press, 1994.

———. *God, Death and Time.* Edited by Jacques Rolland. Translated by Bettina Bergo. Redwood City, CA: Stanford University Press, 2000.

———. "God and Philosophy." In *Basic Philosophical Writings*, edited by Adriaan
T. Peperzak, Simon Critchley, and Robert Bernasconi, 129–48. Bloomington:
Indiana University Press, 1996.

———. "Judaism and the Feminine." In *Difficult Freedom: Essays on Judaism*,
translated by Seán Hand, 30–37. Baltimore, MD: Johns Hopkins University
Press, 1990.

———. "La Substitution." *Revue Philosophique de Louvain* 91, no. 66 (1968):
487–508.

———. "Love and Filiation." In *Ethics and Infinity: Conversations with Phillippe
Nemo*, translated by Richard A. Cohen, 63–72. Pittsburgh, PA: Duquesne
University Press, 1985.

———. "Meaning and Sense." In *Basic Philosophical Writings*, edited by Adriaan
T. Peperzak, Simon Critchley, and Robert Bernasconi, 33–64. Bloomington:
Indiana University Press, 1996.

———. "The Name of a Dog, or Natural Rights." In *Difficult Freedom: Essays
on Judaism*, translated by Seán Hand, 151–53. Baltimore, MD: Johns Hopkins
University Press, 1990.

———. *Oeuvres Complètes*. Vols. 1–2. Edited by Rodolphe Calin and Catherine
Chalier. Paris: Bernard Grasset, 2009.

———. *Otherwise Than Being or Beyond Essence*. Translated by Alphonso Lingis.
Dordrecht: Kluwer Academic Publishers, 1991. Originally published as
Autrement qu'être, ou, Au-delà de l'essence (La Haye: Nijhoff, 1974).

———. "Philosophy, Justice, and Love." In *Entre Nous: On Thinking-of-the-Other*,
translated by Michael B. Smith and Barbara Harshaw, 103–22. New York:
Columbia University Press, 1998. Originally published as "Philosophie, Justice
et Amour." In *Entre Nous: Essais sur le penser-à-l'autre*. Paris: Bernard Grasset,
1991.

———. *Proper Names*. Translated by Michael B. Smith. Stanford, CA: Stanford
University Press, 1996.

———. "Résumé de 'Totalité et infini.'" *Annales de l'université de Paris* (*Sorbonne,
Paris V*) 31 (1961).

———. "The Struthof Case." In *Difficult Freedom: Essays on Judaism*, translated by
Seán Hand, 149–50. Baltimore, MD: Johns Hopkins University Press, 1997.

———. "Substitution." In *Basic Philosophical Writings*, edited by Adriaan T.
Peperzak, Simon Critchley, and Robert Bernasconi, 80–95. Bloomington:
Indiana University Press, 1996.

———. *Time and the Other*. Translated by Richard B. Cohen. Pittsburgh, PA:
Duquesne University Press, 1987.

———. *Totality and Infinity: An Essay on Exteriority*. Translated by Alphonso
Lingis. Pittsburgh, PA: Duquesne University Press, 1995. Originally published as
Totalité et Infini: Essai Sur l'Extériorité. La Haye: Martinus Nijhoff, 1961.

———. "The Trace of the Other." In *Deconstruction in Context*, edited by Mark Taylor and translated by Alphonso Lingis, 345–59. Chicago: University of Chicago Press, 1986.

Levinas, Emmanuel, and Richard Kearney. "Dialogue with Emmanuel Levinas." In *Face to Face with Levinas*, edited by Richard A. Cohen, 13–34. Albany: State University of New York Press, 1986.

Levitt, Laura. *Jews and Feminism: The Ambivalent Search for Home*. New York: Routledge, 1997.

Llewelyn, John. "Am I Obsessed by Bobby? (Humanism of the Other Animal)." In Bernasconi and Critchley, eds., *Re-Reading Levinas*, 234–45.

Lofton, Kathryn. *Consuming Religion*. Chicago: University of Chicago Press, 2017.

Loraux, Nicole. *The Experiences of Tiresias: The Feminine and the Greek Man*. Translated by Paula Wissig. Princeton, NJ: Princeton University Press, 1995.

———. *Mothers in Mourning: With the Essay 'Of Amnesty and Its Opposite.'* Translated by Corinne Pache. Ithaca, NY: Cornell University Press, 1998.

———. *Tragic Ways of Killing a Woman*. Translated by Anthony Forster. Cambridge, MA: Harvard University Press, 1987.

MacCannell, Juliet Flower. *The Regime of the Brother: After the Patriarchy*. London: Routledge; 1991.

Mader, Mary Beth. "Antigone's Line." In *Feminist Readings of Antigone*, edited by Fanny Söderbäck. Albany: State University of New York Press, 2010.

Maimonides. *The Guide of the Perplexed*. Translated by Shlomo Pines. Chicago: University of Chicago Press, 1963.

Malka, Salomon. *Emmanuel Levinas: His Life and Legacy*. Translated by Michael Kigel and Sonja M. Embree. Pittsburgh, PA: Duquesne University Press, 2006.

Marcotte, Amanda. "Don't Be So Shocked by the Deaths on *Game of Thrones*: The Show Is a Classical Tragedy." *Slate*, June 9, 2015, https://slate.com/culture/2015/06 /game-of-thrones-is-a-classical-tragedy-don-t-be-so-shocked-by-the-deaths.html.

Marion, Jean-Luc. *The Erotic Phenomenon*. Translated by Stephen E. Lewis. Chicago: University of Chicago Press, 2005.

McGinity, Keren R. *Still Jewish: A History of Women and Intermarriage in America*. New York: New York University Press, 2012.

McMillen, Edmund. "Binding of Isaac: Origins (IGTM Special Edition Extended Interview)." September 8, 2014. https://www.youtube.com/watch?v= bMqFTuMECeA.

McMillen, Edmund, and Florian Himsl. *The Binding of Isaac*. 2011. https://store .steampowered.com/app/113200/The_Binding_of_Isaac/.

McRuer, Robert. *Crip Theory: Cultural Signs of Queerness and Disability*. New York: New York University Press, 2006.

McWilliams, Wilson Carey. *The Idea of Fraternity in America*. Berkeley: University of California Press, 1973.

Mehta, Samira K. *Beyond Chrismukkah: The Christian-Jewish Interfaith Family in the United States.* Chapel Hill: University of North Carolina Press, 2018.

Meir, Ephraim. "The Meaning of the Abrahamic Adventure in Levinas's Thought." In *Levinas Faces Biblical Figures,* edited by Yael Lin, 19–34. Lanham, MD: Lexington, 2014.

———. *Letters of Love: Franz Rosenzweig's Spiritual Biography and Oeuvre in Light of the Gritli Letters.* New York: Peter Lang, 2006.

Mendes-Flohr, Paul. "Between Sensual and Heavenly Love: Franz Rosenzweig's Reading of the Song of Songs." In *Scriptural Exegesis: The Shapes of Culture and the Religious Imagination: Essays in Honour of Michael Fishbane,* edited by Deborah A. Green and Laura S. Lieber, 310–18. Oxford: Oxford University Press, 2009.

———. Review of *The Kiss of God: Spiritual and Mystical Death in Judaism,* by Michael Fishbane. *History of Religions* 37, no. 2 (1997): 172–74.

Meyer, Eric Daryl. "Gregory of Nyssa and Jacques Derrida on the Human-Animal Distinction in the Song of Songs." In *The Bible and Posthumanism,* edited by Jennifer L. Koosed, 199–223. Atlanta, GA: Society of Biblical Literature, 2014.

Mills, Patricia Jagentowicz. "Hegel's Antigone." In *Feminist Interpretations of G. W. F. Hegel,* edited by Patricia Jagentowicz Mills, 59–88. University Park: Pennsylvania State University Press, 1996.

———. *Woman, Nature, and Psyche.* New Haven, CT: Yale University Press, 1987.

Mitchell, Juliet. *Siblings: Sex and Violence.* Cambridge, UK: Polity, 2003.

Moore, Stephen D. "The Song of Songs in the History of Sexuality." *Church History* 69, no. 2 (June 2000): 328–49.

Morgan, Michael L. *Discovering Levinas.* Cambridge, UK: Cambridge University Press, 2007.

Mosès, Stéphane. *System and Revelation: The Philosophy of Franz Rosenzweig.* Translated by Catherine Tihanyi. Detroit, MI: Wayne State University Press, 1992 [1982].

Moyn, Samuel. "Divine and Human Love: Franz Rosenzweig's History of the Song of Songs." *Jewish Studies Quarterly* 12 (2005): 194–212.

———. *Origins of the Other: Emmanuel Levinas between Revelation and Ethics.* Ithaca, NY: Cornell University Press, 2005.

Nancy, Jean-Luc. *A Finite Thinking.* Edited by Simon Sparks. Stanford, CA: Stanford University Press, 2003.

———. *L'Intrus.* Translated by Susan Hanson. East Lansing: Michigan State University Press, 2002.

New, Melvyn, Robert Bernasconi, and Richard A. Cohen, eds. *In Proximity: Emmanuel Levinas and the Eighteenth Century.* Lubbock: Texas Tech University Press, 2001.

Norton, Anne. *Bloodrites of the Post-Structuralists: Word, Flesh and Revolution.* New York: Routledge, 2002.

Nye, Andrea. "Irigaray and Diotima at Plato's Symposium." In *Feminist Interpretations of Plato*, edited by Nancy Tuana, 197–216. University Park: Pennsylvania State University Press, 1994.

Ochs, Vanessa L. *Sarah Laughed: Modern Lessons from the Wisdom and Stories of Biblical Women*. Philadelphia: The Jewish Publication Society, 2005.

Oliver, Kelly. *Animal Lessons: How They Teach Us to Be Human*. New York: Columbia University Press, 2009.

———. "Paternal Election and the Absent Father." In Chanter, ed., *Feminist Interpretations of Emmanuel Levinas*, 224–40.

Oppenheim, Michael D. "Feminist Jewish Philosophy: A Response." *Nashim: A Journal of Jewish Women's Studies & Gender Issues* 14 (fall 2007): 209–32.

———. *Søren Kierkegaard and Franz Rosenzweig: The Movement from Philosophy to Religion*. PhD diss., University of California, Santa Barbara, 1976.

Ozouf, Mona. "Liberty, Equality, Fraternity." In *Realms of Memory: The Construction of the French Past*, Vol. 3, translated by Arthur Goldhammer, 77–116. New York: Columbia University Press, 1998.

Palmer, Gesine. "'Dying for Love'—Making Sense of an (Unwitting?) Inversion in Franz Rosenzweig's Star of Redemption." *Bamidbar* 4, no. 2 (2019): 28–52.

Pardes, Ilana. *Countertraditions in the Bible: A Feminist Approach*. Cambridge, MA: Harvard University Press, 1992.

———. *The Song of Songs: A Biography*. Princeton, NJ: Princeton University Press, 2019.

Pateman, Carole. *The Sexual Contract*. Cambridge, UK: Polity, 1988.

Peleg, Yaron. "Love at First Sight? David, Jonathan, and the Biblical Politics of Gender." *Journal for the Study of the Old Testament* 30, no. 2 (2005): 171–89.

Perpich, Diane. *The Ethics of Emmanuel Levinas*. Redwood City, CA: Stanford University Press, 2008.

Peskowitz, Miriam. "Engendering Jewish Religious History." *Shofar: An Interdisciplinary Journal of Jewish Studies* 14, no. 1 (fall 1995): 8–34.

Pickstock, Catherine. "The Problem of Reported Speech: Friendship and Philosophy in Plato's *Lysis* and *Symposium*." *Telos* 123 (2002): 35–64.

Plaskow, Judith. *The Coming of Lilith: Essays on Feminism, Judaism, and Sexual Ethics, 1972–2003*. Edited by Judith Plaskow and Donna Berman. Boston: Beacon Press, 2005.

Plato. *Phaedo*. Translated by David Gallop. Oxford: Oxford University Press, 1993.

———. *Symposium*. Translated by Alexander Nehamas and Paul Woodruff. Indianapolis, IN: Hackett, 1989.

Pollak, Ellen. *Incest and the English Novel, 1684–1814*. Baltimore, MD: Johns Hopkins University Press, 2003.

Pollock, Benjamin. *Franz Rosenzweig and the Systematic Task of Philosophy*. Cambridge, UK: Cambridge University Press, 2009.

———. *Franz Rosenzweig's Conversions: World Denial and World Redemption*. Bloomington: Indiana University Press, 2014.

Prell, Riv-Ellen. *Fighting to Become Americans: Jews, Gender, and the Anxiety of Assimilation*. Boston: Beacon Press, 1999.

Puar, Jasbir K. *The Right to Maim: Debility, Capacity, Disability*. Durham, NC: Duke University Press, 2017.

Raphael, Melissa. *The Female Face of God in Auschwitz: A Jewish Feminist Theology of the Holocaust*. London: Routledge, 2003.

Rashkover, Randi. *Revelation and Theopolitics: Barth, Rosenzweig, and the Politics of Praise*. New York: T&T Clark International, 2005.

Ravven, Heidi. "Creating a Jewish Feminist Philosophy." *Anima* 12, no. 2 (1986): 99–112.

Rawlinson, Mary C. "Beyond Antigone: Ismene, Gender, and the Right to Life." In *The Returns of Antigone: Interdisciplinary Essays*, edited by Tina Chanter and Sean D. Kirkland, 101–24. Albany: State University of New York Press, 2014.

Reinhard, Kenneth. "The Ethics of the Neighbor: Universalism, Particularism, Exceptionalism." *Journal of Textual Reasoning* 4, no. 1 (November 2005): 1–21.

Reznik, Larisa. "This Power Which Is Not One: Queer Temporality, Jewish Difference, and the Concept of Religion in Mendelssohn's Jerusalem." *Journal of Jewish Identities* 11, no. 1 (January 2018): 143–77.

Robbins, Jill. *Prodigal Son/Elder Brother: Interpretation and Alterity in Augustine, Petrarch, Kafka, Levinas*. Chicago: University of Chicago Press, 1991.

Robinson, Joanna. "How Tonight's *Game of Thrones* Signaled a Brutal Departure from the Books." *Vanity Fair*, June 10, 2015, https://www.vanityfair.com /hollywood/2015/06/stannis-burns-shireen-game-of-thrones-dance-of -dragons.

Ronell, Avital. "Hannah Arendt Swallows the Lessing-Prize." *MLN* 131, no. 5 (December 2016): 1164–80.

———. *Loser Sons*. Urbana-Champaign: University of Illinois Press, 2012.

———. *Stupidity*. Urbana-Champaign: University of Illinois Press, 2002.

Rose, Gillian. *The Broken Middle: Out of Our Ancient Society*. Oxford, UK: Blackwell, 1992.

———. *Mourning Becomes the Law: Philosophy and Representation*. Cambridge: Cambridge University Press, 1996.

Rosenstock, Bruce. *Philosophy and the Jewish Question: Mendelssohn, Rosenzweig, and Beyond*. New York: Fordham University Press, 2009.

Rosenzweig, Franz. *Briefe und Tagebücher*. Edited by Rachel Rosenzweig and Edith Rosenzweig-Scheinmann. The Hague: Springer, 1979.

———. "The Builders: Concerning the Law." In *On Jewish Learning*, edited by Nahum Glatzer, 72–94. Madison: University of Wisconsin Press, 1955.

———. "Das Neue Denken." *Der Morgen* 1, no. 4 (October 1925): 426–51.

———. *Die 'Gritli'-Briefe: Briefe an Margrit Rosenstock-Huessy*. Edited by Inken Ruhle and Reinhold Mayer. Tübingen: Bilam, 2002.

———. *Franz Rosenzweig: His Life and Thought*. Edited by Nahum Glatzer. Indianapolis, IN: Hackett, 1988.

———. "Lessing's Nathan." In *Cultural Writings of Franz Rosenzweig*, edited and translated by Barbara E. Galli, 105–12. Syracuse, NY: Syracuse University Press, 2000.

———. "The New Thinking." In *Philosophical and Theological Writings*, edited and translated by Paul W. Franks and Michael L. Morgan, 109–39. Indianapolis, IN: Hackett, 2000.

———. *The Star of Redemption*. Translated by Barbara E. Galli. Madison: University of Wisconsin Press, 2005. Originally published as *Der Stern der Erlösung*. Heidelberg: L. Schneider, 1954.

———. "'Urzelle' to the *Star of Redemption*." In *Philosophical and Theological Writings*, edited and translated by Paul W. Franks and Michael L. Morgan, 48–72. Indianapolis, IN: Hackett, 2000.

Rowling, J. K. *Harry Potter and the Deathly Hallows*. Vancouver: Bloomsbury, 2007.

Rubin, Gayle. "The Traffic in Women: Notes on the 'Political Economy' of Sex.'" In *Toward an Anthropology of Women*, edited by Rayna R. Reiter, 157–210. New York: Monthly Review Press, 1975.

Rudavsky, Tamar. "Feminism and Modern Jewish Philosophy." In *The Cambridge Companion to Modern Jewish Philosophy*, edited by Michael Morgan and Peter Gordon, 324–47. Cambridge, UK: Cambridge University Press, 2007.

Samuelson, Norbert. *A User's Guide to Franz Rosenzweig's Star of Redemption*. Richmond, VA: Curzon, 1999.

Sandford, Stella. "Levinas, Feminism and the Feminine." In Bernasconi and Critchley, eds., *The Cambridge Companion to Levinas*, 139–60.

———. "Masculine Mothers? Maternity in Levinas and Plato." In Chanter, ed., *Feminist Interpretations of Emmanuel Levinas*, 180–202.

———. *The Metaphysics of Love: Gender and Transcendence in Levinas*. London: Continuum International Publishing Group, 2000.

Santner, Eric L. *On the Psychotheology of Everyday Life: Reflections on Freud and Rosenzweig*. Chicago: University of Chicago Press, 2001.

Sartre, Jean-Paul. *Existentialism and Humanism*. Translated by Philip Mairet. London: Methuen, 1970.

Schneider, Monique. "*En deçà du visage*." In *Emmanuel Levinas: L'éthique comme philosophie première*, edited by Jean Greisch and Jacques Rolland, 133–53. Paris: Éditions du Cerf, 1993.

Schwab, Katharine. "The Rise of *Buffy* Studies." *The Atlantic*, October 1, 2015. http://www.theatlantic.com/entertainment/archive/2015/10/the-rise-of-buffy-studies/407020/.

Schwartz, Joshua. "Ishmael at Play: On Exegesis and Jewish Society." *Hebrew Union College Annual* 66 (1995): 203–21.

Seery, John E. "Acclaim for *Antigone's Claim* Reclaimed (or, Steiner contra Butler)." In *Judith Butler's Precarious Politics: Critical Encounters*, edited by Terrell Carver and Samuel A. Chambers, 62–76. New York: Routledge, 2008.

Seidman, Naomi. *The Marriage Plot: Or, How Jews Fell in Love with Love, and with Literature*. Stanford, CA: Stanford University Press, 2016.

Shapiro, Susan E. "A Matter of Discipline: Reading for Gender in Jewish Philosophy." In *Judaism Since Gender*, edited by Miriam Peskowitz and Laura Levitt, 158–73. New York: Routledge, 1997.

———. "'And God Created Woman': Reading the Bible Otherwise." In *Levinas and Biblical Studies*, edited by Tamara Cohn Eskenazi, Gary A. Phillips, and David Jobling, 159–93. Atlanta, GA: Society of Biblical Literature, 2003.

———. "Gender and Jewish Philosophy: Introduction." *Bamidbar* 4, no. 2 (2019): 7–9.

———. "Toward a Postmodern Judaism: A Response." In *Reasoning After Revelation: Dialogues in Postmodern Jewish Philosophy*, edited by Steven Kepnes, Peter Ochs, and Robert Gibbs, 77–87. Boulder, CO: Westview Press, 1998.

Shell, Marc. *Children of the Earth: Literature, Politics, and Nationhood*. Oxford: Oxford University Press, 1993.

———. *The End of Kinship: 'Measure for Measure,' Incest, and the Ideal of Universal Siblinghood*. Redwood City, CA: Stanford University Press, 1988.

Sherwood, Yvonne. "And Sarah Died." In *Derrida's Bible (Reading a Page of Scripture with a Little Help from Derrida)*. Edited by Yvonne Sherwood. New York: Palgrave Macmillan, 2004.

———. "Binding-Unbinding: Divided Responses of Judaism, Christianity, and Islam to the 'Sacrifice' of Abraham's Beloved Son." *Journal of the American Academy of Religion* 72, no. 4 (December 2004): 821–61.

———. "A Recently Discovered Letter from Isaac to Abraham (Annotated)." In *Biblical Blaspheming: Trials of the Sacred for a Secular Age*, 179–94. Cambridge, UK: Cambridge University Press, 2012.

Siebers, Tobin. *Disability Theory*. Ann Arbor: University of Michigan Press, 2008.

Sophocles. "Antigone." In *Greek Tragedies*, edited by David Grene and Richmond Lattimore and translated by David Grene, 177–232. Chicago: University of Chicago Press, 1991.

———. "Oedipus the King." In *Sophocles I*, edited by David Grene and Richmond Lattimore and translated by David Grene, 9–76. Chicago: University of Chicago Press, 1991.

Soskice, Janet Martin. *The Kindness of God: Metaphor, Gender, and Religious Language*. Oxford: Oxford University Press, 2007.

Speiser, Ephraim Avigdor. "The Wife-Sister Motif in the Patriarchal Narratives." In *Biblical and Other Studies*, edited by Alexander Altmann, 15–28. Cambridge, MA: Harvard University Press, 1963.

Staehler, Tanja. *Plato and Levinas: The Ambiguous Out-Side of Ethics*. New York: Routledge, 2010.

Stahmer, Harold. "Franz Rosenzweig's Letters to Margrit Rosenstock-Huessy: 'Franz,' 'Gritli,' 'Eugen' and *The Star of Redemption*." In *Der Philosoph Franz Rosenzweig (1886–1929) Internationaler Kongress—Kassel 1986: Band I: Die Herausforderung jüdischen Lernens*, edited by Wolfdietrich Schmied-Kowarzik, 109–37. Freiburg: Verlag Karl Alber, 1988.

Steiner, George. *Antigones*. Oxford: Oxford University Press, 1986.

Stiebert, Johanna. *Fathers and Daughters in the Hebrew Bible*. Oxford: Oxford University Press, 2013.

Stone, Ken. "Animal Difference, Sexual Difference, and the Daughter of Jephthah." *Biblical Interpretation* 24, no. 1 (January 2016): 1–16.

Strauss, Leo. *Leo Strauss on Moses Mendelssohn*. Edited by Martin Yaffe. Chicago: University of Chicago Press, 2012.

Taylor, Charles. *Hegel*. Cambridge, UK: Cambridge University Press, 1977.

Thompson, Jennifer A. *Jewish on Their Own Terms: How Intermarried Couples Are Changing American Judaism*. New Brunswick, NJ: Rutgers University Press, 2013.

Tirosh-Rothschild, Hava. "Dare to Know: Feminism and the Discipline of Jewish Philosophy." In *Feminist Perspectives on Jewish Studies*, edited by Lynn Davidman and Shelly Tenenbaum, 85–119. New Haven, CT: Yale University Press, 1996.

Tirosh-Samuelson, Hava. "Feminism and Gender." In *The Cambridge History of Jewish Philosophy, Volume 2: The Modern Era*, edited by Martin Kavka, Zachary Braiterman, and David Novak, 154–89. Cambridge: Cambridge University Press, 2012.

Torrance, Isabelle. "Antigone and Her Brother: What Sort of Special Relationship?" In *Interrogating Antigone in Postmodern Philosophy and Criticism*, edited by S. E. Wilmer and Audrone Zukauskaite, 240–53. Oxford: Oxford University Press, 2010.

Trible, Phyllis. "Genesis 22: The Sacrifice of Sarah." In *Women in the Hebrew Bible*, edited by Alice Bach, 271–87. New York: Routledge, 1999.

———. *God and the Rhetoric of Sexuality*. Philadelphia: Fortress, 1978.

———. *Texts of Terror: Literary-Feminist Readings of Biblical Narratives*. Minneapolis, MN: Fortress, 1984.

Tuana, Nancy. "Preface." In Chanter, ed., *Feminist Interpretations of Emmanuel Levinas*, xiii–xv.

Valeur, Peter Svare. "Notes on Friendship: Moses Mendelssohn and Gotthold Ephraim Lessing." *Oxford German Studies* 45, no. 2 (2016): 142–56.

Van der Heide, Albert. *"Now I Know": Five Centuries of Aqedah Exegesis*. Cham: Springer International, 2017.

Vasey, Craig R. "Faceless Women and Serious Others: Levinas, Misogyny, and Feminism." In *Ethics and Danger: Essays on Heidegger and Continental Thought*, edited by Arleen B. Dallery and Charles E. Scott, 317–30. Albany: State University of New York Press, 1992.

Vint, Sherryl. *Animal Alterity: Science Fiction and the Question of the Animal*. Liverpool: Liverpool University Press, 2010.

Von Goethe, Johann Wolfgang. *Faust: Part One and Two*. Translated by Carl R. Mueller. Hanover, NH: Smith and Kraus, 2004.

Wallach, Kerry. *Passing Illusions: Jewish Visibility in Weimar Germany*. Ann Arbor: University of Michigan Press, 2017.

Walsh, Carey. "Christianity: Traditional Christian Interpretations of Genesis 22." In *Interpreting Abraham: Journeys to Moriah*, edited by Bradley Beach and Matthew Powell, 27–56. Minneapolis, MN: Fortress, 2014.

Watts Belser, Julia. "Judaism and Disability." In *Disability and World Religions: An Introduction*, edited by Darla Schumm and Michael Stoltzfus, 93–113. Waco, TX: Baylor University Press, 2016.

Weddle, David L. *Sacrifice in Judaism, Christianity, and Islam*. New York: New York University Press, 2017.

Weems, Renita J. *Just a Sister Away: A Womanist Vision of Women's Relationships in the Bible*. San Diego, CA: LuraMedia, 1988.

Wehrs, Donald R. "Levinas, Goethe's *Wilhelm Meisters Lehrjahre*, and the Compulsion of the Good." In New, Bernasconi, and Cohen, eds., *In Proximity: Emmanuel Levinas and the Eighteenth Century*, 215–42.

Weinbaum, Alys Eve. *Wayward Reproductions: Genealogies of Race and Nation in Transatlantic Modern Thought*. Durham, NC: Duke University Press, 2004.

Weissberg, Liliane. "Humanity and Its Limits: Hannah Arendt Reads Lessing." In *Practicing Progress: The Promise and Limitations of Enlightenment*, edited by Richard E. Schade and Dieter Sevin, 187–98. Amsterdam: Brill, 2007.

Welz, Claudia. "Keeping the Secret of Subjectivity: Kierkegaard and Levinas on Conscience, Love and the Limits of Self-Understanding." In *Despite Oneself: Subjectivity and Its Secret in Kierkegaard and Levinas*, edited by Claudia Welz and Karl Verstrynge, 153–226. London: Turnshare, 2008.

———. *Love's Transcendence and the Problem of Theodicy*. Tübingen: Mohr Siebeck, 2008.

Westermann, Claus. *Genesis 12–36: A Commentary*. Translated by John J. Scullion. Minneapolis, MN: Augsburg, 1985.

Wiedemann, Barbara, ed. *Paul Celan, Nelly Sachs: Correspondence*. Translated by Christopher Clark. Riverdale-on-Hudson, NY: Sheep Meadow, 1995.

Wills, David. "Translator's Preface." In *The Gift of Death* by Jacques Derrida, translated by David Wills, vii–viii. Chicago: University of Chicago Press, 1995.

"The Winds of Winter." *Game of Thrones*. Season 6, episode 10, directed by Miguel Sapochnik, written by David Benioff and D. B. Weiss. Aired June 26, 2016, on HBO.

Wolfson, Elliot R. *Alef, Mem, Tau: Kabbalistic Musings on Time, Truth, and Death*. Berkeley: University of California Press, 2006.

———. "Apophasis and the Trace of Transcendence: Wyschogrod's Contribution to a Postmodern Jewish Immanent A/Theology." *Philosophy Today* 55 (November 2011): 334–40.

———. "Asceticism and Eroticism in Medieval Jewish Philosophical and Mystical Exegesis of the Song of Songs." In *With Reverence for the Word: Medieval Scriptural Exegesis in Judaism, Christianity, and Islam*, edited by Jane Dammen McAuliffe, Barry D. Walfish, and Joseph R. Goering, 92–118. Oxford: Oxford University Press, 2003.

———. *Circle in the Square: Studies in the Use of Gender in Kabbalistic Symbolism*. Albany: State University of New York Press, 1995.

———. *A Dream Interpreted within a Dream: Oneiropoiesis and the Prism of Imagination*. New York: Zone Books, 2011.

———. *The Duplicity of Philosophy's Shadow: Heidegger, Nazism, and the Jewish Other*. New York: Columbia University Press, 2018.

———. "Echo of the Otherwise: Ethics of Transcendence and the Lure of Theolatry." In *Encountering the Medieval in Modern Jewish Thought*, edited by James A. Diamond and Aaron W. Hughes, 261–324. Leiden: Brill, 2012.

———. "Facing the Effaced: Mystical Eschatology and the Idealistic Orientation in the Thought of Franz Rosenzweig." *Zeitschrift für Neure Theologiegeschichte* 4 (1997): 39–81.

———. *Giving beyond the Gift: Apophasis and Overcoming Theomania*. New York: Fordham University Press, 2014.

———. "Imagination and the Theolatrous Impulse: Configuring God in Modern Jewish Thought." In *The Cambridge History of Jewish Philosophy: Volume 2: The Modern Era*, edited by Martin Kavka, Zachary Braiterman, and David Novak, 663–703. Cambridge, UK: Cambridge University Press, 2012.

———. *Language, Eros, Being: Kabbalistic Hermeneutics and Poetic Imagination*. New York: Fordham University Press, 2005.

———. "Light Does Not Talk but Shines: Apophasis and Vision in Rosenzweig's Theopoetic Temporality." In *New Directions in Jewish Philosophy*, edited by Elliot R. Wolfson and Aaron W. Hughes, 87–148. Bloomington: Indiana University Press, 2010.

———. "Secrecy, Modesty, and the Feminine: Kabbalistic Traces in the Thought of Levinas." *Journal of Jewish Thought and Philosophy* 14 (2006): 195–224.

———. "Suffering Eros and Textual Incarnation: A Kristevan Reading of Kabbalistic Poetics." In *Toward a Theology of Eros: Transfiguring Passion at the Limits of Discipline,* edited by Virginia Burrus and Catherine Keller, 341–65. New York: Fordham University Press, 2006.

———. *Venturing Beyond: Law and Morality in Kabbalistic Mysticism.* Oxford: Oxford University Press, 2006.

Wolfson, Elliot R., and Aaron W. Hughes. "Introduction: Charting an Alternative Course for the Study of Jewish Philosophy." In *New Directions in Jewish Philosophy,* edited by Elliot R. Wolfson and Aaron W. Hughes, 1–18. Bloomington: Indiana University Press, 2010.

Wright, Tamra. *The Twilight of Jewish Philosophy: Emmanuel Levinas' Ethical Hermeneutics.* Amsterdam: Harwood Academic Publishers, 1999.

Wright, Tamra, Peter Hughes, and Alison Ainley. "The Paradox of Morality: An Interview with Emmanuel Levinas." In *The Provocation of Levinas: Rethinking the Other,* edited by Robert Bernasconi and David Wood and translated by Andre Benjamin and Tamra Wright, 168–80. London: Routledge, 1988.

Wynter, Sylvia. "Unsettling the Coloniality of Being/Power/Truth/Freedom: Towards the Human, After Man, Its Overrepresentation—An Argument." *CR: The New Centennial Review* 3, no. 3 (2003): 257–337.

Wyschogrod, Edith. *Crossover Queries: Dwelling with Negatives, Embodying Philosophy's Others.* New York: Fordham University Press, 2006.

———. "Introduction." In *The Enigma of Gift and Sacrifice,* edited by Edith Wyschogrod, Jean-Joseph Goux, and Eric Boynton, 1–16. New York: Fordham University Press, 2002.

Young, William. *Uncommon Friendships: An Amicable History of Modern Religious Thought.* Eugene, OR: Cascade Books, 2009.

Zank, Michael. "The Rosenzweig–Rosenstock Triangle, Or, What Can We Learn from *Letters to Gritli*?: A Review Essay." *Modern Judaism* 23, no. 1 (2003): 74–98.

Zierler, Wendy. "In Search of a Feminist Reading of the Akedah." *Nashim* 9, no. 1 (2005): 10–26.

Žižek, Slavoj. "From Antigone to Joan of Arc." *Helios* 31, no. 1–2 (2004): 51–62.

INDEX

Abraham: and *Aqedah*, 170–72, 175–79, 187–88, 190–91, 193–94, 196n7, 196n8, 196n11, 200n37, 200n40, 202n49, 202n52, 203n52; and laughter, 79–82, 97n116, 98n119, 98n122, 99n124, 100n128, 100n129; as sibling-spouse, 36–38, 58n97

Adams, Carol J., 88

Adler, Rachel, 80, 99n124, 100n127

Aeschylus, 172–74, 178, 198n29, 199n31

Ainley, Alison, 204n63

Ali, Kecia, 69

Allen, Sarah, 5, 18n26, 69, 75, 101n32

Améry, Jean, 204n65

androgyny, 44, 53n51, 155n17, 159n59, 198n29

Anidjar, Gil, 40, 54n66

animals: and critical animal studies, 55n71, 87n29, 88n35, 218, 222n40, 222n42, 223n44; Derrida on, 68, 87n31, 222n40; and the feminine, 67–69, 70, 88n35; Levinas on, 67–69, 70, 86n28, 87n31, 87n32; and sacrifice, 187–88, 199n32

Antigone (Sophocles), 10, 131–42; Hegel on, 132–42; sister-brother relation in, 131–43; sister-sister relation in, 137, 140–41, 160n67, 161n77, 169, 194n1, 194n2, 194n3

Antigone, Interrupted (Honig), 141, 161n77, 161n78, 169, 193, 194, 194n1, 194n2, 194n3

Aqedah (Genesis): Kierkegaard on, 170–71, 175–79, 185, 196n11, 200n37, 201n40, 202n49; Levinas on, 171–72, 177–79, 185–86, 187–88, 195n8, 201n43, 202n49;

in popular culture, 190–91, 193–94; Rosenzweig on, 195n8, 202n49; and sacrifice, 175–79, 185–87, 202n52

Arendt, Hannah: on fraternity, 9–10, 103, 113–18, 125n65, 126n72, 126n74; on friendship, 10, 103, 113–18, 126n74, 126n76

Aristotle, 111, 115

Atterton, Peter, 68

Augustine, 112

Bal, Mieke, 92n60

Batnizky, Leora, 3, 15n17, 17n21, 32–33, 54n65, 60n112, 118, 128n92, 206n74, 207n88

Beauvoir, Simone de, 4, 7, 18n24

Benhabib, Seyla, 133

Benjamin, Mara: on Jewish philosophy, 2, 214–15; on Levinas, 17n22, 195n8, 208n100; on love, 110; on maternity, 185, 208n100; on Rosenzweig, 17n22, 31, 32, 44, 48n21, 56n85, 62n150, 63n153, 86n22, 167n139, 195n8

Bereishit Rabbah, 37, 99n125

Berman, Lila Corwin, 19n34, 40–41, 215, 216

Bernasconi, Robert, 207n88

Biale, David, 41–42, 47n2, 50n30, 58n107, 61n128

Bienenstock, Myriam, 145, 163n95, 164n99

Bible. *See* Genesis; Judges; Song of Songs

Bilge, Sirma, 41, 128n97

binding of Isaac. *See Aqedah*

Binding of Isaac, The (video game), 189–91

ANDREA DARA COOPER is Leonard and Tobee Kaplan Scholar in Modern Jewish Thought and Culture and Associate Professor in the Department of Religion at the University of North Carolina, Chapel Hill. Her work has appeared in the *Journal of Jewish Thought and Philosophy*, *Oxford Bibliographies In Jewish Studies*, *Religion Compass*, and the *Journal of Jewish Ethics*.

CPSIA information can be obtained
at www.ICGtesting.com
Printed in the USA
LVHW022132161121
703481LV00006B/520